# Localism and Pla

# Localism and Planning

Simon Ricketts

Duncan Field

**Bloomsbury** Professional

Bloomsbury Professional Limited, Maxwelton House, 41–43 Boltro Road, Haywards Heath, West Sussex, RH16 1BJ

© Bloomsbury Professional Limited 2012

Bloomsbury Professional is an imprint of Bloomsbury Publishing Plc

All rights reserved. No part of this publication may be reproduced in any material form (including photocopying or storing it in any medium by electronic means and whether or not transiently or incidentally to some other use of this publication) without the written permission of the copyright owner except in accordance with the provisions of the Copyright, Designs and Patents Act 1988 or under the terms of a licence issued by the Copyright Licensing Agency Ltd, Saffron House, 6–10 Kirby Street, London EC1N 8TS, England. Applications for the copyright owner's written permission to reproduce any part of this publication should be addressed to the publisher.

Warning: The doing of an unauthorised act in relation to a copyright work may result in both a civil claim for damages and criminal prosecution.

Crown copyright material is reproduced with the permission of the Controller of HMSO and the Queen's Printer for Scotland. Any European material in this work which has been reproduced from EUR-lex, the official European Communities legislation website, is European Communities copyright.

A CIP Catalogue record for this book is available from the British Library.

ISBN 978 1 84766 945 2

Typeset by Phoenix Photosetting, Chatham, Kent
Printed and bound in Great Britain by Hobbs The Printers Ltd, Totton, Hampshire

# Foreword

I am delighted to have been asked to write a foreword to this thoughtful book. It is much more than a text book guide to the Localism Act.

The Localism Act is a part of a determined attempt by, initially, the Conservative Party, and subsequently the Coalition Government, to change the relationship between the individual and the State across all aspects of government. The word democracy, in translation, is derived from the Greek words, 'people' and 'power', and much of the Localism Act can be explained within that concept, be it the general power of competence given to local authorities, the empowerment of the community, the abolition of regional spatial strategies, the introduction of neighbourhood planning or the meaningful proportion of Community Infrastructure Levy which will be hypothecated to neighbourhood level.

Our planning system has been described as the best in the world yet, for all that, it has been taken through a series of upheavals with new principal Acts in 1947, 1968, 1971, 1990, 1991, 2004, 2008 and now 2011. It might reasonably be asked how great is the change this time?

There are some themes that are surprisingly constant, albeit that they have stirred great controversy. As long ago as 1923, the then Minister (shortly to serve under Neville Chamberlain as Secretary of State) considered 'that the presumption should always be in favour of the person who wishes to undertake development … It is also particularly desirable that no obstacles should be placed in the way of proposed development, unless it is clearly detrimental to important local needs or interests'.[1]

Thus, the presumption in favour of sustainable development (contained in the new National Planning Policy Framework) is really no more than the return of an old friend in new clothes – for all the excitement that has been generated. In contrast, the National Planning Policy Framework, taken as a whole, does strike a new, and commendably concise, note in a call to action for a planning system with fresh purpose.

Prior to the General Election, and as the Localism Bill travelled through Parliament, the public debate tended to be about power and control and, rather less, about the intrinsic importance of the town planning system.

It is a system which directly, or indirectly, touches every aspect of life and seeks to answer some of the most complex and difficult questions. What size will (or is it a case of should) our population be and what shape would it have? A particularly difficult political question is what size of population is sustainable at national and local levels? How do we reduce carbon; where will our children live; how is employment encouraged; where is the water; where and what is the energy; where should we create roads, railways and airports; how is the stewardship of natural resources to be managed?

---

1 Town Planning (General Interim Development) Order 1922, Ministry of Health Circular 368.

*Foreword*

After the launch of localism, and in the face of the global economic storm, the rise of the importance of growth has served to check some aspects of localism. The final balance has yet to emerge.

The Coalition Government has sought behavioural and cultural change and, even as the Localism Bill was being drafted, that change began to emerge increasingly strongly. For the Act to succeed, high levels of responsibilities will need to be taken up by local authorities, communities (business and the third sector as well as residents) and neighbourhoods through an extensive involvement in, and desire to serve, the wider 'public interest'. This perhaps begs the interesting question as to what constitutes the public interest in the world of localism.

Turning to practicalities, the book breaks down the new legislation into a series of topics explaining each in a clear and open way with useful suggestions of the implications. It, therefore, serves as an excellent guide to the legislation and what to do about it, depending upon one's point of view.

His Honour George Dobry QC wrote that 'it is not so much the system which is wrong, but the way in which it is used. Successful implementation of the proposed measures depends on a change of attitude towards a more positive and constructive approach on all sides'.[2]

These words, written 40 years ago, ring just as true today.

Hugh Bullock BSc FRICS FRTPI FRSA<br>
Senior Partner<br>
Gerald Eve LLP

---

[2] Review of the Development Control System (Interim Report) 1972, (Final Report) 1975, His Hon George Dobry CBE QC Dr Jur (Hon).

# Preface

This book would not have come about if we had not decided that we would embark on a blog, *L is for Localism*,[1] to provide our own factual, although sometimes opinionated, commentary on the passage of the Localism Bill through Parliament from our standpoint as planning law practitioners. *L is for Localism* appeared to strike some sort of chord with the planning and planning law community. The current Government's localism agenda is a vast undertaking and it is sometimes difficult to see the wood for the trees in making sense of the waves of policy announcements and the patchwork of amendments that are sought to be made to the existing system.

We did not fully appreciate when we uploaded our first blog posting on 6 December 2010 quite how controversial the Government's proposals would prove to be. Despite the relatively detailed groundwork that had been done by the Conservatives in establishing their policy position in the run-up to the May 2010 election, the idea in particular that there should be a 'presumption in favour of sustainable development' has generated much controversy. Once the draft National Planning Policy Framework was published in July 2011, a number of organisations, led by the National Trust, became seriously concerned as to the implications of the changes. The Daily Telegraph in particular picked up the baton, starting a 'Hands Off Our Land' campaign.

It is impossible to focus on the Localism Bill, now Act, in isolation. The agenda for change is much wider than that. Nor is it possible to look at 'planning' in isolation from the Government's wider policy objectives, particularly with regard to addressing the country's fiscal deficit and with regard to the Conservatives' 'Big Society' vision.

There has been so much 'spin' as to what is proposed for the planning system that it appears that many have lost the thread as to what the original purposes of the reforms were stated to be and where the process has reached. Whether you, the reader, are a planner, planning lawyer, developer, land owner, community volunteer, conservationist, politician or simply an interested member of the public, this book seeks to recover that thread and to summarise for you the ongoing reforms of the planning system as they are at 6 April 2012.

We have found it challenging to condense the vast amount of material into a manageable volume. The Localism Act itself (referred to throughout as 'the Act') runs to 483 pages. We do not attempt to cover detailed housing law or compulsory purchase compensation reforms. If we have dealt too briefly with any areas which may be of specific interest, we hope that the extensive footnoted references to the underlying material will be some compensation. We are conscious of the differing effects of the Act in England, Wales and the rest of the United Kingdom and refer the reader to Appendix 1 where we set out the

---

1   http://localism.sjberwin.com.

*Preface*

position in detail, rather than deal with each position as we come to it in the body of the text itself.

Aside from our long-suffering families, we would like to thank a number of members of the planning team at SJ Berwin, particularly Juliet Munn, Meeta Kaur, Sarah Bischoff, Peter White, Annabel Cox, Verity Ellis, Hayley Anderson and Carole Lamb. All mistakes are ours alone.

Simon Ricketts and Duncan Field<br>May 2012

# Contents

| | |
|---|---:|
| Foreword | v |
| Preface | vii |
| Abbreviations | xiii |
| Table of statutes | xv |
| Table of statutory instruments | xxi |
| Table of cases | xxiii |

| | |
|---|---:|
| **Chapter 1  Introduction** | **1** |
| The planning system inherited by the new Government | 1 |
| The political background to the May 2010 election insofar as is relevant to the issues that concern us in this book | 2 |
| | |
| **Chapter 2  May 2010 to April 2012, the changes unfold** | **13** |
| | |
| **Chapter 3  Local authorities' powers and duties** | **33** |
| The new 'General Power of Competence' | 33 |
| Transfer and delegation of government functions to local authorities | 36 |
| New governance arrangements | 37 |
| New mayoral arrangements | 38 |
| Predetermination | 39 |
| Standards | 41 |
| Pay accountability | 42 |
| EU fines | 44 |
| Non-domestic rates | 45 |
| | |
| **Chapter 4  Community empowerment** | **47** |
| Local referendums | 47 |
| Community Right to Challenge | 49 |
| Assets of Community Value | 50 |
| | |
| **Chapter 5  Abolition of regional strategies** | **57** |
| Background | 57 |
| Coalition Government's stance | 59 |
| Formal abolition of regional strategies | 63 |
| The duty to co-operate | 65 |
| Changes to local plans regime | 67 |
| | |
| **Chapter 6  Neighbourhood planning** | **69** |
| Building blocks of neighbourhood planning | 70 |
|    Neighbourhood areas | 70 |
|    Formation of neighbourhood areas | 71 |
|    Qualifying bodies | 72 |
|    Neighbourhood Development Orders | 74 |
|    Community Right to Build Orders | 79 |
|    Neighbourhood Development Plans | 80 |
|    Charges and funding | 83 |

*Contents*

| | | |
|---|---|---|
| **Chapter 7** | **Consultation before applying for planning permission** | **85** |
| **Chapter 8** | **Enforcement against breaches of planning control** | **87** |
| Restriction on retrospective applications | | 87 |
| Deliberately concealed breaches | | 87 |
| Removal notices in relation to display structures for unauthorised advertisements | | 89 |
| Action notices to remedy persistent problems with unauthorised advertisements | | 89 |
| Power to remedy defacement of premises | | 89 |
| Increase in penalties and time limits for criminal offences | | 90 |
| **Chapter 9** | **Community Infrastructure Levy** | **91** |
| Legislative basis | | 91 |
| What is the CIL and what can it be used for? | | 91 |
| Who can charge it and who can collect it? | | 92 |
| On what basis must the CIL be charged? | | 93 |
| Charging schedule formulation and adoption procedures | | 94 |
| What is the CIL charged on? | | 96 |
| How is the CIL calculated? | | 96 |
| Who is liable? | | 97 |
| When does liability to pay arise? | | 98 |
| Procedural issues | | 99 |
|    Payment of the CIL | | 100 |
|    Payments in kind | | 101 |
| Relationship between the CIL and planning obligations | | 102 |
| Reliefs and exemptions | | 103 |
|    Exemption for minor development | | 103 |
|    Exemption for charities | | 103 |
|    Social housing relief | | 104 |
|    Exceptional circumstances relief | | 105 |
| Reviews and appeals | | 106 |
|    Review and appeal of chargeable amount | | 106 |
| Who has adopted the levy so far? | | 107 |
| **Chapter 10** | **Nationally Significant Infrastructure Projects** | **109** |
| Background | | 109 |
| Coalition Government's stance | | 111 |
| Abolition of Infrastructure Planning Commission | | 111 |
| National Policy Statements | | 114 |
| Section 35 directions | | 114 |
| Pre-application consultation and publicity requirements | | 114 |
| Other changes | | 115 |
| **Chapter 11** | **London** | **117** |
| Housing and regeneration functions | | 118 |
| Mayoral Development Corporations | | 120 |
| Greater London Authority governance changes | | 124 |
| **Chapter 12** | **Other legislative and administrative changes** | **127** |
| Changes to permitted development rights and review of use classes order | | 127 |
| The planning guarantee and information requirements | | 130 |
| The Chancellor's Autumn Statement 2011, the Penfold Review Implementation Report and the Housing Strategy for England | | 131 |

| | |
|---|---|
| Autumn Statement 2011 | 131 |
| Implementation Report of Penfold Review | 133 |
| Housing Strategy for England | 134 |
| Amendments to the local plan-making process | 135 |
| Changes to the General Development Procedure Order 1995 | 137 |
| Nature Improvement Areas | 138 |

## Chapter 13  Local Enterprise Partnerships, enterprise zones — 139

| | |
|---|---|
| Introduction | 139 |
| Funding | 142 |
| Regional Growth Fund | 142 |
| LEP Capacity Fund | 143 |
| LEP Start-up Fund | 144 |
| Enterprise zones | 144 |
| Business rates discount | 146 |
| Retention of business rates growth by local authorities | 146 |
| Simplified planning approach | 147 |
| Broadband roll-out | 147 |
| Enhanced capital allowances | 148 |
| Additional options | 148 |

## Chapter 14  National Planning Policy Framework — 149

| | |
|---|---|
| Background | 149 |
| The draft NPPF | 149 |
| What made the draft NPPF so different? | 150 |
| Communities and Local Government Select Committee Report | 154 |
| The Environmental Audit Committee Report | 159 |
| The National Planning Policy Framework (final form) | 161 |
| Foreword and Introduction | 165 |
| 1  Building a strong, competitive economy | 168 |
| 2  Ensuring the vitality of town centres | 169 |
| 3  Supporting a prosperous rural economy | 170 |
| 4  Promoting sustainable transport | 170 |
| 5  Supporting high quality communications infrastructure | 171 |
| 6  Delivering a wide choice of high quality homes | 171 |
| 7  Requiring good design | 173 |
| 8  Promoting healthy communities | 173 |
| 9  Protecting Green Belt land | 175 |
| 10  Meeting the challenge of climate change, flooding and coastal change | 176 |
| 11  Conserving and enhancing the natural environment | 177 |
| 12  Conserving and enhancing the historic environment | 178 |
| 13  Facilitating the sustainable use of minerals | 180 |
| Plan-making | 181 |
| Decision-taking | 185 |
| Transitional arrangements for the NPPF | 187 |
| Documents replaced by the NPPF | 188 |
| Documents published alongside the NPPF | 189 |
| Technical Guidance to the NPPF | 189 |
| Planning Policy for Traveller Sites | 191 |
| Government's response to the CLG Select Committee's Report | 192 |
| Concluding thoughts on the NPPF | 195 |

Contents

| | |
|---|---|
| **Chapter 15   Funding LPAs** | **197** |
| Local retention of business rates | 198 |
| Tax Increment Financing | 201 |
| The New Homes Bonus | 202 |
| The proposal that LPAs should be allowed to set their own planning application fees | 203 |
| Community land auctions | 204 |
| Local finance considerations | 205 |
| | |
| **Chapter 16   Navigating the system** | **209** |
| The landowner | 209 |
|   Audit developer interest | 209 |
|   Everybody needs good neighbours | 210 |
|   The promotion of sites | 211 |
|   Unlocking potential | 211 |
|   New designations | 212 |
| The developer | 214 |
|   Community demographics | 214 |
|   Consultation, consultation, consultation | 215 |
|   Collaboration | 217 |
|   The policy landscape | 218 |
|   Turn socio-economic benefits into headline issues | 222 |
| The local planning authority | 223 |
|   L is for local plan | 223 |
|   Resources | 225 |
|   Be open and inclusive | 227 |
|   Ringmaster | 228 |
|   Pitfalls | 229 |
| Local resident/local business | 232 |
|   Initiate or join a Neighbourhood Forum | 232 |
|   Beware the cost of formal localism structures | 233 |
|   Power of opinion | 234 |
|   If you don't ask, you don't get | 235 |
|   Opposition tactics | 236 |
| Concluding thoughts | 238 |
| | |
| **Appendix 1   Territorial extent of the Act** | **241** |
| | |
| **Appendix 2   From a Bill to an Act: The stages undergone by the Localism Bill** | **245** |
| | |
| **Appendix 3   Is it in force?** | **247** |
| | |
| **Appendix 4   List of documents replaced by the NPPF** | **257** |
| | |
| **Index** | **259** |

# Abbreviations

| | |
|---|---|
| **AONB** | Area of Outstanding Natural Beauty |
| **BIS** | Department for Business, Innovation and Skills |
| **CIL** | Community Infrastructure Levy |
| **CRBO** | Community Right to Build Order |
| **DCLG** | Department of Communities and Local Government |
| **DMPO** | Town and Country Planning (Development Management Procedure) (England) Order 2010 (SI 2010/2184) |
| **EAC** | Environmental Audit Committee |
| **GDPO** | Town and Country Planning (General Development Procedure) Order 1995 (SI 1995/419) |
| **GLA** | Greater London Authority |
| **HCA** | Homes and Communities Agency |
| **IPC** | Infrastructure Planning Commission |
| **LDA** | London Development Agency |
| **LDO** | Local Development Order |
| **LEP** | Local Enterprise Partnership |
| **LLDC** | London Legacy Development Corporation |
| **LPA** | Local planning authority |
| **MDA** | Mayoral Development Area |
| **MDC** | Mayoral Development Corporation |
| **MPG** | Minerals Policy Guidance |
| **NDO** | Neighbourhood Development Order |
| **NDP** | Neighbourhood Development Plan |
| **NIA** | Nature Improvement Areas |
| **NPPF** | National Planning Policy Framework |
| **NPS** | National Policy Statement |
| **NSIP** | Nationally Significant Infrastructure Project |
| **PAG** | Practitioners Advisory Group |
| **PAS** | Planning Advisory Service |
| **PEO** | Planning Enforcement Order |
| **PPG** | Planning Policy Guidance |
| **PPS** | Planning Policy Statement |
| **PROD** | Public Request to Order Disposal |

*Abbreviations*

| | |
|---|---|
| **RDA** | Regional Development Agency |
| **RSS** | Regional Spatial Strategy |
| **SAC** | Special Area of Conservation |
| **SPA** | Special Protection Area |
| **TIF** | Tax Increment Financing |

# Table of statutes

| | |
|---|---|
| Business Rate Supplements Act 2009 | 249 |
| Companies Act 2006 | |
| s 1(1) | 122 |
| 1159 | 121, 122 |
| Co-operative and Community Benefit Societies and Credit Unions Act 1965 | 122 |
| Equality Act 2010 | 36, 227 |
| Fire and Rescue Services Act 2004 | |
| s 2, 4 | 43 |
| Freedom of Information Act 2000 | 227, 237 |
| Greater London Authority Act 1999 | 117, 124, 125, 250, 255 |
| s 31 | 118 |
| 39A(2) | 124 |
| (4) | 125 |
| 41(1)(d)–(g) | 253 |
| 42B | 253 |
| 333A, 333D | 119 |
| 333F | 253 |
| (1)–(3) | 253 |
| Pt VIIA (ss 333ZA–333E) | 119 |
| 409 | 125 |
| 424(1) | 122 |
| Greater London Authority Act 2007 | 117 |
| Housing Act 1985 | 250 |
| Housing Act 1996 | 249, 250 |
| Housing and Regeneration Act 2008 | 250 |
| s 17, 18 | 124 |
| Human Rights Act 1998 | 80 |
| Industrial and Provident Societies Act (Northern Ireland) 1969 | 122 |
| Local Democracy, Economic Development and Construction Act 2009 | 59, 60 |
| Pt 5 (ss 70–87) | 60, 61, 220 |
| s 70(1) | 61 |
| 75 | 61 |
| 79(6) | 59, 60, 61 |
| 88 | 37 |
| 103 | 37 |
| Local Government Act 1972 | |
| Pt VA (ss 100A–100K) | 125 |
| s 123 | 123 |
| Local Government Act 2000 | 33, 35, 37, 41, 42, 253 |
| Pt I (ss 1–9A) | 37 |
| s 2 | 253 |
| (2) | 35 |
| 9H–9HE, 9M | 38 |
| 39(2), (3), (6) | 252 |
| Local Government Act 2003 | |
| s 31 | 203 |
| Local Government Finance Act 1988 | 198 |
| s 43 | 249 |
| 47 | 251 |
| Local Government Finance Act 1992 | 48 |
| Local Government, Planning and Land Act 1980 | 55 |
| s 135 | 121 |
| Sch 32 | 144 |
| Localism Act 2011 | 30, 31, 39, 59, 70, 71, 85, 131, 132, 187, 195, 211, 215, 217, 223, 225, 228, 230, 236, 241 |
| Pt 1 (ss 1–47) | 241 |
| Pt 1 Ch 1 (ss 1–8) | 33 |
| s 1 | 212, 251 |
| (1) | 33 |
| (7) | 254 |
| 2 | 33, 251 |
| (1) | 33 |
| (2), (3) | 34 |
| 3 | 33, 34, 251 |
| 4 | 33, 36, 251 |
| (1)–(3) | 34 |
| 5, 6 | 34, 251 |
| 7 | 251 |
| 8 | 251 |
| (2) | 248 |
| 9–14 | 251 |
| Pt 1 Ch 4 (ss 15–20) | 249 |
| s 15 | 36, 248 |
| 16 | 36 |
| 19 | 37, 248 |
| 20 | 248 |
| 21, 22 | 248, 249, 252, 255 |
| 23 | 247 |
| 24 | 249 |

## Table of statutes

Localism Act 2011 – contd
| | |
|---|---|
| s 25 | 39, 40, 227, 248 |
| 26 | 41, 247, 251, 252 |
| 27(1) | 42 |
| (6)(f) | 249 |
| 28 | 42 |
| (1) | 42 |
| 30 | 251 |
| 34 | 42 |
| (1) | 43 |
| 36 | 249 |
| 37 | 247 |
| Pt 1 Ch 8 (ss 38–43) | 248 |
| s 38–43 | 251 |
| 44, 45 | 248 |
| 46 | 252 |
| 47 | 248 |
| Pt 2 (ss 48–57) | 44, 242, 255 |
| s 53, 54 | 44 |
| 55, 56 | 45 |
| Pt 3 (ss 58–67) | 242 |
| s 64 | 252 |
| Pt 4 (ss 68–71) | 45, 242 |
| s 68 | 249 |
| 69 | 45, 251 |
| (1)–(6) | 249 |
| (7)(e) | 249 |
| (8) | 248 |
| 70 | 45, 249 |
| 71 | 45, 248 |
| Pt 5 (ss 72–108) | 47, 242 |
| Pt 5 Ch 1 (ss 72–80) | 47 |
| s 72 | 48, 248 |
| 73–80 | 248 |
| Pt 5 Ch 2 (ss 81–86) | 47, 49, 247 |
| s 81–85 | 234 |
| 86 | 2 34, 247 |
| Pt 5 Ch 3 (ss 87–108) | 47, 50, 247 |
| s 87 | 50, 213, 234 |
| (3) | 52, 213 |
| 88 | 50, 51, 213, 234 |
| (6) | 213 |
| 89, 90 | 234 |
| 91 | 234 |
| (2) | 53 |
| 92 | 213, 234 |
| 93, 94 | 234 |
| 95 | 53, 213, 234 |
| (2)–(5) | 53 |
| 96–98 | 234 |
| 99 | 54, 234 |
| 100 | 52, 234 |
| 101, 102 | 234 |
| 103, 104 | 234, 247 |
| 105 | 234, 248 |
| 106–108 | 234 |
| Pt 6 (ss 109–144) | 242 |

Localism Act 2011 – contd
| | |
|---|---|
| s 109 | 63, 65, 218, 220, 226 |
| (1)(b) | 247 |
| (2) | 247 |
| (3) | 220, 247 |
| (4)–(7) | 247 |
| 110 | 66, 67, 158, 184, 220, 237, 247 |
| 111, 112 | 67, 248 |
| 113 | 67, 137, 248 |
| 114 | 91, 248 |
| 115 | 91, 212, 235, 249 |
| Pt 6 Ch 3 (ss 116–121) | 69 |
| s 116 | 218, 247, 249, 254 |
| 117 | 83, 225, 247 |
| (2)–(5) | 83 |
| (6) | 83 |
| (e) | 83 |
| (7), (8) | 83 |
| 118 | 83, 247 |
| 119 | 84, 247 |
| 120 | 247 |
| 121 | 247, 249, 254 |
| 122 | 185, 215, 226, 234, 238, 247 |
| Pt 6 Ch 5 (ss 123–127) | 87 |
| s 123 | 87, 254 |
| 124 | 88, 226, 254 |
| (2) | 249 |
| 125 | 254 |
| 126 | 90, 254 |
| 127 | 89, 254 |
| Pt 6 Ch 6 (ss 128–142) | 111 |
| s 128 | 111, 112, 113, 252 |
| (1) | 112 |
| (2) | 249 |
| 129 | 112, 113, 249, 252 |
| 130 | 114, 252 |
| 131 | 252 |
| 132 | 252 |
| (10) | 114 |
| 133, 134 | 114, 252 |
| 135, 136 | 115, 252 |
| 137 | 115, 215, 252 |
| 138 | 115, 252 |
| (5) | 249 |
| (9) | 116 |
| 139 | 252 |
| 140 | 116, 252 |
| 141 | 252 |
| 142 | 252 |
| (3) | 249 |
| 143 | 205, 223, 227, 238, 248 |

Localism Act 2011 – *contd*

| | |
|---|---|
| s 143(4) | 238 |
| (5) | 206 |
| 144 | 247 |
| Pt 7 (ss 145–185) | 243 |
| s 145 | 249 |
| 146 | 250 |
| 147(1), (6) | 250 |
| 150 | 250 |
| (1) | 253 |
| (3) | 255 |
| 151–153 | 250 |
| 154 | 250, 252 |
| 155–157 | 252 |
| 158 | 250, 252, 254 |
| 159–161 | 252 |
| 162(1), (2) | 252 |
| (3)(a) | 252 |
| (4), (5) | 252 |
| 163, 164 | 252 |
| 165 | 250, 252 |
| 166 | 252 |
| 168–175 | 247 |
| 176 | 250 |
| 177 | 248 |
| 178 | 250, 252 |
| 179 | 252 |
| 183 | 248 |
| 184 | 254 |
| 185 | 252 |
| Pt 8 (ss 186–231) | 117, 243 |
| Pt 8 Ch 1 (ss 186–195) | 118 |
| s 186 | 118, 250, 252 |
| 187 | 119, 250, 252 |
| 188 | 119, 254 |
| 189 | 252 |
| 190 | 119, 250 |
| 191 | 119, 139 |
| (1) | 252 |
| (2)–(5) | 250 |
| 192 | 119, 254 |
| (2), (5), (6), (8) | 119 |
| (9) | 120 |
| 193, 194 | 250 |
| 195 | 250 |
| (1), (2) | 252 |
| Pt 8 Ch 2 (ss 196–222) | 39, 120, 248 |
| s 197(1) | 250 |
| (3)(e), (f) | 248, 250 |
| (5) | 248, 250 |
| (6) | 120 |
| 198 | 120 |
| 200(1) | 121, 122 |
| (2), (3) | 121 |
| (4) | 122 |
| (6)–(8) | 121 |
| (9) | 122 |
| (10) | 121, 122 |

Localism Act 2011 – *contd*

| | |
|---|---|
| s 201–204 | 122 |
| 205(1), (2) | 122 |
| (4) | 122 |
| 206 | 123 |
| (1)–(4), (6) | 123 |
| 207, 208 | 123 |
| 209 | 123 |
| (3) | 123 |
| (4) | 124 |
| 210–215 | 124 |
| 216 | 122 |
| 217 | 124 |
| (4), (5) | 124 |
| 219, 220 | 124 |
| 223 | 124, 250 |
| 224 | 125, 250 |
| 225, 226 | 125, 254 |
| 227–229 | 125, 255 |
| 230 | 250 |
| 231 | 125, 255 |
| Pt 9 (s 232) | 243 |
| s 232 | 254 |
| Pt 10 (ss 233–241) | 243 |
| s 233 | 247, 252 |
| 234–236 | 247 |
| 237 | 247, 249, 250, 251, 252, 253, 254, 255 |
| 238–241 | 247 |
| Sch 1 | 254 |
| para 2, 3 | 253 |
| Sch 2 | 37, 38, 248, 249, 252, 255 |
| Sch 3 | 249, 252, 255 |
| para 70 | 248 |
| Sch 4 | 41, 251, 252 |
| para 57, 58 | 247 |
| Sch 5 | 248 |
| Sch 6 | 248 |
| Sch 7 | 248 |
| Sch 8 | |
| para 1 | 247 |
| 13(1) | 247 |
| 18, 19 | 247 |
| Sch 9 | 69, 71, 72, 73, 210, 218, 247, 254 |
| Pt 1 (paras 1–4) | 74, 234 |
| para 2 | 210, 225, 232, 237 |
| Pt 2 (paras 5–7) | 80, 81, 234 |
| para 7 | 185, 210, 221, 225, 232, 233, 237 |
| Sch 10 | 69, 74, 185, 210, 221, 225, 232, 233, 237, 247, 249, 254 |

*Table of statutes*

Localism Act 2011 – *contd*
- Sch 11 ............................ 69, 79, 210, 225, 232, 247, 249, 254
  - para 2 ............................ 79
- Sch 12 ............... 69, 247, 249, 254
- Sch 13 ............... 111, 113, 249, 252
- Sch 14 ............................ 254
- Sch 16 ............................ 253
- Sch 17 ............................ 253
- Sch 18 ............................ 248
- Sch 19 ............................ 253
- Sch 20 ........................ 119, 252
- Sch 23 ........................ 253, 255
- Sch 24 ........................ 247, 252
- Sch 25 ........................ 119, 250
  - Pt 1 ............................ 254
  - Pt 2 ............................ 251
  - Pt 3 ............................ 251
  - Pt 4 ........................ 252, 255
  - Pt 5 ............................ 251
  - Pt 6 ............................ 249
  - Pt 7 ............................ 253
  - Pt 8 ............................ 249
  - Pt 10 ........................... 253
  - Pt 14 ........................... 249
  - Pt 15 ........................... 247
  - Pt 17 ........................... 249
  - Pt 18 ........................... 254
  - Pt 19 ........................... 254
  - Pt 20 ...................... 113, 253
  - Pt 21 ........................... 253
  - Pt 26 ........................... 253
  - Pt 27 ........................... 253
  - Pt 29 ........................... 249
  - Pt 30 ........................... 254
  - Pt 31 ........................... 253
  - Pt 32 ........................... 252
  - Pt 33 ........................... 255
  - Pt 34 ........................... 254

Ministers of the Crown Act 1975 .................... 121, 122

New Towns Act 1981 .................. 121

Planning Act 2008 ......... 85, 94, 110, 111, 113, 114, 147, 166
- Pt 3 (ss 14–30) ................... 110
- s 14 ............................. 75
- 33 .............................. 115
- 35, 35A ......................... 114
- 37(3), (4) ...................... 115
- 38, 42 .......................... 115
- 46 ......................... 112, 113
- 47 .............................. 215
  - (1), (2) ...................... 216
  - (6) ........................... 115
- 48, 49 .......................... 215
- 51 .............................. 111

Planning Act 2008 – *contd*
- s 51(2) .......................... 111
- 52, 53 .......................... 115
- 55 ......................... 115, 215
- 62 .............................. 111
- 88 .............................. 115
- 102A, 102B ...................... 116
- 120(2) .......................... 116
- Pt 11 (ss 205–225) ............... 91
- s 206 ...................... 91, 92, 96
- 208 .............................. 97
- 209 .............................. 96
- 211(1) ........................... 93
- 212 .............................. 94
  - (8) ............................ 95
- 212A ............................. 95
- 213 .......................... 95, 96
- 216 .............................. 92
- 216A ............................ 212
- 221 .............................. 91

Planning and Compulsory Purchase Act 2004 .......... 2, 21, 58, 59, 60, 67, 147, 187
- s 1 .............................. 57
- 2 ................................. 1
- Pt 2 (ss 13–37) .................. 224
- s 17 ............................. 224
- 20 ............................... 95
- 33A ........................ 220, 237
- 35 .............................. 137
- Pt 3 (ss 38–39) ................... 57
- s 38 ...................... 2, 57, 81, 152, 186
  - (6) ...................... 162, 220
- 38A .................. 72, 80, 83, 232
  - (1), (2) ....................... 81
  - (3) ................... 81, 221, 225
  - (4), (5) ....................... 81
- 38B ...................... 80, 81, 83, 210, 232
- 38C .................. 80, 83, 232, 233
- 39 ............................... 58
- 40, 41 .......................... 186
- 64 ............................... 95

Public Bodies Act 2011 ............. 139

Regional Assemblies (Preparations) Act 2003 ............... 58

Regulation of Investigatory Powers Act 2000 ................ 15

Town and Country Planning Act 1990 ............... 85, 88, 90, 109, 249
- s 55 .............................. 1
- 56(4) ............................ 99
- 61A–61D ......................... 186
- 61E ..................... 74, 83, 232
  - (1) ............................ 75

## Table of statutes

Town and Country Planning Act
1990 – *contd*

| | |
|---|---|
| s 61E(2) | 78, 82 |
| (4), (5) | 78 |
| 61F | 72, 74, 83, 225, 232, 237 |
| (5) | 73, 232 |
| (9) | 73, 74, 237 |
| 61G | 71, 74, 83, 225, 232, 237 |
| 61H | 74, 78, 82, 83, 232 |
| 61I | 74, 83, 232 |
| 61J | 74, 78, 82, 83, 210, 232 |
| 61K | 74, 75, 83, 210, 232 |
| 61L | 74, 78, 82, 83, 232 |
| (2)(b) | 78 |
| (5) | 78 |
| 61M, 61N | 74, 79, 83, 232 |
| 61O–61Q | 74, 83, 232 |
| 61W | 185, 215 |
| (2), (3) | 238 |
| (4) | 216, 217, 238 |
| 61X | 185, 215 |
| (2) | 238 |
| 61Y | 185, 215 |
| 70 | 205, 206, 223, 227, 238 |
| (2) | 162, 186 |
| (4) | 238 |
| 73 | 98 |
| 73A | 99 |
| 76A(10) | 98 |

Town and Country Planning Act
1990 – *contd*

| | |
|---|---|
| s 77(4) | 98 |
| 79(4) | 98 |
| 97, 100 | 98 |
| 102, 104 | 99 |
| 106 | 101, 102, 105, 217 |
| 171BA–171BC | 226 |
| 225C, 225F, 255A | 89 |
| 288 | 60 |
| Sch 1 | 75, 81 |
| Sch 2 | 75, 81 |
| Sch 4A | 186 |
| Sch 4B | 74, 83 |
| para 1 | 75 |
| 3 | 75, 225 |
| 4 | 75, 76, 233 |
| 5 | 75, 76 |
| 6 | 75, 77 |
| (2), (3) | 77 |
| 7 | 77, 233 |
| 8 | 77 |
| (2) | 77, 78, 82, 185, 221, 232, 237 |
| 9–11 | 77 |
| 14 | 78, 82, 233 |
| 15 | 78, 82 |
| Sch 4C | 79, 83, 232 |
| para 1, 3 | 79 |
| 4 | 232 |
| (5) | 79 |
| 5(6), (7) | 80 |
| 6 | 80 |
| 7 | 225 |

# Table of statutory instruments

Civil Procedure Rules 1998, SI 1998/3132
   Pt 54 (rr 54.1–54.36) ................ 236
Community Infrastructure Levy (Amendment) Regulations 2011, SI 2011/987 ............... 91
Community Infrastructure Levy Regulations 2010, SI 2010/948 ...................... 91, 92, 93, 94, 97, 106, 205, 212
   reg 4 ........................................ 97, 98
   5 ................................................ 99
   6 ................................................ 96
   8 ................................................ 100
   9 ................................................ 98
   12–14 ........................................ 93
   15–17, 19 .................................. 94
   20–24 ........................................ 95
   25, 26, 28 .................................. 96
   31 ........................................ 97, 98
   32, 33 ........................................ 97
   34–36 ........................................ 98
   43, 44, 46, 47 ........................... 103
   48–51 ........................................ 104
   59 ................................................ 92
   61 ................................................ 93
   64 ................................................ 100
   64A ..................................... 100, 106
      (3) ......................................... 100
   65–67 ........................................ 100
   68, 69 ........................................ 101
   69A, 69B .................................. 101
   70, 71 ........................................ 101
   Pt 10 (regs 112–121) ................ 106
   reg 113, 114 ............................. 106
   115–120 .................................... 107
   122, 123 .................................... 102
Conservation of Habitats and Species Regulations 2010, SI 2010/490 ...................... 183, 185
Environmental Information Regulations 2004, SI 2004/3391 .... 63, 227
   reg 9 ........................................ 63
Local Authorities (Contracting Out of Community Infrastructure Levy Functions) Order 2011, SI 2011/2918 ....................... 93
Localism Act 2011 (Commencement No 1 and Transitional Provisions) Order 2011, SI 2011/2896 ............................ 32, 248
Localism Act 2011 (Commencement No 1) (Wales) Order 2012, SI 2012/193 ............... 32, 251
Localism Act 2011 (Commencement No 2 and Transitional and Saving Provision) Order 2012, SI 2012/57 ......... 32, 249, 251
Localism Act 2011 (Commencement No 3) Order 2012, SI 2011/411 ...................... 32, 251
Localism Act 2011 (Commencement No 4 and Transitional, Transitory and Saving Provisions) Order 2012, SI 2012/628 ............... 32, 251, 252, 254
Localism Act 2011 (Commencement No 5 and Transitional, Savings and Transitory Provisions) Order 2012, SI 2012/1008 ................. 32, 253, 254, 255
London Legacy Development Corporation (Establishment) Order 2012, SI 2012/310 ...... 39, 82, 120, 121
Neighbourhood Planning (General) Regulations 2012, SI 2012/637 ............................... 71, 76, 237
   reg 5–7 ...................................... 71
   8–11 ......................................... 73
   12(1), (2) .................................. 74
   21–23 ........................................ 76
   Sch 1 ......................................... 76
Public Contracts Regulations 2006, SI 2006/5 ................... 49
Town and Country Planning (Development Management Procedure) (England) Order 2010, SI 2010/2184 ......... 137, 215
Town and Country Planning (Environmental Impact Assessment) Regulations 2011, SI 2011/1824 .................... 76, 185, 236
   Pt 2 (regs 4–6) .......................... 216
   Pt 4 (regs 13–15) ...................... 216
   Sch 1 ......................................... 75
   Sch 2 ......................................... 75, 80
Town and Country Planning (General Development Procedure) Order 1995, SI 1995/419 ............................. 137

*Table of statutory instruments*

| | |
|---|---|
| Town and Country Planning (Local Planning) (England) Regulations 2012, SI 2012/767 | 135 |
| Pt 2 (reg 4) | 135 |
| reg 5 | 135 |
| 6 | 136 |
| 18 | 136 |
| (2) | 136 |
| 20 | 136 |
| 22(1) | 136 |
| Pt 8 (reg 34) | 137 |
| Town and Country Planning (Mayor of London) Order 2008, SI 2008/580 | 117 |
| Town and Country Planning (General Permitted Development) Order 1995, SI 1995/418 | 130 |
| art 4 | 129 |
| Town and Country Planning (Use Classes) Order 1987, SI 1987/764 | 129, 130 |

# Table of cases

## B

Brent LBC v Risk Management Partners Ltd & London Authorities Mutual Ltd, Harrow London Borough Council [2009] EWCA Civ 490, [2010] PTSR 349, [2010] BLGR 99 .................................................................. 35

## F

Fidler v Secretary of State for Communities & Local Government [2010] EWHC 143 (Admin), [2010] 1 EGLR 94, [2010] 15 EG 96 .................... 88

## G

Ghadami v Harlow District Council [2004] EWHC 1883 (Admin), [2005] BLGR 24, [2005] 1 P & CR 19 .................................................. 41

## N

National Secular Society v Bideford Town Council see R (on the application of National Secular Society) v Bideford Town Council [2012] EWHC 175 (Admin), [2012] Eq LR 326

## R

R v Brent London Borough Council, ex p Gunning (1985) 84 LGR 168 ......... 86
R v Panel for Takeovers & Mergers, ex p Datafin [1987] 1 QB 815 ................. 74
R (on the application of Cala Homes (South) Ltd) v Secretary of State for Communities & Local Government [2010] EWHC 2866 (Admin), [2011] BLGR 204, [2010] 46 EG 116 (CS) ...................................................... 61, 63, 210
R (on the application of Cala Homes (South) Ltd) v Secretary of State for Communities & Local Government [2011] EWHC 97 (Admin), [2011] 1 P & CR 22, [2011] JPL 887 .................................................................. 61, 62
R (on the application of Cala Homes (South) Ltd) v Secretary of State for Communities & Local Government [2011] EWCA Civ 639, [2011] 2 EGLR 75, [2011] 34 EG 68 .................................................................. 219
R (on the application of Harris) v London Borough of Haringey [2009] EWHC 2329 (Admin) ............................................................................................ 40
R (on the application of Lewis) v Redcar & Cleveland Borough Council [2008] EWCA Civ 746, [2009] 1 WLR 83, [2008] BLGR 781 ............................ 40
R (on the application of Williams) v Surrey County Council [2012] EWHC 867 (QB) .................................................................................................. 36
R (on the application of National Secular Society) v Bideford Town Council [2012] EWHC 175 (Admin), [2012] Eq LR 326 ...................................... 36

## S

Secretary of State for Communities & Local Government v Welwyn Hatfield Borough Council (Alan Beesley, interested party) [2011] UKSC 15, [2011] 2 AC 304, [2011] 2 WLR 905 ...................................................... 88, 89

# Chapter 1

# Introduction

This book assumes a general working knowledge of the current planning system in England and Wales. Our focus is the implications of the changes introduced by the incoming coalition Government as a result of the May 2010 election. This first chapter sets the scene for what follows by summarising:

- the planning system inherited by the new Government;
- the political background to the May 2010 election insofar as is relevant to the issues that concern us in this book.

Chapter 2 looks at the gestation of the Localism Act 2011 and the development of the new Government's policies following the May 2010 election, before we then examine in subsequent chapters the various legislative and policy changes in more detail.

## THE PLANNING SYSTEM INHERITED BY THE NEW GOVERNMENT

If one were to summarise the characteristics of the pre-existing system, they might be:

- a statutory structure having its roots in post-war legislation with five tiers of decision-maker and/or decision-making body, those tiers being –
  - the Secretary of State,
  - regional planning bodies,[1]
  - county councils (in parts of the country, a number having been abolished and their functions assumed instead by the relevant Local Planning Authority),
  - borough/district councils/unitary authorities ('Local Planning Authorities' or 'LPAs'),
  - parish/town councils (in place in parts of the country);
- a top-down approach where regional plans, approved by the Secretary of State, set out strategic policies and requirements, with which LPAs and county councils need to comply, in particular in formulating their local development plans;
- non-statutory planning policy guidance and circulars provided by the Secretary of State as a 'material consideration' for authorities to take into account in making planning decisions and making planning policies;
- the relatively minor role played by parish and town councils, again not in place in all areas;
- a development control (recently re-badged 'development management') system whereby 'development' (defined by statute[2]), save for specified

---

1  Introduced in Planning and Compulsory Purchase Act 2004, s 2.
2  Town and Country Planning Act 1990, s 55.

*Introduction*

exceptions, requires planning permission, which is granted by LPAs in accordance with a statutory procedure that provides a right of appeal, administered by the Planning Inspectorate. Decisions are taken in accordance with the development plan (ie the regional plan plus the LPA's adopted plan or plans) unless material considerations dictate otherwise.[3]

What was once a relatively simple administrative structure has become overlain through successive Governments' amendments with a mass of exceptions. The problems are various. For example:

- there have been various political initiatives to stimulate regeneration and economic growth that have given us concepts such as enterprise zones, simplified planning zones, development corporations and other regeneration bodies with varying amounts of planning powers given to them;
- the planning system has been made an important delivery agent for a number of social initiatives such as the provision of affordable housing, the provision of infrastructure and measures to tackle climate change;
- European Union law has imposed additional requirements such as environmental impact assessment and strategic environmental assessment.

The hard copy version of the planning law practitioner's bible, the Encyclopaedia of Planning Law and Practice, now runs to seven fat loose-leaf volumes.

Despite attempts to encourage more public participation ('community engagement' in the jargon), the system has become forbidding in the extreme to non-specialists, with its own impenetrable language and acronyms, a situation that reached its apogee with the replacement of the local plans system in the Planning and Compulsory Purchase Act 2004 with local development frameworks, made up of a series of 'development plan documents' and 'local development documents'.

The problems with the system are easy to identify, less easy to put right. They became the focus of a good deal of attention in the lead-in to the May 2010 election.

## THE POLITICAL BACKGROUND TO THE MAY 2010 ELECTION INSOFAR AS IS RELEVANT TO THE ISSUES THAT CONCERN US IN THIS BOOK

'Decentralisation' and 'the Big Society' were at the heart of the Conservatives' policy formulation ahead of the May 2010 election (an election for which they had plenty of preparation time due to Gordon Brown's late decision in October 2007 not to call an election following his succession as Prime Minister to Tony Blair in June 2007).

Greg Clark, now Minister for Decentralisation and Cities but then head of the Conservative Party's Policy Unit, published *Total Politics: Labour's Command State* in 2003.

---

3   Planning and Compulsory Purchase Act 2004, s 38.

## The political background to the May 2010 election

'We're not the only ones to point to the problems of the centralised state. It's easy enough to bandy around the rhetoric of decentralising reforms – even the Government say they're committed to a "new localism." But until such an abstract concept is turned into something more meaningful, it will never amount to anything more than fine words.'[4]

Conservative think tank, the Policy Exchange is influential in Tory thinking. In 2004 it published a report by journalist Simon Jenkins, entitled *Big Bang Localism*[5] capturing the views of many at the time with regard to the Labour Government's approach:

'After Mr Blair's second victory in 2001, the main agencies of centralism, the Treasury, Cabinet Office and Audit Commission, went near berserk. Public administration was overwhelmed with targetry and inspection. Consultants devised ever more fantastic schemes to fast-track, ring-fence and "silo" policy. One official described Downing Street as like Earl Haig's headquarters in the Great War, mechanically shovelling tens of thousands of inspectors over the top to gain six yards of improved service delivery. The period was one of "chaotic centralism".'

David Cameron assumed leadership of the Conservative party in 2005 and as part of his victory speech he said: 'There is such a thing as society, but it is not the same as the state'. Aside from the clever echo/not-echo of Margaret Thatcher's infamous (although often misconstrued, absent of its context) 'there is no such thing as society', the phrase appears to have been the seed for what became the 'Big Society' idea – 'reducing the role of central Government in favour of local determination and delivery of services'.[6] There is an excellent article by Steve Richards in the Independent, *Can the Big Society work?*[7]

David Cameron put Oliver Letwin in charge of a wide-ranging policy review.

In 2006, the Policy Exchange published another influential report, *Better Homes, Greener* Cities.[8] The report included the following:

'The planning system should be localised, with local authorities being placed in charge of densities, brown vs. green field ratios, design codes and Green Belt designation ... The planning system should be made more flexible, with greater freedom to change between planning designations and an extension of permitted development rights'

---

4   Clark, Greg and Mather, James (eds) (2003) *Total Politics – Labour's Command State*, Conservative Policy Unit, ISBN: 0-9544917-4 (available at http://www.conservatives.com/pdf/totalpolitics0903.pdf [accessed March 2012]), quoted in RTPI's evidence to the CLG Select Committee (1 October 2010) (available at http://www.rtpi.org.uk/download/10514/CLG-SC-Localism-Inquiry-RTPI-Evidence-01.10.10.pdf).
5   Jenkins, Simon (2004) *Big Bang Localism*, Policy Exchange (available at http://www.policyexchange.org.uk/assets/big_bang_localism.pdf [accessed March 2012]), quoted by RTPI, opp cit.
6   Available at http://www.rtpi.org.uk/download/10514/CLG-SC-Localism-Inquiry-RTPI-Evidence-01.10.10.pdf [accessed January 2012].
7   The Independent (8 February 2011) *Can Big Society Work?* (available at http://www.independent.co.uk/news/uk/politics/can-the-big-society-work-2207352.html [accessed December 2011]). Steve Richards has also gone into more detail in a series of four 30 minute programmes on Radio 4, *David Cameron's Big Idea*.
8   Evans, A and Hartwich, O M (2006) *Better Homes, Greener Cities*, Policy Exchange & Localism, quoted by the RTPI, opp cit.

*Introduction*

and that:

> 'Receipts from existing taxes associated with new development, such as Council Tax and business rates, should be hypothecated to the local authority.'

Another influence on Conservative thinking has undoubtedly been emerging work on behavioural thinking. The RTPI has put it as follows:

> 'It derives from Richard H Thaler, Professor of Behavioural Science and Economics at the University of Chicago and an adviser to the Conservative Party. In 2008 he wrote a book with fellow Chicago University Professor, Cass R. Sunstein, called *Nudge*[9] which encapsulated his thinking. It puts forward an approach that it terms "libertarian paternalism" which is achieved through designing and putting into place an "architecture of choice". One of the basic premises of this book is that:
>
>> "In many domains, including environmental protection …., we [argue] that better governance requires less in the way of government coercion and constraint, and more in the way of freedom to choose. If incentives and nudges replace requirements and bans, government will be both smaller and more modest."'

In June 2008, the Conservative Party published a policy paper, *Voluntary Action in the 21st Century*.[10] A now familiar theme was beginning to emerge:

> 'In the post-bureaucratic age, the people who will first perceive the new problems to be solved and discover the best ways to solve them will not be ministers holed up in Whitehall, but the legions of committed individuals, voluntary organisations, social enterprises, commercial companies, communities defined by geography or by shared interest as well as democratic government from neighbourhood councils to Westminster.'

The fruits of the policy review were a series of 'Policy Green Papers' in 2009 and 2010. There has been much focus on Policy Green Paper 14, *Open Source Planning*,[11] published in February 2010 (and of which more later). However, *Open Source Planning* should be read in context. Planning was just one of the policy areas where changes were sought. David Cameron launched *Control Shift: Returning Power to Local Communities* – Policy Green Paper 9[12] on 17 February 2009. This was a comprehensive and wide-ranging document that set out a series of underlying principles and tenets of the Conservatives' policy in relation to the balance between the state, local government and communities.

The document set out a 'five-pillar strategy to shift power away from the central state and firmly back to local people:

---

9   Thaler, Richard H and Sunstein, Cass R (2009) *Nudge*, Penguin Books.
10  Conservative Party Policy Green Paper (June 2008) *Voluntary Action in the 21st Century* (available at http://conservativehome.blogs.com/platform/files/green_paper_booklet.pdf [accessed December 2011]).
11  Conservative Party Policy Green Paper (February 2010) *Open Source Planning* (available at http://www.conservatives.com/News/News_stories/2010/02/~/media/Files/Green%20Papers/planning-green-paper.ashx [accessed December 2011]).
12  Conservative Party Green Paper (February 2009) Control Shift: Returning Power to Local Communities (available at http://www.conservatives.com/~/media/Files/Downloadable%20Files/Returning%20Power%20Local%20Communities.ashx?dl=true [accessed December 2011]).

*The political background to the May 2010 election*

## 1 Giving local communities a share in local growth

Under Labour, central government has tried to drive house-building and development through top-down targets. But councils that encourage house building and new business activity are not guaranteed any financial reward, and can even lose out. Instead of top-down targets, we need a new financial framework which rewards this essential activity. We will:

- enable local authorities to benefit financially when they deliver the housing that local people need;
- give local authorities the right to retain the financial benefits arising from new business activity in their areas;
- give local authorities a new discretionary power to levy business rate discounts; and
- make the local government funding settlement more transparent.

## 2 Freeing local government from central control

We will free councils from the central and regional bureaucracy which drives up our council tax, and ensure local services are delivered according to local need, not the requirements of distant government officials. We will:

- end Whitehall capping powers and give local residents the power to veto high council tax rises via local referendum;
- drastically reduce the centrally imposed bureaucratic burdens that drive up council tax;
- enlarge the freedom of local councils to act in the best interests of residents, by giving them a "general power of competence";
- give local councils greater freedom to determine how they carry out their statutory regulatory duties;
- abolish all process targets applied to local authorities, and free councils from intrusive and ineffective inspection regimes by abolishing the Comprehensive Area Assessment; and
- end all forced amalgamations of local authorities.

## 3 Giving local people more power over local government

We will put more power in the hands of local people and make councillors more accountable to their citizens. We want people to be able to see clearly, and exercise real influence over, what their elected representatives are doing with the power they are trusted with. We will:

- provide citizens in all large cities with the opportunity to choose to have an elected mayor;
- give people the power to instigate referendums on local issues;
- make the police accountable to the people they serve through directly elected commissioners, crime maps and quarterly beat meetings;
- put the power to judge the behaviour of councillors back in the hands of their citizens by abolishing the Standards Board, and repealing rules that prevent councillors representing their constituents' views on local issues;
- permit local authorities to devolve unlimited funding to ward councillors; and
- let local people choose the organisational structures of their local councils.

*Introduction*

**4  Giving local people more ability to determine spending priorities**

We will give local councils the freedom to spend money on the things that matter to local people, and give local communities more power over how money is spent locally. We will:
- give local people greater control over how central government funds are spent in their area;
- phase out ring fencing, so that decisions about how councils spend their budgets are taken by councils and their citizens alone; and
- make it easier for local government to raise money for local projects on the bond market.

**5  Removing regional government**

Under Labour, a distant and remote tier of ineffective regional government has been given increasing control over people's lives. We want to devolve power from regional quangos back down to local councils. We will:
- abolish all regional planning and housing powers exercised by regional government;
- abolish the Government Office for London and devolve its functions to London boroughs or the Mayoralty and Greater London Authority, as appropriate;
- strip the Regional Development Agencies of their powers over planning; and give local governments the power to establish their own local enterprise partnerships to take over development functions from RDAs;
- abandon plans to regionalise fire control (while providing new measures to enhance resilience in the case of a national emergency); and
- replace the Infrastructure Planning Commission with speeded up public enquiries for infrastructure development or private/hybrid legislation for major projects.'

It will be seen that many of these proposals have now made their way into the Act or remain on the Government's policy agenda.

The party's proposals with regard to housing were set out in Policy Green Paper 10, published on 7 April 2009, *Strong Foundations: Building Homes and Communities*.[13] Again, the proposals, taken from the document's executive summary are worth setting out. There is again a striking correlation with the system which is now emerging:

**'Our plans for a more sustainable housing market**

*Community-led housing*

… We will:
- Abolish the unsuccessful regional planning system and the counterproductive regional housing targets;
- Incentivise new house-building by matching local authorities' council tax take for each new house built for six years – with special incentives for affordable housing;

---

13  Conservative Party Policy Green Paper (April 2009) *Strong Foundations: Building Homes and Communities* (available at http://www.conservatives.com/~/media/Files/Green%20Papers/Housing-Green-Paper.ashx?dl=true [accessed December 2011]).

- Allow the creation of entirely new bodies – Local Housing Trusts – with new freedom to develop homes for local people, as long as there is strong community backing;
- Relax the rules that prevent thousands of habitable empty properties being used to house those on local authority waiting lists; and
- Broaden access to the government's databases of surplus public sector land and buildings, to enable members of the public to identify vacant government land that should be available for house-building.

*A planning system that delivers*

… We will:
- Ensure that the views of local residents are genuinely taken into account at the start of the planning process, by making pre-application consultations between developers and local people mandatory for major applications;
- Enable councils to revise their current local plans to protect Green Belt land and prevent the imposition of eco-towns against local wishes;
- Reverse the classification of gardens as brownfield land and allow councils to prevent over-development of neighbourhoods and stop "garden grabbing"; and
- Guarantee that councillors have the freedom to campaign and represent their constituents on planning issues.

*Social housing that helps not hinders*

… We will:
- Pilot "Right to Move", a scheme which allows good social tenants to demand that their social landlord sell their current property and use the proceeds, minus transaction costs, to buy (and thereby bring into the social rented sector) another property of their choice – anywhere in England;
- Re-introduce a comprehensive national mobility scheme for those tenants who wish to move to existing social sector properties;
- Offer good social tenants a 10% equity share in their social rented property, which can be cashed in when they leave the social rented sector;
- Strengthen shared ownership options by encouraging flexible equity stakes, working to get greater private sector involvement in shared ownership, and ensuring that shared ownership buyers are not treated as subprime borrowers;
- Ensure that tenants moving within the social sector keep their Right to Buy discounts;
- Instigate a formal review of waiting lists policy to make the system more fair and transparent; and
- Implement a range of policies to address the problems of homelessness.

*Housing that contributes to a low carbon economy*

… We will:
- Scrap the discredited Home Information Packs (HIPs), liberating Energy Performance Certificates to genuinely help people improve the environmental standing of their property;

## Introduction

- Allow all households to benefit from lower fuel bills with an entitlement to have £6,500 worth of energy efficiency improvements done to their home – the costs being recovered automatically through the household energy bill over a period up to 25 years;
- Permit employers to count carbon reductions they achieve in employees' homes towards their own emissions reduction targets;
- Ensure that every gas and electricity bill contains information which allows each household to compare their energy consumption with average households of a comparable size; and
- Support the "Merton Rule" which gives local authorities the powers to set renewable and low carbon energy targets for new development.'

This was the background against which *Open Source Planning* was published in February 2010. *Open Source Planning's* executive summary pulls no punches. It starts:

> 'The planning system is vital for a strong economy, for an attractive and sustainable environment, and for a successful democracy. At present, the planning system in England achieves none of these goals. It is broken.'

It goes on to walk the tight-rope between encouraging economic growth and decentralisation/localism:

> 'The purpose of the planning system is to reconcile, in the most equitable and efficient way possible, competing economic, social and environmental priorities, at the national and local level.
>
> To rebuild Britain's broken economy, we have to reinvigorate our construction and development industries and the investment that goes with them. Without a transformed planning system, our chances of getting the investment and growth we need will be hampered and possibly crippled, because today's centralised, bureaucratic planning system gives local communities little option but to rebel against Whitehall and regional diktats and, all too often, against the notion of development itself. The result is that far from achieving central targets, we are seeing historically low levels of house building which fail to match the needs of our economy or our society.'

The executive summary stresses the need for 'radical change'. It postulates that '[c]ommunities should be given the greatest possible opportunity to have their say and the greatest possible degree of local control ... [I]f we can enable communities to find their own ways of overcoming the tensions between development and conservation, local people can become proponents rather than opponents of appropriate economic growth'. The document uses computer technology:[14]

> 'Only a radical reboot is going to deliver the planning system that we need to succeed in the years to come.'

The summary talks of enabling local people and local government to 'produce their own distinctive local policies to create communities which are sustainable, attractive and good to live in'. Local people in each neighbourhood would 'be

---

14  The executive summary of *Open Source Planning* defines open source as 'a concept which originated in the software industry, where it aims to make computer programming open to all in a highly flexible and adaptable way. Its values of transparency and free access have held out the chance of opening up the software industry to better quality software at a lower cost than before. We believe this is just the approach our planning system also requires'.

## The political background to the May 2010 election

able to specify what kind of development and use of land they want to see in their area'. There would be a framework of incentives for development.

The document set out a series of radical proposals for reform of the planning system, including:

- A proposed new national planning framework, which would include, in a single document, the main features of all national planning policies, to be debated and voted upon in both Houses of Parliament.
- Abolition of regional planning bodies, policies and targets.
- 'Collaborative democracy' to be adopted in creating local plans. If an area fails to adopt its local plan by a specified deadline, a 'presumption in favour of sustainable development' is to apply.
- To reform the planning appeal system, by permitting third party appeals against grant of planning permission and to reduce developers' rights of appeal narrowing the circumstances in which (a) procedures are followed incorrectly and (b) the local plan is contravened. A mechanism for avoiding consideration of vexatious appeals is also to be introduced. (These proposals have not to date been taken forward.)
- To remove the Planning Inspectorate's powers to alter draft local plans. In the event that there is a direct breach of national planning guidance in a draft local plan, the Planning Inspectorate is to report it to the Secretary of State. If the Secretary of State is of the view that the draft local plan is not in accordance with national planning guidance, then the Council will be required to amend and resubmit its local plan for further consideration, encouraging greater dialogue between developers and the local community in relation to proposed planning applications, including:
  - legislating to ensure that, on projects above a given threshold the local community's view on design is sought, before the planning application is submitted to the Council; and
  - providing developers with the ability to be able to voluntarily compensate immediate neighbours for impacts associated with a planning application, in return for their support in the planning process. (This specific proposal has not to date been taken forward.)
- To reward, through grant funding, LPAs that grant planning permission for affordable homes and new house building.
- To give authorities the ability to abolish local affordable housing targets in local plans.
- To make the proposed Infrastructure Planning Commission a section of the Planning Inspectorate, to be known as the 'Major Infrastructure Unit'. The Unit would make recommendations to the Secretary of State, rather than make the final decision on Nationally Significant Infrastructure Projects.
- To replace the Community Infrastructure Levy with a single, unified local tariff applicable to all residential and non-residential development at graded rates, depending on the size of the development. The proceeds of this tariff would be applied directly to the site-specific impacts and to the community where the development is being undertaken and tariffs would not be charged on affordable housing.
- To legislate to relax restrictions on councillors engaging in discussions with applicants and potential applicants.
- To introduce flexibility into use classes, including:

## Introduction

- – providing an automatic right to change the use of any existing building to an educational use via permitted development; and
- – removing the need for planning permission for the installation of micro-generating equipment.
- To restrict the ability to apply for retrospective planning permission to allow only the rectification of genuine mistakes.
- To undo the changes in Planning Policy Statement 4 *Planning for Sustainable Growth* (December 2009) by re-introducing the 'needs' test and to allow councils to take competition issues into account when formulating their local plans. (These proposals have not to date been taken forward.)
- To create a Conservation Credits scheme, providing incentives for developers to protect bio-diversity.
- To review laws relating to 'blight' to ensure that the means of seeking reimbursement for blight is easier, quicker and that the level of compensation is fair.

The principal author of *Open Source Planning* was John Howell, MP for Henley.[15] He describes some of the background to the preparation of the document in his keynote address to the September 2011 Oxford Joint Planning Law Conference:[16]

> 'In writing Open Source Planning, I and colleagues had well over 100 meetings with regular users of the planning system. [...] We spread our net widely and included environmentalists, lawyers, planners, house builders, specialist developers, infrastructure providers, local councillors, those involved in consultation and of course representatives of local community groups.
>
> The consistent message from all these meetings was:
> - that the planning system was broken; and
> - that the planning system should be vital for a strong economy, for an attractive and sustainable environment, and for a successful democracy.
>
> There was also a strong message that in none of these areas did the planning system achieve these goals.
>
> Given the scale of the problems, we were encouraged widely to take the view that piecemeal reform of the planning system was not an adequate response and that the tinkering with the planning system undertaken by previous Governments was not the answer.'

The proposals set out in *Open Source Planning* and the other policy green papers found their way into the Conservative Manifesto within which 'Building a Big Society' was a central theme.[17]

The twin strands of encouraging growth and encouraging decentralisation are of course not new for the Conservative Party. Hugh Bullock's excellent paper to the 2011 Oxford Joint Planning Law Conference[18] examines the ideological background to the Localism Bill. He draws attention to the statement in Winston

---

15 Currently Parliamentary Private Secretary to Minister for Decentralisation and Cities, Greg Clark.
16 JPL Issue 13 (2011) *Localism and Growth.*
17 Conservative Party Manifesto (April 2010) (available at http://media.conservatives.s3.amazonaws.com/manifesto/cpmanifesto2010_lowres.pdf [accessed December 2011]).
18 JPL Issue 13 (2011) *Localism and Growth.*

## The political background to the May 2010 election

Churchill's 1950 election manifesto: 'The present [planning] machinery is much too cumbersome, too rigid and too slow' and to the pro-growth policies within Circular 22/80 and 14/85. He refers to (now Minister for Decentralisation and Cities) Greg Clark's work in the early 2000s as then head of the Conservative Party Policy Unit, in criticising Blair's Labour Government for its 'command state' where 'centralised bureaucracies took power and control that should properly belong to individuals, communities and professionals'.[19]

For another good analysis of the concept of localism in planning and its origins, we recommend the Royal Town Planning Institute's evidence to the CLG Select Committee, dated 1 October 2010.[20] The evidence contains the following:

'The concept of localism, by other names, is not new to planning. Indeed, it can be said to have been at the heart of planning since planning became a statutory function. The statement below can be seen to embody key aspects of localism:

It is not merely landowners in the area who are affected or even business interests. Too often in the past the objections of a noisy minority have been allowed to drown the voices of other people vitally affected. These too must have their say, and when they have had it, the provisional plan may need a good deal of alteration, but it will be all the better for that since it will reflect actual needs democratically expressed. In the past, plans have been too much the plans of officials and not the plans of individuals, but I hope we are going to stop that.[21]

Interestingly, the statement was made over 60 years ago – by Rt. Hon. Lewis Silkin MP in introducing the Town and Country Planning Bill into the Commons in 1947.

This focus on local communities being given a real opportunity to influence the future of their areas has continued in planning guidance and in practice. In 1968, the Government commissioned Arthur Skeffington MP to hold an inquiry into participation in planning. This report[22] found that:

Planning is a prime example of the need for this participation, for it affects everybody. People should be able to say what kind of community they want and how it should develop: and should be able to do so in a way that is positive and first-hand. It matters to us all that … we can influence the shape of our community so that the towns and villages in which we live, work, learn and relax may reflect our best aspirations.

Current guidance, in the form of Planning Policy Statement (PPS1) Delivering Sustainable Development,[23] states that:

Plans should be drawn up with community involvement and present a shared vision and strategy of how the area should develop to achieve more sustainable patterns of development.'

---

19  Greg Clark, James Mathers (eds) of Conservative Policy Unit (2003) *Total Politics: Labour's Command State.*
20  Available at http://www.rtpi.org.uk/download/10514/CLG-SC-Localism-Inquiry-RTPI-Evidence-01.10.10.pdf [accessed January 2012].
21  Rt Hon Lewis Silkin MP, House of Commons, 3rd Reading of Town and Country Planning Bill, 1947.
22  Ministry of Housing & Local Government *et al* (1969) *People and Planning.*
23  Available at http://www.communities.gov.uk/documents/planningandbuilding/pdf/planningpolicystatement1.pdf [accessed January 2012].

*Introduction*

We have referred earlier to a 'tight-rope between encouraging growth and decentralisation/localism'. Of course this sort of statement assumes that the two objectives cannot be reconciled. The challenges in that regard are significant given the widespread perception that, in the absence of central direction, local communities would often prefer the status quo to the levels of development that are perceived as required from the perspective of housing need or of economic growth and activity. This tension is evident throughout the localism debate. Is it, for example, legitimate to dismiss local concerns about development proposals as 'NIMBY' ('not in my back yard') concerns? Is it consistent with a localism agenda to promote development by way of unelected Local Enterprise Partnerships or Mayoral Development Corporations?

The Liberal Democrats had a less developed policy position going into the May 2010 election, although localism has long been central to Liberal Democrat thinking. Their manifesto and more detailed policy document on the environment contained a number of proposals that, with the benefit of hindsight, were surprisingly consistent with those of the Conservatives, for example:

- to allow a third-party right of appeal in cases where planning decisions go against locally agreed plans;
- to require a local competition test for all planning applications for new retail developments;
- to abolish the Infrastructure Planning Commission and 'return decision-making, including housing targets, to local people';
- to 'stop "garden grabbing", defining gardens as Greenfield sites in planning law so that they cannot so easily be built over';
- to create a 'new designation – similar to Site of Special Scientific Interest status – to protect green areas of particular importance or value to the community'.

It is interesting to complete the picture by looking at the 2010 Labour manifesto.[24] The incumbent government always of course finds it more challenging to arrive at a new package of proposals. What is striking is the level of correlation with the other two main parties. The cover image on the document shows a family taking in an idyllic landscape of fields, hedges and trees with a village in the distance. No talk of a broken system of course: Labour's 'regeneration policies have transformed previously neglected communities and our great cities are among the best in the world'.

The document proposes a regional growth fund, 'a major devolution of power' to 'our core cities and city regions', support for post offices, shops and pubs in rural communities, new powers for local government, with fewer ring-fenced budgets. Councillors would have enhanced scrutiny powers and local residents would be able to petition to demand action. There would be more city regions with directly-elected mayors enjoying London-style powers. A separate document, setting out Labour's plan for housing, proposed giving 'new powers to Parish Councils to provide up to 10–15 new affordable homes in their community, without the need for individual planning applications from the local authority'.

---

24 Labour Party Manifesto (2010) (available at: http://www.labour.org.uk/uploads/TheLabourPartyManifesto-2010.pdf [accessed December 2011]).

## Chapter 2

# May 2010 to April 2012, the changes unfold

The outcome of the 6 May 2010 election was a hung Parliament; only the second UK general election to deliver such a result since the Second World War.[1] We waited until 12 May for the Conservatives and Liberal Democrats to announce that the two parties had reached a 'coalition deal'. An initial seven page document headed *Conservative Liberal Democrat Coalition Negotiations: Agreements Reached 11 May 2010*[2] was published on 12 May 2010. It was expressed to be a document that set out the agreement reached between Conservatives and Liberal Democrats on a range of issues 'that needed to be resolved ... in order for [the parties] to work together as a strong and stable government. It will be followed in due course by a final Coalition Agreement, covering the full range of policy and including foreign, defence and domestic policy issues not covered in this document'.

Section 1 was headed 'Deficit Reduction':

'The parties agree that deficit reduction and continuing to ensure economic recovery is the most urgent issue facing Britain.'

An emergency budget was proposed within 50 days of signing of the Coalition Agreement. A full Spending Review would be held in the Autumn of 2010 'following a fully consultative process involving all tiers of government and the private sector'. Under Section 6, 'Political Reform', it was announced that the 'parties will promote the radical devolution of power and greater financial autonomy to local government and community groups. This will include a full review of local government finance'. Under Section 11, 'Environment', a series of measures were set out which the parties 'agree to implement ... to fulfil our joint ambitions for a low carbon and eco-friendly economy'. A political compromise was set out in relation to nuclear power:

'Liberal Democrats have long opposed any new nuclear construction. Conservatives, by contrast, are committed to allowing the replacement of existing nuclear power stations provided they are subject to the normal planning process for major projects (under a new national planning statement) and provided also that they receive no public subsidy.

We have agreed a process that will allow Liberal Democrats to maintain their opposition to nuclear power while permitting the government to bring forward the national planning statement for ratification by parliament so that new nuclear construction becomes possible.

This process will involve:
- The government completing the drafting of a national planning statement and putting it before parliament;

---

1 The Conservatives won 307 seats, Labour 258 and the Liberal Democrats 57 out of a total of 650 seats. The previous hung Parliament followed the general election in February 1974.
2 Available at http://www.conservatives.com/~/media/Files/Downloadable%20Files/agreement.ashx?dl=true [accessed January 2012].

*May 2010 to April 2012, the changes unfold*

- Specific agreement that a Liberal Democrat spokesman will speak against the planning statement, but that Liberal Democrat MPs will abstain; and clarity that this will not be regarded as an issue of confidence.'

There were no other references to planning reform – plainly matters of detail that were to be left to the subsequent Coalition Agreement, published on 20 May 2010.

In some ways, the Coalition Agreement represented a remarkable achievement, crunching together two parties' pre-election manifestos to arrive at a 'programme for partnership government'.

The foreword to the 20 May 2010 document, jointly written by the Conservatives' leader David Cameron, now Prime Minister, and Liberal Democrats' leader, Nick Clegg, now Deputy Prime Minister, refers in its first substantive paragraph to a shared 'conviction that the days of big government are over; that centralisation and top-down control have proved a failure. We believe that the time has come to dispose power more widely in Britain today; to recognise that we will only make progress if we help people to come together to make life better. In short it is our ambition to distribute power and opportunity to people rather than hoarding authority within government. That way we can build the free, fair and responsible society we want to see'.

There are later references to:

- 'a determination to oversee a radical redistribution of power away from Westminster and Whitehall to Councils, communities and homes across the nation. Wherever possible we want people to call the shots over the decision that affect their lives'; and
- 'Our government will be a much smarter one, shunning the bureaucratic levels of the past and finding intelligent ways to encourage, support and enable people to make better choices for themselves'.

The body of the document contains 11 sections. Section 4, 'Communities and Local Government', is most relevant to this book and we set out its 28 bullet points in their entirety:

- 'We will promote the radical devolution of power and greater financial autonomy to local government and community groups. This will include a review of local government finance.
- We will rapidly abolish Regional Spatial Strategies and return decision-making powers on housing and planning to local councils, including giving councils new powers to stop "garden grabbing".
- In the longer term, we will radically reform the planning system to give neighbourhoods far more ability to determine the shape of the places in which their inhabitants live, based on the principles set out in the Conservative Party publication Open Source Planning.
- We will abolish the unelected Infrastructure Planning Commission and replace it with an efficient and democratically accountable system that provides a fast-track process for major infrastructure projects.
- We will publish and present to Parliament a simple and consolidated national planning framework covering all forms of development and setting out national economic, environmental and social priorities.

*May 2010 to April 2012, the changes unfold*

- We will maintain the Green Belt, Sites of Special Scientific Interest (SSSIs) and other environmental protections, and create a new designation – similar to SSSIs – to protect green areas of particular importance to local communities.
- We will abolish the Government Office for London and consider the case for abolishing the remaining Government Offices.
- We will provide more protection against aggressive bailiffs and unreasonable charging orders, ensure that courts have the power to insist that repossession is always a last resort, and ban orders for sale on unsecured debts of less than £25,000.
- We will explore a range of measures to bring empty homes into use.
- We will promote shared ownership schemes and help social tenants and others to own or part-own their home.
- We will promote "Home on the Farm" schemes that encourage farmers to convert existing buildings into affordable housing.
- We will create new trusts that will make it simpler for communities to provide homes for local people.
- We will phase out the ring-fencing of grants to local government and review the unfair Housing Revenue Account.
- We will freeze Council Tax in England for at least one year, and seek to freeze it for a further year, in partnership with local authorities.
- We will create directly elected mayors in the 12 largest English cities, subject to confirmatory referendums and full scrutiny by elected councillors.
- We will give councils a general power of competence.
- We will ban the use of powers in the Regulation of Investigatory Powers Act (RIPA) by councils, unless they are signed off by a magistrate and required for stopping serious crime.
- We will allow councils to return to the committee system, should they wish to.
- We will abolish the Standards Board regime.
- We will stop the restructuring of councils in Norfolk, Suffolk and Devon, and stop plans to force the regionalisation of the fire service.
- We will impose tougher rules to stop unfair competition by local authority newspapers.
- We will introduce new powers to help communities save local facilities and services threatened with closure, and give communities the right to bid to take over local state-run services.
- We will implement the Sustainable Communities Act, so that citizens know how taxpayers' money is spent in their area and have a greater say over how it is spent.
- We will cut local government inspection and abolish the Comprehensive Area Assessment.
- We will require continuous improvements to the energy efficiency of new housing.
- We will provide incentives for local authorities to deliver sustainable development, including for new homes and businesses.
- We will review the effectiveness of the raising of the stamp duty threshold for first-time buyers.
- We will give councillors the power to vote on large salary packages for unelected council officials.'

There is an important health warning on the final page of the document:

*May 2010 to April 2012, the changes unfold*

'The deficit reduction programme takes precedence over any of the other measures in this agreement, and the speed of implementation of any measures that have a cost to the public finances will depend on decisions to be made in the Comprehensive Spending Review.'

The new Communities and Local Government ministerial team was as follows:

## Secretary of State for Communities and Local Government

Eric Pickles

Mr Pickles has been Conservative MP for Brentwood and Ongar since 1992 and Chairman of the Conservative Party since January 2009. Between 1988 and 1990, he had been leader of Bradford Council.

## Minister for Decentralisation and Cities

Greg Clark

Mr Clark has been Conservative MP for Tunbridge Wells since May 2005, prior to which he was Director of Policy for the Conservative Party from March 2001. In March 2003 he wrote a report that proved important to the party's emerging thinking and positioning in relation to New Labour, *Total Politics – Labour's Command State*.[3]

Mr Clark's ministerial role straddles the Department for Communities and Local Government ('DCLG') and the Department for Business, Innovation and Skills ('BIS'): his initial ministerial role in May 2010 was as Minister for Decentralisation, within DCLG, but this was augmented in July 2011 by an additional role as BIS' Minister for Cities.

## Minister for Housing and Local Government

Grant Shapps

Mr Shapps has been Conservative MP for Welwyn Hatfield since May 2005. He had publically supported David Cameron's leadership campaign and when Cameron became leader in 2005 he assumed the role of Vice-Chairman of the Conservative Party. He is an enthusiastic embracer of social media.[4]

## Parliamentary Under Secretary of State

Andrew Stunell

Mr Stunell has been Liberal Democrat MP for Hazel Grove since 1997. He has an extensive local government background as a former Stockport Metropolitan District Council and Cheshire County Council member.

---

[3] Clark, Greg and Mather, James (eds) (2003) *Total Politics – Labour's Command State*, Conservative Policy Unit, ISBN: 0-9544917-3-4 (available at http://www.conservatives.com/pdf/totalpolitics0903.pdf [accessed December 2011]).

[4] Tweeting as @grantshapps with over 43,000 followers at last count.

## Parliamentary Under Secretary of State

Bob Neill

Mr Neill has been Conservative MP for Bromley and Chislehurst since June 2006. Within a year he joined the Conservatives' shadow Communities and Local Government team and in 2009 he became responsible for planning matters, thereby being seen by many as the mouth-piece for the proposals contained within *Open Source Planning* at many events in the lead-up to the May 2010 election. He has a strong local government background, having served as London Assembly member for Bexley and Bromley between 2000 and 2008 and leader of the Conservative Group on the Assembly.

## Parliamentary Under Secretary of State

Baroness Hanham

Baroness Hanham is a Conservative member of the House of Lords and was leader of the Royal Borough of Kensington and Chelsea from 1989 to 2000.

The Queen's Speech, delivered at the official state opening of Parliament on 25 May 2010, set out the new Government's legislative priorities for the coming year. Her Majesty announced 24 new Bills including a Bill 'to devolve greater powers to Councils and neighbourhoods and give local communities control over housing and planning decisions. Legislation will be introduced to stop uncompleted plans to create unitary Councils'. The Cabinet Office's accompanying briefing note[5] referred to the proposed legislation as the 'Decentralisation and Localism Bill'[6] and we set out the contents of the note as follows:

> 'The Bill would devolve greater powers to councils and neighbourhoods and give local communities control over housing and planning decisions.
>
> **The main benefits of the Bill would be:**
> - Empowering local people.
> - Freeing local government from central and regional control.
> - Giving local communities a real share in local growth.
> - A more efficient and more local planning system.
>
> **The main elements of the Bill are:**
> - Abolish Regional Spatial Strategies.
> - Return decision-making powers on housing and planning to local councils.
> - Abolish the Infrastructure Planning Commission and replace it with an efficient and democratically accountable system that provides a fast-track process for major infrastructure projects.
> - New powers to help save local facilities and services threatened with closure, and give communities the right to bid to take over local state-run services.
> - Abolish the Standards Board regime.

---

5  Details of the Decentralisation and Localism Bill, announced in the Queen's Speech 2010 (available at http://www.number10.gov.uk/news/queens-speech-decentralisation-and-localism-bill/ [accessed December 2011]).

6  A title which appears thereafter to have been shortened without explanation, to the Localism Bill – it would have been a mouthful ...

*May 2010 to April 2012, the changes unfold*

- Give councils a general power of competence.
- Require public bodies to publish online the job titles of every member of staff and the salaries and expenses of senior officials.
- Give residents the power to instigate local referendums on any local issue and the power to veto excessive council tax increases.
- Greater financial autonomy to local government and community groups.
- Create Local Enterprise Partnerships (to replace Regional Development Agencies) – joint local authority-business bodies brought forward by local authorities to promote local economic development.
- Form plans to deliver a genuine and lasting Olympic legacy.
- Outright abolition of Home Information Packs.
- Create new trusts that would make it simpler for communities to provide homes for local people.
- Review Housing Revenue Account.'

The new Prime Minister gave a speech on the economy on 28 May 2010. 'Rebalancing the economy' was one of his main themes:

'So government must get out of the way where it is inhibiting enterprise and it's got to get active in those areas where it is needed. And there's a third, crucial part of our coalition strategy for growth – which is to rebalance our economy.

Today our economy is heavily reliant on just a few industries and a few regions – particularly London and the South East. This really matters. An economy with such a narrow foundation for growth is fundamentally unstable and wasteful – because we are not making use of the talent out there in all parts of our United Kingdom.

We are determined that should change. That doesn't mean picking winners but it does mean supporting growing industries – aerospace, pharmaceuticals, high-value manufacturing, hi-tech engineering, low carbon technology. And all the knowledge-based businesses including the creative industries.

And it doesn't mean ignoring London – in fact we support Crossrail – but it does mean having a plan to breathe economic life into the towns and cities outside the M25.

I was speaking to Lord Heseltine about this – and few people know more about this than he does. He first visited the London Docklands when, in his words, it was "6,000 acres of forgotten wasteland." Today it is one of the wealthiest and most dynamic parts of our capital. His experience was that regeneration only works through public-private, central-local partnerships – the coming together of business, government and councils. So that's what you'll get from us.

An early task will be to reform and refocus regional support and the RDAs.
…

I will be assigning Ministers and senior MPs to some of our biggest cities, with responsibility to work with local communities to help drive forward economic development by making sure blockages in Whitehall are dealt with.

We will give our biggest cities the opportunity to elect executive mayors, powerful local politicians who know the area, who have real clout to drive projects through. And we will give much more power to local councils.

A new general power of competence will make it easier for them to set up banks, develop property, run new services and own assets. And we'll also give them the power to get together with local businesses to form their own local enterprise partnerships, to create the right environment for business investment and chart their economic future.'

Eric Pickles, the new Secretary of State for Communities and Local Government, seemed to relish his new role as the cabinet's plain-speaking northerner. These are some typical extracts from a speech he gave on 11 June 2010:[7]

'A friend of mine, a senator from Wisconsin, once said that "if you don't like the folks, don't be in our business". The previous government didn't like the folks. It didn't trust them. It always believed that it knew best. And we've just had thirteen years of the most centralising government in history. A controlling government, obsessed with targets, inspections and micromanagement. It left local government toothless. Community groups out in the cold. Residents powerless to change anything.

We've all seen the results. Voting rates plummeted – there's no point in voting if nothing changes. No matter who they vote for the council always gets in. There was no room for creativity or innovation in public services. You just followed the rules and ticked the boxes. And the money followed the power: so London and the South East grew at the expense of everywhere else in the country.

So when people ask me about my priorities in Government, I have 3 very clear priorities: localism, and we'll weave that into everything we do from parks to finance to policy. My second priority is localism, and my third is … localism.

Because if you want to restore faith in politics, you make sure that local government is properly accountable to the voters.

If you want to rebuild a fragile national economy, then you don't strangle business with red tape and let bloated regional bodies make all the decisions.

If you want people to feel connected to their communities. Proud of their communities. Then you give people a real say over what happens in their communities. And the power to make a difference.

Because we like the folks. We don't think we know better than they do. And we trust them to know what's best for them.

So we are determined to wrest control from the bureaucrats, the quangos, and central government departments. Taking power pushing it as far away from Whitehall as possible. I want you to understand, I am deadly serious about this.

We are definitely going to do this. We are going to shake up the balance of power in this country. We are going to change the nature of the constitution. Be in no doubt about our commitment to localism. I know I look like an unlikely revolutionary, but the revolution starts here.

---

7   Communities Secretary, Eric Pickles (11 June 2010) Queen's Speech Forum (available at http://www.communities.gov.uk/speeches/corporate/queensspeechforum [accessed December 2011]).

## May 2010 to April 2012, the changes unfold

It won't be in a single action or a single law. It will be through dramatic and bold actions, but also small and incremental changes. Localism is the principle, the mantra, and defines everything we do.

You might think, well, all governments talk like this. But we've proved it by getting on and doing it.

- We've made HIPS history and already the number of homes being put up for sale has gone up by 35 per cent.
- We've given a lifeline to thousands of businesses in ports who had huge backdated business rates hanging over their head.
- We've scrapped the top down housing targets and meaningless regional spatial strategies.
- We've put an end to the "garden grabbing" which has seen acres of land lost to intensive development.
- We've cut the ring fencing and red tape which comes attached to hundreds of millions pounds worth of central government grants.
- We're leading by example in making central government more open, more transparent, more accountable.
- And we're showing we're serious about saving money. Taking pay cuts ourselves, shining the spotlight on public sector pay, and leaving the public to draw their own conclusions.

That's not bad for four weeks work, if I do say so myself. And we have more in store for the next few weeks.

Everything we've done has been about giving up control, restoring the balance of power. So by the time that the localism bill is introduced later in the year, we'll already start to see localism taking shape and becoming a reality.

That bill will go even further in giving voters more power over local government and local spending. It will free up local government from the shackles of central government control. And it will continue the overhaul of the planning system: to put the community back in charge of how their area develops.

But there are three things I want you to understand about localism.

First, if this is going to have an effect, local government has got to be ready to step up to the plate. Seize the opportunities that are coming your way. Don't wait around for us to tell you what to do.

…

Second, localism isn't just about giving power back to local government. We're not talking about a tug of war between you and me.

It's even more important that we push power downwards and outwards to the lowest possible level. Out to the folks themselves.

Because if people know they can make a difference, then there's a reason to stand up and be counted.

We want to make sure people can take control and take responsibility in their street, their estate, their town. Solving problems and taking action for themselves. With neighbourhoods, people working together, as the basis for the big society.

And my third and final point is that this means there has never been a better time to be involved in local government.

No one working in local government signed up to be told what to do for the rest of their lives by Whitehall.

So there is a real opportunity for councillors today:
- to have much more fulfilling, rewarding careers
- to exercise genuine choice and power
- to change the face of their neighbourhoods
- to actually make a difference to people's lives

Local government will no longer be the poodle of central government. And together, we are going to be part of the most radical shake up of power there has been for generations.'

Chancellor George Osborne presented the first budget of the new Government on 22 June 2010.[8] His announcements included:

- The introduction of a simplified planning consents process in specific areas through use of Local Development Orders.[9]
- Confirmation of the Government's intention to scrap Regional Development Agencies, to take effect through a Public Bodies Bill. In their place locally elected leaders, working with business, would lead local economic development in their area in Local Enterprise Partnerships. It was announced that these would be supported by a new Regional Growth Fund for England in 2011/12 and 2012/13.
- Establishment of Infrastructure UK, a Treasury body designed to stimulate greater private sector investment in infrastructure and improve the Government's long-term planning and delivery.
- Encouragement for increased funding for infrastructure projects from the private sector so that public sector investment in infrastructure could be targeted on those projects with the greatest economic benefit and for which private funding is not available.

Disquiet over the pace of some of the changes, particularly the proposed abolition of the regional strategies, was beginning to build. The regional strategies saga is dealt with in more detail in Chapter 5 of this book but it is interesting to note statements made by planning minister Bob Neill in a House of Commons debate in Westminster Hall on 30 June. He referred to advice that had been given by a leading planning barrister, Peter Village QC (advice which ultimately of course was vindicated) that the abolition would be unlawful:

'... however eminent the opinion of Mr Village QC, it was at odds with the opinion of those who advised the DCLG.'

He went on to say that:

'because the arrangements for planning regulations under the previous Government were so complex, Ministers had something of a legal minefield to walk through to ensure that we get it right ... we are determined that we do not have any false starts.'

On 19 July 2010, Prime Minister David Cameron gave a speech in Liverpool on 'Big Society'. He described the 'Big Society agenda' as having three strands: social action, public service reform, and community empowerment. There are

---

8 HM Treasury(2010) *Budget* (available at http://cdn.hm-treasury.gov.uk/junebudget_complete.pdf [accessed December 2011]).
9 A concept originally introduced by the Planning and Compulsory Purchase Act 2004.

## May 2010 to April 2012, the changes unfold

'three techniques we must use to galvanise' the strands: decentralisation ('We must push power away from central government to local government – and we shouldn't stop there…'), transparency and providing finance.

On 6 July 2010, the Secretary of State announced the formal revocation of the regional strategies with immediate effect and on 22 July 2010 he announced the Government's intention to abolish the eight Government Offices for the Regions across England.

The Government's full Spending Review, promised in its initial Coalition Agreement, was published on 20 October 2010. Setting the reduction of the fiscal deficit as an urgent priority to secure economic stability at a time of continuing uncertainty in the global economy, the Spending Review set out a series of cuts across Government departmental budgets averaging 19 per cent over the following four years.

The detailed announcements included:

- Reduction in DCLG's budget in real terms of 33 per cent in the following five years.
- Restatement of the Government's focus on shifting power away from central government to local communities, citizens and independent providers.
- Restatement of the Government's plans to increase the national housing supply by reforming the planning system to make it more efficient, effective and supportive of development. The New Homes Bonus, which works by matching the council tax generated from every new home for each of the following six years, was referred to as a way of incentivising local authorities and communities to be supportive of housing.
- Extension of the Regional Growth Fund to three years and an increase in the fund by £400 million to £1.4 billion.
- Commitment by the Government to a programme to deliver up to 150,000 new affordable homes over the next five years, while reforming the council housing finance system to give local authorities more control over their finances.

This was followed on 28 October 2010 by a White Paper (sponsored by BIS rather than DCLG) entitled *Local Growth: Realising Every Place's Potential*.[10]

The White Paper continued on from commitments made in the June Budget and in the Comprehensive Spending Review. Aside from various local government finance proposals, covered in detail in Chapter 15 of this book, and announcements as to the 24 Local Enterprise Partnerships (LEPs), covered in detail in Chapter 13 of this book, the White Paper also gives an interesting BIS slant to the Government's package of planning reforms. The 'new streamlined planning system' is seen as crucial to attract growth and investment. Neighbourhood plans are referred to as a way to bring forward more development than set out in local plans. Local development plans should be produced by local authorities and used to establish a strategic framework on infrastructure and local economic growth requirements. Additionally, the Government's commitment to right-to-build powers is re-stated, which would allow local communities to deliver small-scale development without the need

---

10 BIS White Paper (October 2010) *Local Growth: Realising Every Place's Potential* (available at http://www.bis.gov.uk/assets/biscore/economic-development/docs/l/cm7961-local-growth-white-paper.pdf [accessed December 2011]).

for planning permission. Local authorities, public bodies and infrastructure providers are warned that a duty may be imposed on them under the Localism Bill to 'cooperate'.

On 10 November 2010, the High Court quashed the attempted abolition of the regional strategies. The Government ploughed on, announcing that their intended abolition was still a material consideration that decision makers would need to take into account and that abolition would follow by way of provisions in the Localism Bill.

By now speculation was mounting as to the timing of the Bill and its likely contents. It was initially expected in late November, but then slipped progressively further back until it finally was deposited in Parliament on 13 December 2010. It was accompanied by an 'Essential Guide'[11] and a 'Media Background Note'.[12]

To the relief of many in the development industry, it did not contain restrictions on the right to appeal and nor did it include third party rights of appeal (both ideas promoted in *Open Source Planning*). However, it was a massive undertaking – 204 clauses and 24 Schedules. Unusually for such a wide ranging piece of legislation, but unsurprisingly given the detailed policy development that had been taking place as already described, the Bill was not first published in draft or preceded by a White Paper. It was therefore to be expected that there would be a series of amendments and refinements as it proceeded through both Houses of Parliament.

We set out at Appendix 2 the steps that the Bill went through in its passage through both Houses of Parliament and the various versions of the Bill that were published.

The first detailed examination of the Bill in the House of Commons took place at Second Reading on 17 January 2011.[13]

On 17 March 2011, the all-party House of Commons Communities and Local Government Select Committee delivered a scathing report into the abolition of regional strategies. Its conclusions and recommendations, following four days of hearings and a substantial body of written evidence, included the following:

- 'We recommend that the Government adopt a more evidence-based and consultative approach to policy making in the future, especially in an area such as planning, where pragmatism and consensus are valuable assets in securing active rather than reluctant consent to new approaches to local involvement in decisions affecting people's everyday lives.'
- 'The peremptory abolition of Regional Spatial Strategies has created a hiatus in the planning framework, which risks producing a damaging inertia. We recommend that the Government issue guidance, as soon

---

11  DCLG (December 2010) *Decentralisation and the Localism Bill* (available at http://www.communities.gov.uk/documents/localgovernment/pdf/1793908.pdf [accessed December 2011]).
12  DCLG (December 2010) *Localism Bill Starts a New Era of People Power* (available at http://www.communities.gov.uk/news/newsroom/1794971 [accessed December 2011]).
13  SJ Berwin LLP (20 January 2011) *L is for Localism Blog* (available at http://localism.sjberwin.com/wp-content/themes/twentyten/2011_01_20.html [accessed December 2011]) summarised the six hour debate in Update 9.

as possible, compliant with the existing law, to assist local authorities and others on how to address the important strategic planning issues covered by RSSs and how to continue work on Local Development Frameworks.'
- 'We recommend that the Government include effective strategic planning arrangements in the Localism Bill, and that it work with all sectors to devise and promulgate an agreed approach to larger-than-local planning across a number of authorities.'
- 'A body of skill and experience has built up over the years, in partnership forums, to shape planning for both aggregate minerals and waste planning. We urge the Government to retain these arrangements, which have shown themselves to be advantageous, cheap and a means of keeping the anxiety over these difficult planning issues to a minimum.'
- 'National targets on environmental issues such as renewable energy will need to be distributed to each local authority preparing a local development framework, following a period of consultation and engagement with interested parties.'
- 'We look forward to the Government bringing forward amendments to the Localism Bill which will provide a framework for local authorities to work within, outlining what actions local authorities should take in their duty to cooperate, how they measure success or failure, how parties may insist on the delivery of what has been agreed, and default options if there is inadequate cooperation.'
- 'We are pleased that the Government has not advocated giving planning powers to LEPs. LEPs are not under any compulsion to consider environmental or social issues or to consider the multitude of interests that concern planning. Their primary purpose is "enterprise", which as an advocacy function cannot sit comfortably with statutory democratic regulation.'
- 'We welcome the Government's recognition of the need for more homes. We especially welcome its intention of ensuring that more homes are built in total than were built immediately before the recession, and of building 150,000 affordable homes over the next four years (although this is not an exceptional number by historic standards). However, we question whether either of these aspirations will be achievable under the Government's current proposals for the planning system.'
- 'No evidence was produced to support the Government's view that local authorities will achieve comparable rates of house building to those in the past, let alone an increase. If the evidence of success fails to materialise very quickly, the Government is going to have to review its selection of levers of influence. We recommend that the Government report back to the House in two years' time on the extent to which the measures it is taking are achieving the aim of increasing the rates of building of both affordable and market homes.'
- 'We recommend that the Government ensure that the New Homes Bonus scheme keeps the local development plan at its heart, where planning decisions are based on sound evidence and judged against criteria which include issues of sustainability. It should do so by explicitly linking the Bonus to homes provided for in the local plan following robust assessments of housing need. We agree that it should be paid only when those homes are actually built.'

- 'We recommend that the Government redesign the New Homes Bonus so that it better rewards the meeting of demonstrable need for affordable housing.'
- 'We recommend that the Government bring forward proposals which will ensure that robust and consistent evidence to support local development plans is produced and regularly updated in the most effective and efficient manner. It is not acceptable for Ministers to abdicate their responsibilities in this regard by leaving all the responsibility with under-resourced and under-skilled local planning authorities.'

Chancellor George Osborne's 23 March 2011 Budget once again stressed the role of the planning system in encouraging enterprise and growth. The documents published on Budget day included *The Plan for Growth*.[14] The statements most relevant to planning included the following:

- A new presumption in favour of sustainable development, so that the default answer to development is 'yes', unless it would compromise key sustainability principles in national policy. Draft wording was promised for May 2011.
- A new National Planning Policy Framework (NPPF) containing planning policies to deliver key economic social and environmental objectives, which would include the presumption in favour of sustainable development. A draft NPPF would be published for consultation later in the year.
- A steer from the Government that in planning decisions significant weight should be attached to supporting the economic recovery: the Government's policy is to ensure the planning system does everything it can to support growth. Local authorities should also press ahead with up to date development plans that set out the 'opportunities for growth'.
- A request from the Government that if developments have stalled due to extensive planning obligations negotiated in more buoyant market conditions, local authorities should reconsider these in light of changed circumstances and policy tests and modify the obligations where possible to allow development to proceed.
- Changes to the Localism Bill so that businesses would be able to bring forward neighbourhood plans and neighbourhood development orders and to ensure that Neighbourhood Forums and parish councils would have to consult local businesses as well as residents on these matters.
- Allowing the use of previously developed land to be chosen locally and removing nationally imposed targets for the proportion of development that should be built on previously developed land; however, Green Belt policy restrictions would remain.
- Piloting a land auction model, beginning with public sector land. This would allow councils to ask landowners to name a price for selling their land and to have 18 months within which they can purchase land at that price; the council would then be able to auction the land to developers on the basis of an acceptable planning use and keep any profits.
- Streamlining planning applications and related applications for other consents by removing bureaucracy from the system and speeding

---

14  HM Treasury (March 2011) *The Plan for Growth* (available at http://cdn.hm-treasury.gov.uk/2011budget_growth.pdf [accessed December 2011]).

## May 2010 to April 2012, the changes unfold

it up, including a new 12-month guarantee for the processing of all planning applications (including any appeal). It would also involve implementation of the Penfold Review.

- Revising environmental impact assessment procedures to make them clearer and remove unnecessary work.
- Ensuring a fast track planning process for major infrastructure applications.
- Consultation on proposals to make it easier to convert commercial premises (Classes B1, B2 and B8) to residential use (Class C3). The Government would also look at expanding permitted development rights for minor commercial development.
- Working with local authorities to expedite planning decisions for surplus public sector land which is suitable for housing (including surplus military land).
- Looking at the role of Local Enterprise Partnerships in the planning system.
- Strengthening the proposed local authority duty to co-operate on planning to ensure they demonstrate that they have planned for key sub-national infrastructure.

This list was perhaps the strongest sign yet of a more balanced approach seeking to temper the power that localism was to deliver into the hands of local authorities and neighbourhoods. Here were promises of policy and law to establish a pro-growth agenda, to which neighbourhoods and local authorities would need to work; indeed some measures, such as facilitating changes of use to residential and extending permitted development rights, would take more matters out of their remit altogether.

At the same time, the Government also announced the following 11 new urban enterprise zones (each falling within the area of a Local Enterprise Partnership): Birmingham and Solihull; Leeds City Region; Sheffield City Region; Liverpool City Region; Greater Manchester; West of England; Tees Valley; North Eastern; the Black Country; Derby/Derbyshire/Nottingham/Nottinghamshire; and the Royal Docks in East London, which was chosen by the Mayor. In addition, the Government commenced a competitive process for other Local Enterprise Partnerships to establish ten more enterprise zones across England (a total of 21).

Amendments to allow for business neighbourhoods were introduced on 11 May 2011. The report stage of the Bill was set for 17 May 2011, with the third Reading the following day. Numerous Government amendments were made but most controversial was the introduction of a new clause 15, which sought to require 'local finance considerations' to be taken into account in the determination of planning applications. This issue is covered in Chapter 15 of this book.

On 15 June 2011, DCLG published a statement on the presumption in favour of sustainable development.[15] The statement indicated 'an approach that the Government could take … It … will help to inform discussion about the way [the presumption] would operate'.

---

15 DCLG (June 2011) *Presumption in favour of sustainable development* (available at http://www.communities.gov.uk/planningandbuilding/planningsystem/planningpolicy/presumptionfavour/ [accessed December 2011]).

'... the Government's clear expectation is that we move to a system where the default answer to development is "yes", except when this would compromise the key sustainable development principles set out in national planning policy.'

'There is a presumption in favour of sustainable development at the heart of the planning system, which should be central to the approach taken to both plan-making and decision-taking. Local planning authorities should plan positively for new development, and approve all individual proposals wherever possible.

Local planning authorities should:
- Prepare local plans on the basis that objectively assessed development needs should be met, and with sufficient flexibility to respond to rapid shifts in demand or other economic changes
- Approve development proposals that accord with statutory plans without delay and
- Grant permission where the plan is absent, silent, indeterminate or where relevant policies are out of date

All of these policies should apply unless the adverse impacts of allowing development would significantly and demonstrably outweigh the benefits, when assessed against the policy objectives in the National Planning Policy Framework taken as a whole.'

The NPPF was published in draft on 25 July 2011. Perhaps the level of anticipation can be measured by the excitement of many earlier in the month when a leaked version of an earlier draft, marked '13 June 2011, version 4' gained wide circulation on the internet.

Publication of the draft NPPF became a significant media issue and indeed, unexpectedly for many of us, gave planning more headlines and column inches in the national media than had ever previously been the case. One early protagonist was national charity the National Trust. The day after the draft NPPF was published, National Trust's director-general, Dame Fiona Reynolds, was on the war path. The National Trust's statement read as follows:

**'Government reforms threaten green spaces**

"Planning is for people, not for profit," says Director-General, Dame Fiona Reynolds

The National Trust today signalled our grave concerns over the Government's planning reforms, warning that the proposed changes could lead to unchecked and damaging development in the undesignated countryside on a scale not seen since the 1930s.

The draft of the National Planning Policy Framework (NPPF), published by the Government yesterday, contains a core presumption that the default answer to any proposed development will be "yes".

This finally sounds the death-knell to the principle established in the 1940s that the planning system should be used to protect what is most special in the landscape, creating a tool to promote economic growth in its stead.

We have criticised the Government's focus throughout its consultation document on economic growth, which sends the message that schemes which deliver this alone will be enough to get planning permission. This will focus developers' and local authorities' attention on the narrow grounds of short-term financial gain, rather than delivering the wider public benefit that good planning can deliver.

We believe that the town and country planning system, as a whole, has served the country well.

It has enabled growth by guiding development to the places that need it, while protecting open countryside, preventing sprawl and safeguarding designated areas and historic buildings.

> "Those planning principles remain as necessary today as when they were first established. Weakening protection now risks a return to the threat of sprawl and uncontrolled development that so dominated public debate in the 1930s."

> "The National Trust believes in growth as we all do – but not at any cost. Development that works must pass a triple bottom line test – by showing that it meets the needs of people and the environment as well as the economy.

> Despite some warm words to this effect, the document makes it clear that development is to be encouraged, even urging local authorities to promote more development than is in the plan and over-allocate land for housing."

**Fiona Reynolds, National Trust Director-General.**

> "The Government's proposals allow financial considerations to dominate, and with this comes huge risk to our countryside, historic environment and the precious local places that people value."

We believe the tone and language of the NPPF and consultation document is wrong on several counts:
- the reversal of development controls in the public interest comes at too high a price. The NPPF's concept of sustainable development puts too little weight on benefiting people and the environment.
- the removal of much detailed guidance to local authorities leaves too much power in the hands of developers who will only need to show that their proposals will deliver growth for other important considerations – for example impact on communities, nature and landscape, and the environment – to be pushed aside.
- local people will have to rely on a development plan to protect what they treasure and shape where development should go. Yet only some local authorities have development plans in place and many local authorities and neighbourhood groups do not have the resources and specialist skills to create plans that genuinely integrate social, environmental and economic considerations. If there is no up to date development plan, planning applications will automatically get consent.

Fiona Reynolds concluded

> "The National Trust shares the Government's commitment to localism but it has got the changes to planning wrong. We urge a rethink of the NPPF before we throw the baby out with the bathwater.'"

We deal with the issues specific to the draft NPPF in more detail in Chapter 14. However, with the spotlight of the media and various planning and pressure group commentators now on the changes, and eager to tweet 24/7 on every twist and turn of the debate, calm discussion of the issues became more difficult. The potential intellectual tension, denied by the government, between the 'localist' and 'growth' agendas, became a more real political tension between those who began to see the Government's planning reforms as harmful to heritage and the countryside (and inappropriately driven by business agendas) and those who saw the reforms as necessary to achieve growth and delivery of homes.

In the meantime, the Bill had concluded its Committee Stage in the House of Lords and there were further significant changes: The main changes introduced in the Lords affected referendums and assets of community value. With regard to referendums, the concept was introduced of a 'special-case petition'. A special-case petition is a petition to hold a referendum where:

- the local authority's chief finance officer estimates that the cost of holding a referendum in response to the petition would be more than five per cent of the amount last calculated by that authority (before it received the petition) as its council tax requirement for the financial year in which the petition is received;
- the relevant officer of the local authority considers that the matter to which the referendum question relates has been or has substantially been the subject of at least one local or other referendum held in the previous four years in the area to which the petition relates; or
- the relevant officer of the local authority considers that there is a statutory process which gives members of the public an opportunity to make representations in relation to the subject matter of the petition and those adversely affected by the process have a statutory right of appeal in respect of the substance of the issues concerned or a statutory right to instigate a review of the substance of the issues concerned (judicial review or a complaint to the Ombudsman will not suffice).

In these circumstances the holding of referendums would be discretionary.

In relation to assets of community value, the surrender of a leasehold interest in an asset with at least 25 years to run would no longer trigger the notification requirements and an opportunity for the community to bid for the interest. In addition, a new clause was added to the Bill which provided for the local authority to inform the owner of an asset of a request from a community interest group to be treated as a potential bidder as soon as practicable following its receipt. Finally, a new duty of cooperation between local authorities was introduced, where any land of community value straddled different local authority areas.

Amendments were introduced to allow for business orientated neighbourhoods or 'business areas'.

Changes were made to the proposed power for local planning authorities to obtain a planning enforcement order where the normal time limits for enforcement had passed but a breach of planning control had been concealed. This power would now only apply in relation to *deliberate* concealment and not inaction.

A further change to planning enforcement was made to address concerns that had been expressed to the Government about land owners who are served with an enforcement notice when they, themselves, may be the victims of unauthorised development on their land. Local planning authorities would now have an ability to send a letter of assurance to the person concerned; this would

## May 2010 to April 2012, the changes unfold

indicate that in the circumstances the authority considered that the person was not at risk of being prosecuted if the enforcement notice were not to be complied with. Such a letter of assurance could be withdrawn if circumstances change.

Amendments were made in relation to Nationally Significant Infrastructure Projects to ensure that if the previous stages completed early, the three month deadline for reporting or for decision making (as the case may be) was to be calculated from that earlier date and, in relation to acceptance of applications, rather than forcing each application to adhere to rigid criteria, an amendment was made which would allow the Secretary of State to use his discretion to accept any application which he considered had been prepared to a satisfactory standard. This would allow him to accept applications with minor or technical flaws.

An entirely new Part 8 was added to the Bill covering aspects of compulsory purchase compensation in relation to land in England.

First, where actual or expected planning permission is taken into account in assessing the value of the land, it was to be assumed that the scheme underlying the compulsory purchase order was cancelled on the date on which notice of the order was first made but otherwise the valuation should take into account the planning permission or the prospect of planning permission existing on the relevant valuation date. This would obviate the need to refer back to planning policies in existence on the assumed date of cancellation of the compulsory purchase order (often some ten to 15 years before the valuation date).

Secondly, this part of the Bill introduced new provisions to deal with certificates of appropriate alternative development for land in England. In particular, the provisions introduced a new right of appeal to the Lands Chamber of the Upper Tribunal against a certificate issued by a local planning authority (as opposed to the existing position where the appeal is to the Secretary of State).

Aside from this, a number of amendments were made to Part 6 of the Bill (housing) covering the creation of tenancies of social housing by deed and registration of tenancies of social housing at the Land Registry, swaps of secure and assured tenancies, succession by a new tenant following death of the original tenant of social rented property, tenancy deposit schemes and a new exemption for co-operatives from the requirement for houses in multiple occupation to be licensed. In relation to London, changes were introduced relating to the delegation of functions by the Mayor to mayoral development corporations and the political restrictions to which staff in mayoral development corporations would be subject.

The Act finally gained Royal Assent on 15 November 2011.

The main further changes since House of Lords Committee stage were as follows:

The provisions that would have required local authorities to hold a referendum whenever requested to do so by five per cent or more of the local electorate were dropped.

The scope of the Community Right to Challenge may now go beyond services run by local authorities and could potentially include the right to challenge government departments to run local services that they are providing. There is also an obligation to specify a timescale for the procurement exercise on the authority that is compelled to tender the opportunity to run services under these provisions.

Assets of community value have now been defined in the Act rather than leaving this for later regulations. To be an asset of community value, either (1) the land or building must have an actual current use that is not ancillary and furthers the social well-being or social interests of the local community, or (2) in the recent past the building must have had an actual use which was not ancillary and furthered the social well-being or social interests of the local community and it is realistic to think that within the next five years it could have a use which is not ancillary and furthers (whether or not in the same way as before) the social well-being or social interests of the local community. In this context 'social interests' means cultural, recreational or sporting interests.

Certain disposals are also now exempt from the moratorium on disposal that normally applies when the land or building is included on the register of assets. These include: gifts; disposals pursuant to entitlement under a will or intestacy; disposals by personal representatives under a will to raise money to pay debts, taxes, costs or other entitlements; disposals within a family; disposal of land only part of which is listed as a community asset; disposal as part of the transfer of a business as a going concern; disposal pursuant to the requirements of a trust; and disposals by reason of a person becoming or ceasing to become a trustee or a partner in a partnership.

Finally, the timescales for notification of disposals and the moratorium periods were added. These are: six months prior notice of disposal; six week for requests to be treated as a bidder to be made by community interest groups; and 18 months as the protection period for a particular disposal after notification of proposed disposal has been given to a local authority.

The Act still provides for the abolition of the Regional Strategies but flexibility was introduced to enable all or part of a regional strategy (and all or part of a direction saving structure plan policies) to be revoked.

The purposes for which the Community Infrastructure Levy ('CIL') can be used were widened still further in the final stages of the Bill, to allow for funding in certain circumstances of things other than infrastructure and in relation to infrastructure funding not only for its provision but also its improvement, replacement, operation or maintenance.

The Government felt the need to answer critics who alleged that the inclusion in statute of the need to have regard to relevant local finance considerations when determining planning applications elevated those considerations above all others; clarification was added to the effect that this did not alter whether regard is to be had to a particular consideration in a planning application or the weight to be given to a consideration.

Whilst the Act was clearly a major milestone for the Government's reform of the planning system, there is no indication of any slow-down in the Government's proposals for further reform. This was amply demonstrated in Chancellor George Osbourne's third Budget, on 21 March 2012. The announcements relevant to localism and planning included the following:

- The long awaited final version of the NPPF would be published on 27 March 2012 and would apply to plan-making and planning decisions from that date with appropriate arrangements for implementation and the effect on local authorities' local plans. The Chancellor stated that the

## May 2010 to April 2012, the changes unfold

NPPF would contain a 'powerful presumption in favour of sustainable development [ ... ] and will localise choice about the use of previously developed land, ending nationally imposed targets'.

- Further announcements on measures to deregulate and simplify the planning system including reduced information requirements for planning applications, amendments to the Use Classes Order and permitted development rights to make changes of use easier by April 2013 and clarification of the Government's 12-month guarantee for processing planning applications.
- New permitted development rights for micro-renewable energy.
- New legislation would remove the duplication in the consenting regime for nationally significant infrastructure developments caused currently by the need for the Special Parliamentary Procedure in certain circumstances.
- The Government would make up to £150 million available for large scale projects in core cities through Tax Incremental Financing ('TIF'). Details of a competition for the allocation of TIF funding will be announced next month.
- The Government would be accelerating the release of public sector land and anticipated that it would meet its objective to dispose of land with the capacity to build over 100,000 homes by April 2014.
- Enhanced capital allowances would be made available from 1 April 2012 for the London Royal Docks Enterprise Zone. Enhanced capital allowances will be made available for sites in Local Enterprise Zones in Scotland (Irvine, Nigg and Dundee) and at Deeside in North Wales. Such measures are also currently being considered for Northern Ireland.
- Lord Heseltine will 'undertake an independent review of how spending departments and other relevant public sector bodies interact with the private sector, and assess their capacity to deliver pro-growth policies'.

At the beginning of his budget speech the Chancellor strongly criticised the current planning regime stating that:

> 'You can't earn your future if you can't get planning permission [ ... ] global businesses have diverted specific investments that would have created hundreds of jobs in some of the most deprived communities in Britain to countries like Germany and the Netherlands, because they couldn't get planning permission here.'

The majority of the Act came into force on 6 April 2012, although a number of provisions were the subject of earlier commencement orders.[16] We set out in Appendix 3 a list of the provisions which are in force as at 6 April 2012.

---

16 The Localism Act 2011 (Commencement No 1 and Transitional Provisions) Order 2011 (SI 2011/2896), The Localism Act 2011 (Commencement No 2 and Transitional and Saving Provision) Order 2012 (SI 2012/57), The Localism Act 2011 (Commencement No 1) (Wales) Order 2012 (SI 2012/193), The Localism Act 2011 (Commencement No 3) Order 2012 (SI 2011/411), The Localism Act 2011 (Commencement No 4 and Transitional, Transitory and Saving Provisions) Order 2012 (SI 2012/628) and The Localism Act 2011 (Commencement No 5 and Transitional, Savings and Transitory Provisions) Order 2012 (SI 2012/1008) (all available at http://www.legislation.gov.uk/ [accessed March 2012]).

# Chapter 3

# Local authorities' powers and duties

## THE NEW 'GENERAL POWER OF COMPETENCE'

It is surely symbolic of the Government's objectives that the very first provision of the Localism Act extends the general powers of local authorities: Ch 1, Pt 1, s 1(1) provides that a 'local authority has power to do anything that individuals generally may do'. Subject to limitations set out in sections 2 to 4, an authority may do anything under this provision in any way it chooses, including: (a) in the UK or elsewhere, (b) for commercial purposes or otherwise with or without charge, and (c) for the benefit of the authority itself, its area, persons resident or present in its area or even for some other benefit unrelated to its area.

This power benefits English local authorities, including any parish council that meets any conditions prescribed by order of the Secretary of State for these purposes. For those authorities, the general power of competence will supersede the general well-being powers under the Local Government Act 2000, which will now be limited in their application to local authorities in Wales.

The explanatory notes[1] to the Act describe the section as providing that the 'power may be used in innovative ways'.

DCLG's Media Background Note summarises the new general power of competence as follows:

> 'The general power of competence will provide local authorities, including certain parish councils, with all the same powers that an individual generally has, which will enable them to do anything apart from that which is specifically prohibited. This measure will mean that local councils will have new freedoms to run services free from Whitehall diktat. It will to give local authorities confidence in their legal capacity to act on behalf of their communities and to act in their own interest to generate efficiencies and savings. It will provide more freedom for councils to innovate and work together with others to drive down costs. It will give them increased confidence to set up banks, develop property, run new services and own assets.'

The Act sets out a number of limits on the exercise of the general power of competence as follows:

- if there is overlap between an existing power and the new power, it will be subject to the same restrictions as the existing power (s 2(1));
- if a local authority is subject to an existing statutory limitation then it remains subject to it (but will only be subject to any future limitation which is expressly applied to the general power, as the provisions make

---

1 Localism Act 2011, Explanatory Notes (available at http://www.legislation.gov.uk/ukpga/2011/20/notes/contents [accessed March 2012]).

a distinction between restrictions contained in 'pre-commencement' legislation and 'post-commencement' legislation) (s 2(2));
- the new power does not itself include power to make or alter certain arrangements for the discharge of local authority functions and local authority governance (s 2(3));
- where under the new power a service is provided by the local authority to a person but not for a commercial purpose, the authority can only charge for the service if (a) that service is not required to be provided under any other statutory provision, (b) the person concerned has agreed to the service, and (c) generally the authority does not otherwise have a specific power to charge. This is subject to the general principle that over the relevant financial year the income from charges for the relevant service must not exceed the cost of its provision (s 3);
- an authority may only rely on the new power to do things for a commercial purpose if they are things which the authority could also do, under the same power, for a purpose which is not commercial (s 4(1));
- in doing things for a commercial purpose authorities must do so through a company (s 4(2));
- an authority may not do things for a commercial purpose in relation to any person, if it is required to do those things in relation to that person pursuant to a statutory provision (s 4(3)).

Section 5 provides the Secretary of State with powers to make supplemental provisions to amend, repeal, revoke or disapply a provision where he considers that it restricts a local authority from exercising the general power of competence. The Secretary of State may also restrict a local authority from exercising the general power of competence or limit this power by making it subject to conditions.

The Secretary of State may only make supplemental provisions if certain conditions are met, including:[2]

- the effect of the provision is proportionate to the policy objective that the provision is intended to secure;
- a fair balance is struck between the public interest and the interests of any person adversely affected by it; and
- the provision does not remove any necessary protection.

The extent to which local authorities are truly empowered by the Act is dependent on how the Government actually implements these provisions: it is the Secretary of State – through his order making powers – who will decide on the extent to which those restrictions are lifted.

Conversely, if local authorities are empowered to act through these new provisions, then will their activities be adequately supervised through the Secretary of State's residual order-making powers? Given the extent of public expenditure cuts, local authorities will surely try to push at the boundaries of the new power in order to achieve budget-driven outcomes. Public law will to some extent keep local authorities in check – as public bodies, they can be held to account through judicial review if they misuse their powers – for example, if they apply them irrationally or in a way which is vitiated by bias or with a closed mind. So it may be the courts which will ultimately police and help to define how far local authorities can go.

2   Localism Act 2011, s 6.

## The new 'General Power of Competence'

The new general power of competence replaces the well-being power set out in the Local Government Act 2000 which states that:

> 'Every local authority are to have power to do anything which they consider is likely to achieve any one or more of the following objects –
> (a) the promotion or improvement of the economic well-being of their area,
> (b) the promotion or improvement of the social well-being of their area, and
> (c) the promotion or improvement of the environmental well-being of their area.'[3]

The brave talk about empowered authorities sounds rather familiar. The 2000 Act's well-being power was introduced to widen the freedoms for local authorities to act in the face of previous concerns as to the operation of the 'ultra vires' doctrine. The guidance provided at the time of the 2000 Act stated that '… the Government's purpose in introducing the well-being power is to reverse that tradition of cautious approach, and to encourage innovation and other joint working between local authorities and their partners to inspire communities' quality of life'.

A recent judgment of the Court of Appeal in *Brent LBC v Risk Management Partners Limited and London Authorities Mutual Limited and Harrow London Borough Council*[4] created nervousness within local authorities about the true extent of the 2000 Act's well-being power. This case concerned London Authorities Mutual Limited ('LAML') a company limited by guarantee which had been set up by ten London boroughs for the purpose of providing themselves with cheaper insurance. The case was brought at first instance by an independent insurance provider which had submitted a tender for the provision of insurance in response to an invitation to tender from the London Borough of Brent. The contract was awarded to LAML which had not taken part in the tender process. At first instance the High Court held that the Council had no power to become a member of LAML or make payments to it.

The Court of Appeal agreed. Pill LJ held that:

> 'While the setting up of a company may, subject to limitations, come within the well-being power, I doubt whether participation in an insurance company with a view to seeking cheaper insurance premiums, circumscribed as it would be by those limitations, does so. In any event, I am not persuaded that participation in an insurance enterprise which involves giving guarantees to the company and assuming what could be very substantial liabilities to other local authorities comes within the well-being power. That power does not extend to a power to enter into the complex and somewhat speculative attempt to save money which is the mainspring of the LAML arrangement. The guarantees and degree of speculation involved, in my view take the activity proposed beyond what Parliament intended by the well-being clause.'[5]

DCLG's view is that, by removing the reference to social, environmental and economic wellbeing, the new power can 'significantly increase the confidence

---

3　Local Government Act 2000, s 2(1).
4　[2009] EWCA Civ 490.
5　*Brent LBC v Risk Management Partners Limited and London Authorities Mutual Limited and Harrow London Borough Council* [2009] EWCA Civ 490, Lord Justice Pill at para 119.

*Local authorities' powers and duties*

of local authorities, enabling them to consider more innovative approaches to service delivery and efficiency savings'.[6]

It should be noted that, however widely the courts interpret the general power of competence, local authorities will of course always remain subject to other regimes such as the EU public procurement rules and the European Convention on Human Rights, as well as traditional principles of administrative law.

The proposed general power of competence has recently become unexpectedly topical, following the judgment of Ouseley J in *National Secular Society v Bideford Town Council*[7] on 17 February 2012. Ouseley J held that a parish council's practice, common to many local authorities, of saying prayers at the start of its formal meetings was unlawful on the basis that the council had no statutory power either to hold prayers as part of a formal council meeting or to summon councillors to a meeting at which prayers were on the agenda. DCLG issued a press statement on 17 February 2012 indicating that in response to the ruling the Secretary of State had 'fast-tracked and personally signed a Parliamentary Commencement Order so the new power can be exercised by all major local authorities in England from today and following due Parliamentary process for parishes by April', giving councils 'the vital legal standing that should allow them to continue to hold formal prayers at meetings where they wish to do so'.

Another example of the pitfalls that remain for local authorities was provided, just as this book went to press, by *R (on the application of Lucy Williams and Nicholas Dorrington) v Surrey County Council*[8] where Mr Justice Wilkie ruled that a county council's attempt to replace paid staff at ten libraries with volunteers was unlawful in that the county council had failed to have due regard to its duties under the Equality Act 2010 in relation to the need for training on equality issues.

## TRANSFER AND DELEGATION OF GOVERNMENT FUNCTIONS TO LOCAL AUTHORITIES

Chapter 4 of the Act contains a series of provisions that enable the transfer and delegation of government functions to local authorities.

Under s 15, the Secretary of State may make a provision transferring a local public function from the local authority whose function it is to a permitted authority if that authority would be capable of properly exercising this function. This power may only be used by the Secretary of State in order to promote economic development or wealth creation or increase local accountability for the relevant public function.

Under s 16, a Minister of the Crown may transfer any of his functions to a permitted authority as long as the authority is capable of exercising it. This power is not available however if the function relates to the making of

---

6 DCLG (2011) *Localism Bill: General Power of Competence – Impact Assessment* (available at http://www.communities.gov.uk/publications/localgovernment/localismcompetence [accessed December 2011]).
7 [2012] EWHC 175.
8 *R (on the application of Lucy Williams and Nicholas Dorrington) v Surrey County Council* [2012] EWHC 867 (QB).

regulations or other instruments of a legislative character or a power to fix fees or charges.

A 'permitted authority' is defined for the purpose of these provisions as a county council, district council, economic prosperity board established under the Local Democracy, Economic Development and Construction Act 2009, s 88 or a combined authority established under s 103 of that Act.

In order for a function to be transferred or delegated, the Secretary of State and/or minister must have consulted the relevant permitted authority and the authority must have consented to take on the function. When considering whether to make an order transferring a function to a permitted authority, the Secretary of State must lay the draft order before Parliament and have regard to:

'(a)  any representations,
 (b)  any resolution of either House of Parliament, and
 (c)  any recommendations of a committee of either House of Parliament charged with reporting on the draft order'[9]

that are made within 60 days of a draft order being published. After this 60-day period has passed, the Secretary of State must make Parliament aware of any representations that have been made. If both Houses of Parliament approve the draft order by resolution then the Secretary of State may make the Order.

## NEW GOVERNANCE ARRANGEMENTS

Currently, all councils in England (apart from very small shire district councils[10]) must be governed in one of two ways as set out in the Local Government Act 2000:

- directly elected mayor and cabinet; or
- indirectly elected leader and cabinet.

In the Coalition Agreement,[11] the Government committed to 'allowing councils to return to the committee system, should they wish to'.[12] Section 21 and Sch 2 of the Act make amendments to the Local Government Act 2000, Pt 1 so that local authorities in England will be able to operate through:

- executive arrangements;
- a committee system; or
- prescribed arrangements.

Schedule 2 also permits the Secretary of State to allow further systems of governance if these would be an improvement on the prescribed systems.

The changes seek to allow local authorities to decide for themselves how they should go about their business.

---

9   Localism Act 2011, s 19.
10  DCLG (2011) *Localism Bill: Giving Councils Greater Freedom over their Governance Arrangements – Impact Assessment* (available at http://www.communities.gov.uk/publications/localgovernment/localismgovernance [accessed March 2012]).
11  HM Government (2010) *The Coalition: Our Programme for Government* (available at http://www.cabinetoffice.gov.uk/sites/default/files/resources/coalition_programme_for_government.pdf [accessed March 2012]).
12  HM Government (2010) *The Coalition: Our Programme for Government,* page 12 (available at   http://www.cabinetoffice.gov.uk/sites/default/files/resources/coalition_programme_for_government.pdf [accessed March 2012]).

*Local authorities' powers and duties*

In order to change governance structures, a local authority will need to pass a resolution to that effect. Where a referendum was used to create the current system, a referendum must be used to depart from it.[13] In order to prevent local authorities constantly changing their systems of governance, there are safeguards that prevent a local authority from passing a resolution to change the system within five years of a previous resolution.

It remains to be seen whether many authorities will instigate these changes, which are voluntary. The Government itself does not believe that more than five to ten per cent of councils will adopt the committee system of governance.[14]

## NEW MAYORAL ARRANGEMENTS

Schedule 2 of the Act also provides for the introduction of directly elected mayors by inserting new ss 9H to 9HE into the Local Government Act 2000.

Section 9HB provides that the Secretary of State may by regulations determine when elections for mayors may or not take place. The term of office for an elected mayor is to be four years unless the Secretary of State determines otherwise.

The Government has committed to creating directly elected mayors in 12 cities across England (to be known as mayoral cities[15]), in addition to the existing arrangements in London. The majority of cities are to hold public referendums to determine whether they should have mayors and, if this proposal is met with approval, a mayor should be elected shortly thereafter. Any person in an area eligible to vote for the election of councillors and who is a registered voter in that area will be able to vote in a referendum for a mayor. The Secretary of State may make provisions about the conduct of such referendums, although these must be approved by the Electoral Commission before they are introduced.

The Secretary of State has declared that the referendums in the mayoral cities will be held on 3 May 2012. Leicester will not be holding a referendum as it already has an elected mayor. Liverpool City Council has voted to bypass the referendum and the city will vote for a mayor on 3 May 2012.

The Secretary of State is also able to issue an order, where a mayor has been elected, for public functions to be transferred to the mayor. On 1 November 2011 the DCLG published a consultation paper on proposals related to the transfer of power to mayors. The current proposals are that the transfer of such powers should be locally led. The cities themselves would therefore be required to make recommendations about which powers they would like to see transferred to their mayors. Certain public functions, such as in respect of NHS health facilities will not be transferable. The Government hopes that 'direct elections for Mayors will ensure the leadership of our largest City councils is accountable, visible and has a clear mandate from the City'.[16]

---

13  Local Government Act 2000, s 9M introduced by Localism Act 2011, Sch 2.
14  DCLG (2011) *Localism Bill: Giving Councils Greater Freedom over their Governance Arrangements – Impact Assessment* (available at http://www.communities.gov.uk/publications/localgovernment/localismgovernance [accessed March 2012]).
15  Birmingham, Bradford, Bristol, Coventry, Leeds, Leicester, Liverpool, Manchester, Newcastle upon Tyne, Nottingham, Sheffield and Wakefield.
16  Communities and Local Governments (1 November 2011) *What can a Mayor do for your City? – A Consultation*, page 6.

Liverpool's Mayor, for example, will be at the centre of a new £130 million 'city deal' for Liverpool. Although its grant funding isn't contingent on the election of a mayor, the Government has made it clear that it believes that a mayor will provide the accountability required for the new powers and funds to be passed down from central Government.

The new city deal for Liverpool will also allow the Mayor of Liverpool to establish the first Mayoral Development Corporation ('MDC') outside London. MDCs are specifically designed to secure the regeneration of an area, and any powers assigned to such a body must be for this purpose or incidental to this purpose. Under the Act, an MDC may become the local planning authority for the relevant area[17] and is able to carry out a number of other functions in order to secure regeneration. These powers include, amongst others, that it may provide or facilitate the provision of infrastructure, acquire and dispose of land, provide financial assistance and grant discretionary relief from business rates. (Please see Chapter 11 for a more detailed explanation of MDCs).

On 6 February 2012, the Mayor of London announced the first London MDC under Pt 8, Ch 2 of the Act, the London Legacy Development Corporation ('LLDC'). LLDC has taken over the role of the Olympic Park Legacy Company and will, from 1 April 2012, be responsible for the regeneration legacy of the Olympic Park after the end of the Games. The LLDC will also manage some of the Thames Gateway Development Corporation's Assets and will be directly accountable to Londoners through the Mayor. The Government considers that this accountability is essential in order to secure locally led regeneration. The LLDC was established by the London Legacy Development Corporation (Establishment) Order 2012 (SI 2012/310).

## PREDETERMINATION

'Pre-determination' is shorthand for the administrative law principle developed by the courts that a decision taken by a public body is unlawful if the decision-maker approached the decision with a closed mind. Section 25 of the Act seeks to give effect to the Conservatives' pre-election pledge set out in its Green Paper titled *Open Source Planning*[18] that:

> 'We will legislate to ensure that councillors (while being properly prevented from advancing personal interests) have the freedom to campaign and represent their constituents, and then speak and vote on those issues without fear of breaking the rules of "pre-determination".'[19]

In reality the provision does no more than reflect the view already taken by the courts – that 'predisposition' does not equate to 'predetermination'. Section 25 does not give carte blanche for councillors and developers to do things now which would previously have led to the risk of a permission being quashed on the grounds of predetermination. But, associated with the abolition of the Standards Board (see below) and the new general power of competence, it

---

17  Although this is apparently not proposed for the Liverpool MDC.
18  The Conservative Party (February 2010) *Open Source Planning* (available at http://www.conservatives.com/News/News_stories/2010/02/~/media/Files/Green%20Papers/planning-green-paper.ashx [accessed December 2011]).
19  The Conservative Party (February 2010) *Open Source Planning,* page 17 (available at http://www.conservatives.com/News/News_stories/2010/02/~/media/Files/Green%20Papers/planning-green-paper.ashx [accessed December 2011]).

does provide a clear indication of the Government's direction of travel: fewer unnecessary constraints on local government.

Section 25 provides that a 'decision-maker is not to be taken to have had, or have appeared to have had, a closed mind when making the decision just because ... the decision-maker had previously done anything that directly or indirectly indicated what view the decision-maker took, or would or might take, in relation to a matter, and ... the matter was relevant to the decision'. It is interesting to see this principle spelled out in legislation, but the section would not in our view prevent decisions being struck down by the courts in exactly the same instances as they might previously have been struck down – where the decision-maker's conduct leads the court to conclude that he had a closed mind. Even without s 25, permissions were not struck down simply because of the decision-maker's previous conduct – more was needed than that. The courts have taken a pragmatic approach, eg Pill LJ in *R (on the application of Kevin Paul Lewis) v Redcar & Cleveland Borough Council*:[20]

> 'Councillors are elected to implement, amongst other things, planning policies. They can properly take part in the debates which lead to planning applications made by the Council itself. It is common ground that in the case of some applications they are likely to have, and are entitled to have, a disposition in favour of granting permission. It is possible to infer a closed mind, or the real risk a mind was closed, from the circumstances and evidence. Given the role of councillors, clear pointers are, in my view, required if that state of mind is to be held to have become a closed, or apparently closed, mind at the time of decision.
>
> It is for the court to assess whether Committee members did make the decision with closed minds or that the circumstances give rise to such a real risk of closed minds that the decision ought not in the public interest be upheld. The importance of appearances is, in my judgment, generally more limited in this context than in a judicial context ... [The] appearance created by a Councillor voting for a planning project he has long supported is, on analysis, to be viewed in a very different way.'[21]

In the same case Rix LJ continued as follows:

> 'So the test would be whether there is an appearance of predetermination, in the sense of a mind closed to the planning merits of the decision in question. Evidence of political affiliation or of the adoption of policies towards a planning proposal will not for these purposes by itself amount to an appearance of the real possibility of predetermination, or what counts as bias for these purposes.'[22]

These principles were applied by Lindblom J at first instance in *R (on the application of Harris) v London Borough of Haringey*.[23] Whilst the judge's ruling was overturned on other grounds, his decision on predetermination was not interfered with, where he held that the chair of the planning committee's views on development of the site, expressed many years previously, were an indication of legitimate predisposition rather than unlawful predetermination.

---

20 [2008] EWCA Civ 746.
21 [2008] EWCA Civ 746, para 63.
22 [2008] EWCA Civ 746, para 96.
23 [2009] EWHC 2329.

*Standards*

This outcome may be contrasted with that in a case with more extreme facts such as *Ghadami v Harlow District Council*,[24] in which the chair of the planning committee had gone so far as to telephone an objector and threaten compulsory purchase, where the court proceeded to quash the permission.

To the extent that this provision will have any effect on the courts' current approach, it should be noted that the section applies to 'members of all councils in England and Wales to which there are direct elections' – so in any event will not apply to decisions taken by officers under delegated powers. Nor does it apply to the Secretary of State or inspectors and so will not be relevant in call-in or appeal situations.

## STANDARDS

Schedule 4 of the Act, which is brought into effect by s 26, abolishes the Standards Board for England and codes of conduct made by local authorities under the Local Government Act 2000, making good on a promise set out in the *The Coalition – Our Programme for Government*[25] to 'abolish the Standard Board regime'.[26] The Government's position is that 'an unelected non-departmental public body regulating a centrally prescribed conduct regime for councillors is against the principles of localism'.[27] The Act also abolishes the independent First-tier Tribunal (Local Government Standards in England) to which the Standard Board referred cases for determination.

The Government's impact assessment states that only '28% of the 6000 complaints made to the Standards Board between May 2008 and March 2010 were recommended for investigation'.[28] The Government hopes that, by allowing local authorities to govern the conduct of their staff themselves, the amount of 'frivolous and malicious'[29] complaints will reduce. Further, although the cost of closing down the Standards Board is estimated at £19.6 million, the Government believes that DCLG will save £6 million a year in running costs.[30]

---

24 [2004] EWHC 1883.
25 HM Government (2010) *The Coalition: Our Programme for Government* (available at http://www.cabinetoffice.gov.uk/sites/default/files/resources/coalition_programme_for_government.pdf [accessed March 2012]).
26 HM Government (2010) *The Coalition: Our Programme for Government,* page 12 (available at http://www.cabinetoffice.gov.uk/sites/default/files/resources/coalition_programme_for_government.pdf [accessed March 2012]).
27 DCLG (2011) *Localism Bill: The Abolition of the Standards Board Regime, Clarification of the Law on Predetermination and the Requirement to Register and Declare Interests, Impact Assessment,* page 8 (available at http://www.communities.gov.uk/publications/localgovernment/localismstandardsboard [accessed December 2011]).
28 DCLG (2011) *Localism Bill: The Abolition of the Standards Board Regime, Clarification of the Law on Predetermination and the Requirement to Register and Declare Interests, Impact Assessment,* page 1 (available at http://www.communities.gov.uk/publications/localgovernment/localismstandardsboard) [accessed December 2011].
29 DCLG (2011) *Localism Bill: The Abolition of the Standards Board Regime, Clarification of the Law on Predetermination and the Requirement to Register and Declare Interests, Impact Assessment,* page 1 (available at http://www.communities.gov.uk/publications/localgovernment/localismstandardsboard [accessed December 2011]).
30 DCLG (2011) *Localism Bill: The Abolition of the Standards Board Regime, Clarification of the Law on Predetermination and the Requirement to Register and Declare Interests, Impact Assessment,* page 10 (available at http://www.communities.gov.uk/publications/localgovernment/localismstandardsboard [accessed December 2011]).

*Local authorities' powers and duties*

None of the roles of the Standards Board will transfer to any other bodies and, from its abolition on 31 March 2012, cases have been returned to the monitoring officer of the local authority in question to be dealt with internally.

Understandably, concerns have been raised about a possible reduction in the standard of governance once local authorities are able to regulate themselves. Section 27(1) states that 'a relevant authority must promote and maintain high standards of conduct by members and co-opted members of the authority'. A relevant authority is held to mean most English authorities including county, borough and parish councils, English fire and rescue authorities, the Council of the Isles of Scilly and English and Welsh policy authorities.

In a change from the original Bill, the Act requires that relevant authorities must adopt a code of conduct for their members that must, when viewed as a whole, be consistent with the following principles:

- selflessness;
- integrity;
- objectivity;
- accountability;
- openness;
- honesty; and
- leadership.[31]

These principles are of course familiar tenets from the Local Government Act 2000 code of conduct, based on principles established by Lord Nolan in his report on *Standards in Public Life*.[32]

The code of conduct must include provisions relating to the manner in which conflicts of interest should be recorded and, other than for parish councils, arrangements that allow for the investigation of breaches of the code.

A relevant authority must also establish and maintain a register of interest of its members and co-opted members. This register must be available for inspection by the public and any member or co-opted member must enter any disclosable pecuniary conflict of interests that they may have within 28 days of becoming a member. The relevant authority's monitoring officer will be responsible for maintaining this register, however each member will be responsible for entering their interests on the register. Section 34 of the Act makes it a criminal offence if a member or co-opted member fails to register a disclosable interest or if they provide false or misleading information as regards any disclosable interest. The maximum penalty for committing such an offence is a fine of up to £5,000 and disqualification for up to five years. As such, any breaches of this requirement must be reported to the police and will then be investigated by the magistrates court.

## PAY ACCOUNTABILITY

Section 28 of the Act requires every relevant authority to prepare a pay policy statement every year from 2012/2013 onwards. For this section a relevant authority is defined as:

---

31  Localism Act 2011, s 28(1).
32  Committee on Standards in Public Life (2001) *The First Seven Reports – A Review of Progress* (available at http://www.public-standards.gov.uk/Library/OurWork/First7Reports_ProgressReviewSummary.pdf [accessed March 2012]).

(a) a county council;
(b) a county borough council;
(c) a district council;
(d) a London borough council;
(e) the Common Council of the City of London in its capacity as a local authority;
(f) the Council of the Isles of Scilly;
(g) the London Fire and Emergency Planning Authority;
(h) a metropolitan county fire and rescue authority; or
(i) a fire and rescue authority constituted by a scheme under the Fire and Rescue Services Act 2004, s 2 or a scheme to which s 4 of that Act applies.[33]

The Government has published guidance which states that a pay policy statement is a 'statement that must articulate the authority's own policies towards a range of issues relating to the pay of its workforce, particularly its senior staff (or "chief officers") and its lowest paid employees'.[34] These statements must be approved by the full council and be published on the authority's website.

The requirement for the publication of pay policy statements is in response to the Hutton Review of Fair Pay in the Public Sector Report published in March 2011. One of the findings of the interim report was that:

'Although rises in pay for public sector executives are not matching the rise in private sector pay, it has been increasing faster than pay for public sector low earners – begging the question of whether this has been proportional. Pay ratios in the public sector have also increased over the last decade, with pay for top earners in most public sector workforces increasing faster than for bottom earners since 2001.'[35]

The interim report indicated that over 800 local government employees are in the top one per cent of earners in the country (although these figures were quoted as being indicative and not definitive).[36] The requirements set out in this chapter of the Act and in the associated guidance are designed to increase transparency as regards pay in these authorities by:

- ensuring that pay policy statements are available to the public;
- requiring full council approval of each pay policy statement ensuring that all members are aware of the authority's approach to pay;
- requiring that all offers of salaries over £100,000 to a new member of staff are voted on by the full council;
- introducing a measure of fairness by publishing policies for remuneration for the most highly paid staff alongside those for lower paid positions;

---

33 Localism Act 2011, s 34(1).
34 DCLG (November 2011) *Openness and Accountability in Local Pay: Draft Guidance under Section 40 of the Localism Act*, page 1 (available at http://www.communities.gov.uk/documents/localgovernment/pdf/2031774.pdf [accessed March 2012]).
35 HM Treasury (March 2011) *Hutton Review of Fair Pay in the Public Sector: Final Report*, para 1.7 (available at http://www.hm-treasury.gov.uk/d/hutton_fairpay_review.pdf [accessed December 2011]).
36 HM Treasury (December 2010) *Hutton Review of Fair Pay in the Public Sector: Interim Report*, page 41 Chart 2.F (available at http://www.hm-treasury.gov.uk/d/hutton_interim_report.pdf [accessed December 2011]).

*Local authorities' powers and duties*

- publishing the authority's pay multiple (the ratio between the highest paid authority and the lowest paid);
- setting out how decisions are made in respect of bonuses, performance related pay and redundancy packages.

## EU FINES

Part 2 of the Act gives the Government the power to pass on to a local authority any fines issued against the Government for failure to comply with any European legislation, if the local authority's behaviour led to the fine. Although the UK has never received an EU fine, the Government's justification for the need for such a provision, as set out in the impact assessment relating to this provision, is stated to be as a consequence of a recent situation where an unnamed local authority was investigated for breach of EU procurement rules in respect of a major town centre redevelopment and was said to have refused to fully cooperate with the investigation.[37]

Initial versions of these provisions in the Bill caused disquiet within local authorities as ministers were to have sole authority to pass any fines downwards.[38] Amendments made were designed to ensure that there is a more rigorous system in place, namely:

- A minister must designate the relevant authority by a Parliamentary Order approved by both Houses of Parliament. This designation must identify the EU sanctions that the designation relates to and set out the activities of the authority which led to the designation. Before making such a designation the minister must consult with the authority. Where an EU sanction has been imposed, and at least one authority has been designated, the Government must establish an independent panel which must consist of members who have the suitable qualifications, expertise or experience.[39]
- Before any payment is required the Government must, after consultation with the panel, issue a warning notice to the authority. This notice must identify the relevant EU sanction, the amount that the local authority is required to pay and the proposed timetable for payments. The notice must also invite the authority to make representations to the independent panel.[40]
- Once a warning notice has been issued and the panel has considered any representations made, the panel must report to the Government. After having considered the report, the Government must then determine whether the local authority's actions caused or contributed to the breach of EU law resulting in the sanction, and the proportion that the local authority should contribute to the fine. Before a final notice is issued,

---

37 DCLG (January 2011) *Localism Bill: Payment of European Union Infraction Fines by Local and Public Authorities, Impact Assessment*, case discussed on page 7 (available at http://www.communities.gov.uk/documents/localgovernment/pdf/1829681.pdf [accessed December 2011]).
38 For example at http://www.local.gov.uk/web/10161/localism-act/-/journal_content/56/10161/3100124/ARTICLE-TEMPLATE [accessed March 2012].
39 Localism Act 2011, s 53.
40 Localism Act 2011, s 54.

the Government must consider a number of factors including the effect of the fine on the authority's finances.[41]
- A final notice must then be issued which must identify the EU sanction, the payments required from the local authority and the action of the local authority which resulted in the fine.[42]

France was recently fined €20 million, with a further fine of €58 million for every further six months of non-compliance with EU fishing legislation. The provisions in this part of the Act therefore carry potentially significant consequences for local authorities.

## NON-DOMESTIC RATES

Part 4, ss 69 and 70 of the Act amend the Local Government Finance Act 1988 to provide for discretionary relief if a hereditament is occupied for the purpose of a not-for-profit organisation, club or society or one whose main purpose is charitable, philanthropic or religious or otherwise involved in education, social welfare, science or the fine arts. Discretionary relief will also be available for small businesses. There will also be no change in the relief of rates for charities. Part 4, s 71 of the Act discharges any obligation to repay backdated rates if the rates are backdated by 33 months or more in the 2005 ratings list and were due to the splitting out of a larger rateable property. This provision relates to the backdating of non-domestic rates for a number of properties brought about by the Ports Review, carried out by the Valuation Office between 2006 and 2008. This review brought to light mistakes in the rates being applied to certain properties resulting in a number of large properties being subdivided and non-business rates being retrospectively charged to these newly divided business properties.

This imposition of backdated rates, due in no way to fault on behalf of the occupiers, was considered by many to be unjust, not least because these repayments were requested at the height of the recession. The previous Government acknowledged this unfairness and extended the repayment term from the usual 14 days to up to eight years with interest free instalments. The May 2010 Coalition Agreement stated that savings made by cutting certain non front line services 'can be used to support jobs, for example through the cancelling of some backdated demands for business rates'.

The Government's proposed reforms to the business rates system so as to allow an element of local retention of business rates are set out in Chapter 15.

---

41  Localism Act 2011, s 55.
42  Localism Act 2011, s 56.

# Chapter 4

# Community empowerment

Part 5 of the Localism Act covers:

Chapter 1: Council tax referendums and other changes to the council tax system (we will only cover referendums – the rest is outside the scope of this book).
Chapter 2: Community Right to Challenge
Chapter 3: Assets of Community Value

*Open Source Planning* was silent on these proposals, although the Conservative Party's *Control Shift* Policy Green Paper set out that 'if voters want to see something done in their area, they'll be able to force it on to the agenda'[1] and that:

> 'Our vision of localism is one where power is decentralised to the lowest possible level. For services which are used individually, this means putting power in the hands of individuals themselves. Where services are enjoyed collectively, they should be delivered by accountable community groups; or, where the scale is too large or those using a service too dispersed, by local authorities themselves, subject to democratic checks and balances. It is important to note that this green paper deals mainly with this third stage of localism – to local authorities.'[2]

The Coalition Agreement stated:

> 'We will give residents the power to investigate local referendums on any local issue'[3]

and

> 'We will introduce new powers to help communities save local facilities and services threatened with closure, and give communities the right to bid to take over local state-run services'.

## LOCAL REFERENDUMS

When the Bill was first laid before Parliament, it proposed a duty on local authorities to hold local referendums on local issues where the local electorate petitioned for one, and for the outcome of those referendums to be taken into account.

The proposal was that a local authority would be required to hold a referendum between two and 12 months of the request if the following conditions were met:

---

1 The Conservative Party (2009) *Control Shift: Returning Power to Local Communities*, page 2.
2 The Conservative Party (2009) *Control Shift: Returning Power to Local Communities*, page 8.
3 HM Government (2010) *The Coalition: Our Programme for Government*, page 27 (available at http://www.cabinetoffice.gov.uk/sites/default/files/resources/coalition_programme_for_government.pdf [accessed March 2012]).

## Community empowerment

- it received a valid petition signed by at least five per cent of the local government electors in the authority's area;
- a member of the authority made the request;
- the petition sets out a question that the petitioners want to be asked; and
- the local authority resolved that it was appropriate.

The authority could only refuse to hold a referendum on certain specified grounds that were set out in the Bill:

- if action in response to the outcome of the referendum question would be likely to lead to an unlawful action;
- if the matter in question was not a local matter over which the authority or any partner authority had any influence or which affected the area of any of its inhabitants;
- if it related to anything specified in a Government order; or
- if the petition or request was vexatious or abusive.

What constituted a 'local issue' was to be prescribed in regulations to be made by the Secretary of State, which would also set out how referendums should be run. Although the outcome of the referendum was not binding, as soon as practicable after the result of the referendum was known, the LPA had to consider what steps it should take to give effect to the result.

The provisions were promoted by the Government as a way to address concern that local electors across England lacked a general mechanism through which they could influence local decision making and make their views known.[4]

However, as the Bill progressed through the House of Lords, the 18 provisions relating to local referendums were removed.

Although the power to call a referendum on any issue of local nature has been removed, the Act still provides for community referendums to be held in relation to council tax increases. Section 72 inserts a new Chapter into the Local Government Finance Act 1992, which provides for a duty to hold a referendum where the amount of council tax for a financial year is 'excessive'.

Whether council tax for a financial year is excessive is to be determined by the relevant council tax billing authority, in accordance with principles for excessive council tax to be set by the Secretary of State and approved by a resolution of the House of Commons. Where a billing authority has determined that its council tax for a financial year is excessive, it must hold a local referendum. The billing authority must produce substitute calculations which would not be considered to be excessive, which will have effect if the majority of persons participating in the referendum do not approve the excessive amount of council tax.

The other specified areas of the Act which provide for referendums to be held are in relation to the making of neighbourhood development plans, neighbourhood development orders, community right to build orders and in relation to changes in local authority governance arrangements.

---

4  DCLG (2010) *Localism Bill: Media Background Note* (available at http://www.communities.gov.uk/documents/newsroom/word/1795339.doc [accessed March 2011]).

## COMMUNITY RIGHT TO CHALLENGE

Part 5, Ch 2 of the Act creates the new Community Right to Challenge. The Community Right to Challenge can perhaps be best summarised by reference to the Coalition Agreement, where the Government set out to 'introduce new powers to help communities save local facilities and services threatened with closure, and give communities the right to bid to take over local state-run services.'[5] It is based on the premise that local assets should be kept in public use and part of local life. Greg Clark, Minster for Decentralisation and Cities, has stated that 'many local authorities already recognise the unique role that [community] groups can play in designing and delivering local services – often offering new ideas, a deeper understanding of service users' needs, and good value for taxpayers' money. In other places, however, sensible suggestions can fall on deaf ears.'[6]

The Community Right to Challenge enables voluntary or community bodies, charitable trusts, parish councils and council workers[7] (referred to in Pt 5, Ch 2 of the Act as 'relevant bodies') to challenge the provision of services provided by or on behalf of a county council, district councils and London borough councils or 'such other person or body as may be prescribed by the Secretary of State by regulations'[8] (referred to in Pt 5, Ch 2 of the Act as 'relevant authorities') by making an expression of interest to run that service.

The relevant authority must consider and either accept (with or without modification) or decline an expression of interest in relation to the running of a particular service submitted by the relevant body, based upon the consideration of whether the provision of the service by the relevant body might promote or improve the social, economic or environmental well-being of the authority's area. Where the expression of interest is accepted, a 'procurement exercise' must be undertaken for the challenged service in line with the normal procedures, in which the relevant bodies that made the expression of interest can bid. Clearly the extent and formality of the procurement process to be followed will be dictated partly by the requirements of the Public Contracts Regulations 2006.

In early versions of the Bill, almost all other detail required was left for subsequent secondary legislation. DCLG consulted in early 2011[9] on more detailed proposals. It sought views mainly on:

- whether particular services that are subject to the right should be exempted;[10]

---

5   HM Government (2010) *The Coalition: Our programme for Government,* page 12 (available at http://www.cabinetoffice.gov.uk/sites/default/files/resources/coalition_programme_for_government.pdf [accessed March 2012]).
6   DCLG (Feburary 2011) *Proposals to Introduce a Community Right to Challenge – A Consultation Paper,* page 10.
7   And any other public body specified by the Secretary of State in regulations.
8   And any other public body specified by the Secretary of State in regulations.
9   DCLG (February 2011) *Proposals to Introduce a Community Right to Challenge: Consultation Paper* (available at http://www.communities.gov.uk/documents/localgovernment/pdf/1835810.pdf [accessed November 2011]).
10  DCLG (February 2011) *Proposals to Introduce a Community Right to Challenge: Consultation Paper,* section 2 (available at http://www.communities.gov.uk/documents/localgovernment/pdf/1835810.pdf [accessed November 2011]).

*Community empowerment*

- whether the right should be extended to other bodies carrying out a function of a public nature;[11]
- whether there should be a fixed minimum period –
  (i) during which a local authority must consider an expression of interest,[12]
  (ii) during which it must reach a decision,[13]
  (iii) between an expression of interest being accepted and a relevant authority initiating a procurement exercise;[14]
- what information should be included in an expression of interest;[15] and
- what the grounds on which an expression of interest can be rejected should be.[16]

The Secretary of State's power to specify the time periods has been removed and instead an obligation has been placed on the relevant authority to specify and publish a timescale for the acceptance of an expression of interest and the commencement of a procurement exercise.

## ASSETS OF COMMUNITY VALUE

Sitting alongside the Community Right to Challenge is the Community Right to Buy, established by Pt 5, Ch 3 of the Act. The Community Right to Buy is based on the concept of giving local people 'the opportunity to take control of assets and facilities in their neighbourhoods by levelling the playing field by providing the time for them to prepare a proposal'.[17] It gives local communities a chance to bid for listed assets when they come up for sale, to give the opportunity for property deemed to be of community importance to come under local control.

Local authorities, which for the purpose of Pt 5, Ch 3 are district councils, county councils, London borough councils, the Common Council of the City of London and the Council of the Isles of Scilly (and in Wales, a county council or county borough council),[18] are required by s 87 of the Act to maintain a list of land in their area that is of community value. Section 88 defines land that is of community value as follows:

---

11 DCLG (February 2011) *Proposals to Introduce a Community Right to Challenge: Consultation Paper*, section 3 (available at http://www.communities.gov.uk/documents/localgovernment/pdf/1835810.pdf [accessed November 2011]).
12 DCLG (February 2011) *Proposals to Introduce a Community Right to Challenge: Consultation Paper*, section 4 (available at http://www.communities.gov.uk/documents/localgovernment/pdf/1835810.pdf [accessed November 2011]).
13 DCLG (February 2011) *Proposals to Introduce a Community Right to Challenge: Consultation Paper*, section 6 (available at http://www.communities.gov.uk/documents/localgovernment/pdf/1835810.pdf [accessed November 2011]).
14 DCLG (February 2011) *Proposals to Introduce a Community Right to Challenge: Consultation Paper*, section 8 (available at http://www.communities.gov.uk/documents/localgovernment/pdf/1835810.pdf [accessed November 2011]).
15 DCLG (February 2011) *Proposals to Introduce a Community Right to Challenge: Consultation Paper*, section 5 (available at http://www.communities.gov.uk/documents/localgovernment/pdf/1835810.pdf [accessed November 2011]).
16 DCLG (February 2011) *Proposals to Introduce a Community Right to Challenge: Consultation Paper*, section 7 (available at http://www.communities.gov.uk/documents/localgovernment/pdf/1835810.pdf [accessed November 2011]).
17 DCLG (2011) *Assets of Community Value: Policy Statement,* page 5 (available at http://www.communities.gov.uk/publications/localgovernment/assetscommunityvaluestatement [accessed March 2012]).
18 The Secretary of State may by order amend the definition of local authority for the purpose of Pt 5, Ch 3 of the Act.

## Assets of Community Value

**'88 Land of community value**
(1) For the purposes of this Chapter but subject to regulations under subsection (3), a building or other land in a local authority's area is land of community value if in the opinion of the authority –
   (a) an actual current use of the building or other land that is not an ancillary use furthers the social wellbeing or social interests of the local community, and
   (b) it is realistic to think that there can continue to be non-ancillary use of the building or other land which will further (whether or not in the same way) the social wellbeing or social interests of the local community.
(2) For the purposes of this Chapter but subject to regulations under subsection (3), a building or other land in a local authority's area that is not land of community value as a result of subsection (1) is land of community value if in the opinion of the local authority –
   (a) there is a time in the recent past when an actual use of the building or other land that was not an ancillary use furthered the social wellbeing or interests of the local community, and
   (b) it is realistic to think that there is a time in the next five years when there could be non-ancillary use of the building or other land that would further (whether or not in the same way as before) the social wellbeing or social interests of the local community.
(3) The appropriate authority may by regulations –
   (a) provide that a building or other land is not land of community value if the building or other land is specified in the regulations or is of a description specified in the regulations;
   (b) provide that a building or other land in a local authority's area is not land of community value if the local authority or some other person specified in the regulations considers that the building or other land is of a description specified in the regulations.
(4) A description specified under subsection (3) may be framed by reference to such matters as the appropriate authority considers appropriate.
(5) In relation to any land, those matters include (in particular) –
   (a) the owner of any estate or interest in any of the land or in other land;
   (b) any occupier of any of the land or of other land;
   (c) the nature of any estate or interest in any of the land or in other land;
   (d) any use to which any of the land or other land has been, is being or could be put;
   (e) statutory provisions, or things done under statutory provisions, that have effect (or do not have effect) in relation to –
     (i) any of the land or other land, or
     (ii) any of the matters within paragraphs (a) to (d);
   (f) any price, or value for any purpose, of any of the land or other land […]'

Voluntary or community organisations with a local connection, as well as parish councils in England and community councils in Wales, can nominate to include in the list particular assets that they consider to be of community value. Regulations will set out the meaning of 'voluntary or community body' and the conditions that have to be met for a person to have a local connection. The September 2011 Policy Statement on the Community Right to Buy states that '"local voluntary and community body" will be defined as a body, other than a public or local authority, which may be incorporated or unincorporated, must not be run primarily for profit, and must have a primary purpose concerned with the local authority's area, or the neighbourhood in which the asset is situated where this is in more than one authority's area. We will set out the full definition in regulations.'[19]

The asset will be included on the list if the local authority is of the opinion that the current use of the asset furthers the social wellbeing or social interests of the local community, that the use is not an ancillary one and that it is realistic that the use of the asset in this way can continue.

In February 2011, DCLG carried out a public consultation[20] in relation to the Community Right to Buy, seeking views on, among other things:

- whether local authorities should decide what constitutes an asset of community value (based on a broad definition of asset of local community benefit and a list of excluded assets, including residential properties);
- the length of the moratorium period,[21] which should give community groups reasonable time to develop a viable bid without disproportionately interfering with an owner's property rights;
- the right for asset owners to appeal against a local authority's decision to list their asset; and
- the opportunity for owners to claim compensation for costs arising as a direct result of the operation of the scheme.

DCLG published in September 2011 its Policy Statement on *Assets of Community Value*, which in its own words, 'sets out the way forward on the issues following the consultation'.[22] It recognises that there are some categories of land that should be excluded from being listed and that these will be set out in regulations. DCLG has indicated that it intends to exclude the following:[23]

- residential premises including sites for mobile homes and boats (which will not include properties such as shops or pubs which have living quarters above them); and
- operational land used for transport infrastructure or some other related purposes by statutory undertakers.

Pursuant to s 100 of the Act, inclusion of land in the list of Assets of Community Value takes effect as a local land charge. Section 87(3) provides that land included will be removed from the list five years after its original

---

19 DCLG (2011) *Assets of Community Value: Policy Statement,* page 7 (available at http://www.communities.gov.uk/publications/localgovernment/assetscommunityvaluestatement [accessed March 2012]).
20 Available at http://www.communities.gov.uk/publications/localgovernment/righttobuyconsultation [accessed March 2012].
21 See further below.
22 DCLG (2011) *Assets of Community Value: Policy Statement* (available at http://www.communities.gov.uk/publications/localgovernment/assetscommunityvaluestatement [accessed March 2012]).
23 DCLG (2011) *Assets of Community Value: Policy Statement,* pages 6 and 7 (available at http://www.communities.gov.uk/publications/localgovernment/assetscommunityvaluestatement [accessed March 2012]).

entry in the list. Pursuant to s 91(2), local authorities must give written notice of the inclusion or removal of an asset on the list to the owner of the land, any occupiers of the land, and the person who made the nomination. An owner of land to be listed has the right to ask to request the local authority to review its decision to include his land in the list. DCLG has indicated that it will specify in regulations that an owner of land listed will also have a right of appeal to an independent tribunal, against the outcome of the review by the local authority.[24]

The Act prevents a 'relevant disposal' of a listed asset being made, unless certain specific conditions have been met. A 'relevant disposal' is defined in section 95 as:

- a disposal of the freehold estate in land with vacant possession; and
- the grant or assignment of a leasehold estate in land with at least 25 years to run which is granted or assigned with vacant possession.

A number of disposals are exempt under the Act from the definition of 'relevant disposal', including the following:

- transfers made other than for value;
- transfers of land between members of the family;
- transfers resulting from the inheritance of land;
- transfers resulting from sales of land to pay estate debts;
- transfers resulting from the resignation or death of trustees of a trust or partners in a firm;
- transfers between trustees, between a trust and a settler, and between a trust and a beneficiary;
- transfers related to business transactions of a going concern, where the intention is to continue the existing use of the asset; or
- transfers where the listed asset forms part of a larger estate.

DCLG has indicated that it will provide for further exemptions in regulations, including exempting transfers between connected companies.[25]

The relevant disposal may only proceed if each of the following conditions set out in section 95(2) to (5) have been fulfilled:

Condition A: The owner must have notified the local authority in writing of his intention to enter into a relevant disposal of the land;

Condition B: Either –
(i) the interim moratorium period has ended (being six weeks from the date the local authority has been notified in writing of the intention of the owner to enter into a relevant disposal of land) without the local authority having received a written request that a community group be considered as a potential bidder in relation to the land, or
(ii) the full moratorium period has ended (being six months from the date the local authority has been notified in writing of the intention of the owner to enter into a relevant disposal of land), and

---

24 DCLG (2011) *Assets of Community Value: Policy Statement,* page 7 (available at http://www.communities.gov.uk/publications/localgovernment/assetscommunityvaluestatement [accessed March 2012]).

25 DCLG (2011) *Assets of Community Value: Policy Statement,* page 9 (available at http://www.communities.gov.uk/publications/localgovernment/assetscommunityvaluestatement [accessed March 2012]).

## Community empowerment

Condition C: The protected period has not ended (being 18 months from the date the local authority has been notified in writing of the intention of the owner to enter into a relevant disposal of land).

These moratorium periods are designed to give community groups sufficient time to decide whether to put forward an expression that they wish to be considered as bidders, and if so, to prepare their bid. Community groups have six weeks following the notification that the owner is selling a listed asset and in which to request to be considered as a potential bidder. If no one comes forward in those six weeks, the asset can be disposed of. However, where a group expresses an interest, the full six month moratorium period is triggered, so that a bid can be put together by the community group.

There is no obligation for the owner to sell its listed asset to the local community and unlike the Community Right to Buy scheme in Scotland, the Community Right to Buy does not confer a formal right of first refusal. Further, where the listed asset is not sold at the end of the interim or full moratorium period, the asset may be sold within the remainder of the 18-month period without triggering another delay.

In its September 2011 Policy Statement on *Assets of Community Value*, DCLG has indicated that it intends that 'where there is a community interest group wishing to purchase a particular asset, and able to pay the price determined by the owner, the owner should have the option of disposing of the asset to that group without waiting till the end of the window to do so. This would allow local authorities to continue to make asset transfers to community interest groups without being restricted by the moratorium, and thus provides an opportunity for community interest groups to have a 'right of first offer.'[26] DCLG considers that 'community interest group' for this purpose should be defined in regulations and expects it to be defined as a parish council, or a body whose primary purpose is concerned with the local authority's area, or the neighbourhood in which the asset is situated where this is in more than one authority's area and which is:

- a company limited by guarantee;
- an Industrial and Provident Society (either a co-operative or a community benefit society);
- a community interest company; or
- any other body which is registered as a charity, including a charitable incorporated organisation.

Section 99 of the Act provides for the Secretary of State to make regulations to provide for compensation in connection with the operation of the right, which DCLG has proposed will apply to any owners for loss and expense incurred as a result of listing and complying with the procedures required by the scheme.

As mentioned above, a scheme already operates in Scotland that has some similarities. It allows 'communities with a population of less than 10,000 in Scotland to apply to register an interest in land and the opportunity to buy that

---

26 DCLG (2011) *Assets of Community Value: Policy Statement,* page 10 (available at http://www.communities.gov.uk/publications/localgovernment/assetscommunityvaluestatement [accessed March 2012]).

## Assets of Community Value

land when it comes up for sale.'[27] Guidance issued by the Scottish Government on the Scottish Community Right to Buy[28] states that the right in Scotland:

> 'provides CBs [community bodies] with a pre-emptive right to buy the land in which they have registered a community interest. To date, CBs have registered an interest in land including fields, woodlands, and a range of other assets such as buildings, for example churches, a school, and a community centre. The [Land Reform (Scotland)] Act also allows CBs to place registrations on salmon fishings and mineral rights (except mineral rights to oil, coal, gas, gold or silver) which are owned separately from the land with which they are associated.'[29]

The Scottish regime contains detailed and complex requirements, both for the process of applying to register land, and the process of proceeding with a purchase. For example, to register land as being of community interest, the community body must demonstrate it has the support of at least ten per cent of the community and must submit detailed maps showing among other things the boundaries of the community and land to be registered. Once the registered land comes up for sale and the community body has confirmed that it wishes to exercise its right to buy, an independent valuer will be appointed to determine the market value of the land. The community body must then ballot the community on the purchase and secure a majority in favour of the purchase of the land. The results of the ballot must be submitted to the Scottish Ministers, together with a feasibility study or business plan and evidence of compliance with other requirements, including that the community body's proposals to use the land are compatible with furthering the achievement of sustainable development, and that the purchase is in the public interest. Scottish lawyer Malcolm Combe has commented as follows on a case concerning unsuccessful attempts by a community body in Scotland, the Kinghorn Community Land Association 2005, to register land for the purposes of the right to buy:

> 'While there may be nothing in law to stop further applications, a community could be forgiven for becoming thoroughly fed up with the whole process. The Kinghorn community has been active for some time, incorporating its first company on 15 December 2004. Some five years later, no land has been acquired by the community under the auspices of the Act. While the legislation may be radical in outlook, its application has not been. As previously noted, a restrictive approach to the Act's operation makes a challenging process more challenging still. The experience at Kinghorn Loch does little to alter that view.'[30]

The Assets of Community Value mechanism is to be distinguished from a 'public request to order disposal' ('PROD'), the existing little-used mechanism contained in the Local Government, Planning and Land Act 1980. Members of the public have the right to request an order from the Secretary of State for

---

27 The Scottish Government *Community Right to Buy* (see http://www.scotland.gov.uk/Topics/farmingrural/Rural/rural-land/right-to-buy/Community [accessed March 2012]).
28 The Scottish Government (2009) *Part 2 of the Land Reform (Scotland) Act 2003: Community Right to Buy – Guidance: Còir Coimhearsnachd Air Ceannachd – Stiùireadh* (available at http://www.scotland.gov.uk/Publications/2009/06/08101427/0 [accessed March 2012]).
29 The Scottish Government (2009) *Part 2 of the Land Reform (Scotland) Act 2003: Community Right to Buy – Guidance: Còir Coimhearsnachd Air Ceannachd – Stiùireadh*, page 1 (available at http://www.scotland.gov.uk/Publications/2009/06/08101427/0 [accessed March 2012]).
30 Malcolm M Combe (2010) *Access to Land and Land Ownership* (available at Edin LR 2010, 14(1), 106–113).

## Community empowerment

public authority owned land, which they believe to be vacant or underused, to be sold to enable it to be brought back into use. Such a request must include details of why the applicant believes that:

(a) the land is vacant or underused;
(b) there are no suitable publicly tested plans in place to reclaim the land, or are likely to be in the foreseeable future; and
(c) why the land should be disposed of in order to enable it to be brought back into use.

The Government has developed an on-line tool for members of the public to use, known (confusingly, given the various similar-sounding mechanisms!) as the Community Right to Reclaim Land, to provide information about empty land and buildings throughout communities for the purposes both of PROD and Assets of Community Value.[31] Information currently held on separate databases will be brought together in order to make it easier to find out the owner of vacant land in a particular area. In a February 2011 press release, Grant Shapps, the Housing Minister, states that:

> '... we are introducing a new Right to Reclaim Land. Under our plans, communities will no longer be kept in the dark about what land is available; instead they will be able to see at the click of a button what local opportunities there are for development. And rather than requests to use that land being blocked and ignored, ordinary people who make a case to improve their local area will be listened to.'[32]

In order to further encourage the use of PROD, DCLG published on its website on 5 October 2011 the PROD request form and a short explanatory note as to how the power should be used.[33]

---

31 DCLG website, see http://www.communities.gov.uk/housing/housingsupply/righttoreclaim/ [accessed February 2012].
32 DCLG (2 February 2011) *Press Release – Grant Shapps: Communities to be Given a Right to Reclaim Land* (available at http://www.communities.gov.uk/news/corporate/1833082 [accessed February 2012]).
33 DCLG (5 October 2011) *Public Request to Order Disposal: Request Form* (available at http://www.communities.gov.uk/publications/housing/prodrequestform [accessed February 2012]).

# Chapter 5

# Abolition of regional strategies

## BACKGROUND

Since the Planning and Compulsory Purchase Act 2004 ('PCPA 2004'), Pt 3 came into force in September 2004, regional strategies have comprised part of the statutory development plan for the purposes of PCPA 2004, s 38. Prior to PCPA 2004, regional planning policy was set out in non-statutory regional planning guidance, which was prepared in accordance with Planning Policy Guidance Note 11, *Regional Planning*.[1] Regional strategies under PCPA 2004 had to 'set out the Secretary of State's policies (however expressed) in relation to the development and use of land within the region'.[2] They were to 'provide a broad development strategy for the region for a fifteen to twenty year period'[3] and should:

- articulate a spatial vision of what the region will look like at the end of the period of the strategy and show how this will contribute to achieving sustainable development objectives;
- provide a concise spatial strategy for achieving that vision, defining its main aims and objectives, illustrated by a key diagram, with the policies clearly highlighted;
- address regional or sub-regional issues that will often cross county or unitary authority and, on occasion, district boundaries, and take advantage of the range of development options that exist at that level. The regional strategy should not address local issues which should be the subject of a [local development document];
- be consistent with and supportive of other regional frameworks and strategies, including the regional sustainable development framework and the regional cultural, economic and housing strategies;
- be specific to the region – whilst it should have regard to national policies it should not simply repeat them nor resort to platitudes. It should provide spatially specific policies applying national policies to the circumstances of the region;
- be locationally but not site specific, while not going into the level of detail more appropriate to a local development document;
- be focused on delivery mechanisms which make clear what is to be done by whom and by when;
- provide a clear link between policy objectives and priorities, targets and indicators. It should be monitored annually against the delivery of its priorities and the realisation of its vision for the region, and reviewed as appropriate;

---

1 DETR (October 2000) Planning Policy Guidance Note 11: *Regional Planning*.
2 Planning and Compulsory Purchase Act 2004, s 1.
3 DCLG (7 September 2004) Planning Policy Statement 11: *Regional Spatial Strategies*, para 1.3 (available at http://webarchive.nationalarchives.gov.uk/+/http://www.communities.gov.uk/publications/planningandbuilding/pps11spatial [accessed March 2012]).

## Abolition of regional strategies

- apply the test of adding value to the overall planning process; and
- contribute to the achievement of sustainable development in line with PCPA 2004, s 39.[4]

In defence of the Coalition Government's accusations that the regional tier of planning is undemocratic, it is worth remembering that, prior to the introduction of PCPA 2004, the Labour Government published in 2002 a White Paper entitled *Your Region, Your Choice*,[5] in which it 'delivered' its 'manifesto commitment to provide for directly elected regional assemblies in those regions that want them'.[6] The Government envisaged that 'where voters choose to have an elected assembly this will mean that, for the first time, decisions affecting the region will be taken by a body that is directly accountable to the regional electorate rather than to Ministers and the UK Parliament.'[7] Where elected regional assemblies were in place, powers in key areas such as economic development, spatial planning and housing would be devolved to them from government offices and other public bodies, including the development of regional strategies. The Regional Assemblies (Preparations) Act 2003 was subsequently enacted to permit referendums to be held to create directly elected regional assemblies in line with the White Paper. The first referendum for a regional assembly, which took place in the North East of England in November 2004, resulted in a dramatic defeat for the principle of regional assemblies, with a total number of 696,519 people (78 per cent) voting against the plans and only 197,310 (22 per cent) voting in favour.[8] As a result of the clear indication that the public did not want a regional assembly, and accusations of it only constituting a 'white elephant', any plans for further referendums on directly elected regional assemblies were dropped.[9]

Instead, in July 2007, the then Government published its *Review of Sub-national Economic Development and Regeneration*, in which it was recognised that 'the regional tier has an important role in developing overall strategy, identifying priorities and opportunities for growth. More policy and funding decisions should be devolved from the centre. However, accountability arrangements need to be clearer and simplification is required.' In this regard, the Government proposed to 'move to a single integrated regional strategy which sets out the economic, social and environmental objectives for each region' and 'place on the Regional Development Agencies the executive responsibility, on behalf of the region, for developing the integrated regional strategy, working closely with local authorities and other partners'.[10]

---

4 DCLG (7 September 2004) Planning Policy Statement 11: *Regional Spatial Strategies*, para 1.7 (available at http://webarchive.nationalarchives.gov.uk/+/http:/www.communities.gov.uk/publications/planningandbuilding/pps11spatial [accessed March 2012]).
5 DCLG (2002) *Your Region, Your Choice: Revitalising the English Regions* (available at http://www.communities.gov.uk/publications/regeneration/yourregionyour [accessed March 2012]).
6 DCLG (2002) *Your Region, Your Choice: Revitalising the English Regions*, Preface (available at http://www.communities.gov.uk/publications/regeneration/yourregionyour [accessed March 2012]).
7 DCLG (2002) Your Region, Your Choice: Revitalising the English Regions, para 4.3 (available at http://www.communities.gov.uk/publications/regeneration/yourregionyour [accessed March 2012]).
8 BBC (2004) *North East Votes 'No' to Assembly* (available at http://news.bbc.co.uk/1/hi/uk_politics/3984387.stm [accessed March 2012]).
9 BBC (2004) *Prescott Rules Out Regional Polls* (available at http://news.bbc.co.uk/1/hi/uk_politics/3992435.stm [accessed March 2012]).
10 HM Treasury (2007) *Review of Sub-national Economic Development and Regeneration*, page 9.

Subsequently, and with the coming into force of the Local Democracy, Economic Development and Construction Act 2009, the separate concepts established under PCPA 2004 of a regional spatial strategy (setting out the Secretary of State's policies in relation to development and use of land) and the regional economic strategy (produced by regional development agencies), became single documents, known as regional strategies.

## COALITION GOVERNMENT'S STANCE

On 6 July 2010, the Secretary of State announced by way of a letter to Chief Planning Officers[11] the formal revocation of regional strategies with immediate effect. The intention to abolish the regional strategies had been set out in the pre-election Green Paper, *Open Source Planning*, where the Conservative Party committed to 'abolishing the entire bureaucratic and undemocratic tier of regional planning, including the Regional Spatial Strategies and national and regional building targets'[12] and had made its way into the Coalition Government's *Programme for Government*, where the Government set out to 'rapidly abolish Regional Spatial Strategies and return decision-making powers on housing and planning to local councils, including giving councils new powers to stop "garden grabbing"'.[13]

Although the drive to shift power to the local level was an important factor in the Government's aim to abolish regional strategies, a significant driver for the abolition of regional strategies was the Government's view of housing targets, the Government's view being that, in line with the localism agenda, LPAs, rather than regional planning bodies or the Government, should be responsible for establishing the right level of housing provision in their area, and for identifying long-term supply of housing land, without the burden of regionally set housing targets.[14] The guidance issued with the letter to Chief Planning Officers confirmed that regional strategies had been revoked under the Local Democracy, Economic Development and Construction Act 2009, s 79(6), which permits the Secretary of State, if it thinks it is necessary or expedient, to revoke a regional strategy or such parts of a regional strategy as he thinks appropriate, and that the legal basis for the abolition of the overall system in the longer term would be the Localism Act.

The guidance was intended to provide clarification on the impact of the revocation of regional strategies. It contained the following paragraph:

'4. **How will this affect planning applications?**

In determining planning applications local planning authorities must continue to have regard to the development plan. This will now consist only of:

---

11   DCLG (6 July 2011) *Letter to Chief Planning Officers: Revocation of Regional Spatial Strategies* (available at http://www.communities.gov.uk/publications/planningandbuilding/letterregionalstrategies [accessed March 2012]).
12   Conservative Party Policy Green Paper 14 (2010) *Open Source Planning*, page 2 (available at http://www.conservatives.com/News/News_stories/2010/02/New_homes_and_jobs_through_Open_Source_Planning.aspx [accessed March 2012]).
13   Cabinet Office (2010) The Coalition: Our Programme for Government, page 11 (available at http://www.cabinetoffice.gov.uk/news/coalition-documents [accessed March 2012]).
14   DCLG (6 July 2011) *Letter to Chief Planning Officers: Revocation of Regional Spatial Strategies* (available at http://www.communities.gov.uk/publications/planningandbuilding/letterregionalstrategies[accessed March 2012]).

## Abolition of regional strategies

- Adopted DPDs;
- Saved policies; and
- Any old style plans that have not lapsed.

Local planning authorities should also have regard to other material considerations, including national policy. Evidence that informed the preparation of the revoked Regional Strategies may also be a material consideration, depending on the facts of the case.

Where local planning authorities have not yet issued decisions on planning applications in the pipeline, they may wish to review those decisions in light of the new freedoms following the revocation of Regional Strategies. The revocation of the Regional Strategy may also be a material consideration.'

This put developers in an awkward position as many had been promoting, over a long period, large schemes designed to accommodate housing targets set out in regional strategies.

Cala Homes was an example of such a developer – it had been promoting a scheme for 2,000 residential homes with associated infrastructure and facilities on 87 acres of farmland at Barton Farm, Winchester for a number of years. Much of Cala's case rested on the need for additional housing in Hampshire to meet policy requirements in the relevant regional strategy, the South East Plan. The relevant local policy stated that the development of the site 'will only be permitted if the Local Planning Authority is satisfied that a compelling justification for additional housing in the Winchester district has been identified by the Strategic Planning Authorities …'. Cala Homes had appealed against the non-determination of the planning application by Winchester City Council, whose position was that it was now able to determine the application without the framework of regional numbers and plans and that accordingly it was free to conclude that the site did not need to be released for housing. The public inquiry into the appeal was suspended in light of the Government's announcement of the formal revocation of regional strategies in June 2010 and Cala Homes commenced judicial review proceedings against the Secretary of State, arguing that the Secretary of State had acted unlawfully by revoking regional strategies without primary legislation and prior to the putting into place of transitional arrangements.[15] The High Court's judgment, published in November 2010, quashed the Government's decision to revoke regional spatial strategies ('RSSs') under the Local Democracy, Economic Development and Construction Act 2009, s 79(6). The Court found that the Government had used s 79(6) for an improper purpose, concluding:

'The LDEDCA 2009 maintains in place, with some modifications, the whole elaborate machinery set up by Parliament under the PCPA 2004 to create a new statutory tier of regional planning guidance in the form of Regional Spatial Strategies, now re-named as Regional Strategies. I refer to some particular features of the regime set out in Part 5 of the 2009 Act below, but the main and critical point is that there is no sufficient indication in section 79(6) of the 2009 Act that Parliament intended to reserve to the Secretary

---

15 Two more developers also issued proceedings under the Town and Country Planning Act 1990, s 288 in relation to decisions taken by the Secretary of State following the purported revocation of RSSs. The first, Catesby Property Group, was appealing the refusal of its proposal to build a mixed use development in Bude, Cornwall. The second, Colonnade Land, had its proposal for a development of up to 326 homes at Coombes Farm in Rochford, Essex, refused.

of State a power to set that whole elaborate structure at nought if, in his opinion, it was expedient or necessary to do so because it was not operating in the public interest. If Parliament had intended to create such a power for the Secretary of State – something akin to a Henry VIII clause, since the practical effect of it would be to grant the Secretary of State power to denude primary legislation of any practical effect, without having to seek the approval of Parliament for such a course by passing further legislation – it would in my opinion undoubtedly have used much clearer language to achieve that effect and would have given the provision far greater prominence than section 79(6) has, tucked away as a final sub-section in a provision otherwise dealing with revision of Regional Strategies. A contrast may be drawn in that regard between the location of section 79(6) in Part 5 of the 2009 Act and the prominence given to section 70(1) as the leading provision in Part 5, which sets the scene for the provisions which follow in that Part and is the basis for the whole elaborate framework which that Part puts in place. A number of subsidiary points may be made in support of this fundamental point, as set out below;

...

The provisions in Part 5 of the 2009 Act requiring Regional Strategies to be published, making provision for the public to have opportunities to make representations regarding their drafting (including, where appropriate, at examinations in public) and for community involvement in the preparation of such planning policy guidance (see section 75) are all strong indications as to the importance which Regional Strategies are intended to have in the operation of the planning system and for the guidance of the public. These are important means of ensuring public participation in the creation of planning policy and transparency in relation to such policy, and it is not plausible to suppose that Parliament intended that they should be capable of being simply by-passed by action taken by the Secretary of State under section 79(6), which carries with it no procedural protections or requirements at all.'[16]

As a result of this judgment, regional strategies returned to their status as part of the development plan. However, in response, the Government's Chief Planner, Steve Quartermain, published on 10 November 2010 (the same day the judgment was published) a statement and letter to local planning authorities reiterating that the Government's intention to abolish regional strategies through the introduction of the Localism Act remained a material consideration to be taken into account by local planning authorities in planning decisions.[17] In response, Cala Homes launched a second application for judicial review, this time challenging the lawfulness of this advice.

On 7 February 2011, the High Court delivered its ruling on the second judicial review.[18] Mr Justice Lindblom dismissed the claim for judicial review, finding that the statement of the Chief Planner was not unlawful or irrational. He

---

16 *Cala Homes (South) Ltd v Secretary of State for Communities and Local Government* [2010] EWHC 2866 (Admin), para 52.
17 DCLG (10 November 2010) *Letter to Chief Planning Officers: Revocation of Regional Spatial Strategies* (available at http://www.communities.gov.uk/publications/planningandbuilding/letterabolitionregional [accessed March 2012]).
18 *R (Cala Homes (South) Limited v Secretary of State for Communities and Local Government (No.2)* [2011] EWHC 97 (Admin).

## Abolition of regional strategies

decided that the statement merely advised authorities, when determining planning decisions to which regional strategies were relevant, to take into account the Government's intention to reform the existing planning system. There was no inconsistency between the fact that regional strategies formed part of the development plan and the concept that the Government's intention to abolish them was a material consideration. Mr Justice Lindblom also held that it was at least desirable, if not necessary, for the Government's position in relation to regional strategies to be made known once the decision in the earlier judicial review proceedings had become public, to avoid creating further uncertainty.

Cala Homes unsuccessfully appealed to the Court of Appeal.[19] Lord Justice Sullivan stated that:

> '[Counsel for Cala Homes] submitted that if the proposed abolition was a material consideration it would be irrational to give it any weight at this stage. However, Mr. Mould's [Counsel for the Secretary of State's] submissions have persuaded me that where the issue is one of weight rather than materiality, "never say never" is the appropriate response to a submission that, as a matter of law, any decision-maker in any case would be bound to give no significant weight to a potentially material factor. Mr. Mould fairly acknowledged that even within the minority of cases in which the proposed abolition of regional strategies will be relevant, there may well be very few cases in which it would be appropriate at this stage of the Parliamentary and SEA process to give any significant weight to the proposal. But the Chief Planner's letter is concerned with the whole of the period prior to the enactment of the Localism Bill (if it is enacted), and the position will change as it progresses, or fails to progress. Even now there might be finely balanced cases where the very slight prospect of a very substantial policy change might just tip the balance in favour of granting or refusing planning permission. Mr. Mould gave the hypothetical example of a large-scale residential proposal (which he referred to as a "new town", but the point would equally apply to a proposed extension of an existing settlement), which is proposed to be developed over the next 15–20 years, to which there are very strong site-specific objections, and where the sole justification for granting planning permission is the need to meet the requirement for residential development over the next 20 years in the regional strategy. In such a case it would not be irrational for the decision maker to give some weight to the prospect, however uncertain, that the regional policy justification for granting permission for such a long-term proposal may cease to exist within the short term. In such a case, to give even a very little weight to the prospect of a change in policy might be to give that factor "significant" weight, significant in the sense that it might tip the balance in favour of refusing permission. This hypothetical example may well be an extreme case, but it does illustrate why it would not be safe for the Court to assume that at this stage there are no circumstances in which any decision-maker could rationally give some weight to the proposed abolition of regional strategies. In view of the uncertainty created by the legal obstacles referred to above (para. 31) any decision-maker who does think it appropriate to give some weight to the Government's proposal when determining an application or an appeal would be well-advised to give very

---

19  *R (Cala Homes (South) Limited) v Secretary of State for Communities and Local Government (No 2)* [2011] EWHC 97 (Admin).

## FORMAL ABOLITION OF REGIONAL STRATEGIES

Section 109 of the Act gives the Secretary of State the power to revoke the whole or any part of a regional strategy. The words 'or any part of' were introduced at a late stage to address a further complication the Government now faces. From soon after the Government announced its intention to abolish regional strategies, legal commentators have questioned whether in fact strategic environmental assessment would be required under the Strategic Environmental Assessment Directive,[20] on the basis that assessment is required of any modifications of any 'plan or programme'. The issue was raised in the first *Cala Homes* judgment, with Mr Justice Sales finding that:

'All the existing Regional Strategies were made the subject of environmental assessment before they were adopted, no doubt because of the practical impact that they would inevitably have by setting part of the framework for decision-making in planning cases. I can see no sound basis for the contention put forward by the Secretary of State that revocation of Regional Strategies does not equally require at least consideration under Regulation 9 whether similar detailed environmental assessment is required. The revocation of a Regional Strategy may have as profound practical implications for planning decisions as its adoption in the first place. Thus the purposive approach to the interpretation of the 2004 Regulations referred to above supports the same conclusion.

I would add that I also consider that there is force in the alternative analyses proposed by the Claimant, to the effect that a Regional Strategy is itself a relevant "plan" for the purposes of the 2004 Regulations, and that revocation of that "plan" either amounts to a modification of such "plan" (applying a purposive interpretation of the Regulations, since it is difficult in the context of the object of the SEA Directive and Regulations to see why significant but lesser changes to a Regional Strategy should require there to be an environmental assessment, but that if the change takes the extreme form of revocation of the Regional Strategy that requirement should suddenly fall away) or to the adoption of a new relevant "plan", namely the local development plan documents standing alone, to be read without reference to the Regional Strategy.

On a straightforward reading of the 2004 Regulations in the present context, therefore, I consider that the Secretary of State acted unlawfully by purporting to revoke the South East Plan Regional Strategy without first at least conducting a screening assessment under Regulation 9.'[21]

In a written statement to the House of Commons on 5 April 2011,[22] Bob Neill MP, Parliamentary Under-Secretary of State for Communities and Local

---

20 Directive 2001/42/EC of 27 June 2001 on the Assessment of the Effects of Certain Plans and Programmes on the Environment.
21 *Cala Homes (South) Ltd v Secretary of State for Communities and Local Government* [2010] EWHC 2866 (Admin), paras 62–64.
22 Daily Hansard (2011) (available at http://www.publications.parliament.uk/pa/cm201011/cmhansrd/cm110405/wmstext/110405m0001.htm [accessed March 2012]).

*Abolition of regional strategies*

Government, announced the Government's intention to undertake strategic environmental assessment 'on a voluntary basis', 'to assess whether there are any significant environmental effects of revoking each regional strategy ... subject to Royal Assent [of the Act], the revocation of each individual regional strategy will be commenced after the assessment process has been completed'.

Pursuant to this statement, the Government is currently in the process of carrying out strategic environmental assessment in relation to the likely significant environmental effects of the revocation of the seven existing regional strategies (and the non-statutory regional planning guidance for the South West). On 20 October 2011, it published, for consultation, environmental reports in relation to the revocation of each regional strategy and the regional planning guidance. Bob Neill commented that 'these reports make it clear that revoking the Plans will protect communities and the environment from top down pressure to build on the Green Belt.' The environmental reports for the revocation of the seven existing regional strategies[23] find as follows in relation to the likely significant environmental effects of the revocation:

> 'The revocation of the Plan would decentralise planning powers to local authorities, freeing them to work with their local communities to deliver sustainable development. To support them in both delivering for their local communities and addressing strategic cross-border issues, the Government is proposing a duty on public bodies to co-operate on planning concerns that cross administrative boundaries. Local authorities will be expected to work collaboratively with other bodies to ensure that strategic priorities across local boundaries are properly co-ordinated and clearly reflected in individual local plans. They will be expected to demonstrate that this is the case when their local plans are examined in public.
>
> The environmental effects of revoking the Plan would reflect future decisions by local authorities, taken individually and collectively. Whilst the environmental effects cannot therefore be predicted in detail at this point, it is clear that the revocation of regional strategies and their top-down targets will provide opportunities for securing environmental benefits because their revocation would remove certain current policies which present a threat to local environments. For example, revocation would remove the top-down pressure on local authorities to review the extent of their Green Belt. Across England this would have been likely to effect more than thirty areas. Protecting the Green Belt brings many environmental benefits including safeguarding the countryside and preventing urban sprawl.
>
> In overall terms, it is reasonable to anticipate that decisions taken locally will look to maximise positive environmental outcomes for the local area. However, even if there were circumstances where this was not the case, strong protections for the environment set out in national planning policy and, in many cases, provided for by national and European legislation means it is highly unlikely that there would be any significant adverse environmental effects resulting from the revocation.'[24]

---

23 All bar the environmental assessment for the revocation of the regional planning guidance for the South West, although this also concludes that it is highly unlikely that there would be any significant adverse environmental effects resulting from its revocation.

24 The environmental reports for each RSS and for the regional planning guidance for the South West are available at http://www.communities.gov.uk/planningandbuilding/planningenvironment/strategicenvironmentassess/ [accessed March 2012].

## The duty to co-operate

As already set out in the written statement to Parliament, the Government has reiterated that it hopes to proceed with the final abolition of each individual regional strategy as soon as the assessment process has been completed.[25]

Baroness Hanham in a House of Lords debate in relation to the abolition of regional strategies and (what was to become) s 109 confirmed that:

> 'the Government intend to lay orders in Parliament revoking the existing regional strategies and saved structure plan policies as soon as possible after Royal Assent of the Bill, subject to the outcome of the environmental assessment process. In the mean time, councils should press ahead in preparing up-to-date local plans. These plans will be important in defining strategic priorities and setting the context for neighbourhood plans. Up-to-date local plans also provide councils with the opportunity to control how development and growth are planned in their area and they provide the basis for planning decisions. Until they are revoked by order, local plans must be in general conformity with regional strategies which remain part of the development plan.'[26]

## THE DUTY TO CO-OPERATE

The Government envisages that regional planning issues will in the future be dealt with through the co-operation of local authorities on strategic matters. The Act introduces a duty that requires that LPAs, county councils or anyone else prescribed to cooperate with each other in relation to the preparation of development plan documents or other local development documents, and the preparation of marine plans, where they relate to 'strategic matters'. Greg Clark in the House of Commons commented that the Act:

> 'replaces the regional arrangements that have been in place for some years and introduces instead a duty to co-operate that brings local authorities together in a more natural way. Rather than giving an administrative solution to some of the problems, it allows people to collaborate, discuss and come to resolutions of larger than local issues.'[27]

In response to the Communities and Local Government Select Committee's Report on the abolition of regional strategies, which found that 'the peremptory abolition of Regional Spatial Strategies has created a hiatus in the planning framework, which risks producing a damaging inertia'[28] and recommended (among other things) that 'the Government must ensure that the beneficial and positive aspects of Regional Spatial Strategies, in particular for integrating infrastructure, economic development, housing, data collection

---

25 DCLG (20 October 2011) *Government Moves Ahead with Plans to Abolish Regional Plans and Protect the Green Belt* (available at http://www.communities.gov.uk/news/newsroom/2012247 [accessed March 2012]).
26 Hansard, 12 October 2011, cols 1769–1770.
27 Hansard, 17 May 2011, col 261.
28 Communities and Local Government Select Committee (March 2011) *Abolition of Regional Spatial Strategies: A Planning Vacuum*, page 14 (available at http://www.parliament.uk/business/committees/committees-a-z/commons-select/communities-and-local-government-committee/publications/ [accessed March 2012]).

*Abolition of regional strategies*

and environment protection, are not swept away, but are retained in any new planning framework,[29] the Government stated that:

> 'We are fully committed to effective strategic planning and we have provided a statutory framework for this through the duty to co-operate. But we want councils to be free to respond in the most effective way to the issues that matter to them and their communities so we will not impose a rigid and centrally directed system for planning on crossboundary issues. *Local councils are perfectly capable of addressing strategic issues locally*, working with adjoining authorities and other bodies as needed. The National Planning Policy Framework will set out the Government's policies on local plans and their role in planning for wider cross boundary issues through the duty to co-operate. Local plans will need to demonstrate conformity with national policy that will be tested as part of the local examination. We anticipate that these wider issues will include policies on economic development, housing supply, strategic infrastructure provision and environmental management.'[30]

The new duty to co-operate is found in s 110 and states that local planning authorities, county councils and other bodies with statutory functions must engage constructively, and on an ongoing basis, with each other in respect of the preparation of:

- development plan documents;
- other local development;
- marine plans; and

any activities that support the preparation of the above, including matters related to sustainable development that would have significant wider impacts.

The bodies caught by these provisions will be expected to consider the activities of other bodies that may interact with their activities and must be able to evidence the existence of such co-operation when submitting their development plan documents for inspection.

Further regulations setting out the type of bodies that will be caught by this duty, and guidance in respect of its operation, are expected.

Baroness Young of Old Scone (a cross-bencher and formerly chief executive of the Environment Agency) commented in the House of Lords debate on an amendment to what was to be s 110:

> 'The importance of this duty is indubitable and there has been considerable discussion about it. The mechanism for strategic planning is now only the duty to co-operate. It is new and the only mechanism, so it is important, not just for strategic infrastructure and economic development, that the duty to co-operate applies. It should take proper account of issues that need to be planned on a wider basis than a single authority, such as adaptation to climate change, flood risk, coastal erosion, biodiversity and other environmental measures.

---

29  Communities and Local Government Select Committee (March 2011) *Abolition of Regional Spatial Strategies: A Planning Vacuum*, page 9 (available at http://www.parliament.uk/business/committees/committees-a-z/commons-select/communities-and-local-government-committee/publications/ [accessed March 2012]).
30  Government response to the Communities and Local Government Committee's Report on the Abolition of Regional Strategies, June 2011, page 4 (available at http://www.communities.gov.uk/publications/planningandbuilding/responseabolitionregional [accessed March 2012]).

To give two examples: river basin management plans need to operate on a wider basis than a single authority and they are a statutory requirement under European law. Likewise, landscape scale biodiversity can often be resolved by two or more authorities working together. The Government's Natural Environment White Paper and the importance of landscape scale land management for conservation have already been outlined in the ecosystem assessment that the Government conducted. There are many reasons why it is really important, because this is now the only mechanism for strategic planning at a higher level than a single authority that this duty to co-operate works.

It is doubly important now because the national planning policy framework has no spatial element to it. It is simply a set of policies that do not refer to any particular part of land or the country. Since the regional spatial strategies are disappearing there must therefore be a stronger duty for adequate co-operation between local authorities.'[31]

DCLG's view is that the duty to cooperate should not be applied retrospectively and that draft development plan documents that were submitted for examination prior to s 110 coming into force on 15 November 2011 are not required to comply with the duty.[32]

## CHANGES TO LOCAL PLANS REGIME

Sections 111 to 113 of the Act make relatively minor changes to the PCPA 2004 local development plans regime.

Section 111 has the effect of removing the requirement for LPAs to submit their draft local development schemes for the Secretary of State's approval (or, in London, to the Mayor of London). Authorities will simply have to publish up to date information on the scheme for the public.

Section 112 allows LPAs to request the examiner of a draft development plan document, during the examination, to recommend modifications that could make the document suitable for adoption. It also gives LPAs an element of flexibility in dealing with recommended modifications proposed by an independent examiner to a draft development plan document. Previously the LPA was required to incorporate all of the examiner's recommended modifications. Section 112 allows the LPA, in relation to recommended modifications that (taken together) do not materially affect the policies in the plan, to adopt the plan with additional modifications if the additional modifications (taken together) do not materially affect the policies that would be set out in the document if it was adopted just with the examiner's main modifications. The prohibition on an LPA withdrawing a draft development document once it has been submitted for independent examination has also been removed.

Section 113 removes the duty on LPAs to submit an annual monitoring report to the Secretary of State. They must simply publish the information at least annually direct to the public.

---

31 Hansard Debate, 12 October 2011, at cols 1774–1775. The amendment tabled that led to this discussion was not accepted.
32 Planning magazine (10 February 2012), page 8.

## Chapter 6

# Neighbourhood planning

*Open Source Planning* set out the Conservative party's aims to transform a 'broken' planning system to one that 'enables local people to shape their surroundings in a way that, while heeding global and national environmental constraints – carbon, biodiversity, landscape, heritage – is also sensitive to the history and character of a given location'.[1] The Coalition Agreement adopted the commitment to carry out a 'radical reboot', stating that the new Government would radically reform the planning system to 'give neighbourhoods far more ability to determine the shape of the places in which their inhabitants live, based on the principles set out in the Conservative Party publication *Open Source Planning*'.[2] The Localism Act legislates this 'radical shift in the balance of power' aiming to 'decentralise power as far as possible'.[3]

Part 6, Ch 3 and Schs 9 to 12 of the Act introduce a neighbourhood tier of planning in England which sits below that of districts or boroughs and which will see neighbourhood plans becoming 'the new building blocks of the planning system with communities having the power to grant planning permission if a majority of electors are in favour'.[4] *A Plain English Guide to the Localism Act* explains neighbourhood planning as follows:

> 'Instead of local people being told what to do, the Government thinks that local communities should have genuine opportunities to influence the future of the places where they live …
>
> Neighbourhood planning will allow communities, both residents, employees and business, to come together through a local parish council or neighbourhood forum and say where they think new houses, businesses and shops should go – and what they should look like.
>
> These plans can be very simple and concise, or go into considerable detail where people want. Local communities will be able to use neighbourhood planning to grant full or outline planning permission in areas where they most want to see new homes and businesses, making it easier and quicker for development to go ahead.

---

1. The Conservative Party (2010) *Open Source Planning*, page 1 (available at http://www.conservatives.com/News/News_stories/2010/02/New_homes_and_jobs_through_Open_Source_Planning.aspx [accessed March 2012]).
2. The Conservative Party (2010) *Open Source Planning*, page 11 (available at http://www.conservatives.com/News/News_stories/2010/02/New_homes_and_jobs_through_Open_Source_Planning.aspx [accessed March 2012]).
3. DCLG Press Notice (December 2010) *Localism Bill Starts a New Era of People Power* (available at http://www.communities.gov.uk/news/regeneration/1794971 [accessed March 2012]).
4. Eric Pickles MP (13 December 2010) *Written Parliamentary Statement on the Localism Bill* (available at http://www.communities.gov.uk/statements/corporate/localismbill [accessed March 2012]).

*Neighbourhood planning*

Provided a neighbourhood development plan or order is in line with national planning policy, with the strategic vision for the wider area set by the local planning authority, and with other legal requirements, local people will be able to vote on it in a referendum. If the plan is approved by a majority of those who vote, then the local authority will bring it into force.'[5]

## BUILDING BLOCKS OF NEIGHBOURHOOD PLANNING

The Act introduces several new concepts which underpin the principles of neighbourhood planning. The key bodies involved in neighbourhood planning are 'qualifying bodies' – which are parish councils and either possible or actual Neighbourhood Forums.

Neighbourhood Forums are community groups established for the express purpose of promoting or improving the social, economic and environmental well-being of an area, whether or not they are also established for the purpose of promoting the carrying on of trades, professions or other business. They must be designated as Neighbourhood Forums by the local authority in respect of a designated neighbourhood or business area. However, they cannot be designated for an area that includes the whole or any part of the area of a parish council.

The key neighbourhood planning tools, which can be initiated by qualifying bodies, include:

- Neighbourhood Development Plans, which will set out policies in relation to the development and land use in defined neighbourhood areas;
- Neighbourhood Development Orders, which will grant either full or outline planning permission for development specified in the order in relation to the particular neighbourhood area without the need for planning applications; and
- Community Right to Build Orders, which are a particular type of neighbourhood development order, and permit development on a specific site within the neighbourhood area without the need for planning permission.

### Neighbourhood areas

Neighbourhood areas are key to neighbourhood planning: they define the geographical limits of neighbourhood plans and orders.

Neighbourhood areas are designated by LPAs within their administrative area following a successful application by a relevant body. There can be no overlap between neighbourhood areas, so it is a case of first come, first served. A relevant body is a parish council, or an actual or possible Neighbourhood Forum.

---

5   DCLG (November 2011) *A Plain English Guide to the Localism Act*, page 15 (available at http://www.communities.gov.uk/publications/localgovernment/localismplainenglishupdate [accessed March 2012]).

## Formation of neighbourhood areas

In October 2011, the Government consulted on draft neighbourhood planning regulations setting out further detail on the mechanics of neighbourhood planning.[6] This consultation closed on 5 January 2012 and on 6 March 2012 the Neighbourhood Planning (General) Regulations 2012 (SI 2012/637) ('Neighbourhood Planning Regulations') were laid before Parliament. These came into force on 6 April 2012. Although the Government stated that its approach to the regulations was to impose 'the minimum of requirements on communities to free them from unnecessary process and to encourage them to get involved', they do formalise the procedures which should be followed.

Under the Neighbourhood Planning Regulations, reg 5, a neighbourhood area application must include the following:

- a map setting out the area to which the application relates;
- a statement explaining why this area should be designed as a neighbourhood area; and
- a statement that the body making the application qualifies as a relevant body under the Act.[7]

As soon as possible after receiving an area application from a relevant body, the LPA must publish the application on their website and in such other manner as they consider likely to bring the application to the attention of the people who live, work and carry on business in the area. This publication of information must contain details of how representations can be made and by when these must be received by the LPA (which must not be less than six weeks from when the application was first published).[8]

When deciding whether to create a neighbourhood area, the LPA must have regard to the desirability of designating the whole of the area as a neighbourhood area whilst considering the preservation of existing neighbourhood area boundaries. If the application is refused, the LPA must give reasons for this refusal. Where a valid application is made but the LPA does not believe that the area is appropriate for designation as a neighbourhood area, the LPA must ensure that all, or part of, the nominated area is included in an existing, or a soon to be designated, neighbourhood area.

As soon as a neighbourhood area is designated, the LPA must publish on its website and in any other manner which it considers likely to bring to the designation to the attention of the people who live, work or carry on business in the area:

(a) the name of the neighbourhood area;
(b) a map which identifies the area; and
(c) the name of the relevant body who applied for the designation.

Where an application for designation is refused, a document setting out this decision and a statement of reasons must be published by the relevant LPA.[9]

---

6 DCLG (13 October 2011) *Neighbourhood Planning Regulations: Consultation* (available at http://www.communities.gov.uk/publications/planningandbuilding/planningregulationsconsultation [accessed March 2012]).
7 Ie under the Town and Country Planning Act 1990, s 61G as inserted by the Localism Act 2011, Sch 9.
8 Neighbourhood Planning (General) Regulations 2012 (SI 2012/637), reg 6.
9 Neighbourhood Planning (General) Regulations 2012 (SI 2012/637), reg 7.

Whenever an LPA exercises its powers to designate a neighbourhood area, it must consider whether it should designate the area concerned as a business area. These are neighbourhood areas where, having regard to such matters as may be prescribed, the LPA considers that the area is wholly or predominantly business in nature.

As originally drafted, the Localism Bill did not include provisions for business areas and thereby assumed that only areas that were residential in character would be able to take advantage of the new neighbourhood planning powers. The British Property Foundation and the British Chambers of Commerce lobbied heavily to ensure that the neighbourhood planning provisions also catered for areas which are largely commercial in character, and subsequent amendments made throughout the process of the Bill through Parliament now ensure business areas are treated equally to residential areas.

## Qualifying bodies

Qualifying bodies are parish councils, or an organisation or body designated as a Neighbourhood Forum, authorised for the purposes of a Neighbourhood Development Order or Neighbourhood Development Plan to act in relation to a neighbourhood area as a result of the Town and Country Planning Act 1990, new s 61F (in relation to Neighbourhood Development Orders) and the Planning and Compulsory Purchase Act 2004, new s 38A (in relation to Neighbourhood Development plans).[10]

Parish councils have traditionally been seen as the most local level of government and it is no surprise they have been credited with such a major role in the neighbourhood planning tier. Parish councils have a responsibility for the well-being of their local community and can exercise a number of other local functions. They consist of a number of councillors who are elected by local people. As a body, a parish council is subject to the ordinary duties of public authorities and so must act reasonably and within its powers, as its decisions, actions or failures to act in relation to the exercise of a public function can be challenged by way of judicial review like those of any other public authority.

A Neighbourhood Forum must be established expressly for the purposes of promoting or improving the social, economic and environmental well-being of an area that consists of or includes the neighbourhood area concerned (it may also be established for the express purpose of promoting the carrying on of business in the neighbourhood area but not exclusively so). Membership to a Neighbourhood Forum must be open to individuals living or working in the neighbourhood area and elected members of a council whose area falls within the neighbourhood area. It must have at least 21 members, have a written constitution, and will need to comply with conditions prescribed in regulations.

The initial version of the Bill contained a requirement for Neighbourhood Forums to have a minimum of only three members. However, as Baroness Hanham commented:

> 'in response to concerns raised in Committee in the Commons regarding the legitimacy of a neighbourhood forum, especially about the number of members, we amended the Bill to increase the minimum membership requirement for forums from three people to 21 and to ensure that

---

10   Both provisions are inserted by the Localism Act 2011, Sch 9.

## Building blocks of neighbourhood planning

membership is drawn from across the community ... Our expectation and hope is that a forum of 21 people will not be just a forum of 21 people; the intention is to involve the whole neighbourhood. There will be a leading group in the forum, but it will not be exclusive and cut out other residents who live in the area – after all, it is their area and they need to be talked to. A number of people will bring forward plans and then discuss and consult on them.'[11]

When an organisation or body submits an application for a Neighbourhood Forum this application must include:

- the name of the proposed Neighbourhood Forum;
- a copy of the proposed Forum's written constitution;
- the name of the neighbourhood area to which the application relates and a map identifying the area;
- the contact details of at least one member of the Neighbourhood Forum to be made public;
- a statement setting out how the proposed Neighbourhood Forum meets the conditions set out in the Localism Act (the conditions in the Town and Country Planning Act 1990, s 61F(5) as inserted by Sch 9 of the Act).[12]

As soon as possible after receiving an application for the designation of a Neighbourhood Forum, the LPA must publish details of the application on their website, and in any other manner as it considers likely to bring the application to the attention of people who live, work or carry out business in the area. The LPA must also publicise the fact that no other Neighbourhood Forum may be designated for that neighbourhood area until the relevant application is withdrawn or expires and how to make representations in respect of the application including the deadline for these, which must be at least six weeks from the date on which the application is first publicised.[13]

There can only be one Neighbourhood Forum per neighbourhood area: a local authority may designate a Neighbourhood Forum for a neighbourhood area 'only if that area does not consist of or include the whole or any part of the area of a parish council' and if a Neighbourhood Forum has been designated and not withdrawn or expired, the LPA can decline to consider any Neighbourhood Forum application for the same neighbourhood area.[14]

As soon as possible after a designation has been made, an LPA must publicise this designation and, where a designation is refused, the LPA has to publicise its decision and give reasons.[15] An LPA can withdraw a designation where the Forum is no longer meeting the conditions of or criteria for their designation but must give reasons for such a decision.[16] In addition, a designation ceases to have effect at the end of five years (without affecting the validity of neighbourhood development orders or plans). It is also open to a Neighbourhood Forum to give notice to an LPA that it no longer wishes to be designated as the Neighbourhood

---

11 Hansard Debate, 19 July 2011, col 1215.
12 Neighbourhood Planning (General) Regulations 2012 (SI 2012/637), reg 8.
13 Neighbourhood Planning (General) Regulations 2012 (SI 2012/637), reg 9.
14 Neighbourhood Planning (General) Regulations 2012 (SI 2012/637), reg 11.
15 Neighbourhood Planning (General) Regulations 2012 (SI 2012/637), reg 10.
16 Town and Country Planning Act 1990, s 61F(9), inserted by Localism Act 2011, Sch 9.

*Neighbourhood planning*

Forum for a neighbourhood area in which case the LPA has to withdraw the designation.[17]

Baroness Hanham asserted in the House of Lords debates on the proposed neighbourhood planning provisions in the Bill that Neighbourhood Forums would not be not public bodies and that their purpose would be to form themselves in order to make a neighbourhood plan and subsequently, when they had done that, to disband, so they would have a 'shortish' life.[18] However, in our view it is highly likely that Neighbourhood Forums will be considered to be public bodies – at least for the purposes of judicial review. It is well-established that all bodies exercising functions of a public law nature are susceptible to a challenge by way of judicial review. Guidance was set out by the Court of Appeal in *R v Panel for Takeovers and Mergers, ex parte Datafin*[19] to the effect that even a privately established panel was susceptible to judicial review because it in fact operated as an integral part of a governmental framework (in this case for regulating takeovers and mergers), and those affected had to submit to its jurisdiction. Neighbourhood Forums will be taking on functions of a public nature and will be established pursuant to statutory provisions; these are characteristics of a public body. It would also be odd if – unlike their neighbourhood planning counterparts, parish councils – they were to remain unaccountable to the courts for the exercise of any neighbourhood planning administrative function (such as approval of details under a Neighbourhood Development Order). Where, in practice, Neighbourhood Forums will be less exposed is in relation to the administrative decisions in the neighbourhood planning process that are most likely to be subject to challenge; this is because those decisions (the making of plans and orders) reside still with LPAs.

## Neighbourhood Development Orders

Schedule 9, Pt 1 and Sch 10 of the Act insert new ss 61E to 61Q and Sch 4B into the Town and Country Planning Act 1990 to make provision for Neighbourhood Development Orders ('NDOs'), one of the new planning tools introduced by the Act. As set out in new s 61E(2), an NDO grants planning permission in relation to a particular neighbourhood area, for development specified in the NDO or for a class of development specified in the NDO. New s 61J adds that an NDO may make provisions in relation to:

- all land in the neighbourhood area specified in the order;
- any part of that land; or
- a specific site in that neighbourhood area.

An NDO:

- may not grant planning permission for any development which already has planning permission; and
- may not relate to more than one neighbourhood area.

---

17 Neighbourhood Planning (General) Regulations 2012 (SI 2012/637), reg 12(1). Regulation 12(2) goes on to require that an LPA publicises the withdrawal of a designation under reg 12(1) or the Town and Country Planning Act 1990, s 61F(9).
18 Hansard Debate, 17 October 2011, cols 56–57.
19 [1987] 1 QB 815.

## Building blocks of neighbourhood planning

Planning permission granted by an NDO can be conditional as set out in the order, or unconditional. The Town and Country Planning Act 1990, new s 61K provides that NDOs cannot grant planning permission in relation to:

- minerals;
- aggregates;
- waste matters;
- Sch 1 environmental impact assessment projects;[20]
- Nationally Significant Infrastructure Projects;[21] or
- other classes of development which the Government can prescribe.

As Baroness Hanham stated when supporting proposed amendments to the neighbourhood planning provisions of the Act in the House of Lords:

> 'our position is that we have excluded development types and classes which, due to their scale and complexity, are inappropriate to be given planning permission through a neighbourhood development order. These include nationally significant infrastructure projects and county minerals and waste applications, which are far too big for a neighbourhood to consider.'[22]

It is perhaps odd then that 'Schedule 2 development'[23] is not also excluded from the scope of NDOs – since it still includes development projects which can have significant environmental impacts and can be just as large or significant as Sch 1 projects. It also means that potentially very large scale urban development projects could in the future be permitted through neighbourhood development orders – unless expressly excluded by the Government in regulations.

Pursuant to new s 61E(1), any qualifying body[24] is entitled to initiate a process for the purpose of requiring a local planning authority in England to make an NDO. The Town and Country Planning Act 1990, new Sch 4B, para 1 sets out the requirements of a proposal for an NDO. The qualifying body must submit to the LPA a draft of the NDO and a statement which contains a summary of the proposals and sets out why the NDO should be made in the proposed terms. The Secretary of State may also prescribe the form of any such proposals in regulations which may also require other documents and information to accompany proposals for an NDO. Paragraph 3 requires LPAs to provide advice and assistance to qualifying bodies in developing proposals for NDOs. This does not include a duty to provide financial assistance.

Schedule 4B, paras 4 to 6 set out further requirements for proposals for NDOs. Paragraph 4 gives further power to the Secretary of State to make regulations as to requirements that must be complied with before proposals for an NDO may

---

20 This refers to development projects set out in the Town and Country Planning (Environmental Impact Assessment) Regulations 2011 (SI 2011/1824), Sch 1 which implements Council Directive 85/337/EEC on the Assessment of Certain Public and Private Projects on the Environment – now consolidated into Directive 2011/92/EU (the 'EIA Directive'). Schedule 1 sets out a series of large development projects, in relation to which environmental impact assessment must always be carried out prior to approval being granted. Such development projects include large crude oil refineries, large industrial or agricultural plants, waste water treatment plants and other large industrial installations.
21 As defined in the Planning Act 2008, s 14 as including airport-related development, the construction of harbour facilities and highway-related development.
22 Hansard Debate, 19 July 2011, col 1215.
23 Ie development in the Town and Country Planning (Environmental Impact Assessment) Regulations 2011 (SI 2011/1824), Sch 2 for which consideration must be given whether or not to require environmental impact assessment in any given case.
24 It will be remembered that a 'qualifying body' is a parish council or a Neighbourhood Forum.

## Neighbourhood planning

be submitted to a local planning authority or fall to be considered by a local planning authority.

The Neighbourhood Planning Regulations,[25] reg 21 requires that a qualifying body, prior to submitting a proposal for an NDO or Community Right to Build Order ('CRBO') to the LPA, must publicise in a manner that is likely to bring it to the attention of people who live, work or carry on business in the relevant neighbourhood area:

- details of the proposals;
- details of where and when the proposals may be inspected;
- details of how to make representations; and
- the deadline for the receipt of those representations (which should not be less than six weeks after the date of first publication of the proposal).

The qualifying body must also consult a number of bodies set out in Sch 1 to the Regulations, which include:

- any parish council or Neighbourhood Forum who may be affected by the proposals;
- any relevant consultation body, including English Heritage, the Civil Aviation Authority and the Secretary of State for Defence;
- any person, who 21 days before the proposal for the order is submitted, the qualifying body considered to be an owner or a tenant of the relevant land; and
- the LPA.

As soon as possible after receiving the order proposal, the LPA must publicise it, and if relevant the environmental statement submitted in accordance with the Environmental Impact Regulations.[26]

The Town and Country Planning Act 1990, new Sch 4B, para 4 also requires that the power to make such regulations should be exercised to secure that prescribed requirements as to consultation with and participation by the public must be complied with before a proposal for an NDO may be submitted to a local planning authority, and that a consultation statement (containing the details of those consulted, a summary of the main issues raised and any other prescribed information in relation to that consultation and participation) must accompany the proposal submitted to the LPA. The Neighbourhood Planning Regulations, reg 22 contains a list of information that must accompany the submission of a proposal for an NDO or CRBO – this includes the consultation statement, a statement explaining how the proposal meets the basic conditions for a NDO or CRBO and (among other things) a plan or statement identifying the land to which the proposal relates. Regulation 23 contains requirements for the LPA to publicise the proposal for an NDO or CRBO – with the duty being to 'publicise in such a manner as it considers is likely to bring the application to the attention of people who live, work or carry on business in the area to which the application relates'.

Pursuant to Sch 4B, para 5, an LPA may decline to consider a repeat proposal. A proposal for an NDO is to be considered a repeat proposal where, in the last two years, the LPA has refused the same or a similar proposal or that proposal

---

25 The Neighbourhood Planning (General) Regulations 2012 (SI 2012/637).
26 Town and Country Planning (Environmental Impact Assessment) Regulations 2011 (SI 2011/1824).

## Building blocks of neighbourhood planning

did not get sufficient votes in the referendum, and the LPA considers that there has been no significant change in relevant considerations since the refusal of the proposal or the holding of the referendum.

Schedule 4B, para 6 sets out the matters which the LPA must consider prior to the proposal for an NDO to be referred to independent examination. The LPA must be satisfied that the procedural requirements set out under the Act have been met. These requirements include, for example, that the authority must be authorised to act in respect of the neighbourhood area (ie if part of the area included in the proposal is under the control of another authority, consent from the other authority must be received) and that the proposal and all of the accompanying documents meet with all the requirements set out above. If the LPA is not satisfied that these requirements have been met then it must refuse the application and set out the reasons for this refusal to the qualifying body.

Schedule 4B, paras 7 to 11 prescribe the process that must be followed for the independent examination of the proposal for an NDO. Under para 7, once satisfied with compliance with paras 6(2) and (3), the LPA must submit the draft NDO for independent examination. An LPA may appoint an independent examiner only with the agreement of the qualifying body. The Secretary of State has the final say as to who the examiner should be when no agreement can be reached between the LPA and the qualifying body. An examiner must be independent of the qualifying body and the LPA, must not have an interest in any land that may be affected by the draft NDO, and must have appropriate qualifications and experience.

The matters which the examiner must consider in his examination of the draft NDO are set out in Sch 4B, para 8 and include whether the NDO is appropriate having regard to national policy, whether it is appropriate to make the order having special regard to the desirability of preserving any listed building or any features of special architectural or historic interests and to the desirability of preserving or enhancing the character or appearance of any conservation area, whether it contributes to the achievement of sustainable development, whether it is in general conformity with the strategic policies of the local development plan and whether the making of the order would be compatible with EU law.

Generally, the examination will take the form of written representations, although pursuant to para 9 the examiner may call a public hearing and receive oral representations about a particular issue at the hearing where he considers it necessary to ensure adequate examination of the issue or to give a person a fair chance to put a case (or in such other cases as may be prescribed). Schedule 4B, para 10 requires the examiner to make a reasoned report on the draft order containing recommendations either that (i) the draft order be submitted to a referendum; that (ii) modifications specified in the report be made to the draft order and that the modified order be submitted to a referendum; or that (iii) the proposal for the order be refused. The modifications that the examiner may recommend may relate only to:

- modifications that the examiner considers need to be made to secure that the draft order meets the basic conditions mentioned in para 8(2);
- modifications that the examiner considers need to be made to secure that the draft order is compatible with the Convention Rights;[27]

---

27 Ie the rights in the European Convention on Human Rights.

## Neighbourhood planning

- modifications that the examiner considers need to be made to secure that the draft order complies with the provision made by or under ss 61E(2), 61J and 61L (which regulate what might be included in an NDO);
- modifications specifying a period under s 61L(2)(b) or (5) (time limits for approvals and commencement of development); and
- modifications for the purpose of correcting errors.

The examiner's report, where it recommends that the order is submitted to referendum, must also recommend whether the area for the referendum should extend beyond the neighbourhood area to which the order relates (and if so, what that area should be). Following independent examination, the LPA must, if satisfied that the draft order meets the basic conditions of para 8(2), is compatible with Convention Rights and complies with the provisions made by or under ss 61E(2), 61J and 61L (or would be if modifications were made to the draft order), hold a referendum in accordance with para 14 and (where the neighbourhood area is designated as a business area under section 61H) an additional referendum in accordance with para 15. Paragraphs 14 and 15 set out the detailed requirements of who is entitled to vote in the referendums and who is responsible for holding the referendum.

Under para 14, an individual is eligible to vote in a referendum if, at the date of the referendum, they are entitled to vote in the election of a local councillor or the council in that area and if their election address is in that area. Registered non-domestic rate payers are entitled to vote in a neighbourhood area designated as a business area (although regulations may be implemented which would allow other persons to vote in such a referendum).

Under new ss 61E(4) and (5), an LPA to which a proposal for the making of an NDO has been made must make the NDO if more than half of those who vote in each referendum that is held vote in favour of the order (unless it considers that it would breach EU law or the European Convention on Human Rights). If two referendums take place (because the NDO related to a neighbourhood area designated as a business area) but in only one of the referendums more than half vote in favour of the order, the LPA may (but need not) make the NDO.

In relation to the examination and referendum processes, Baroness Hanham stated that:

> 'residents will always be able to have a say in the development of proposals at independent examination and in the referendum at the end of the process. It will be very much in the interest of the neighbourhood forums to see that they have consulted with the people who live in their area and they have given them an opportunity to comment and be part of what is being proposed. Otherwise, if they put it to a referendum they are not going to win it, which would probably not be quite what they had in mind. Where proposals will affect people living on the periphery of a neighbourhood area, it will be possible for the local authority to extend the referendum area to include those people in the vote.'[28]

Despite the changes introduced to allow businesses to take part in neighbourhood planning, the system still seems skewed in favour of local residents over businesses. The discretion given to LPAs in business areas to decide whether to make the NDO where two referendums take place and only one results in a vote

---

28  Hansard Debate, 19 July 2011, col 1217.

in favour of the NDO, means that an NDO could be frustrated if local residents vote against it – even where the area is predominantly business in nature and the majority of the business voters vote in favour of it. In addition, it is noteworthy that there is no provision for investors or landowners to have a vote unless they are also a business ratepayer.

New ss 61M and 61N provide for the Secretary of State (and an LPA, with the consent of the Secretary of State), to revoke an NDO. An LPA may also at any time, with the consent of the qualifying body that initiated the NDO, modify an NDO for the purpose of correcting errors. Judicial review may also be brought within six weeks of the day on which the decision to make the NDO is published.

## Community Right to Build Orders

Schedule 11 of the Act inserts a new Sch 4C into the Town and Country Planning Act 1990 to make provision for the making of Community Right to Build Orders ('CRBOs'), a particular type of NDO providing for community-led, site-specific development. New Schedule 4C, para 1 specifies that that the provisions of the Town and Country Planning Act relating to NDOs also have effect in relation to CRBOs subject to the provisions of the new Sch 4C. It further clarifies that CRBOs are a specific type of NDO, distinguished by the fact that (i) they must be made pursuant to a proposal by a community organisation; (ii) they will grant planning permission for specified development in relation to a specified site in the specified neighbourhood area; and (iii) the specified development does not exceed prescribed limits.[29] The prescribed limits may be by reference to the area in which the development is to take place, the number or type of operations or uses of land constituting the development, or any other factor.

A 'community organisation' for the purposes of CRBOs is defined in new Sch 4C, para 3 as a body corporate established for the express purpose of furthering the social, economic and environmental well-being of individuals living, or wanting to live, in a particular area, and which meets such other conditions in relation to its establishment or constitution as may be prescribed.

Paragraph 4 provides that a community organisation is authorised for the purposes of a CRBO to act in relation to a neighbourhood area (whether or not any part of the neighbourhood area falls within the area of a parish council) if the area for which the community organisation is established consists of or includes the neighbourhood area and, at the time the proposal for the CRBO is made, more than half the members of the organisation live in the neighbourhood area.

There are limited grounds on which an LPA can decline to consider a proposal for a CRBO or NDO – para 4(5) sets out that this may occur where:

- another proposal has been made for a CRBO or other NDO;
- the other proposal is outstanding; and
- the authority considers that the development and site to which the proposals relate are the same or substantially the same.

---

29  Localism Act 2011, Sch 11, para 2.

*Neighbourhood planning*

Paragraph 5(6) specifies that where the LPA declines to consider the proposal, it must notify the person making the proposal of that fact and of their reasons for declining to consider it. Paragraph 5(7) requires a proposal for a CRBO to state that it is a proposal for such an order.

Further grounds of refusal are set out in the Town and Country Planning Act 1990, new Sch 4C, para 6 – an LPA must decline to consider a proposal for a CRBO if it considers that:

- the specified development falls within Annex 2 to the EIA Directive[30] and is likely to have significant effects on the environment by virtue of factors such as its nature, size or location and taking into account any relevant criteria mentioned in Annex 3 of the EIA Directive; or
- the specified development is likely to have significant effects on a qualifying European site (whether alone or in combination with other plans or projects) and is not directly connected with or necessary to the management of that site.

The CRBO provisions have been amended substantially since the concept was initially promoted. The Government initially proposed that in order for a Right to Build scheme to be passed, a 90 per cent majority would be needed at the referendum stage. On 22 September 2010, Grant Shapps announced that this threshold would be lowered to 75 per cent. However in the Act only a simple majority is required. This lower threshold is designed to encourage more, and quicker, development. However it perhaps does not sit entirely comfortably with Grant Shapps's September 2010 statement that development would only be allowed under these provisions if there is the 'support of the overwhelming majority of the wider community'.

The Government has stated that the CRBO powers are to be used in both urban and rural areas throughout England and envisages that the powers will be exercised to enable developments such as 'additional housing to meet the demand of future generations, new shops where communities want to offer low rent deals to local convenience stores or farm shops, or a new community hall or sports facilities'. Local communities will be able to decide how they wish to take their developments forward and what types of organisations they wish to partner with to enable the development to take place (such as property developers and housing associations).

As with other forms of NDO, there is a requirement for independent examination and a referendum.

The LPA must comply with the recommendations in the examiners' report and is only authorised to make changes to the order to rectify minor errors and ensure compliance with EU obligations and the Human Rights Act.

## Neighbourhood Development Plans

Schedule 9, Pt 2 of the Act contains provisions in relation to Neighbourhood Development Plans ('NDPs') and inserts new ss 38A to 38C into the Planning and Compulsory Purchase Act 2004. NDPs, once formally made, will form part

---

30  Directive 85/337/EEC on the Assessment of the Effects of Certain Public and Private Projects on the Environment, now consolidated into Directive 2011/92/EU. See also the Town and Country Planning (Environmental Impact Assessment) Regulations 2011 (SI 2011/1824), Sch 2.

of the local development plan for the purposes of the Planning and Compulsory Purchase Act 2004, s 38. As such, when deciding planning applications, LPAs will have to determine them in accordance with policies in NDPs (as well as their own development plan documents) unless material considerations indicate otherwise. The National Planning Policy Framework also provides that, once made, the policies contained in an NDP take precedence over existing non-strategic policies in the local plan for that neighbourhood where they are in conflict.[31]

The Planning and Compulsory Purchase Act 2004,[32] new s 38B contains further requirements in relation to the provisions that may be made by NDPs. Importantly, an NDP may only relate to one neighbourhood area, and a neighbourhood area may only have one NDP. Accordingly, provided that the policies of an NDP are in general conformity with the strategic policies in the development plan for the area and meet other basic conditions, it is again a case of first come first served – so the most organised parish council or neighbourhood forum will ensure that their vision of their neighbourhood is approved.

Where the policy set out in a development plan conflicts with any other part of the plan, the policy will take precedence, and like NDOs, NDPs cannot cover minerals, aggregates or waste matters, Sch 1 environmental impact assessment projects or Nationally Significant Infrastructure Projects. Again, Sch 2 environmental impact assessment projects are not excluded – as we commented earlier on in this section in relation to NDOs, this means that NDPs could still make provision for very significant development projects.

The Act also makes provision for further regulations by which the Government can prescribe other matters which should or should not be included within the scope of NDPs.

The Planning and Compulsory Purchase Act 2004, new s 38A(1)[33] specifies that 'any qualifying body is entitled to initiate a process for the purpose of requiring a local planning authority in England to make a neighbourhood development plan'. Sub-section (2) clarifies that a 'neighbourhood development plan' is a plan which sets out policies (however expressed) in relation to the development and use of land in the whole or any part of a particular neighbourhood area specified in the plan. Baroness Hanham, supporting an amendment made in the House of Lords to this subsection to clarify that NDP policies can apply to all or part of a neighbourhood area, stated that:

> 'there are no unnecessary, top-down restrictions: neighbourhood development plans can be as simple or as ambitious as the community wants to make them. They can include policies covering the whole area, or could have just one or two policies focused on a specific site, such as a high street or valued green space.'[34]

Section 38A(3) applies the procedure to NDOs to the making of NDPs. Sub-sections (4) and (5) specify that an LPA will be required to make an NDP after

---

31 DCLG (March 2012) *NPPF*, para 185 (available at http://www.communities.gov.uk/documents/planningandbuilding/pdf/2116950.pdf [accessed April 2012]). See further Chapter 14.
32 Inserted by the Localism Act 2011, Sch 9, Pt 2.
33 Also inserted by the Localism Act 2011, Sch 9, Pt 2.
34 Hansard Debate, 17 October 2011, col 58.

*Neighbourhood planning*

a referendum is held and more than half of those voting have voted in favour, unless policies in the NDP would be incompatible with any EU obligation or the European Convention on Human Rights. As with NDOs, where the LPA is satisfied that the draft plan meets the basic conditions of the Town and Country Planning Act 1990, new Sch 4B, para 8(2), is compatible with Convention rights and complies with the provisions made under new ss 61E(2), 61J and 61L of the 1990 Act, the LPA must hold a referendum in accordance with Sch 4B, para 14 and, where the area is designated as a business area, an additional referendum under para 15. Where two referendums were held (because the NDP relates to a neighbourhood area designated as a business area under the Town and Country Planning Act 1990, new s 61H), and in one of those referendums (but not the other) more than half of those voting have voted in favour of the NDP, the LPA may (but need not) make the NDP.

This requirement to hold at least one referendum if the LPA is satisfied that the proposed NDP meets all the relevant criteria does appear to be in contrast to what Parliament may have intended. In a debate in the House of Lords on 17 October 2011, Baroness Hanham stated that:

> 'Where there is agreement on the neighbourhood plan between the neighbourhood forum and the local council under the local development plan, a referendum does not have to take place. As long as they are all in agreement and are all working to the same end, the local authority can accept that the neighbourhood plan conforms with the local development plan and therefore does not require a referendum. Referendums need to be held where the local neighbourhood forum is putting forward a new plan which may or may not conform to a local development order or the national planning framework.'[35]

It may be that the Government has in mind that the LPA can simply progress the document as its own area action plan in these circumstances.

As with NDOs, NDPs will also be subject to independent examination and, following adoption, can be challenged by way of judicial review, with a six weeks' deadline. The examiner will have to consider whether the NDP is appropriate, having regard to national policy, whether it contributes to the achievement of sustainable development, whether it is in general conformity with the strategic policies in the local development plan, and whether the NDP is in conformity with EU obligations. Although clearly it is important that the NDPs do not conflict with other planning policies already in place, there are foreseeable difficulties in ensuring that NDP policies are in 'general conformity with strategic policies in the local development plan'. First, often there will not be a 'black and white' answer on conformity. Secondly, where an LPA's development plan policies are relatively broad and non-site specific, this requirement could be a relatively simple hurdle to overcome but may nonetheless give rise to policies in the NDP which do not sit well with certain aspects of the local plan. Thirdly, where an LPA's development plan policies set site-specific land-use objectives or housing targets, it is difficult to see how the Government's aims of allowing local people to shape their neighbourhoods can be fulfilled unless they simply adhere to the development plan.

---

35 Explanatory memorandum to the London Legacy Development Corporation (Establishment) Order 2012 (SI 2012/310) (available at http://www.lawtel.com/MyLawtel/Documents/AI0120310 [accessed February 2012]).

## Charges and funding

Section 117 of the Act permits the Secretary of State, with the consent of the Treasury, to make regulations so that LPAs can impose charges to meet the expenses they have incurred or expect to be incurring in connection with the exercise of their neighbourhood planning functions. Their neighbourhood planning functions for this purpose are held by s 117(2) to include the exercise of any of their functions under any provision made by or under:

- any of the Town and Country Planning Act 1990, new ss 61E to 61Q or new Schs 4B or 4C (neighbourhood development orders and community right to build orders);
- any of the Planning and Compulsory Purchase Act 2004, new ss 38A to 38C (neighbourhood development plans); or
- s 117 itself.

Section 117(3) further sets out that the regulations to be made by the Secretary of State must secure that:

- the charges are payable in relation to development for which planning permission is granted by a neighbourhood development order made under the Town and Country Planning Act 1990, s 61E;
- the charges become payable when the development is commenced (determined in accordance with the regulations); and
- the charges are payable to local planning authorities.

Section 117(4) provides that the regulations to be made may authorise that the charges to be imposed may be decided by LPAs for their area. Where this is the case, the LPA may not charge for its neighbourhood planning functions until it has published a charging schedule setting out the amounts it will charge for development in its area. Where the regulations authorise charges to be imposed by LPAs, the regulations must also make provision for the approval and publication of a charging document, and must set out matters to which the LPA must have regard in setting the charges, and what expenditure must be disregarded when setting the charges. The regulations must also authorise LPAs to set different charges for different cases, circumstances or areas; and authorise the LPA to make exceptions.

Section 117(5) requires the regulations to make provision about liability to pay a charge. Sub-section (6) sets out that the regulations may include provisions in respect of liability including issues in respect of partial liability, joint liability, the liability of owners and developers (among others) and the apportionment and transfer of liability.

Sub-section (7) defines, for the purpose of s 117(6)(e), an owner and a developer of land. An 'owner' of land is to be taken to be a person who owns an interest in land, and a 'developer' as a person who is wholly or partly responsible for carrying out development. Sub-section (8) provides further detail on what the regulations should contain in relation to appeals relating to the apportionment of liability, including the procedure and time limits for appeals and any costs awards in respect of those appeals.

Section 118 contains further detail on what the regulations to be made pursuant to s 117 must contain in relation to the collection of charges, for example in respect of payment by instalments, repayments in the case of overpayment and

*Neighbourhood planning*

the enforcement of the charges imposed by regulation including provisions for the imposition of interest, penalties and surcharges.

Section 119 sets out supplementary provisions in relation to the procedures that may be followed in connection with charges imposed under the regulations. In particular these provisions must include details of procedures to be followed by the LPA if they are to start imposing charges, including provisions for consultation.

The Act also permits the Secretary of State to do anything he considers appropriate for the purpose of publicising or promoting the making of neighbourhood development orders and plans; and for the purpose of giving advice and assistance to anyone in relation to the making of proposals for neighbourhood development orders and plans. This may include the provision of financial assistance (or the making of arrangements for its provision) to any body or other persons; and the making of agreements or other arrangements with any body or other person (under which payments may be made to the person).

## Chapter 7

# Consultation before applying for planning permission

The Localism Act introduces an amendment to the Town and Country Planning Act 1990 which requires developers to consult with local communities affected by proposed development and to take consultation responses into account before making planning applications. The duty of pre-application consultation for larger developments was first promoted in *Open Source Planning* but as a concept it is not new, given its introduction in the development consent system for Nationally Significant Infrastructure Projects under the Planning Act 2008.

The Act requires that the prospective applicant publicises the proposed application in such manner as he reasonably considers is likely to bring the proposed application to the attention of a majority of the persons who live at, or otherwise occupy, premises in the vicinity of the land. Specific persons must also be consulted. The consultation responses must be taken into account when deciding whether to make the application in the same form as that consulted upon.

The prospective applicant must also set out how he may be contacted by persons wishing to comment 'or collaborate with the applicant on the design of the proposed development', and give such information about the proposed timetable for the consultation as is sufficient to ensure that persons wishing to comment on the proposed development may do so in good time.

A subsequent development order will set out the types of application to which the pre-application consultation duty will apply. The Government has indicated that the pre-application consultation requirement is likely to apply to large scale developments, being residential developments with the potential to provide 200 or more new residential units, or (where the number of residential units to be constructed is not specified) with a site area of four hectares or more; and other developments which would provide 10,000 square metres of new floor space or with a site area of two hectares or more.[1]

The development order will also require any application to which the pre-application consultation duty applies to be accompanied by a pre-application consultation report. This must contain details of how the duty has been complied with, details of the responses received to the consultation, and how the responses received have been taken into account.

In the January 2011 impact assessment published in relation to the compulsory pre-application consultation duty to be introduced by the Bill, the Government expressed the hope that the new duty will (i) increase community engagement in the planning system and allow communities the opportunity to shape their

---

1 DCLG (2011) *Pre-application Consultation with Communities* (available at http://www.communities.gov.uk/planningandbuilding/planningsystem/preapplicationconsultation/ [accessed March 2012]).

*Consultation before applying for planning permission*

neighbourhoods; (ii) reduce the costs of the planning process and speed up the system; and (iii) increase the number of high quality, major applications agreed.

Although this new duty may be seen, particularly by developers, to be an additional burden, in practice pre-application consultation is already undertaken for most major developments in England. However, pre-application consultation is, in most instances, currently carried out as a matter of good practice or at most in fulfilment of a policy commitment or planning application validation requirement, as distinct from a statutory duty. We go on to consider this further in Chapter 16 but we do think this duty will introduce fertile ground for hardened objectors who will use it to challenge planning permissions in the courts, particularly early on when compliance with the duty will not have been tested.

Key issues are likely to be the scope of consultation and its timing, the adequacy of publicity arrangements, and the adequacy of the response to the consultation by the developer. It will be interesting to see whether the 'Sedley' criteria for consultation (named after the submission of Stephen Sedley QC in *R v Brent London Borough Council, ex parte Gunning*[2]) are taken into account by the courts when deciding whether the new duty to consult under the Act has been satisfied. These require that:

- consultation is undertaken while proposals are still at a formative stage;
- adequate information is provided to enable consultees to properly respond;
- adequate time is allowed for consultees to properly respond; and
- conscientious consideration is given to the responses to the consultation.

The Government's Code of Practice on Consultation,[3] which commits a number of public sector organisations and governmental departments who have signed up to it to a set of standards when they undertake formal consultation exercises, may also provide useful guidance. This contains seven principles of consultation that those bodies should adhere to:

- Formal consultation should take place at a stage when there is scope to influence the policy outcome.
- Consultations should normally last for at least 12 weeks with consideration given to longer timescales where feasible and sensible.
- Consultation documents should be clear about the consultation process, what is being proposed, the scope to influence and the expected costs and benefits of the proposals.
- Consultation exercises should be designed to be accessible to, and clearly targeted at, those people the exercise is intended to reach.
- Keeping the burden of consultation to a minimum is essential if consultations are to be effective and if consultees' buy-in to the process is to be obtained.
- Consultation responses should be analysed carefully and clear feedback should be provided to participants following the consultation.
- Officials running consultations should seek guidance in how to run an effective consultation exercise and share what they have learned from the experience.

2   [1985] 84 LGR 168.
3   HM Government (July 2008) *Code of Practice on Consultation* (available at http://www.bis.gov.uk/policies/bre/consultation-guidance [accessed March 2012]).

# Chapter 8

# Enforcement against breaches of planning control

Part 6, Ch 5 of the Localism Act toughens the planning enforcement regime in a number of respects.

## RESTRICTION ON RETROSPECTIVE APPLICATIONS

The first new enforcement power, set out in s 123 of the Act, enables LPAs to decline to determine an application for planning permission if an enforcement notice has already been served in relation to that development or part of that development.

Similarly, an appeal against an enforcement notice may not be brought on the ground that, if there was a breach of planning control, planning permission should be granted for the unauthorised works or use where a planning application for the works or use has already been made but is still within its statutory determination period.

Bob Neill, Parliamentary Under Secretary of State for Communities and Local Government, stated in the House of Commons that this provision is:

> 'not intended to restrict the rights of those who are genuinely seeking retrospective permission. We accept that applications for retrospective planning permission are a legitimate part of the planning system. Sometimes, they are necessary, because we are all aware of a person who in good faith genuinely made an error and carried out a development without realising that permission was needed ... the objective in the clause is to tighten up the rules where an abuse takes place.'[1]

## DELIBERATELY CONCEALED BREACHES

The Act permits an LPA to set aside the time limit within which it would usually have to enforce against breaches of planning control in a situation where there has been deliberate concealment of a planning control breach. Normally, an LPA has only four years to take enforcement action from the date of substantial completion of operational development carried out without authorisation (and change of use to use as a single dwelling house), and ten years to act from the date of breach by unauthorised change of use of any building or breach of condition. After these dates, the unauthorised development or change of use is immune from enforcement.

Deliberate concealment of breaches of planning control has been a sensitive issue for LPAs, illustrated by two recent, well-publicised, cases.

---

1   Hansard, 1 March 2011, col 725.

*Enforcement against breaches of planning control*

The first case concerned a Mr Beesley,[2] who constructed a building on green belt land which from the outside appeared to be a hay barn pursuant to a planning permission that he had obtained, but which comprised a three bedroom dwelling house. Mr Beesley and his family lived in the building continually for four years from 2002 to 2006. In 2006, Mr Beesley applied for a certificate of lawfulness of use of the building as a dwelling house on the basis that more than four years had passed since use of the building had changed from use as a barn to a dwelling house. The LPA refused to grant the certificate, a decision which was eventually appealed to the Supreme Court. The Supreme Court found that there had been no change of use because the building was not initially constructed as a barn, but as a dwelling house. The Supreme Court also commented that even if there were a change in use, Mr Beesley's dishonest conduct meant that he could not rely on the statutory enforcement limit. This was because statutes were to be construed to the effect that no one should be allowed to profit from his own wrongdoing.

The second case concerned the construction by a Mr Fidler[3] of a dwelling house without planning permission. For four years, Mr Fidler hid the building from the LPA behind walls of straw bales and tarpaulin. Once the four year period had expired in 2006, Mr Fidler removed the wall of straw to reveal the large dwelling house, only to be served with an enforcement notice requiring the house to be demolished, which was subsequently appealed to the Court of Appeal. The Court of Appeal found that the time period for enforcement action had not actually expired because it ran from the time of 'substantial completion' which it found to have occurred when the straw bales and tarpaulin were removed in 2006. As such, the statutory period for enforcement had not expired.

Section 124 of the Act amends the Town and Country Planning Act 1990 so as to allow LPAs to apply to the Magistrates' Court for a Planning Enforcement Order ('PEO') in circumstances where there may have been a breach of planning control. If a PEO is made, the LPA is given one year and 22 days to take enforcement action, regardless of whether the normal four or ten years' enforcement deadline has passed. A PEO will only be granted where the magistrates' court is satisfied on the balance of probabilities that the apparent breach of planning control of any of the matters constituting the apparent breach has (to any extent) been deliberately concealed by any person or persons.

The court must be satisfied that the apparent breach, or any of the matters constituting the apparent breach, has 'to any extent' been deliberately concealed by any person or persons. What constitutes deliberate concealment has not been defined by the Act. It is worth noting that the Bill, as originally drafted, required not deliberate concealment, but that the actions of a person had resulted in or contributed to full or partial concealment of the apparent breach. A person's actions were to be taken to include any representations made by that person and any inaction on the person's part. As the Bill progressed through the House of Lords, an amendment was tabled to ensure that the EPOs could only be made where the breach had been deliberately concealed, so that the new provisions should be aimed only at the worst cases of concealment.[4]

---

2 *Secretary of State for Communities and Local Government v Welwyn Hatfield Borough Council* [2011] UKSC 15.
3 *Fidler v Secretary of State for Communities and Local Government and Reigate & Banstead Borough Council* [2010] EWHC 143 (Admin).
4 Hansard, 19 July 2011, col 1304.

It is questionable whether these new provisions were needed at all, given the Supreme Court's ruling in the *Beesley* case, which post-dated the initial versions of the Bill.

## REMOVAL NOTICES IN RELATION TO DISPLAY STRUCTURES FOR UNAUTHORISED ADVERTISEMENTS

Section 127 creates a new s 255A to be inserted into the Town and Country Planning Act 1990 to allow LPAs to remove and dispose of any display structure in their areas which in their view is used for the unauthorised display of advertisements. First, they will have to serve a removal notice on the owner of the land on which the display structure is situated, specifying a time by which the display structure must be removed. If it has not been possible to identify the person responsible for erecting or maintaining the structure, the LPA may fix a removal notice to it. Where the notice has not been complied with, the LPA will be able to remove the display structure itself and recover its costs of removing the structure.

## ACTION NOTICES TO REMEDY PERSISTENT PROBLEMS WITH UNAUTHORISED ADVERTISEMENTS

Section 127 of the Act also inserts a new s 225C into the Town and Country Planning Act 1990 to allow an LPA which has reason to believe that there is a persistent problem with the display of unauthorised advertisements on the surface of any building, wall, fence or other structure or erection or any apparatus or plant to serve an action notice on the owner or occupier of the land on which the surface is situated. The notice must give at least 28 days for specified 'reasonable' measures to be taken to prevent or reduce the frequency of the display of unauthorised advertisements on the structure. The LPA may carry out the measures itself and recover its reasonably incurred expenses in doing so from the person who has required by the action notice to do so. There is the right to appeal against the notice on the following grounds:

- that there is no problem with the display of unauthorised advertisements on the surface concerned or any such problem is not a persistent one;
- that there has been some informality, defect or error in, or in connection with, the notice;
- that the time within which the measures specified in the notice are to be carried out is not reasonably sufficient for the purpose;
- that the notice should have been served on another person.

## POWER TO REMEDY DEFACEMENT OF PREMISES

The Town and Country Planning Act 1990, new s 225F, inserted by s 127 of the Act, gives LPAs the power to remedy the defacement of premises where they consider unauthorised advertisements to be 'detrimental to the amenity of the area or offensive' and 'readily visible from a place to which the public have access'. In these circumstances, LPAs may serve a notice requiring the occupier to remove or obliterate the sign by a time specified in the notice. If the notice is not complied with, the LPA will be able to remove or obliterate the advertisement itself (and recover its costs in so doing).

*Enforcement against breaches of planning control*

## INCREASE IN PENALTIES AND TIME LIMITS FOR CRIMINAL OFFENCES

Section 126 of the Act amends the Town and Country Planning Act 1990 to increase the maximum penalty for a breach of a condition notice from £1,000 to £2,500 in England.

The Act also introduces time limits for bringing proceedings for an offence of non-compliance with tree preservation regulations. Under these provisions, proceedings must be brought within six months of sufficient evidence of the offence coming to the prosecutor's knowledge but within three years of the offence taking place. The same timescales are also introduced for proceedings brought for contravening regulations on the control of advertisements.

# Chapter 9

# Community Infrastructure Levy

The Community Infrastructure Levy ('CIL') is a charge arising on development granted by planning permission. Local authorities in England and Wales may charge it and use it to raise money from owners and developers of land, to fund infrastructure to support the development of its area. Local authorities wishing to charge the CIL must produce a charging schedule setting out the rates at which it will charge it, in pounds per square metre.

The Government's view is that this tariff-based approach is fairer, faster and more certain and transparent than the current system for capture of developer contributions, namely planning obligations, which is lengthy and subject to negotiation. In contrast the CIL is not subject to any negotiation. Government research states that only six per cent of all planning permissions brought any contribution to infrastructure costs required as a result of development and anticipates that the CIL has the potential to raise an estimated £1 billion a year of funding by 2016.

## LEGISLATIVE BASIS

The legislative basis for the CIL is found in the Planning Act 2008 ('PA 2008'), Pt 11 as amended by ss 114 and 115 of the Localism Act[1] and the Community Infrastructure Levy Regulations 2010 (SI 2010/948), as amended by the Community Infrastructure Levy (Amendment) Regulations 2011 (SI 2011/987), (the 'CIL Regulations'). The CIL Regulations came into force in April 2010 and the amendments came into force on 6 April 2011.

Guidance made pursuant to PA 2008, s 221 was issued by DCLG in March 2010 in *Charge Setting and Charging Schedule Procedures* (the 'DCLG Guidance').

In October 2011, DCLG issued a consultation document setting out further proposals for reform of the CIL Regulations.[2] The consultation period ended on 30 December 2011 but the Government has not yet issued any further announcements.

## WHAT IS THE CIL AND WHAT CAN IT BE USED FOR?

The CIL is a charge in respect of development. PA 2008, s 206 empowers the Secretary of State to make regulations providing for the imposition of a CIL and in making the regulations is required to ensure that the overall purpose of the CIL is to ensure that costs incurred in supporting the development of an area

---

1   Localism Act 2011, s 114 came into force on 16 November 2011 and s 115 came into force on 15 January 2012.
2   DCLG (October 2011) *Community Infrastructure Levy: Detailed Proposals and Draft Regulations for Reform Consultation* (available at http://www.communities.gov.uk/publications/planningandbuilding/cilreformconsultation [accessed March 2012]).

can be funded by owners or developers of land. This must be done in a way that does not make the development economically unviable.[3]

The CIL Regulations must require that authorities that charge the CIL use it to support development by funding the provision, improvement, replacement, operation or maintenance of infrastructure.[4] The CIL Regulations may also specify maintenance and operational activities (including operational activities of a promotional kind) in connection with infrastructure that may be funded by the CIL. Infrastructure includes roads and other transport facilities, flood defences, schools and other educational facilities, medical facilities, sporting and recreational facilities and open spaces. An authority charging the CIL may use the CIL it has raised to fund infrastructure outside its area, provided it supports the development of its area. In London, the Mayor's CIL must be applied to funding roads or other transport facilities including, in particular, funding for Crossrail.[5]

Following amendments introduced by the Act, there are now also regulation-making powers aimed at requiring authorities charging the CIL to pass funds raised through the CIL to other bodies; those funds may be applied to infrastructure or any other matter that supports development by addressing the demands that it places on the areas that host it, by those other bodies. Regulations may set out details for this process including the area in which it will apply, the bodies it will apply to, the amount and timings of payments, things that may or may not be funded, monitoring, accounting and reporting responsibilities of charging authorities, and when funding is to be returned to the charging authority. Regulations may also allow that the authority applies some or all of the CIL raised in an area to the same extended matters, but only where they are not required to pass that proportion of the CIL to other bodies.

Although the legislative provisions are drafted very broadly, the intention with respect to these provisions was given some further detail in the October 2011 consultation document issued by DCLG. It included consultation on the issue of how to require charging authorities to pass on a proportion of funds received through the CIL to other bodies. In the consultation, the Government states its intention is to require authorities to allocate a 'meaningful proportion' of the CIL revenue to the local elected council for the area, where development will take place. The consultation sought views on who should receive these 'neighbourhood funds', the proportion to be passed on, timing, reporting and monitoring of payments and the relationship between neighbourhood funds and planning obligations.

The consultation also sought views on whether the CIL should be permitted to fund affordable housing either in isolation or in combination with s 106 obligations.

## WHO CAN CHARGE IT AND WHO CAN COLLECT IT?

The CIL may be charged by 'charging authorities' and a local planning authority is the charging authority for its area, subject to certain exceptions as follows: the Mayor of London is the charging authority for Greater London, *in addition*

---

3 Planning Act 2008, s 206.
4 Planning Act 2008, s 216.
5 Community Infrastructure Levy Regulations 2010 (SI 2010/948), reg 59.

## On what basis must the CIL be charged?

to local planning authorities; the Broads Authority is the charging authority for the Broads; and the Council of the Isles of Scilly is the charging authority for the Isles of Scilly.

The CIL is collected by 'collecting authorities' and charging authorities are the collecting authority for the CIL charged in their areas, subject to the following:

- In relation to the CIL charged by the Mayor of London, the London borough council in whose area the development giving rise to the CIL is located, is the collecting authority for that CIL.
- A county council is a collecting authority for the CIL charged in its area in respect of developments for which it grants planning permission.
- The Homes and Communities Agency, urban development corporations and enterprise zone authorities can agree with charging authorities that they will collect the CIL in respect of development for which they grant planning permission.

Following the coming into force of the Local Authorities (Contracting Out of Community Infrastructure Levy Functions) Order 2011 (SI 2011/2918) on 7 December 2011, charging and collecting authorities are permitted to contract out any of their functions in relation to the setting, charging, collection, enforcement and spending of the CIL. However, they may not contract out of key functions concerning preparing, implementing and withdrawing a charge for their areas. In practice this means they must still carry out any function where a meeting of the authority is required to approve something.

## ON WHAT BASIS MUST THE CIL BE CHARGED?

An authority intending to charge the CIL must issue a document called a charging schedule, which sets out rates or other criteria by reference to which the amount of the CIL chargeable for development is to be calculated.[6]

In setting its CIL rates, the charging authority must aim to strike an appropriate balance between the desirability of funding infrastructure from the CIL, taking into account other actual and expected sources of funding, and the potential effect taken as a whole of the imposition of the CIL on the economic viability of development across its area. It may also have regard to the administrative expenses in connection with it.[7] (Up to five per cent of CIL funds can be spent on costs incurred in administering the CIL.[8]) In relation to the potential effects of imposition of the CIL on economic viability, a London borough must take into account any CIL charged by the Mayor of London.[9]

The charging authority can determine the format and content of a charging schedule[10] but the rates must be set out in pounds per square metre. A charging authority can set differential rates for different zones in which development is situated or by reference to different uses.[11] However, the DCLG Guidance makes clear that differences in rates need to be justified by reference to the economic viability of development and not by reference to the costs of infrastructure. In

---

6 Planning Act 2008, s 211(1).
7 Community Infrastructure Levy Regulations 2010 (SI 2010/948), reg 14.
8 Community Infrastructure Levy Regulations 2010 (SI 2010/948), reg 61.
9 Community Infrastructure Levy Regulations 2010 (SI 2010/948), reg 14.
10 Community Infrastructure Levy Regulations 2010 (SI 2010/948), reg 12.
11 Community Infrastructure Levy Regulations 2010 (SI 2010/948), reg 13.

connection with this, it warns against setting differential rates in such a way as may give rise to notifiable state aid, an element of which is selective advantage.

The charging authority must use 'appropriate available evidence' to inform preparation of the charging schedule and the CIL Regulations may make provisions as to what constitutes appropriate evidence. As this is an amendment to PA 2008 introduced by the Act, the CIL Regulations do not as yet contain any detail on this and neither have any other regulations yet been made. However, the DCLG Guidance gives further details in relation to the necessary evidence base for charging schedules. The Government expects appropriate evidence to include an up-to-date development strategy for the area, which should normally be in a draft or adopted core strategy in England, local plan document in Wales or the London Plan in the case of the Mayor of London.

A charging authority needs to consider the infrastructure it needs, ideally drawing directly from information from the infrastructure planning underpinning its development plan, and funding available from other sources, in order to identify its infrastructure spending gap. Additional bespoke infrastructure planning can be undertaken if it is considered that the existing plan is not sufficiently current or weak, but its purpose is not to challenge the soundness of an adopted development plan.

## CHARGING SCHEDULE FORMULATION AND ADOPTION PROCEDURES

An authority intending to issue or revise a charging schedule must prepare a preliminary draft and consult certain other specified local planning authorities or local authorities, local business people in the relevant area, and (where the authority considers it appropriate) voluntary bodies or bodies representing local business people.[12] It must take account of any representations received before publishing the draft charging schedule that it intends to submit for examination in accordance with PA 2008, s 212. It must then publish the draft charging schedule in the manner set out in the CIL Regulations.[13]

The charging authority has to appoint an examiner to examine the draft charging schedule before it can approve it.[14] Any person can make representations on a draft charging schedule and they can request the right to be heard by the examiner.[15] The CIL Regulations, reg 19 sets out the various documents that must be submitted with the draft charging schedule to the examiner, which includes any representations made and a statement of any modifications the charging authority made to the draft charging schedule after it was published.

In examining the draft charging schedule, an examiner must consider whether the various factors that the charging authority must have regard to in setting its CIL rates have been complied with (as set out in PA 2008 and the CIL Regulations) and must make recommendations and give reasons for his recommendations in relation to the schedule. The recommendations that he can make are as follows:

---

12  Community Infrastructure Levy Regulations 2010 (SI 2010/948), reg 15.
13  Community Infrastructure Levy Regulations 2010 (SI 2010/948), reg 16.
14  Planning Act 2008, s 212.
15  Community Infrastructure Levy Regulations 2010 (SI 2010/948), reg 17.

## Charging schedule formulation and adoption procedures

- that the draft be rejected if he considers that the drafting requirements have not been complied with and this cannot be remedied by modifications;
- that the draft be approved with certain modifications, where the drafting requirements have not been complied with but this can be remedied by making modifications; or
- that the draft be approved.[16]

The examiner must consider any representations received in relation to the draft charging schedule and any person who makes representations must be heard by the examiner if they request to do so. (Where modifications are made to a draft charging schedule after it has been published and a person makes representations in relation to those modifications, they may request to be heard by the examiner but only in relation to those modifications.)[17] The examiner decides how a hearing is to be conducted including deciding the amount of time to be allowed for hearing representations, and he may refuse to allow representations at the hearing if he considers that they are irrelevant, frivolous, vexatious or repetitious.

There are provisions allowing two or more charging schedules to be examined as part of the same examination if charging authorities who prepared the schedules agree. Examinations of charging schedules may also be carried out jointly with an examination of a development plan document under the Planning and Compulsory Purchase Act 2004, s 20 or examination of a local development plan under the Planning and Compulsory Purchase Act 2004, s 64. In relation to Greater London, a charging schedule may be examined jointly with an examination in public of the Mayor's spatial development strategy.[18]

The examiner must submit his recommendations and reasons in writing to the charging authority and the charging authority must publish them in accordance with and in the manner set out in PA 2008, s 212(8) and the CIL Regulations, reg 23. Errors in the examiner's report may be corrected, provided those errors are 'correctable errors' which either do not alter the substance of the recommendations or reasons, or which must be corrected to make the recommendations consistent with the reasons given for the recommendations. This is permitted where the draft charging schedule has not been approved by the charging authority and the examiner may correct the error of his own volition or if requested to do so by the charging authority.[19]

A charging authority must then approve its charging schedule but can only do so where an examiner has made recommendations and the charging authority has had regard to those recommendations and the reasons for them. As such, it cannot approve a charging schedule if the examiner has recommended rejection, but may approve a charging schedule if it incorporates modifications if and as required by the examiner. (Where a charging schedule is approved by a charging authority and it has made modifications to remedy any non-compliance with the drafting requirement identified by the examiner, it must publish a report setting out how the approved schedule remedies the non-compliance the examiner identified.)[20]

---

16 Planning Act 2008, s 212A.
17 Community Infrastructure Levy Regulations 2010 (SI 2010/948), regs 20 and 21.
18 Community Infrastructure Levy Regulations 2010 (SI 2010/948), reg 22.
19 Community Infrastructure Levy Regulations 2010 (SI 2010/948), reg 24.
20 Planning Act 2008, s 213.

A charging authority must publish the charging schedule on its website as soon as practicable after it has approved it and advertise it in the manner set out in the CIL Regulations, reg 25. A charging authority must approve a charging schedule at a meeting of the authority and by a majority of votes of members present. In the case of the Mayor of London, he must approve the charging schedule personally.

The CIL Regulations also make provision for correcting errors in an approved charging schedule. Only 'correctable errors' may be corrected and these are defined as follows:

- errors which, corrected, will have no effect on the amount of CIL chargeable in respect of any given chargeable development; or
- errors which would have the effect mentioned above but the correction is required in order to give effect to the modifications to the draft charging schedule recommended by the examiner.

The charging authority must correct the error either of its own volition or if requested to do so in writing by any person but it cannot do so after the end of six months from the date of approval of the schedule.[21]

A charging schedule approved under PA 2008, s 213 cannot come into effect before the day after it is published.[22]

## WHAT IS THE CIL CHARGED ON?

A charging authority may charge a CIL in respect of development of land in its area.[23] Development means anything done by way of or for the purpose of creating a new building or anything done to or in respect of an existing building.[24] However, this excludes any such works done to buildings into which people do not normally go or buildings into which people only go intermittently for the purpose of inspecting or maintaining plant or machinery. It also excludes a change of use of a single dwelling house to use as two or more separate dwelling houses; and any work done to an existing building involving an increase to the gross floor space for which permission is only required because of a development order.[25]

## HOW IS THE CIL CALCULATED?

The amount of CIL payable, the 'chargeable amount', must be calculated by the collecting authority in accordance with the CIL Regulations, reg 40. The following points are of note in relation to the formulae:

- The chargeable amount is the aggregate of the amounts of the CIL chargeable at each of the rates applicable at the time planning permission first permits the chargeable development in the area in which it will be built.
- Below £50 a chargeable amount is deemed to be zero.

---

21 Community Infrastructure Levy Regulations 2010 (SI 2010/948), reg 26.
22 Community Infrastructure Levy Regulations 2010 (SI 2010/948), reg 28.
23 Planning Act 2008, s 206.
24 Planning Act 2008, s 209.
25 Community Infrastructure Levy Regulations 2010 (SI 2010/948), reg 6.

- Any floor space (measured in gross internal area) of existing buildings which will form part of the completed chargeable development is deducted, as is any floor space of existing buildings which is demolished before completion of the chargeable development, from the net area calculated to be chargeable to the CIL. However, in both cases the existing buildings floor space and the demolished floor space must have been on the land and in lawful use on the date on which planning permission first permits the chargeable development. It will be considered to be in use if part of the building has been in use for a continuous period of at least six months within the period of 12 months ending on the day that planning permission first permits the chargeable development.

It is not entirely clear in the CIL Regulations as to whether the reference to being in use for at least six months of the 12 months prior to the permission that first permits the chargeable development means in actual physical occupation for the six months or in lawful use for the six months. However it seems likely to require both, and in any event it would prudent to assume so.

The CIL is subject to indexation, to the year in which the planning permission was granted.

## WHO IS LIABLE?

A person can assume liability to pay the CIL in respect of a proposed development, before development commences and in accordance with any relevant procedural provisions contained in the CIL Regulations.[26] Any person wishing to assume liability in relation to chargeable development must submit an assumption of liability notice to the collecting authority[27] on a form published by the Secretary of State and liability is deemed to have been assumed on the date on which the notice is received. The collecting authority must send an acknowledgement of receipt. Assumption of liability cannot occur after the chargeable development has commenced except by transfer of assumed liability. Assumption of liability can be withdrawn any time before commencement of the chargeable development by giving notice.

Assumed liability may be transferred by submitting a liability transfer notice to the collecting authority on a Secretary of State's form, which must be received before the date on which the final payment of CIL is due in respect of the chargeable development. Liability is assumed to be transferred on the date on which the collecting authority receives the form.[28]

Where no-one has assumed liability and the chargeable development is commenced in reliance on a planning permission, liability is apportioned between each material interest in the land.[29] A 'material interest' is defined in the CIL Regulations as a freehold estate or a leasehold estate which has more than seven years left to run on the day after which planning permission first permits a chargeable development.[30] Calculation of the apportioned CIL amount

---

26  Planning Act 2008, s 208.
27  Community Infrastructure Levy Regulations 2010 (SI 2010/948), reg 31.
28  Community Infrastructure Levy Regulations 2010 (SI 2010/948), reg 32.
29  Community Infrastructure Levy Regulations 2010 (SI 2010/948), reg 33.
30  Community Infrastructure Levy Regulations 2010 (SI 2010/948), reg 4.

for which each material interest is liable must be carried out by the collecting authority in accordance with the CIL Regulations, reg 34, and the formula is based on the value of each material interest in relation to the aggregate values of all the relevant material interests.

An 'owner' for the purposes of the CIL Regulations is a person who owns a material interest[31] and it is the owner who is liable to pay the amount of the CIL apportioned to his material interest in these circumstances. There are also provisions enabling a collecting authority to obtain information from an owner of a material interest in order to assist it in apportioning liability, through issue of an information notice.[32]

The collecting authority may also decide to transfer a liability to pay the CIL to owners of land where it cannot recover the CIL from a person who has assumed liability, despite having made all reasonable efforts to do so.[33]

Joint owners of an interest in land are each jointly and severally liable to the CIL, as are two or more persons who have assumed liability in respect of a chargeable development.

## WHEN DOES LIABILITY TO PAY ARISE?

A person who assumes liability in accordance with the CIL Regulations, reg 31, is liable on commencement of the chargeable development to pay CIL equal to the chargeable amount less any relief granted.[34]

'Chargeable development' is the development for which planning permission is granted subject to certain further provisions including the following:

- In the case of outline permissions permitting implementation in phases, each phase is a separate chargeable development.
- In the case of permissions granted under the Town and Country Planning Act 1990 ('TCPA 1990'), s 73 which amend a condition on an existing planning permission so as to extend the time within which development may be commenced, the chargeable development is the development which was permitted under the existing planning permission.[35]

A planning permission is any of the following:

- Full and outline planning permission including permissions granted under TCPA 1990, ss 73 (permission to development land without compliance with conditions previously attached) and 73A (permission for development already carried out).
- Planning permissions granted by the Secretary of State under the above provisions as applied to him by TCPA 1990, ss 76A(10), 77(4) and 79(4).
- A planning permission granted or modified on an appeal against an enforcement notice.
- A planning permission modified under TCPA 1990, s 97 or 100.

---

31  Community Infrastructure Levy Regulations 2010 (SI 2010/948), reg 4.
32  Community Infrastructure Levy Regulations 2010 (SI 2010/948), reg 35.
33  Community Infrastructure Levy Regulations 2010 (SI 2010/948), reg 36.
34  Community Infrastructure Levy Regulations 2010 (SI 2010/948), reg 31.
35  Community Infrastructure Levy Regulations 2010 (SI 2010/948), reg 9.

*Procedural issues*

- A planning permission granted by an order under TCPA 1990, s 102 or 104.
- A development consent order.
- A general consent, where this means permissions granted by development orders, local development orders, simplified planning zone schemes, development with government authorisation or enterprise zone schemes and development authorised by an Act of Parliament.[36] (General consents can therefore relate to development that benefits from permitted development rights and does not need express permission from a local planning authority.)

It does not include temporary planning permissions.

Development is commenced on the earliest date on which any material operation is carried out. 'Material operation' has the same meaning as in TCPA 1990, s 56(4).[37]

This is subject to the following exceptions:

- Development commences on the day planning permission is granted if a temporary planning permission had previously been granted for the same development.
- Permission granted under TCPA 1990, s 73A (planning permission for development already carried out) or under a grant or modification of permission on an appeal against an enforcement notice, commences on the day planning permission for that development is granted or modified as the case may be.

## PROCEDURAL ISSUES

The collecting authority must issue a 'liability notice' as soon as practicable after the date on which a planning permission first permits development.

Planning permission first permits development on the day that planning permission is granted but subject to the following:

In the case of outline planning permission, permission first permits development on the date of the final approval of the last reserved matter.

In the case of outline planning permissions which permit developments to be implemented in phases, planning permission first permits a phase of the development on the date of the final approval of the last reserved matter associated with that phase.

In the case of a full planning permission which is subject to conditions requiring further approvals to be obtained from the LPA before development can commence, planning permission is granted on the day final approval is given.

In the case of a general consent on the day on which the collecting authority receives a notice of chargeable development submitted to it in accordance with

---

36 Community Infrastructure Levy Regulations 2010 (SI 2010/948), reg 5.
37 'Material operation' means the construction works in relation to the erection of a building, demolition, digging of a trench for foundations, laying of any underground main or pipe to the foundations, any operation in the course of laying out or constructing a road or part of a road and any change in the use of any land which constitutes material development.

## Community Infrastructure Levy

reg 64 or if no notice is submitted, on the date on which the last person is served with a notice of chargeable development in accordance with reg 64A(3).[38]

Where planning permission is granted by way of a general consent, a notice of chargeable development must be submitted to the collecting authority setting out the land to which it relates, any buildings in use which are to be demolished before completion of the chargeable developments, any buildings in use which will be part of the chargeable development on completion and the development which is the subject of the notice. (A building is considered in use if part of that building has been in use for a continuous period of at least six months within a 12-month period ending on the day the notice is submitted.)[39]

Where no notice has been submitted and the collecting authority considers development has commenced (and no relevant exemption applies), it must issue a notice on each owner of the relevant land and a liability notice.[40]

The liability notice must be on a form published by the Secretary of State and must include a description of the chargeable development, the date on which it was issued and the chargeable amount. It must also state the amount of any charitable relief or relief for exceptional circumstances granted or, in the case of social housing relief, the particulars of each person benefiting from the relief and the amounts of relief each is getting.

The collecting authority must serve the liability notice on the following:

- the relevant person – in the case of a general consent this is the person who has submitted a notice of chargeable development, in the case of planning permission granted subject to the condition requiring further approval, the person who applied for that approval and in all other cases the applicant for planning permission;
- any person that has assumed liability to pay the CIL;
- each owner of the relevant land.

A liability notices ceases to have effect once all outstanding amounts due have been paid.[41] The chargeable amount payable is a local land charge but ceases to be one once all outstanding amounts have been paid.[42]

## Payment of the CIL

When planning permission is granted for a chargeable development, a 'commencement notice' must be submitted to the collecting authority by the day on which the chargeable development commences. It must be submitted on a form published by the Secretary of State and must identify the liability notice issued in respect of the chargeable development, the intended commencement date and any other particulars specified on the form.[43]

A person submitting a commencement notice must serve a copy of it on each person that is an owner of the relevant land. The collecting authority must send an acknowledgement of receipt to the person submitting it.

---

38 Community Infrastructure Levy Regulations 2010 (SI 2010/948), reg 8.
39 Community Infrastructure Levy Regulations 2010 (SI 2010/948), reg 64.
40 Community Infrastructure Levy Regulations 2010 (SI 2010/948), reg 64A.
41 Community Infrastructure Levy Regulations 2010 (SI 2010/948), reg 65.
42 Community Infrastructure Levy Regulations 2010 (SI 2010/948), reg 66.
43 Community Infrastructure Levy Regulations 2010 (SI 2010/948), reg 67.

## Procedural issues

If a commencement notice is not submitted or the collecting authority believes that the chargeable development was commenced earlier than the intended commencement date set out on a commencement notice it has received, it must determine the day on which a chargeable development was commenced, the 'deemed commencement date'.[44]

The collecting authority must then serve a 'demand notice' on each person liable for the CIL setting out various details including the amount payable by each person and the date on which it or instalments are due.[45] The person served with a demand notice can request that the collecting authority make a declaration that he is not required to pay the amount of CIL for which he is liable until works are commenced on the land in which he has a material interest.[46]

A charging authority that intends to allow the CIL to be payable in instalments must publish an instalment policy, setting out the number of instalments payments, the amount payable in any instalment, when instalments are due and any minimum amount of the CIL below which the CIL may not be paid in instalments.[47] Where no instalment policies apply, the CIL is payable in full 60 days after the intended commencement date of the chargeable development. Where an amount payable is not paid by its due date and is outstanding, the CIL balance will fall due immediately.[48]

Other circumstances in which the amount of the CIL is payable in full are as follows:

- It is payable in full on the intended commencement date if nobody has assumed liability, and the collecting authority has received a commencement notice but has not determined a deemed commencement date for the chargeable development.
- It is payable in full on the deemed commencement date where the collecting authority determines a deemed commencement date.
- Any amount outstanding is due in full immediately where the collecting authority transfers liability to the owners.[49]

## Payments in kind

A charging authority can accept 'land payments' to satisfy any CIL liability. A land payment is an acquisition of land from a person liable to pay the CIL on commencement of a chargeable development. The charging authority must aim to ensure that the acquired land is used to provide or facilitate the provision of infrastructure to support development in its area.

It cannot accept a land payment unless it is acquiring the land itself, the person from whom the land is being acquired has assumed liability to pay the CIL and an agreement to make the land payment is entered into before the chargeable development is commenced. The agreement must be in writing and set out the value of the land to be acquired and may not form part of their planning obligation under TCPA 1990, s 106. The value of the land must be determined

---

44 Community Infrastructure Levy Regulations 2010 (SI 2010/948), reg 68.
45 Community Infrastructure Levy Regulations 2010 (SI 2010/948), reg 69.
46 Community Infrastructure Levy Regulations 2010 (SI 2010/948), reg 69A.
47 Community Infrastructure Levy Regulations 2010 (SI 2010/948), reg 69B.
48 Community Infrastructure Levy Regulations 2010 (SI 2010/948), reg 70.
49 Community Infrastructure Levy Regulations 2010 (SI 2010/948), reg 71.

by an independent person and is the price that it might reasonably be expected to obtain if sold on the open market on the date of valuation.

## RELATIONSHIP BETWEEN THE CIL AND PLANNING OBLIGATIONS

The CIL Regulations, regs 122 and 123 provide the legislative basis that is intended to establish the relationship between the CIL and s 106 agreements once the CIL is adopted in an area. However, similar restrictions will apply after 6 April 2014 for authorities that have not adopted the CIL.

Regulation 122 applies to decisions or determinations to grant planning permission for development and states that planning obligations or s 106 agreements can only constitute a reason for granting planning permission if an obligation meets the following tests:

- necessary to make the development acceptable in planning terms;
- directly related to the development; and
- fairly and reasonably related in scale and kind to the development.

This codifies some of the tests originally set out in Circular 5/05 on *Planning Obligations*. DCLG guidance document entitled *Community Infrastructure Levy: An Overview* (May 2011) states the intention is to clarify the purpose of planning obligations in the light of the CIL and reinforce their purpose in seeking only essential contributions rather than more general contributions which are better suited to the CIL. The effect is therefore to render it unlawful to take a planning obligation into account when determining a planning application for development of the kind that could be subject to the CIL, if the obligation does not meet these tests.

Regulation 123 states that a planning obligation cannot be taken into account when determining a planning application for development capable of being charged the CIL, to the extent that it provides for funding or provision of infrastructure projects or of the type that a charging authority has published on its website as being infrastructure it intends to fund through the CIL. In the absence of such a list any infrastructure (as defined) may be funded by the CIL.

The intention with reg 123 is to prevent charging authorities from charging for infrastructure under both the CIL and in planning obligations. A charging authority can publish on its website a list of infrastructure it intends to fund through the CIL but if it does not publish a list, then the default assumption is that the authority is intending to use the CIL to fund any infrastructure capable of being funded by it; this means that an authority cannot then seek any s 106 contribution for this infrastructure, thereby encouraging authorities to publish a list. For shrewd charging authorities these lists are likely to be quite focused and short, in order to ensure that they can continue to have recourse to s 106 agreements on as wide a range of benefits and contributions as possible.

Regulation 123 also states that a planning obligation cannot be taken into account when determining an application where it provides for funding or provision of infrastructure capable of being subject to the CIL and where five or more planning obligations have been entered into on or after 6 April 2010 that also provide for funding or provision of the same project or type of infrastructure. This provision is intended to prevent pooling of s 106

## Reliefs and exemptions

contributions towards infrastructure capable of being funded by the CIL. For other items, such as affordable housing, that are not capable of being funded by the CIL, there is no limit on the numbers of obligations that may be pooled.

# RELIEFS AND EXEMPTIONS

## Exemption for minor development

There is no liability to CIL if a gross internal area on a development comprising new buildings or enlargement of existing buildings is less than 100 square metres. However, this exemption does not apply where the development consists of dwellings.

## Exemption for charities

The owner of a material interest in the relevant land is exempt from paying the CIL if it is a charitable institution and the chargeable development will be used for charitable purposes (and will be occupied or in the control of the charitable institution).[50] In general terms, 'relevant land' is the land to which the planning permission relates. A similar exemption applies where a chargeable authority chooses to offer discretionary charitable relief to a charitable institution, where the whole or greater part of a chargeable development will be held as an investment from which the profits are applied for charitable purposes.[51] If a charging authority wishes to make discretionary charitable relief available in its area, it must first publish a document stating that the relief is available and setting out its policy for giving relief in such circumstances.[52]

These reliefs do not apply if the material interest is owned jointly with another person who is not a charitable institution or if the exemption from liability would constitute state aid. However if a charitable institution would normally be exempt on the basis that the chargeable development will be used for charitable purposes but for the fact that its exemption constitutes state aid, it can still be eligible for relief if discretionary charitable relief is available and the collecting authority is satisfied that the state aid is not notifiable.

In addition, discretionary relief may not be granted if the charitable institution intends to occupy the chargeable development and use it for trading activities, other than the sale of donated goods where the proceeds of sale are applied to the institution's charitable purposes.

In order to benefit from charitable relief, a claim must be submitted to the collecting authority in the manner specified.[53] There are also provisions for 'claw back' where charitable relief is granted and circumstances change such that the eligibility requirements are no longer met after that relief is granted, and this occurs within a period of seven years from the date on which the chargeable development is commenced. If this occurs, the relief granted is withdrawn and

---

50 Community Infrastructure Levy Regulations 2010 (SI 2010/948), reg 43.
51 Community Infrastructure Levy Regulations 2010 (SI 2010/948), reg 44.
52 Community Infrastructure Levy Regulations 2010 (SI 2010/948), reg 46.
53 Community Infrastructure Levy Regulations 2010 (SI 2010/948), reg 47.

the owner of the interest is then liable to pay CIL equal to the level of relief that has been withdrawn.[54]

## Social housing relief

Chargeable development intended as social housing is eligible for relief from the CIL. To be eligible it must comprise 'qualifying dwellings' (in whole or in part) which are ones which satisfy at least one of the following conditions:

- Condition 1 (relates to social rented accommodation) – dwellings let by a private registered provider of social housing, a registered social landlord or a local housing authority under any of the tenancies specified in reg 49.
- Condition 2 (relates to low cost home ownership dwellings) – dwellings occupied according to statutory shared ownership arrangements, where the initial share in the dwelling must not exceed 75 per cent of the total value, the rent payable must be no more than three per cent of the unsold interest and the rise in annual rent must be limited to the rate of inflation plus 0.5 per cent.

The amount of relief is calculated according to formulae set out in reg 50. In order to obtain the relief, a claim must be submitted to the collecting authority by an owner of the relevant land who has assumed liability to pay the CIL in respect of the chargeable development. It must be submitted on the appropriate form and received before commencement of the chargeable development. A relief assessment must be submitted with the claim which identifies the qualifying dwellings, their gross internal area and the calculation of the qualifying amount, and this must be accompanied by evidence of compliance with the conditions set out above. The collecting authority must inform the claimant of its decision and give reasons. If relief is granted, a chargeable development can cease to be eligible if a commencement notice is not submitted before the chargeable development is commenced, or if the claimant withdraws or transfers its assumption of liability.[55]

Relief attaching to a qualifying dwelling transfers whenever the land on which it is built or is to be built is sold prior to it being made available for occupation. The seller must notify and give details of the sale to the collecting authority so that the collecting authority can calculate the relief for the dwellings being transferred and transfer the relief to the new beneficiary, ie the new owner. It will also then calculate and issue a revised notice of relief to the beneficiary on the remainder of the chargeable development.

Social housing relief can be withdrawn when there is any change in circumstance that results in a qualifying dwelling ceasing to be a qualifying dwelling, and that happens within seven years from commencement of development. The amount of relief withdrawn must be paid by the beneficiary (and not an occupier). Sale of a qualifying dwelling does not constitute a disqualifying event if the proceeds of the sale are spent on another qualifying dwelling.

---

54 Community Infrastructure Levy Regulations 2010 (SI 2010/948), reg 48.
55 Community Infrastructure Levy Regulations 2010 (SI 2010/948), reg 51.

## Exceptional circumstances relief

A charging authority may grant relief for exceptional circumstances from liability to pay the CIL if it appears to the authority that there are exceptional circumstances which justify doing so and that it considers it expedient to do. However it can only grant relief if it has made relief for exceptional circumstances available in its area; a s 106 agreement has been entered into in respect of the planning permission which connects the chargeable development and the charging authority considers that the cost of complying with s 106 is greater than the charge from the CIL payable; requiring payment of the charge would have an unacceptable impact on the economic viability of development; and granting relief would not constitute a notifiable state aid.

A charging authority which wishes to make exceptional circumstances relief available in its area must issue and publish a statement which gives notice that the relief is available and the date on which it will begin accepting claims for the relief.

A claim for relief must be submitted by an owner of material interest on the appropriate form and must be received by the charging authority before commencing the chargeable development. It must be accompanied by the following:

- an independent assessment of the cost of complying with the planning obligation;
- an independent assessment of the economic viability of the chargeable development;
- an explanation of why payment of the chargeable amount would have an unacceptable impact on the economic viability; and
- where there is more than one material interest in the land, an apportionment assessment.

The charging authority must make its decision on the claim as soon as practicable and inform the claimant in writing of its decision on the amount of relief granted.

In London, both the borough and the Mayor may charge the levy and therefore both are able to offer exceptional circumstances relief. Where the Mayor has decided to make it available on his CIL, although the claim must still be submitted to the borough, the borough must refer the claim and supporting documentation to the Mayor. Where both the borough and the Mayor have made relief available, the borough must first consider whether to offer the relief, and if so, how much. It then only refers the claim to the Mayor where the relief it proposes to give does not make acceptable the impact of the CIL on the economic viability of the development.

The chargeable development can cease to be eligible for exceptional circumstances relief if, before the chargeable development is commenced, charitable or social housing relief is granted, an owner of a material interest makes a material disposal of that interest, or the chargeable development is not commenced within 12 months from the date on which the charging authority issues its decision on the claim.

## REVIEWS AND APPEALS

There are a number of provisions in the CIL Regulations permitting reviews and appeals to be made on a range of matters and issues.[56]

## Review and appeal of chargeable amount

An 'interested person' can request a review of the calculation of a chargeable amount provided it is made in writing to the collecting authority no later than 28 days after the liability notice stating the chargeable amount subject to the request for review was issued.[57] Representations may be submitted with the review and the collecting authority must consider any such representations. Within 14 days of the date on which the collecting authority received a request for the review (the 'review start date'), the collecting authority must notify the person that requested the review of its decision and give reasons. The collecting authority can either confirm the original chargeable amount or calculate a revised amount.

A review of a decision cannot be requested once relevant development has been commenced. A request for a review also cannot be made if a claim for relief had been submitted to the charging authority and has not been withdrawn.

A person who has requested a review and is aggrieved at the decision on the review or is not notified of the decision within the requisite 14 days, may appeal to the 'appointed person' on the grounds that the revised chargeable amount or the original chargeable amount as the case may be has been calculated incorrectly.[58] The appointed person is a valuation officer or district valuer. An appeal must be made within 60 days of the date of the liability notice which stated the original chargeable amount and only one appeal may be made. An appeal cannot be made if the relevant development has been commenced.

Any review or appeal will lapse if the relevant development is commenced before a decision has been given.

Where an appeal is allowed, the appointed person must calculate a revised chargeable amount.

'Interested persons' that can make a request for a review or an appeal are as follows:

- the person who has assumed liability to pay the CIL;
- in the case of a general consent, the person who submitted a notice of chargeable development;
- in the case of planning permission granted subject to a condition requiring further approval to be obtained before commencing development, the person who has applied for that approval;
- the person who applied for planning permission; and
- a person who has been served with a notice of chargeable development in accordance with reg 64A.

The CIL Regulations also provide for appeals to be made in relation to the following matters:

---

56 Community Infrastructure Levy Regulations 2010 (SI 2010/948), Pt 10.
57 Community Infrastructure Levy Regulations 2010 (SI 2010/948), reg 113.
58 Community Infrastructure Levy Regulations 2010 (SI 2010/948), reg 114.

- Apportionment of liability – a person who disagrees with the decision of the collecting authority on the apportionment of liability with respect to an owner's material interest in land may appeal.[59]
- An interested person who disagrees with the decision of the collecting authority to grant charitable relief may appeal on the ground that it incorrectly determined the value of the interest in the land in respect of which the claim was allowed.[60]
- A person who is aggrieved at the decision of the collecting authority to impose a surcharge may appeal on a number of grounds as set out in the relevant regulation.[61]
- A person on whom a demand notice is served which states a deemed commencement date may appeal on the ground that the collecting authority has incorrectly determined that date.[62]
- A person who is aggrieved at a decision of a collecting authority to impose a CIL stop notice may appeal on the basis that the collecting authority did not send a warning notice before imposing the CIL stop notice or that the chargeable development in respect of which the CIL stop notice was imposed has not commenced.[63]

There are various procedural requirements that must be complied with in relation to making appeals.[64]

## WHO HAS ADOPTED THE LEVY SO FAR?

In December 2010, the Government invited all English local authorities to apply to become part of the CIL front runners project, aimed at supporting local authorities to develop the best approach to implementation in their area. Eight authorities were accepted and, of these, three have so far adopted charging schedules. Newark and Sherwood District Council adopted their schedule on 1 December 2011, and Shropshire Council and the London Borough of Redbridge adopted their charging schedules on 1 January 2012.

The Mayor of London's draft charging schedule underwent examination in 2011 and on 27 January 2012 the independent examiner's report was received recommending that his charging schedule be approved. The Mayor's CIL came into effect on 1 April 2012. It is charged on most developments in London at the following rates:

- Zone 1 Boroughs at £50 per square metre: Camden, City of London, City of Westminster, Hammersmith & Fulham, Islington, Kensington & Chelsea, Richmond upon Thames, Wandsworth;
- Zone 2 Boroughs at £35 per square metre: Barnet, Brent, Bromley, Ealing, Greenwich, Hackney, Haringey, Harrow, Hillingdon, Hounslow, Kingston upon Thames, Lambeth, Lewisham, Merton, Redbridge, Southwark, Tower Hamlets;

---

59 Community Infrastructure Levy Regulations 2010 (SI 2010/948), reg 115.
60 Community Infrastructure Levy Regulations 2010 (SI 2010/948), reg 116.
61 Community Infrastructure Levy Regulations 2010 (SI 2010/948), reg 117.
62 Community Infrastructure Levy Regulations 2010 (SI 2010/948), reg 118.
63 Community Infrastructure Levy Regulations 2010 (SI 2010/948), reg 119.
64 Community Infrastructure Levy Regulations 2010 (SI 2010/948), reg 120.

*Community Infrastructure Levy*

- Zone 3 Boroughs at £20 per square metre: Barking & Dagenham, Bexley, Croydon, Enfield, Havering, Newham, Sutton, Waltham Forest.

Development used wholly or mainly for the provision of medical health services or for the provision of education as a school or college or else as an institution of higher education is subject to nil rates. The Mayor does not provide any exceptional circumstances relief.

# Chapter 10

# Nationally Significant Infrastructure Projects

## BACKGROUND

The Labour Government in its 2007 planning White Paper, *Planning for a Sustainable Future*[1] set out detailed proposals to improve the way Nationally Significant Infrastructure Projects ('NSIPs') progressed through the planning system under the Town and Country Planning Act 1990. The white paper built on the recommendations made in the 2006 Barker and Eddington Reports,[2] which both called for the introduction of a new system for dealing with major infrastructure projects. The Labour Government set out its support for 'Eddington's three stage process, in which:

- ministers would set strategic objectives for national infrastructure development up front, integrating economic, social and environmental goals in order to deliver sustainable development;
- promoters would then develop project proposals within a clear strategic framework, and subject to requirements to consult the public to ensure that promoters are adequately prepared for the issues likely to arise; and
- decisions on applications would be taken by an independent commission comprising well respected experts using more focused inquiry procedures that would provide more accessible opportunities for participation.'[3]

In the White Paper, and concurrent consultation on the proposals contained within the White Paper,[4] the Government proposed to:

'– produce, following thorough and effective public consultation and Parliamentary scrutiny, national policy statements to ensure that there is a clear policy framework for nationally significant infrastructure which integrates environmental, economic and social objectives to deliver sustainable development;
– provide greater certainty for promoters of infrastructure projects and help them to improve the way that they prepare applications by making better advice available to them; by requiring them to consult publicly on proposals for development; and by requiring early and

---

1  HM Government (21 May 2007) *Planning for a Sustainable Future* (available at http://www.communities.gov.uk/archived/publications/planningandbuilding/planningasustainablefuture [accessed March 2012]).
2  HM Treasury (December 2006) *Barker Review of Land Use Planning, Final Report*, Annex A and Sir Rod Eddington, DfT (December 2006) *The Case for Action*, Appendix 4A.
3  HM Government (21 May 2007) *Planning for a Sustainable Future*, para 2.10 (available at http://www.communities.gov.uk/archived/publications/planningandbuilding/planningasustainablefuture [accessed March 2012]).
4  HM Government (21 May 2007) *Planning for a Sustainable Future* (available at http://www.communities.gov.uk/archived/publications/planningandbuilding/planningasustainablefuture [accessed March 2012]).

- effective engagement with key parties such as local authorities, statutory bodies, and relevant highway authorities;
- streamline the procedures for infrastructure projects of national significance by rationalising the different consent regimes and improving the inquiry procedures for all of them;
- clarify the decision making process, and achieve a clear separation of policy and decision making, by creating an independent commission to take the decisions on nationally significant infrastructure cases within the framework of the relevant national policy statement;
- improve public participation across the entire process by providing better opportunities for public consultation and engagement at each stage of the development consent process; improving the ability of the public to participate in inquiries by introducing a specific "open floor" stage; and, alongside the introduction of the new regime, providing additional funding to bodies such as Planning Aid.'[5]

The White Paper led to the formulation and subsequent entry into force of the Planning Act 2008, which established the Infrastructure Planning Commission (the 'IPC') and alongside it a discreet regime for the approval of NSIPs against new National Policy Statements ('NPSs') in the areas of energy, water, transport, waste and waste water. While in this book we will not be covering the detail of the regime, the system put into place by the 2008 Act can be summarised as follows:

What constitutes an NSIP was to be determined in accordance with the Planning Act 2008, Pt 3 and by reference to different thresholds for the scale of different types of infrastructure projects. If a proposal was an NSIP, it had to be determined in accordance with the new regime established under the Planning Act 2008. The Secretary of State also had the ability to direct that infrastructure projects which did not qualify as NSIPs by reference to the thresholds of the Planning Act 2008, should nevertheless be dealt with under the IPC regime.

Approval was to be granted by way of development consent order, which in certain circumstances could include compulsory purchase powers and other powers to facilitate the proposed development.

The IPC was to examine applications for development consent for NSIPs and, where a relevant National Policy Statement for the type of infrastructure the subject of the application was in force, the IPC would also be responsible for deciding applications. Where no National Policy Statement was in force for the type of infrastructure the subject of the application, the IPC had only a reporting function and the Secretary of State retained the decision-making power.

NPSs were to be formulated, consulted on, and had to comply with certain parliamentary requirements. They would set the policy framework within which the IPC would exercise its decision-making powers.

A timetable for the decision-making process was established by the Act, comprising a deadline of six months for the examination procedure and further deadline of three months for a decision to be made by the IPC (or three months for a report by the IPC and a further three months for a decision by the Secretary of State, if applicable).

---

5   HM Government (21 May 2007) *Planning for a Sustainable Future,* pages 3 and 4 (available at http://www.communities.gov.uk/archived/publications/planningandbuilding/planningasustainablefuture [accessed March 2012]).

## COALITION GOVERNMENT'S STANCE

Even in opposition, the parties that would subsequently form the coalition Government had long criticised the IPC, as being democratically unaccountable. After the General Election, as early as June 2010, the DCLG released on its website a statement by Decentralisation Cities Minister Greg Clark, announcing that the 'unelected quango' would be replaced by a 'new democratic, fast track system for decision making on major infrastructure projects to support the UK's return to economic growth' where 'Ministers, not unelected commissioners, will take the decisions on new infrastructure projects critical to the country's future economic growth'.[6]

## ABOLITION OF INFRASTRUCTURE PLANNING COMMISSION

The Coalition Agreement provided that the IPC would be replaced with an 'efficient and democratically accountable system that provides a fast-track process for major infrastructure projects'.[7] This has since been legislated for by Pt 6, Ch 6 of the Localism Act, in particular s 128 which came into force on 31 March 2012.

The Secretary of State now decides on all applications for development consent and the examination and reporting functions of the IPC are accommodated within a new division of the Planning Inspectorate (known as the National Infrastructure Directorate).[8]

Schedule 13 of the Act sets out the necessary amendments to the Planning Act 2008 (and other acts) to give effect to the transfer of functions from the IPC to the Secretary of State. As an example, they allow the Secretary of State (rather than previously, the IPC) to appoint an inspector or a panel of between three to five inspectors, who will examine applications and make recommendations to the Secretary of State. The Secretary of State (subject to specified exceptions) must take into account the relevant National Policy Statement when deciding applications.

Other amendments to the Planning Act 2008 provide for the Secretary of State to charge fees in connection with specified functions, including the giving of advice in accordance with the Planning Act 2008, s 51. Section 51, however, is more substantively amended so that the Secretary of State may by regulations set out that any advice given by him must be disclosed 'to other persons or to the public generally'. Section 51(2), which prevented the IPC from giving advice about the merits of any particular application for development consent order is effectively repealed, leaving the Secretary of State free to give such advice. At Report Stage in the House of Lords, it was stated that:

> 'where the IPC has issued a screening or scoping opinion or has authorised someone to serve a notice under Section 62 of the Planning Act, these actions

---

6 DCLG (29 June 2010) *Major Infrastructure Stays on Fast-track as Planning Quango Closes* (available at http://www.communities.gov.uk/news/corporate/1626220 [accessed March 2012]).
7 HM Government (2010) *The Coalition: Our Programme for Government*, page 11 (available at http://www.cabinetoffice.gov.uk/sites/default/files/resources/coalition_programme_for_government.pdf [accessed March 2012]).
8 The functions of the IPC website can now be found at http://www.infrastructure.planningportal.gov.uk.

will generally stand as authorised after transition as the IPC was the body with legal authority to carry out those actions at the time. Screening and scoping opinions and authorisations to obtain information about interests in land will not have to be given again.'[9]

Section 129 of the Act gives power to the Secretary of State to make directions concerning the transitional arrangements for applications for development consent that have already been submitted and are under consideration by the IPC at the time s 128 comes into force:

**'129 Transitional provisions in connection with abolition**

(1) The Secretary of State may, in connection with the operation of the abolition provisions, give a direction about the handling on and after the abolition date of –
- (a) an application received by the Infrastructure Planning Commission before the abolition date that purports to be an application for an order granting development consent under the Planning Act 2008,
- (b) a proposed application notified to the Commission under section 46 of that Act before the abolition date, or
- (c) an application received by the Secretary of State on or after the abolition date where –
  - (i) the application purports to be an application for an order granting development consent under that Act, and
  - (ii) proposed application that has become that application was notified to the Commission under section 46 of that Act before the abolition date.

(2) A direction under subsection (1) may (in particular) –
- (a) make provision about the effect on and after the abolition date of things done before that date;
- (b) provide for provisions of or made under the Planning Act 2008 to apply on and after that date as they applied before that date, with or without modifications specified in the direction;
- (c) provide for provisions of or made under that Act to apply on and after the abolition date with modifications specified in the direction;
- (d) make provision for a person who immediately before the abolition date –
  - (i) is a member of the Commission, and
  - (ii) is a member of the Panel, or is the single Commissioner, handling an application for an order granting development consent under that Act,
  
  to be, or to be treated as being, a member of the Panel that under Chapter 2 of Part 6 of that Act, or the appointed person who under Chapter 3 of that Part, is to handle the application on and after the abolition date;
- (e) take other transitional provision and savings;
- (f) make provision binding the Crown.

(3) In this section –
"the abolition date" means the date on which section 128(1) comes into force;

---

[9] Hansard, 17 October 2011, col 109 (available at http://www.publications.parliament.uk/pa/ld201011/ldhansrd/text/111017-0003.htm [accessed March 2012]).

## Abolition of Infrastructure Planning Commission

"the abolition provisions" means section 128, Schedule 13 and Part 20 of Schedule 25.'

In December 2011, the DCLG issued a statement on its website[10] in relation to the transitional arrangements to 'ensure that major infrastructure cases transfer seamlessly from the Infrastructure Planning Commission to the Planning Inspectorate'. It announced that the Secretary of State's direction was currently being drafted and would be published in draft in advance of the abolition of the IPC. The Government set out the approach being taken in drafting this direction:

'The direction may only apply to applications, or proposed applications, where notice has been given under section 46 of the Planning Act 2008 that a promoter intends to make an application under that Act. Applications which have not yet reached that stage will not have engaged with the regime sufficiently to require a direction (a direction will not be needed where the Commission has issued a screening or scoping opinion, or has authorised entry onto land – Commission authority for these matters will still stand after transition).

The Government intends the direction to be structured in two parts. The first part will make general provision in respect of those projects for which a section 46 notice has been given as of the date of abolition, to the effect that:
- anything done in relation to those projects for the purpose of complying with the Planning Act 2008 is to be treated as if it had been done under the legislation as amended
- anything done by or in relation to the Infrastructure Planning Commission shall be treated as if it had been done by or in relation to the Secretary of State

The second part will deal with any provision that needs to be made for individual cases, should specific provision be necessary (for example to ensure that, notwithstanding the abolition of the Commission, the consideration of a particular application can continue without a change in persons appointed).

Until the Localism Act is commenced, promoters are expected to continue to act in compliance with the Planning Act 2008 as it presently stands. Section 129 permits the Secretary of State to apply the 2008 Act with modifications, and he will consider using this power to ensure that promoters have properly complied with any requirements that are subsequently modified by the Localism Act.

Promoters of projects are encouraged to liaise closely with the Commission in the weeks leading up to abolition to ensure that any activity carried out in this period is carefully planned, and to enable all necessary matters to be accounted for in the direction. This will help to ensure the transitional period passes smoothly.'

The Infrastructure Planning (Transitional Provisions) Direction 2012[11] came into force on 1 April 2012 and reflected this approach.

---

10 DCLG (December 2011) *Transition to the Planning Act as Amended by the Localism Act 2011* (available at http://www.communities.gov.uk/planningandbuilding/planningsystem/transitionplanningact/ [accessed March 2012]).
11 Available at http://www.infrastructure.independent.gov.uk/wp-content/uploads/2012/03/120309-Direction-major-infrastructure-projects.pdf [accessed April 2012].

## NATIONAL POLICY STATEMENTS

Additionally, the Act introduces changes to the procedure for NPSs. NPSs set out the national policy framework for large energy, water, transport, waste and waste water infrastructure projects. Section 130 of the Act establishes a period of 21 sitting days (which can be extended by the Secretary of State by laying before the House of Commons a statement to that effect) after any final NPS has been laid before Parliament for the House of Commons to resolve to approve (or not proceed with) the NPS. However, an NPS will pass this Parliamentary hurdle if the 21 sitting days have passed either without a resolution not to proceed or with the NPS being expressly approved by the House. The Act also introduces changes to the publicity and consultation requirements for draft NPSs: non-material modifications can be made to draft NPSs without the parliamentary requirements being triggered again, although any amendments that materially affect the policy set out in the original NPS will have to comply with the parliamentary requirements. Further, the 21-day sitting period can be extended by the Secretary of State by a further 21 days or less by laying before Parliament a statement to this effect.

The amendment to the Planning Act 2008 also changes the local authorities that will need to be consulted on a draft NPS: councils sharing a boundary with another ('neighbouring authorities') will need to be consulted only if either they adjoin a lower tier district council or a unitary authority in whose area a proposal is located or they are county councils or unitary authorities themselves and adjoin another county council in whose area a proposal is located.

## SECTION 35 DIRECTIONS

The Act also makes changes to the power of the Secretary of State under the Planning Act 2008, s 35 to direct that an infrastructure project not meeting the thresholds for NSIPs contained in the 2008 Act, should nonetheless be treated as one of national significance requiring development consent. Pursuant to s 132 of the Act, such directions can be made at any time and the applicant will no longer have to wait until a formal application has been made for the project under the normal planning regime to request that the proposal be considered as an NSIP. The amendments also introduce a timescale for dealing with requests for the Secretary of State to exercise the powers of direction – a decision must be made within 28 days of the date the request is made (unless the Secretary of State has asked for further information from the applicant, in which case a decision must be made within 28 days of that information being provided).[12]

## PRE-APPLICATION CONSULTATION AND PUBLICITY REQUIREMENTS

Section 133 of the Act sets out changes to pre-application consultation for NSIPs. Developers bringing forward an application for development consent for an NSIP will only have to consult neighbouring authorities if either they adjoin a lower tier district council or a unitary authority in whose area a proposal is located or they are county councils or unitary authorities themselves and adjoin another county council in whose area a proposal is located. Additionally, s 134

---

12  Planning Act 2008, new s 35A inserted by Localism Act 2011, s 132(10).

*Other changes*

makes a change to the requirement in the Planning Act 2008, s 47(6) concerning the duties of an applicant to publicise its community consultation statement setting out how it proposes to consult the local community: such an applicant must no longer 'publish' the statement, but instead must 'make the statement available for inspection by the public in a way that is reasonably convenient for people living in the vicinity of the land' and must put a notice in a local newspaper stating where and when it can be inspected.

## OTHER CHANGES

Further changes introduced by the Act include the following:

- The Planning Act 2008, s 33 provides that where development consent is required, other consents listed are not required. Section 131 of the Act amends this provision to allow for the Secretary of State to amend the list of consents not required as a result of the making of a development consent order.
- The Planning Act 2008, s 38, which permits the Secretary of State to prescribe model provisions for incorporation into a development consent order, is repealed.
- Section 135 amends the Planning Act 2008, s 52 to allow the Secretary of State to authorise an applicant for an NSIP to serve notice requiring owners of interests in the land to be used for the NSIP to specify people they believe will seek compensation in connection with the construction or operation of the NSIP.
- Section 136 amends the Planning Act 2008, s 53 to extend rights of entry onto land in order to survey it for the purposes of complying with requirements for environmental impact assessment or habitats regulations assessment (which includes taking samples) without requiring prior compliance with the pre-application consultation requirement set out in the Planning Act 2008, s 42.
- Section 137 amends the Planning Act 2008, s 55 in relation to the validation of applications for development consent. Applications no longer need to give reasons for any failure to follow applicable guidance and instead must be of a standard that the Secretary of State considers 'satisfactory' (although in deciding what is satisfactory, the Secretary of State must have regard to the extent to which the application complies with the requirements as to form and contents set out in the Planning Act 2008, s 37(3), and the extent to which any applicable guidance given under s 37(4) has been followed).
- Section 138 provides that only a reduced number of local authorities (see above) need to be notified of an accepted application. Once an application has been made, the applicant, interested parties, and each statutory party and the reduced number of local authorities will need to be notified. Any of the parties notified may then ask to become interested parties. The definition of interested parties for the purposes of applications for development consent is also amended. In addition to the applicant, the local authority in whose area the development is located and a person who has made a relevant representation, anyone who had to be notified of the acceptance of an application and anyone who the examining authority has decided should be an interested party (in

accordance with the Planning Act 2008, new ss 102A and 102B[13]) and who has requested to become an interested party, will be an interested party. The Planning Act 2008, s 88 is also amended so that only the same reduced number of local authorities, and 'statutory parties' (along with the applicant and interested parties), must be invited to the preliminary meeting that must be held following the making of an initial assessment of the principal issues arising on an application.

- Section 140 amends the Planning Act 2008, s 120(2), so that in order for development consent to be granted, the approval of the Secretary of State or any other person may be required.

---

13 Inserted by Localism Act 2011, s 138(9). This makes provision for certain categories of persons to request that they become 'interested parties' for the purpose of the decision-making procedure. The benefits of becoming an interested party are briefly that such a party has the opportunity to make formal representations, attend the preliminary meeting to comment on examination procedures, request an open floor hearing, attend an open floor or specific hearing or request to speak at a hearing.

# Chapter 11

# London

Part 8 of the Localism Act contains a series of legislative changes that relate specifically to London. In this Chapter we address the following:

1 changes to housing and regeneration functions in London;
2 Mayoral Development Corporations;
3 Greater London Authority governance changes.

London has a unique governance structure. Its directly elected Mayor leads the Greater London Authority ('GLA'). The GLA has a series of duties under the Greater London Authority Acts 1999 and 2007 in relation to transport, planning and development, housing, economic development and regeneration, culture, health inequalities, environmental issues, culture and tourism. The Mayor's spatial development strategy for London, known as the London Plan, is part of the strategy development plan for London. London boroughs'[1] plans need to be in general conformity with it and its policies guide decisions on planning applications by the boroughs and by the Mayor. Following abolition of the regional strategies outside of London it will have a unique role in providing strategic regional guidance to the London boroughs. In many ways London is immune from many of the effects and uncertainties of localism – the boroughs will still operate within a regional structure. Any planning application of 'potentially strategic importance'[2] has to be referred to the Mayor who may, subject to detailed constraints, direct the borough to refuse it, or may call it in for his own determination.

Within the GLA 'family' of administrative bodies are the London Development Agency ('LDA'), Transport for London, the London Fire and Emergency Planning Authority and the Metropolitan Police Authority.

The concept of an elected London-wide strategic body has been sometimes controversial. The Greater London Council was abolished by the last Conservative Government in 1985. The GLA was created in 2000[3] and Ken Livingstone, the last leader of the Greater London Council, was elected as first London Mayor on 4 May 2000. After two terms in office, he was beaten in the May 2008 mayoral election by Conservative Boris Johnson.

The GLA's powers were initially focused on housing, skills, planning and waste but were widened in 2007.

On 30 April 2010, the Conservative Party published *A New Settlement for London's Government*.[4] The document indicated that, for Conservatives:

---

1 We use the phrase 'London boroughs' to mean the 32 London boroughs and the Corporation of the City of London.
2 Defined in the Town and Country Planning (Mayor of London) Order 2008 (SI 2008/580).
3 Under the Greater London Authority Act 1999 following a referendum held on 7 May 1998.
4 The Conservative Party (30 April 2010) *A New Settlement for London's Government*.

'driving local accountability is a key part of our local government agenda and it is therefore time to look at how we strengthen London's devolutionary settlement for Londoners. We are determined to bring forward a better settlement for London and that means giving the Mayor the powers that Londoners expect him to have. It also means looking at whether we can go further in pushing down powers to the London boroughs, where local communities can and should make their own decisions when they do not have a pan-London, strategic influence.'

The proposals in the document covered four main areas: housing and regeneration, the Port of London Authority, rail franchises, and the Olympics Legacy.

Until it was abolished by the new coalition Government shortly after the May 2010 general election, the Government Office for London, one of nine regional government offices across England, was the primary means for central Government oversight and control over the workings of London local government.

A 'devolution package for London'[5] was delivered to the Secretary of State on 23 July 2010 jointly by the Mayor of London, London Councils and the London Assembly, which helped to set a detailed set of proposals for change and further devolution of powers, responding to the new Government's policy agenda. The document set out various proposals, divided into three categories: where the three bodies were in agreement, where there was disagreement, and where further discussion would be necessary to achieve jointly agreed proposals. The priorities for the Mayor were stated to be 'the transfer of Homes and Communities Agency London and London Development Agency functions and resources to the Greater London Authority and the establishment of the Olympic Park Legacy Company as a Mayoral Development Corporation'.

The priorities from London Councils were stated to be 'to bring resources and decisions as close to Londoners as possible ... reinforced by greater borough representation on pan-London bodies'.

The priority for the London Assembly was stated to be 'that robust transparency and accountability arrangements are embedded in any devolution package. The Assembly's powers should be strengthened in relation to the Mayor's strategies and budget'.

## HOUSING AND REGENERATION FUNCTIONS

Part 8, Ch 1 of the Act makes specific provision in relation to the GLA's housing and regeneration functions and governance.

The GLA's general power of competence to do anything in support of promoting economic development and wealth creation, promoting social development and improving the environment in Greater London, is currently limited in a number of respects by the Greater London Authority Act 1999, s 31. Section 186 removes limitations on the GLA incurring expenditure in providing housing and education services (although the GLA will still not be able to sponsor – or facilitate the sponsorship of – Academy schools).

---

5  The Mayor of London, London Councils and the London Assembly (23 July 2010) *Devolution Package for London*.

## Housing and regeneration functions

Section 187 gives new housing and regeneration functions to the GLA by amending the Greater London Authority Act 1999, Pt 7A. The new provisions allow the GLA to compulsorily acquire land where authorised by the Secretary of State and to allow it to override easements and apply for a public right of way to be extinguished, for housing and regeneration purposes; and prohibit the GLA from disposing of land held for housing and regeneration purposes for less than the best consideration which can reasonably be obtained (unless the Secretary of State consents). There are further detailed changes to the GLA's housing functions which are beyond the scope of this book.

Section 188 of the Act makes changes to the Greater London Authority Act 1999, ss 333A and 333D relating to the London housing strategy, to reflect that the GLA will now be responsible for exercising housing functions in Greater London rather than the Homes and Communities Agency ('HCA').

Pursuant to s 190, the Secretary of State can make schemes to transfer property, rights and liabilities from the HCA or the Secretary of State to the GLA, a functional body, a subsidiary company of the GLA, the Secretary of State, a London Borough, the Common Council of the City of London, or any other person specified by order of the Secretary of State.

The Act provides for the transfer of the LDA's functions to the GLA. Section 191 and Schs 20 and 25 abolish the LDA. The Secretary of State is empowered to make schemes for the transfer of property, rights and liabilities of the LDA to the GLA, a functional body, a subsidiary company of the GLA, the Secretary of State, a London borough council, the Common Council of the City of London or any body specified by order made by the Secretary of State. The Secretary of State must consult the Mayor of London about the contents of any proposed transfer scheme.

Section 192 amends the Greater London Authority Act 1999 to transfer the duty to prepare and publish an economic development strategy for London from the LDA to the Mayor. Pursuant to s 192(2), the economic development strategy must contain:

- the Mayor's assessment of the economic conditions of Greater London; and
- the Mayor's policies and proposals for the economic development and regeneration of Greater London, including the Mayor's strategy for –
  - promoting business efficiency, investment and competitiveness in Greater London,
  - promoting employment in Greater London, and
  - enhancing the development of skills relevant to employment in Greater London.

When preparing or revising the economic development strategy, the Mayor of London is required to consult bodies representing London employers and employees.

Pursuant to s 192(5) and (6), the Secretary of State may give guidance to the Mayor of London about the matters to be covered by the economic development strategy or the issues to be taken into account in preparing or revising. The Mayor of London must have regard to that guidance. Section 192(8) allows the Secretary of State to direct the Mayor to make such revisions of the strategy as may be specified in the direction where the Secretary of State considers that the economic development strategy for London (or any part of it) is inconsistent with national policies, or that the economic development strategy for London or its implementation is having, or is likely to have, a detrimental effect on any area outside Greater London. Section 192(9) requires the Mayor to revise the economic development strategy for London in accordance with the direction.

## MAYORAL DEVELOPMENT CORPORATIONS

Part 8, Ch 2 of the Act introduces new powers to designate Mayoral Development Areas ('MDAs') in Greater London where, after consultation with interested bodies, the Mayor considers it expedient for furthering one of the GLA's principal purposes (ie the purposes of promoting economic and social development and improving the environment). The Mayor must submit the proposal to the London Assembly for at least 21 days. The Assembly may only veto it by a two-thirds vote.

Section 198 requires that once the Secretary of State has been notified of the designation of an MDA in accordance with s 197(6), he must by order establish a Mayoral Development Corporation ('MDC') for the designated MDA.

At the report stage of the House of Lords, Lord Jenkin of Roding (a former Secretary of State for the Environment in the 1980s under Margaret Thatcher) stated in relation to the powers to create MDAs and MDCs:

> 'Anybody with experience of development corporations, such as the London Docklands Development Corporation and other development corporations outside London, will recognise their hugely important role in urban regeneration in often very run-down areas. One essential characteristic that led to the success of these development corporations, not least the LDDC, was the provision that they had to be planning authorities and therefore had full authority over planning in their areas. In the 1980s this enabled my noble friend Lord Heseltine and my noble and learned friend Lord Howe of Aberavon to trigger what we must all agree has been the most amazing regeneration of what was then the almost derelict area of London docks. My role came later, as Secretary of State for the Environment, and with my late friend Nicholas Ridley, then Secretary of State for Transport, we were responsible for promoting both London City Airport and the Docklands Light Railway. These have transformed the Docklands area and indeed much of east London. Therefore, it is no surprise that the Mayor of London, Boris Johnson, supported by the Greater London Assembly, has persuaded the Government to include mayoral development corporations in the Bill. This is what Chapter 2 of Part 7 of the Bill is all about. As with all those who are concerned with the development and future of London, I warmly welcome most of this chapter.'[6]

On 6 February 2012, the Mayor of London announced that the London Legacy Development Corporation ('LLDC') will become the first London MDC and will take over the role of the Olympic Park Legacy Company for the regeneration of the Olympic Park. LLDC has been established by the London Legacy Development Corporation (Establishment) Order 2012 (SI 2012/310) with the following overall aims:

---

6  Hansard, 12 September 2011, cols 505–506.

## Mayoral Development Corporations

- '• to deliver integrated land management and town planning necessary to implement a coherent plan for the Olympic Park and surrounding area (which overlaps four separate local planning authorities);
- to maximise the receipts available from the development of the Olympic Park within a clear regeneration framework;
- to offer clear legacy leadership, accountable management, and a single point of contact for development partners and potential investors;
- to be in place and operational before the Olympic Games begin; and
- to reflect the Government's localism policy, which aims to ensure that power should be exercised at the lowest practical level, by transferring political control, funding and direction to the elected Mayor of London.'[7]

North Tottenham has also been promoted as a potential MDA.[8]

Pursuant to s 200(1) to (3) and (6), the Secretary of State may at any time, but only having undertaken consultation with affected bodies, make a scheme transferring to an MDC property, rights and liabilities held by:

- a London borough council;
- the Common Council of the City of London in its capacity as a local authority;
- the Homes and Communities Agency;
- a development corporation established under the New Towns Act 1981 for a new town, all or part of whose area is in Greater London;
- an urban development corporation[9] for an urban development area, all or part of which is in Greater London;
- the Olympic Delivery Authority;
- any company, or other body corporate, which is a wholly-owned subsidiary[10] of the Olympic Delivery Authority;
- any company, or other body corporate,[11] which –
  - is a subsidiary of the Olympic Delivery Authority,
  - is a subsidiary of at least one other public authority,[12] and
  - is not a subsidiary of any person who is not a public authority;[13]
- a Minister of the Crown[14] or a government department;

---

7   Explanatory memorandum to the London Legacy Development Corporation (Establishment) Order 2012 (SI 2012/310) (available at http://www.lawtel.com/MyLawtel/Documents/ AI0120310 [accessed February 2012]).
8   Haringey Council (24 March 2011) Press release *New Mayoral Development Corporation for North Tottenham* (available at http://www.haringey.gov.uk/index/news_and_events/latest_news/new_mayoral_development_corporation.htm [accessed March 2012]).
9   Pursuant to Localism Act 2011, s 200(1), 'urban development corporation' means a corporation established by an order under Local Government, Planning and Land Act 1980, s 135.
10  Pursuant to Localism Act 2011, s 200(7), 'wholly-owned subsidiary' has the meaning given by Companies Act 2006, s 1159.
11  Pursuant to Localism Act 2011, s 200(8), a body corporate ('C') is a 'subsidiary' of another person ('P') if P, or P's nominee, is a member of C, or C is a subsidiary of a body corporate that is itself a subsidiary of P.
12  Pursuant to Localism Act 2011, s 200(10), 'public authority' means a public body or a Minister of the Crown or other holder of a public office.
13  Pursuant to Localism Act 2011, s 200(10), 'public authority' means a public body or a Minister of the Crown or other holder of a public office.
14  Pursuant to Localism Act 2011, s 200(10), 'Minister of the Crown' has the same meaning as in the Ministers of the Crown Act 1975.

- any company, all the shares in which are held by a Minister of the Crown;[15]
- any company whose members –
  - include the Mayor and a Minister of the Crown,[16] and
  - do not include anyone who is neither the Mayor nor a Minister of the Crown;[17]
- any other person specified by order of the Secretary of State.

Pursuant to s 200(4), the Mayor of London may at any time make a scheme transferring to an MDC property, rights and liabilities of –

- the Greater London Authority;
- a functional body[18] other than that MDC; or
- a company[19] that is a subsidiary of the Greater London Authority.

Conversely, s 216 allows the Mayor of London to make a scheme for the transfer upon such terms as he considers appropriate of any property, rights or liabilities which are vested in an MDC to:

(a) the Greater London Authority;
(b) a functional body other than the MDC concerned;
(c) a company that is a subsidiary[20] of the Greater London Authority;
(d) a London borough council;
(e) the Common Council of the City of London; or
(f) any other person.

Section 201 sets out MDCs' objects and powers. An MDC has the object of securing the regeneration of its area and 'may do anything it considers appropriate' to that end.

Subsequent provisions set out a series of specific powers. Section 202 allows the Mayor to decide that the MDC for the area is to be the local planning authority for the purposes of plan-making, development control and/or neighbourhood planning.

Section 203 allows an MDC to arrange for all or part of its planning functions to be carried out by the relevant borough council.

Section 204 allows the Mayor to remove or restrict the use of powers which have been given to an MDC.

Section 205(1) and (2) permit an MDC to provide infrastructure (including by way of acquisition, construction, conversion, improvement and repair) and to facilitate the provision of infrastructure. Infrastructure is defined in s 205(4) to mean water, electricity, gas, telecommunications, sewerage or other services;

---

15  Pursuant to Localism Act 2011, s 200(10), 'Minister of the Crown' has the same meaning as in the Ministers of the Crown Act 1975.
16  Pursuant to Localism Act 2011, s 200(10), 'Minister of the Crown' has the same meaning as in Ministers of the Crown Act 1975.
17  Pursuant to Localism Act 2011, s 200(10), 'Minister of the Crown' has the same meaning as in Ministers of the Crown Act 1975.
18  Pursuant to Localism Act 2011, s 200(1), 'functional body' has the meaning given by Greater London Authority Act 1999, s 424(1).
19  Pursuant to Localism Act 2011, s 200(9), 'company' means: (a) a company within the meaning given by Companies Act 2006, s 1(1), or (b) a society registered or deemed to be registered under the Co-operative and Community Benefit Societies and Credit Unions Act 1965 or the Industrial and Provident Societies Act (Northern Ireland) 1969.
20  'Subsidiary' has the meaning given by the Companies Act 2006, s 1159.

## Mayoral Development Corporations

roads or other transport facilities; retail or other business facilities; health, educational, employment or training facilities; social, religious or recreational facilities; cremation or burial facilities, and other community facilities.

Section 206 permits a MDC to regenerate or develop land,[21] to bring about the more effective use of land,[22] provide buildings or other land,[23] and to carry out any of the following activities in relation to land:

- acquiring, holding, improving, managing, reclaiming, repairing or disposing of buildings, other land, plant, machinery, equipment or other property;
- carrying out building and other operations (including converting or demolishing buildings); and
- creating an attractive environment.[24]

It may either carry out these functions itself or facilitate others to carry them out.

Section 206(6) clarifies that for the purposes of s 206:

- reference to a 'building' is reference to a building or other structure (including a house-boat or caravan), or any part of a building or other structure (including a house-boat or caravan);
- 'developing' includes redeveloping;
- 'improving', in relation to buildings, includes refurbishing, equipping and fitting out;
- 'providing' includes providing by way of acquisition, construction, conversion, improvement or repair.

Section 207 permits an MDC to acquire land in its area or elsewhere by agreement. It may also acquire land, and new rights over land, in its area or elsewhere in Greater London compulsorily, if the Secretary of State authorises it to do so, which includes the power to acquire new rights over land and power to acquire land compulsorily for giving in exchange for that land or those new rights.

The Mayor of London's consent must be obtained to any compulsory purchase order which is submitted to the Secretary of State for confirmation.

Section 208 gives MDCs the same powers as the Homes and Communities Agency in relation to acquired land, although the power to extinguish public rights of way is only exercisable with the consent of the Mayor.

Analogous to the restriction on local authorities imposed by the Local Government Act 1972, s 123, s 209 imposes a duty on an MDC not to dispose of land for less than the best consideration which can reasonably be obtained, unless the Mayor of London consents. This duty does not apply to a disposal by way of a short tenancy if the disposal consists of the grant of a term of not more than seven years, or the assignment of a term which, at the date of assignment, has not more than seven years to run. Section 209(3) prevents an MDC from disposing of land which has been compulsorily acquired by it unless the Mayor

---

21  Localism Act 2011, s 206(1).
22  Localism Act 2011, s 206(2).
23  Localism Act 2011, s 206(3).
24  Localism Act 2011, s 206(4).

of London consents. Other than these restrictions, s 209(4) provides that an MDC may dispose of land held by it in any way it considers appropriate.

Additionally, MDCs are able to:

- enter and survey land under the Housing and Regeneration Act 2008, ss 17 and 18;[25]
- adopt private streets where any street works have been executed in an MDA which was or has since become a private street;[26]
- carry on any business and, with the consent of the Mayor of London, form or acquire interests in bodies corporate, although the MDC must ensure that no subsidiary of the MDC engages in an activity which the MDC would not be required or permitted to carry on and that no subsidiary of the MDC borrows from a person other than the MDC, or raises money by the issue of shares or stock to a person other than the MDC, without the consent of the Mayor;[27] and
- with the consent of the Mayor, give financial assistance in any form to any person subject to such terms and conditions as the MDC considers appropriate.[28]

Under s 214 of the Act, the Mayor can decide, following consultation, that the MDC should have the power to grant discretionary relief from business rates rather than the relevant local authority.

Sections 219 and 220 allow for the Mayor of London to give guidance and/or directions to an MDC as to the exercise of any of its functions. Prior to issuing or revoking any guidance and directions, the Mayor of London must consult such persons as he considers appropriate. MDCs must, in exercising their functions, have regard to any guidance given to them under ss 219 and 220.

Section 215 requires the Mayor of London to review from time to time whether existing MDCs should be kept in existence. Where no property, rights or liabilities are vested in an MDC, the Mayor of London can, under s 217, request the Secretary of State to revoke the order he made under s 198 that established the MDC. Upon receipt of such a request, the Secretary of State must make an order giving effect to the request. Where such an order is made, s 217(4) and (5) provide that:

- the MDC is dissolved on the coming into force of the order; and
- that the Mayor must revoke the designation of the MDA for which the MDC was established, publicise the revocation and notify the Secretary of State of the revocation.

## GREATER LONDON AUTHORITY GOVERNANCE CHANGES

Section 223 inserts a new section into the Greater London Authority Act 1999 to permit ministers to delegate to the Mayor of London any of their 'eligible functions'. Pursuant to the Greater London Authority Act 1999, new s 39A(2), eligible functions are those which:

---

25 Localism Act 2011, s 210.
26 Localism Act 2011, s 211.
27 Localism Act 2011, s 212.
28 Localism Act 2011, s 213.

## Greater London Authority governance changes

- do not consist of a power to make regulations or other instruments of a legislative character or a power to fix fees or charges; and
- are considered by the Secretary of State to be functions that can appropriately be exercised by the Mayor.

New s 39A(4) imposes consultation requirements, so that a minister, prior to delegating any functions to the Mayor of London, must consult:

- each London borough council;
- the Common Council; and
- the Assembly.

A minister may revoke a delegation at any time, and the Greater London Authority Act 1999, s 409, which allows a Minister to transfer associated property, rights or liabilities, is amended so that these are transferred back if a delegation is revoked.

Section 224 amends the Greater London Authority Act 1999 so that where the GLA carries on specified activities for a commercial purpose (to be defined in regulations yet to be made), it may do so only through a taxable body such as a subsidiary company of the Authority.

Pursuant to s 225 of the Act, the six statutory environmental strategies that the Mayor of London is currently required to prepare (on biodiversity; municipal waste management; climate change mitigation and energy; adaptation to climate change; air quality, and ambient noise) are to be merged into one, to be known as the London Environment Strategy. Section 226 revokes the requirement to publish reports every four years on the state of the environment in Greater London.

Sections 227, 228 and 229 amend the provisions relating to the Mayor's strategies:

- s 227 requires the Mayor, when preparing a strategy, to take into account the need for consistency with EU obligations and other international obligations and national policies;
- s 228 removes the obligation on the Mayor to consult the functional bodies and the Assembly before public consultation; and
- s 229 introduces a new veto power for the London Assembly over a strategy proposed by the Mayor where a two-thirds majority of the Assembly opposes it. The veto does not apply where a change to a strategy is made to comply with a direction from the Secretary of State.

Section 231 extends, with minor modifications, the provisions of the Local Government Act 1972, Pt 5A which provides for public access to local authority meetings and documents, to Transport for London.

# Chapter 12

# Other legislative and administrative changes

The Government's *Plan for Growth*, published in March 2011 alongside the Budget, stated that 'the current planning system is holding back UK growth and jobs', that 'it is overly bureaucratic, costly for business, and unresponsive to demand'[1] and that 'the Government will make radical changes to the planning system to support job creation and growth. By creating a planning system, supported by powerful financial incentives, that makes the right land available in the right place for development, it will deliver commercial development, vital infrastructure and housing that the country needs'.[2] A series of actions designed to drive 'sustainable economic growth through national planning policy'[3] were set out. Measures that were not subject of previous announcements included:

- consulting on proposals to make it easier to convert commercial premises to residential; and
- introducing a number of measures to streamline the planning applications and related consents regimes to remove bureaucracy from the system and speeding it up, including a 12-month guarantee for the processing of all planning applications, including appeals.[4]

Many of the proposals in *Plan for Growth* are covered by other chapters of this book. This chapter will focus on the two proposals referred to above and to other recent legislative changes introduced by the Government since coming into power.

## CHANGES TO PERMITTED DEVELOPMENT RIGHTS AND REVIEW OF USE CLASSES ORDER

*Plan for Growth* states as follows:

'2.22 The Government wants to identify more opportunities to exempt development from the planning system, where the impacts are likely to be acceptable, to both encourage and make it easier to develop. As part of this, the Government will consult on a proposal to allow changes of use, without the need to apply for planning permission, from classes B1, B2 and B8 (business, general industrial and storage) to class C3 (residential). This will support our urgent need to increase the supply of housing ...'[5]

---

1   HM Treasury (March 2011) *The Plan for Growth*, page 43 (available at http://www.hm-treasury.gov.uk/ukecon_growth_index.htm [accessed March 2012]).
2   HM Treasury (March 2011) *The Plan for Growth*, page 43 (available at http://www.hm-treasury.gov.uk/ukecon_growth_index.htm [accessed March 2012]).
3   HM Treasury (March 2011) *The Plan for Growth*, page 43 (available at http://www.hm-treasury.gov.uk/ukecon_growth_index.htm [accessed March 2012]).
4   HM Treasury (March 2011) *The Plan for Growth*, pages 43 to 49 (available at http://www.hm-treasury.gov.uk/ukecon_growth_index.htm [accessed March 2012]).
5   HM Treasury (March 2011) *The Plan for Growth*, pages 45 and 46 (available at http://www.hm-treasury.gov.uk/ukecon_growth_index.htm [accessed March 2012]).

*Other legislative and administrative changes*

2.23 The Government will also conduct an urgent review of the Use Classes Order and associated permitted development rights, such as the ability to transfer uses between different categories of commercial premises and from residential to commercial use, which will enable full consideration of the role the Use Classes system plays in encouraging growth.'[6]

Following this, in April 2011, DCLG published a consultation paper on proposals to relax permitted development rights to enable changes of use from commercial to residential.[7] The Government identified the lack of land available for residential development as the key barrier to increasing housing supply, and stated that it is 'proposing action on three fronts:

- To provide for the change from commercial (B use classes) to residential (C3 use class) without the need to apply for planning permission. This responds to the recognised and urgent need to increase housing supply at a national level and recognises the fact that, in general, housing is likely to have fewer wider land-use impacts than commercial uses. Proposals are set out in this consultation document.
- A call to local communities and local authorities to use imaginatively the powers they already have to relax planning constraints locally to target local issues, encourage development, support local economic strategies and make best use of existing properties.
- To remove unnecessary barriers to change of use through a wider review of how change of use and permitted development is managed within the planning system. This will include consideration of how the system could be liberalised in ways other than to promote housing supply.'[8]

The main proposal set out in the consultation was to introduce permitted development rights to allow changes of use from B1 uses, which include offices, research and development premises and light industry, to C3 use (dwelling houses), without the need for planning permission. The Government stated that 'removing the burden and costs associated with such applications and establishing the principle that change of use between these classes is permitted should encourage developers to bring forward more proposals for housing'.[9] The Government also considered that there was a strong case for making changes of use from B2 (general industrial) and B8 (storage and distribution) to C3 (dwelling house) permitted development.

The paper stated that 'B1 uses are most likely to be located in suitable locations for housing and that in many cases existing premises will lend themselves to

---

6 HM Treasury (March 2011) *The Plan for Growth*, page 46 (available at http://www.hm-treasury.gov.uk/ukecon_growth_index.htm [accessed March 2012]).
7 DCLG (April 2011) *Relaxation of Planning Rules from Change of Use from Commercial to Residential* (available at http://communities.gov.uk/publications/planningandbuilding/relaxationchangeconsultation [accessed March 2012]).
8 DCLG (April 2011) *Relaxation of Planning Rules from Change of Use from Commercial to Residential*, page 2 (available at http://communities.gov.uk/publications/planningandbuilding/relaxationchangeconsultation [accessed March 2012]).
9 DCLG (April 2011) *Relaxation of Planning Rules from Change of Use from Commercial to Residential*, page 7 (available at http://communities.gov.uk/publications/planningandbuilding/relaxationchangeconsultation [accessed March 2012]).

conversion to housing without the need for extensive external works'.[10] The Government believes 'that in general, the market will make sensible decisions about where land is classified as B2 and B8 is and is not suitable for residential development – homes in unsuitable locations will clearly be much harder to sell'.[11] However, 'given that some changes of use may take place as a result of these proposals which prove not to be successful in market terms, we think it is important to allow land to revert to its original B use class as long as it does so within five years of having changed as a result of this policy'.[12]

The Government further stated that any significant local planning impacts (such as impacts on amenity, housing mix, transport and noise) could be mitigated by local authorities issuing Art 4 directions[13] (the effect of which would withdraw permitted development rights for specific types of development or in certain areas where local authorities consider that the permitted development rights would be inappropriate), or by the Government attaching standard conditions to the permitted development rights to mitigate the impacts. Thresholds could also be imposed, so that buildings above a certain threshold would not benefit from the permitted development rights. The Government also proposed that listed buildings and scheduled monuments, safety hazard zones, development where an environmental impact assessment is required and development on land affected by contamination should be excluded from the permitted development rights. The Government would review the proposals after three years.

In June 2011, the Government published an 'issues paper' seeking views and evidence from interested parties on whether and in what way it would be beneficial to amend the way in which changes of use are currently handled within the planning system with the aim of identifying the possible improvements that could be made to further extend the deregulation benefits of the Town and Country Planning (Use Classes) Order 1987 ('Use Classes Order').[14] The issues paper identified the Use Classes Order and the General Permitted Development Order as the two tools available to reduce both time and cost burdens on businesses created by the requirement for planning permission for changes of use of land and buildings. It posed a series of questions, including the following:

(a) Should a material change of use continue to be considered as development requiring planning permission? If not, what alternative approach might be used?
(b) Are the current classes of use in the Use Classes Order still appropriate?
(c) Does the current operation of the Use Classes Order (allowing changes between uses in the same use class without planning permission) go

---

10 DCLG (April 2011) *Relaxation of Planning Rules from Change of Use from Commercial to Residential,* page 9 (available at http://communities.gov.uk/publications/planningandbuilding/relaxationchangeconsultation [accessed March 2012]).
11 DCLG (April 2011) *Relaxation of Planning Rules from Change of Use from Commercial to Residential,* page 10 (available at http://communities.gov.uk/publications/planningandbuilding/relaxationchangeconsultation [accessed March 2012]).
12 DCLG (April 2011) *Relaxation of planning rules from change of use from commercial to residential,* page 10 (available at http://communities.gov.uk/publications/planningandbuilding/relaxationchangeconsultation [accessed March 2012]).
13 Directions under the Town and Country Planning (General Permitted Development) Order 1995 (SI 1995/418), Art 4.
14 DCLG (25 June 2011) *How Change of Use is Handled in the Planning System – Tell Us what You Think: Issues Paper* (available at http://www.communities.gov.uk/publications/planningandbuilding/changeuseissues [accessed March 2012]).

*Other legislative and administrative changes*

      far enough to remove inappropriate barriers to growth and allow for potential changes of use that boost the economy?
- (d) How should ancillary uses be treated within the Use Classes Order?
- (e) Should the change of use of a building be allowed on a temporary basis without the need for planning permission?

No further details on the outcome of either of the proposals relating to the General Permitted Development Order or the Use Classes Order have yet been published.

A minor change is proposed to the General Permitted Development Order as part of the Government's response[15] to the Portas review: the space over a shop could be converted into two flats without the need for planning permission rather than the current limit of one.

## THE PLANNING GUARANTEE AND INFORMATION REQUIREMENTS

*Plan for Growth* stated that one of the key measures to help make the UK one of the best places in Europe in which to do business would be an increase in the proportion of planning applications approved and dealt with on time.[16] The Government introduced the concept of the 'planning guarantee' so that 'planning applications will not have to spend more than 12 months in total with decision-making bodies, where a timely appeal is made'.[17]

Further to the announcements in the *Plan for Growth* in July 2011, the Government's Chief Planner, Steve Quartermain wrote to Chief Planning Officers of LPAs in England to draw their attention to a DCLG statement on the planning guarantee.[18] This explained that although most applications are determined within the statutory time limits, a small minority of applications, 3,200 applications in the financial year 2010/11, took over 52 weeks.[19] It was announced that, although both the introduction of the planning guarantee and measures to reduce the amount of information required to accompany planning applications would be subject to full consultation in the Autumn of 2011, ahead of those consultations the Government wished to provide an explanation of how the planning guarantee would operate to enable LPAs and affected parties to consider the implications. The statement explained that the planning guarantee would:

> 'establish clear time limits within which an application should be dealt with by the determining bodies (both the local planning authority and, where cases go to appeal, the Planning Inspectorate). Councils and the

---

15  DCLG (30 March 2012) *High Streets at the Heart of our Communities: The Government's Response to the Mary Portas Review*.

16  HM Treasury (March 2011) *The Plan for Growth*, page 6 (available at http://www.hm-treasury.gov.uk/ukecon_growth_index.htm [accessed March 2012]).

17  HM Treasury (March 2011) *The Plan for Growth*, page 46 (available at http://www.hm-treasury.gov.uk/ukecon_growth_index.htm [accessed March 2012]).

18  DCLG (29 July 2011) *Letter to Chief Planning Officers: Planning Guarantee and Information Requirements* (available at http://www.communities.gov.uk/publications/planningandbuilding/letterplanningguarantee [accessed March 2012]).

19  DCLG (2011) *The Planning Guarantee and Information Requirements* (available at http://www.communities.gov.uk/planningandbuilding/planningsystem/planningpolicy/planningguarantee/ [accessed March 2012]).

Planning Inspectorate will both need to make timely decisions to ensure that the Guarantee is delivered. The Planning Inspectorate already has a service standard of completing 80 per cent of cases within 26 weeks, so one approach to the Guarantee would be for a similar maximum period for the time that cases spend with local planning authorities. This would not alter the statutory requirements for local authorities to determine planning applications within 8 or 13 weeks, or the right for applicants to appeal if cases are not determined within those timescales, but would establish some absolute limits so that a one year Guarantee could be met.'

The clock would start once a valid application was received by an LPA and would stop once a decision notice was issued. If that decision notice were to be appealed, the clock would start again once the Planning Inspectorate validated the appeal, and stop once again once the appeal was determined. The statement set out that 'applications handled via a planning performance agreement could also be excluded, as such agreements already offer more certainty for the applicant about the timescale for determining their application'. Performance reports will be published regularly, measuring LPAs and the Planning Inspectorate against the planning guarantee, with the expectation that public availability of such reports will 'act to drive up standards'.

The DCLG's statement further set out that 'applicants frequently complain that they are asked to produce information that is of only marginal relevance, and may be very expensive to produce'. While it recognised that decision makers needed to have all appropriate information available to take decisions on planning applications, it wished to 'revisit' its policy and guidance on information submitted alongside planning applications to 'focus on what is really necessary and cut out what isn't'.

To date, no consultations document has been issued in relation to the planning guarantee or the proposal to review policy and guidance on information requirements.

## THE CHANCELLOR'S AUTUMN STATEMENT 2011, THE PENFOLD REVIEW IMPLEMENTATION REPORT AND THE HOUSING STRATEGY FOR ENGLAND

### Autumn Statement 2011

The Chancellor's Autumn Statement, published in November 2011,[20] contained a series of further announcements in relation to planning reforms that the Government committed to implement in addition to the Localism Act and the National Planning Policy Framework. The announcements included the following:

'**1.98** The Government is also reforming the planning and consenting regime, which can significantly delay infrastructure projects and add to their delivery cost. This has been cited as a key reason for UK infrastructure being more expensive to build than in other European countries. In response to the Penfold Review, the Government will:

---

20 HM Treasury (November 2011) *Chancellor's Autumn Statement* (available at http://www.hm-treasury.gov.uk/as2011_documents.htm [accessed March 2012]).

*Other legislative and administrative changes*

- ensure the key consenting and advisory agencies have a remit to promote sustainable development as soon as the National Planning Policy Framework is finalised. This will ensure that these bodies consider the impact of their decisions on sustainable economic growth and swiftly approve consents when it is appropriate to do so; and
- introduce a 13-week maximum timescale for the majority of non-planning consents, to speed up the consenting process and give certainty to developers. This will take immediate effect for government agencies.

**1.99** In addition, the Government will:
- ensure that there is a more effective mechanism for applicants to obtain an award of costs, if there is an appeal against refusal of a planning permission where a statutory consultee has acted unreasonably, through measures to be implemented in summer 2012. The Government will also improve the performance of the key statutory consultees in responding swiftly to applications. This will include key statutory bodies bringing forward an improvement plan by spring 2012;
- build more flexibility into the new major infrastructure planning process, particularly in the pre-application phase, by summer 2012, as part of a light touch review of the process responding to feedback from users of the regime; and
- ensure that compliance with the Habitats and Wild Birds Directives does not lead to unnecessary costs and delays to development, while continuing to support the Directives' objectives.[21] The Government is reviewing the Directives as currently implemented in England by Budget 2012 and is committed to tackling blockages for developments where compliance is particularly complex or has large impacts. In addition, the Government has announced progress on specific projects where compliance has already proved problematic, including Falmouth Harbour.

**1.100** These measures will complement the Government's wider reforms of the planning system. The Government has already made substantial progress through the Localism Act 2011 and the publication of the draft National Planning Policy Framework, which sets out a presumption in favour of sustainable development. Building on these reforms, the Government will:
- review planning appeals procedures, seeking to make the process faster and more transparent, improve consistency and increase certainty of decision timescales. Proposals will be brought forward for implementation in summer 2012;
- consult on a proposal to allow the reconsideration of those planning obligations agreed prior to April 2010 where development is stalled; and
- consult on proposals to allow existing agricultural buildings to be used for other business purposes such as offices, leisure and retail space, to make it easier for rural businesses to find the premises they need to expand.'

---

21 Defra has announced that it will publish recommendations in this regard by Budget 2012. More information is available at http://www.defra.gov.uk/rural/protected/habitats-wildbirds-review/.

## Implementation Report of Penfold Review

The Penfold Review was carried out in 2009 and 2010 by Adrian Penfold, Head of Planning and Environment at the British Land Company plc, who was appointed by BIS to review the legislative framework for non-planning consents. These are defined as consents which must be granted alongside, but separate to, planning consents in order for a development to take place (eg highways, environmental and heritage consents). Such consents are often blamed for holding up, or discouraging, development as the processes involved in applying for and receiving them are often highly complex, lengthy and costly. The main aim of the Report was 'to identify opportunities to deregulate, as a means of supporting business investment in development'.[22]

The final report, published in July 2010, identifies frequently required non-planning consents and assesses their impact on development in order to increase the efficiency of the system and attempt to reduce any barriers to development. The report is split into different sections which include identifying the problems presented by non-planning consents, challenging current working practices, simplifying the process for receiving consents for development and improving the interaction between planning and non-planning consents.

Alongside the Chancellor's 2011 Autumn Statement, BIS published a report on the implementation of the Penfold Review.[23] The Penfold Review involved an assessment of the efficiency of the regime of non-planning development consents (such as highways, environmental and heritage consents) which are often viewed as unnecessarily increasing the uncertainty, delay and cost of development projects. The Penfold Review made 12 recommendations to the Government on how it could simplify and streamline the non-planning consent regime. In the November 2011 Implementation Report, the Government stated that it wishes to support the Autumn Statement's growth agenda, by ensuring that the non-planning regimes operate in the most flexible and simplified way possible, while delivering the objectives they are designed for. In this regard, it contained commitments that the Government will legislate so that:

(a) the extent of a listed building's special interest is legally defined in its list entry. This will mean that only those parts of a building that contribute to its special interest are protected by regulation, removing the requirement to apply for a consent for works that impact other parts of the building;

(b) developers can seek a five-year certificate of immunity from listing or scheduling at any time (currently, certificates can only be obtained in relation to listing and after a planning application has been submitted);

(c) owners of listed buildings can enter into statutory management agreements with local authorities to enable works set out in that agreement to be undertaken without the need for separate listed building consent. This would simplify redevelopment works to a group of listed buildings or works to frequently changing buildings;

---

22 Adrian Penfold (July 2010) *Penfold Review of Non-Planning Consents*, page i (available at http://www.bis.gov.uk/penfold [accessed March 2012]).
23 Adrian Penfold (July 2010) *Penfold Review of Non-Planning Consents*, page i (available at http://www.bis.gov.uk/penfold [accessed March 2012]).

*Other legislative and administrative changes*

(d) conservation area consents are no longer required when demolishing unlisted buildings. However, planning permission will be required and demolishing an unlisted building in a conservation area without planning permission will be an offence.

In relation to highway consents, the Government stated that it will consult on options to improve the operation of stopping up orders and the interaction between highways consents and the planning system where development is proposed. It will also pilot a scheme of prior approval for Natural England's species licences, to give developers the option of applying for a species licence prior to planning permission to speed up the subsequent process. It will also consult on options for reducing the duplication between rights of way consents and the planning system as part of a wider consultation on rights of way reforms.

In addition, the Implementation Report states that the Government intends to reform the remits of the key consenting and advisory bodies (the Environment Agency, Natural England, English Heritage, the Highways Agency and the Health and Safety Executive) to include the promotion of sustainable development and that the Government expects that, as a consequence, these bodies will consider the impact of their decisions on sustainable economic growth and the viability of economically significant projects and will swiftly approve consents when it is appropriate to do so.

## Housing Strategy for England

Also in November 2011, the Government published its Housing Strategy for England.[24] The Strategy sets out a number of initiatives aimed to encourage the housing market, including:

(a) Supporting a housebuilder indemnity fund led by the Home Builders Federation and the Council of Mortgage Lenders which will back a scheme which aims to provide up to 95 per cent loan to value mortgages on new build properties. Housebuilders will deposit 3.5 per cent of the value of each new home into the indemnity fund and the Government will provide an additional guarantee as support for the loan. The Government has made initial provisions for the scheme to support the sale of 100,000 new homes.
(b) A proposal to consult on an initiative allowing developers of stalled developments to require local authorities to reconsider s 106 Agreements agreed before April 2010. The Government will ensure that any appeals resulting from this process are dealt with promptly.
(c) The launch of a £400 million Get Britain Building Investment Fund which will provide financial support to small and medium sized construction firms in an effort to encourage the development of stalled sites. A prospectus, providing details of the fund and inviting bids, will be published before the end of 2011.
(d) An aim to release land with the capacity to build up to 100,000 new homes from public sector land banks. The Strategy states that the Government is committed to accelerating the release of this land for

---

24 HM Government (November 2011) *Laying the Foundations: A Housing Strategy for England* (available at http://www.communities.gov.uk/publications/housing/housingstrategy2011 [accessed March 2012]).

new development, including through 'build now, pay later' schemes. Tony Pidgley, chairman of the Berkeley Group, will lead a small advisory group that will provide practical advice on the release of key surplus public sector sites which face infrastructure, site mitigation and planning challenges preventing their development. Further, data on almost all Government land and holdings will be published in order to allow communities and developers to identify land with development potential.
(e) Local authorities will be encouraged to work with public sector landowners to make arrangements for planning permission for certain public sector sites before they are put up for public auction. The proceeds of any subsequent sale will then be divided between the local authority and the landowner.
(f) In order to provide new homes and ensure the long term stability of the housing market, the Government plans to encourage locally planned large scale development. In order to encourage such large scale schemes, the Government will run a nationwide competition, the details of which will be published separately in 2012.

## AMENDMENTS TO THE LOCAL PLAN-MAKING PROCESS

The Town and Country Planning (Local Planning) (England) Regulations 2012 (SI 2012/767) ('the Local Planning Regulations') came into force on 6 April 2012.

The Local Planning Regulations, Pt 2 sets out a definition of the bodies to which the new 'duty to co-operate' on planning issues will apply:

(a) the Environment Agency;
(b) the Historic Buildings and Monuments Commission for England;
(c) Natural England;
(d) the Mayor of London;
(e) the Civil Aviation Authority;
(f) the Homes and Communities Agency;
(g) Primary Care Trusts;
(h) Office of Rail Regulation;
(i) Transport for London;
(j) integrated transport authorities;
(k) highway authorities; and
(l) the Marine Management Organisation.

The Local Planning Regulations, reg 5 contains a new definition of development plan documents which states that the following are to be prepared as local development documents:

'any document prepared by a local planning authority individually or in cooperation with one or more other local planning authorities, which contains statements regarding one or more of the following:
(i) the development and use of land which the local planning authority wish to encourage during any specified period;
(ii) the allocation of sites for a particular development or use;
(iii) any environmental, social and economic objectives which are relevant to the attainment of the development and use of land mentioned in paragraph (i); and

*Other legislative and administrative changes*

>   (iv) development management and site allocation policies, which are intended to guide the determination of applications for planning permission.'

Documents that are to be prepared as local development documents are:

>   '(a) any document which:
>   >   (i) relates only to part of the area of the local planning authority;
>   >   (ii) identifies that area as an area of significant change or special conservation; and
>   >   (iii) contains the local planning authority's policies in relation to the area; and
>   (b) any other document which includes a site allocation policy.'

The Local Planning Regulations, reg 6 specifies that any document that falls within these descriptions will comprise a local plan, save for documents only containing statements as to environmental, social or economic objectives. Part 6 sets out the requirements that an LPA must meet when preparing such a plan.

Regulation 18(2) sets out the bodies which the LPA must notify, and invite to make representations, during the preparation of a local plan. These bodies include:

>   '(a) such of the specific consultation bodies as the local planning authority considers may have an interest in the subject of the proposed local plan;
>   (b) such of the general consultation bodies as the local planning authority considers appropriate; and
>   (c) such residents or other persons carrying out business in the local planning authority's area from which the local planning authority considers it appropriate to invite representations.'

When submitting the draft local plan to the Secretary of State, the local planning authority must submit the following documents as set out in reg 22(1):

>   '(a) the sustainability appraisal report;
>   (b) a submissions policies map if the adoption of the local plan would result in changes to the adopted policies map;
>   (c) a statement setting out –
>   >   (i) which bodies and persons the local planning authority invited to make representation under Regulation 18;
>   >   (ii) how these bodies and persons were invited to make representations under Regulation 18;
>   >   (iii) how any representations made pursuant to Regulation 18 have been taken into account;
>   >   (iv) if representations were made pursuant to Regulation 20, the number of representations made and a summary of the main issues raised in those representations; and
>   >   (v) if no such representations were made in Regulation 20, that no such representations were made;
>   (d) copies of any representations made in accordance of Regulation 20; and
>   (e) any supporting documents as in the opinion of the local planning authority are relevant to the preparation of the local plan.'

The regulations also specify the processes that must be followed during the independent examination of the local plan, and for the adoption, withdrawal or revocation of any local plan.

Section 113 of the Act removes the requirement imposed on LPAs by the Planning and Compulsory Purchase Act 2004, s 35 to prepare monitoring reports on the implementation of local development schemes and the achievement of their local plan policies. However, it still requires LPAs to prepare monitoring reports as prescribed by regulations. The Local Planning Regulations, Pt 8 sets out what needs to be included in such monitoring reports including details of CIL receipts, the number of neighbourhood plans that have been adopted, and action taken under the duty to cooperate. Part 9 also requires that such monitoring information is to be made available online and in council offices as soon as it becomes available, rather than in annual reports.

## CHANGES TO THE GENERAL DEVELOPMENT PROCEDURE ORDER 1995

In October 2010, the Town and Country Planning (Development Management Procedure) (England) Order 2010 (SI 2010/2184) (the 'DMPO') came into force, which consolidated all amendments made to the Town and Country Planning (General Development Procedure) Order 1995 (SI 1995/419) up to 6 April 2010 (the 'GDPO'). The DMPO also restructured the provisions of the GDPO to more accurately reflect the actual stages that applicants go through when submitting planning applications.[25] The DMPO introduced a change to allow applicants with partially implemented outline planning permissions to apply for a replacement planning permission with a new time limit where the development permitted was clearly intended at the time of the initial permission to be implemented in phases, and any one of those phases has commenced. The DCLG, in a letter to Chief Planning Officers published in September 2010 which attached a question and answer document,[26] stated that this change was made to respond to concerns raised by applicants that amendments to the GDPO brought forward in 2009 did not apply to outline planning permissions that were being implemented in phases and where at least one phase had already commenced. The explanatory memorandum to the DMPO further explains that the changes introduced in 2009 to the GDPO permitted the time limits for implementation of existing planning permissions to be extended, through the grant of a replacement planning permission prior to expiry of the original permission. The replacement planning permission would be identical to the original planning permission, save for allowing for a longer period of implementation. For such new applications, no design and access statement had to be submitted, and the requirements for consultation were also modified. However, the amended procedure did not apply to planning permissions that had to be implemented in phases where one or more phases had already commenced. As such, the DMPO corrected this to ensure that replacement planning permissions can also

---

25 DCLG (9 September 2010) Questions and answer document attached to the *Letter to Chief Planning Officers: The Town and Country Planning (Development Management Procedure) Order 1995* (available at http://www.communities.gov.uk/publications/planningandbuilding/letterdevelopmentmanagement [accessed March 2012]).

26 DCLG (9 September 2010) *Letter to Chief Planning Officers: The Town and Country Planning (Development Management Procedure) Order 1995* (available at http://www.communities.gov.uk/publications/planningandbuilding/letterdevelopmentmanagement [accessed March 2012]).

*Other legislative and administrative changes*

be applied for and granted where the original planning permission requires phasing and at least one phase has been commenced.

## NATURE IMPROVEMENT AREAS

On 7 June 2011 the Government published the Natural Environment White Paper *The Natural Choice: Securing the Value of Nature*. This White Paper outlined the Government's vision for the natural environment over the next 50 years and contained proposals to protect and improve the natural environment, grow a green economy and reconnect people and nature. The natural environment is defined broadly to cover living things in all their diversity: wildlife, rivers and streams, lakes and seas, urban green space and open countryside, forests and farmed land.

Nature Improvement Areas ('NIAs') were one of the proposals contained within the White Paper. These are areas where the opportunities and benefits for the whole ecological network justify focused efforts on a grand scale. In February 2012, Caroline Spelman, the Secretary of State for Environment, Food and Rural Affairs, announced the introduction of 12 NIAs in England. The NIAs were chosen through a Department for Environment, Food and Rural Affairs competition from a total of 76 bids and propose a wide variety of different wildlife and nature projects. The newly announced NIAs are:

- Birmingham and Black Country Living Landscape;
- Dark Peak (in the Peak District);
- Dearne Valley Green Heart;
- Greater Thames Marshes;
- Humberhead Levels;
- Marlborough Downs;
- Meres and Mosses of the Marches (in Cheshire);
- Morecambe Bay Limestone and Wetlands;
- Nene Valley;
- Northern Devon;
- South Downs Way Ahead; and
- Wild Purbeck.

The NIAs will each receive a portion of £7.5 million in order to create and restore habitats and to encourage local people to become involved in the nature of these areas. They will also be identified in local plans.

## Chapter 13

# Local Enterprise Partnerships, enterprise zones

## INTRODUCTION

In the June 2010 Budget it was announced that:

> 'The Government will enable locally-elected leaders, working with business, to lead local economic development. As part of this change, Regional Development Agencies will be abolished through the Public Bodies Bill. A White Paper later in the summer will set out details of these proposals. As part of this, the Government will ... support the creation of strong local enterprise partnerships, particularly those based around England's major cities and other natural economic areas, to enable improved coordination of public and private investment in transport, housing, skills, regeneration and other areas of economic development;'[1]

The eight Regional Development Agencies ('RDAs') outside the Greater London area are abolished by way of the Public Bodies Act 2011. The London Development Agency's abolition will come about on the day that s 191 of the Localism Act comes into force.

On 29 June 2010, the Secretary of State for Business, Innovation and Skills and the Secretary of State for Communities and Local Government jointly wrote to local authorities and local business leaders inviting proposals for LEPs[2] by 6 September 2010. The letter set out their envisaged role, governance structure and size of LEPs as follows:

> **'Role**
>
> We anticipate that local enterprise partnerships will wish to provide the strategic leadership in their areas to set out local economic priorities. A clear vision is vital if local economic renewal is to be achieved. The Coalition Government is determined to rebalance the economy towards the private sector. We regard local enterprise partnerships as being central to this vision.
>
> Partnerships will therefore want to create the right environment for business and growth in their areas, by tackling issues such as planning and housing, local transport and infrastructure priorities, employment and enterprise and the transition to the low carbon economy. Supporting small business start-ups will therefore be important. They will want to work closely with universities and further education colleges, in view of their importance to local economies, and with other relevant stakeholders. In some areas,

---

1　HM Government (June 2010) *Budget 2010* (available at http://www.direct.gov.uk/prod_consum_dg/groups/dg_digitalassets/@dg/@en/documents/digitalasset/dg_188581.pdf [accessed December 2011]).
2　Secretary of State for Business, Innovation and Skills and the Secretary of State for Communities and Local Government (6 September 2010) *Letter re Proposals for Local Enterprise Partnerships* (available at http://www.communities.gov.uk/documents/localgovernment/pdf/1626854.pdf [accessed November 2011]).

tourism will also be an important economic driver. Further details will be set out in the forthcoming White Paper.

**Governance**

To be effective partnerships, it is vital that business and civic leaders work together. We believe this would normally mean an equal representation on the boards of these partnerships and that a prominent business leader should chair the board. We would, however, be willing to consider variants from this, such as where there is an elected mayor responsible for the area, if that is the clear wish of business and council leaders in the partnership area. The governance structures will need to be sufficiently robust and clear to ensure proper accountability for delivery by partnerships.

**Size**

We have been concerned that some local and regional boundaries do not reflect functional economic areas. We wish to enable partnerships to better reflect the natural economic geography of the areas they serve and hence to cover real functional economic and travel to work areas.

To be sufficiently strategic, we would expect that partnerships would include groups of upper tier authorities. If it is clearly the wish of business and civic leaders to establish a local enterprise partnership for a functional economic area that matches existing regional boundaries, we will not object. We will welcome proposals that reflect the needs of every part of England, not least areas that are economically more vulnerable. Government is keen to work closely with and through capable local enterprise partnerships which meet these criteria.'

On 7 September 2010, details were published of 56 proposals[3] and, on 28 October 2010, 24 bids were announced as successful.[4] A further 15 LEPs have been announced since that date.

The LEPs that have been announced so far are:[5]

- Black Country;
- Buckinghamshire Thames Valley;
- Cheshire and Warrington;
- Coast to Capital;
- Cornwall and Isles of Scilly;
- Coventry and Warwickshire;
- Cumbria;
- Dorset;
- Enterprise M3 (North Hampshire/West Surrey);
- Gloucestershire;
- Greater Birmingham and Solihull;
- Greater Cambridgeshire and Greater Peterborough;
- Greater Manchester;

---

3   DCLG (7 September 2010) *Proposals re Local Enterprise Partnerships* (available at http://www.communities.gov.uk/news/corporate/1708630 [accessed November 2011]).
4   Department for Business, Innovation and Skills (28 October 2010) *Report: New Plan for Local Growth* (available at http://bis.gov.uk/news/topstories/2010/Oct/local-growth [accessed November 2011]).
5   Department for Business, Innovation and Skills (available at http://www.bis.gov.uk/policies/economic-development/leps [accessed October 2011]).

- Heart of the South West;
- Hertfordshire;
- Humber;
- Lancashire;
- Leeds City Region;
- Leicester and Leicestershire;
- Lincolnshire;
- Liverpool City Region;
- London;
- The Marches – Shropshire and Herefordshire;
- New Anglia;
- Northamptonshire;
- North Eastern;
- Nottingham, Nottinghamshire, Derby, Derbyshire;
- Oxfordshire;
- Sheffield City Region;
- Solent;
- South East;
- South East Midlands;
- Stoke and Staffordshire;
- Swindon and Wiltshire;
- Tees Valley;
- Thames Valley Berkshire;
- West of England;
- Worcestershire; and
- York and North Yorkshire.

The *Local Growth* White Paper[6] published on 28 October 2010 stated that LEPs 'will provide the clear vision and strategic leadership to drive sustainable private sector-led growth and job creation in their area. [The Government will] particularly encourage partnerships working in respect to transport, housing and planning as part of an integrated approach to growth and infrastructure delivery'. It envisaged that LEPs 'could take on a diverse range of roles, such as:

- working with Government to set out key investment priorities, including transport infrastructure and supporting or coordinating project delivery;
- coordinating proposals or bidding directly for the Regional Growth Fund;
- supporting high growth businesses, for example through involvement in bringing together and supporting consortia to run new growth hubs […];
- making representation on the development of national planning policy and ensuring business is involved in the development and consideration of strategic planning applications;
- lead changes in how businesses are regulated locally;
- strategic housing delivery, including pooling and aligning funding streams to support this;

---

6 HM Government (28 October 2010) *Local Growth: Realising Every Place's Potential* (available at http://www.bis.gov.uk/assets/biscore/economic-development/docs/l/cm7961-local-growth-white-paper.pdf [accessed November 2011]).

- working with local employers, Jobcentre Plus and learning providers to help local workless people into jobs;
- coordinating approaches to leveraging funding from the private sector;
- exploring opportunities for developing financial and non-financial incentives on renewable energy projects and Green Deal; and
- becoming involved in delivery of other national priorities such as digital infrastructure.'

A number of the RDAs' former functions will now be dealt with on a national level. These include the responsibility for access to finance, such as venture capital funds, and policies where economies of scale exist on a national level or where consistency on national delivery is important. A number of the RDAs' roles are also being scrapped completely.

The new LEPs have been chosen to represent economic areas rather than geographical regions. There may be a number of different LEPs in a certain area and in these circumstances then there is no reason why a local authority should not be able to participate in several LEPs.

The board of each LEP should be made up of an equal number of representatives from local government and from business. The Government recommends that a prominent local business leader should be the chairperson. However this is simply a guide and if, for example, the relevant area has an elected mayor then it may be appropriate for the mayor to take on the responsibility as the chair if they have the full support from the board.[7]

The structure of LEPs will not be defined in legislation.

> 'Governance structures will need to be sufficiently robust and clear to ensure proper accountability for delivery. Partnerships will differ across the country in both form and functions in order to best meet local circumstances and opportunities. A partnership may need legal personality or a specified accountable body in some circumstances, such as if it wished to own assets or contract to deliver certain functions. The constitution and legal status of each partnership will be a matter for the partners, informed by the activities that they wish to pursue.'[8]

## FUNDING

LEPs will be expected to fund their day-to-day running costs and are encouraged to 'consider how they can obtain the best value for public money by leveraging in private sector investment'. They have a number of potential Government funding sources available to them.

## Regional Growth Fund

The Government has established a regional growth fund that will provide a total of £1.4 billion between 2011 and 2014 to projects that attract private sector

---

7  Letter from Vince Cable and Eric Pickles to Local Authority Leaders and Business Leaders and Local Authority Chief Executive Offices (29 June 2010).
8  HM Government (28 October 2010) *Local Growth: Realising Every Place's Potential* (available at http://www.bis.gov.uk/assets/biscore/economic-development/docs/l/cm7961-local-growth-white-paper.pdf [accessed November 2011]).

investment creating economic growth and sustainable employment.[9] This fund is particularly aimed at LEPs in regions that are 'heavily dependent on public sector support'.[10] LEPs will have to compete with other local bodies for the funding. For example, in round two of bidding, successful bids were awarded to, amongst others, the University of Leicester, Derby City, Visit England and the Portsmouth Naval Base Property Trust as well as private businesses and LEPs.[11]

The first round of bidding for Regional Growth Fund monies ended on 21 January 2011 with £450 million of funds allocated to 50 successful bids. Round 2 of bidding ended on 1 July 2011 with £950 million of funds allocated to 119 successful bids.[12] The Government expects that this funding will leverage over £7.5 million of private sector investment, helping create 330,000 jobs.[13] Round 3 of bidding has now opened with a closing date of 13 June 2012 for all bids.

## LEP Capacity Fund[14]

This fund is set aside specifically for LEPs. However, it is relatively small with only £4 million to be allocated within the next four years. Any LEP will be able to bid for a share of this money but they must be able to prove that they can match the amount bid for with private sector investment. This money is not to be used to fund a LEP's running costs.

The first allocation of £1 million closed on 31 March 2011. A further allocation was launched in Autumn 2011, the remaining with £3 million available. The first round called for bids that:

- address a gap in the intelligence available to LEPs on business needs and barriers to growth;
- facilitate business engagement and interaction with the LEP; or
- boost board capacity to prioritise actions which will support business-led growth and jobs within the LEP area. Bids were not considered for secretariat support.[15]

---

9   Department for Business, Innovation and Skills *Frequently Asked Questions* (available at http://www.bis.gov.uk/policies/economic-development/regional-growth-fund/faq [accessed October 2011]).
10  Department for Business, Innovation and Skills *Additional Information* (available at http://www.bis.gov.uk/policies/economic-development/regional-growth-fund/additional-information [accessed October 2011]).
11  Department for Business, Innovation and Skills *Additional Information* (available at http://www.bis.gov.uk/policies/economic-development/regional-growth-fund/additional-information [accessed October 2011]).
12  Department for Business, Innovation and Skills *Successful Second Round Bids* (available at http://www.bis.gov.uk/policies/economic-development/regional-growth-fund/successful-2nd-round-bids [accessed November 2011]).
13  Department for Business, Innovation and Skills *Regional Growth Fund* (available at http://www.bis.gov.uk/RGF [accessed March 2012]).
14  Department for Business, Innovation and Skills *Capacity Fund* (available at http://www.bis.gov.uk/policies/economic-development/leps/capacity-fund [accessed November 2011]).
15  Department for Business, Innovation and Skills (February 2011) *BIS Local Enterprise Partnership Capacity Fund Guidance Note* (available at http://www.bis.gov.uk/assets/biscore/economic-development/docs/l/11-739-local-enterprise-partnership-capacity-fund-guidance.pdf [accessed November 2011]).

*Local Enterprise Partnerships, enterprise zones*

The first round was heavily oversubscribed with the amount requested amounting to £2,307,522 from 33 LEPs.[16] These bids were assessed by BIS with advice from a panel of external stakeholders. A methodology was established for allocating the money which involved providing a score from one to three for each project, separating out projects if several were included in one bid, for quality and value for money. No LEP received more than £48,000.

## LEP Start-up Fund[17]

£5 million was made available in May 2011 as a one-off pot to help LEPs to put in place their core operating capacities in order to enable them to become self-sustaining. Any LEP that had a board in place by this date was eligible to bid for a part of the fund, although it had to meet a number of criteria to prove that it was capable of being operational and sustainable. The amount of bids received totalled around £5.5 million with only two established LEPs choosing not to bid.[18] All bids had to be received by 30 June 2011.

Examples of the type of infrastructure that the bids could be put towards included:

- office rental;
- equipment;
- staff training; and
- IT support.[19]

The LEP start-up fund could not be used to fund activities that were already ongoing, with the idea behind this fund being that the money should be used to help the LEP get on its feet and begin operating.

## ENTERPRISE ZONES

Enterprise zones are clearly not a new concept. The legislative framework for them is contained within the Local Government, Planning and Land Act 1980, Sch 32. Under this Act, District Councils, London Borough Councils and Urban Development Corporations may be invited by the Secretary of State to prepare a scheme for an enterprise zone. Such an invitation would specify the area for which the scheme may be prepared and may contain directions for the drawing up of the scheme. Once the scheme is prepared in accordance with this schedule the relevant body may adopt it. The scheme must then be sent to the Secretary of State and published so that it may be inspected by the public. Any person may question the validity of the scheme. Once the consultation period has passed, the Secretary of State may designate the area as an enterprise zone.

On 5 March 2011, George Osborne announced in a speech to the Conservative Spring conference that the Budget would introduce enterprise zones to 'parts

---

16 Department for Business, Innovation and Skills *Capacity Fund* (available at http://www.bis.gov.uk/policies/economic-development/leps/capacity-fund [accessed November 2011]).
17 Department for Business, Innovation and Skills *Start up Fund* (available at http://www.bis.gov.uk/policies/economic-development/leps/lep-start-up-fund [accessed November 2011]).
18 Department for Business, Innovation and Skills *Start up Fund* (available at http://www.bis.gov.uk/policies/economic-development/leps/lep-start-up-fund [accessed November 2011]).
19 BIS *Local Enterprise Partnership Start-up Fund Guidance Note* (February 2011) (available at http://www.bis.gov.uk/assets/biscore/economic-development/docs/l/11-907-local-enterprise-partnership-start-up-guidance.pdf [accessed November 2011]).

## Enterprise zones

of Britain that have missed out in the last ten years'.[20] Accordingly the first round of the latest generation of enterprise zones were announced in the Budget 2011,[21] chosen with a focus on city regions, and the second on 17 August 2011.[22] The table below sets out the confirmed enterprise zones and the associated LEP.

| Local Enterprise Partnership | Enterprise zone |
| --- | --- |
| *First wave* | |
| Black Country | i54 and Darlaston |
| Derby, Derbyshire, Nottingham and Nottinghamshire | Nottingham (Boots Campus) |
| Greater Birmingham and Solihull | Birmingham (Birmingham City Centre) |
| Greater Manchester | Manchester (Airport) |
| Leeds City Region | Leeds (Lower Aire Valley) |
| Liverpool City Region | Liverpool (Mersey Waters) |
| London | London (Royal Docks) |
| North Eastern | River Tyne and Nissan site |
| Sheffield City Region | Sheffield (The Modern Manufacturing and Technology Growth Area) |
| Tees Valley | Tees Valley Enterprise Zone |
| West of England | Bristol (Temple Quarter) |
| *Second wave* | |
| Cornwall and the Isles of Scilly | Newquay Aerohub |
| Greater Cambridge and Greater Peterborough | Alconbury Airfield |
| Hull and Humber | Humber Estuary Renewable Energy Super Cluster |
| Leicester and Leicestershire | MIRA Technology Park |
| Liverpool City Region | Daresbury Science Campus |
| New Anglia | Great Yarmouth and Lowestoft |
| Oxfordshire | Science Vale UK |
| Solent | Daedalus Airfield |
| South East Midlands | Northampton Waterside |
| The Marches | Rotherwas Enterprise Zone |
| South East | Sandwich and Harlow |

20 The Conservative Party (5 March 2011) *George Osborne: We're Building a Better Future for Britain* (available at http://www.conservatives.com/News/Speeches/2011/03/George_Osborne_speech_to_Spring_Forum_2011.aspx [accessed January 2012]).
21 HM Treasury (June 2011) *Budget 2011*, para 1.10 (available at http://cdn.hm-treasury.gov.uk/2011budget_complete.pdf [accessed November 2011]).
22 DCLG (17 August 2011) *The Government Announces 11 New Enterprise Zones to Accelerate Local Growth, as Part of the Plan for Growth* (available at http://www.communities.gov.uk/news/newsroom/1967595 [accessed November 2011]).

*Local Enterprise Partnerships, enterprise zones*

The Welsh Government has so far announced the creation of seven separate enterprise zones in Wales, each with a specific industry focus:

- Cardiff Central Business District – with a focus on the financial services sector;
- Ynys Mon (Anglesey) – with a focus on the energy sector;
- Deeside – with a focus on the advanced manufacturing sector;
- St Athan – with a focus on the aerospace sector;
- Ebbw Vale – with a focus on the automotive sector;[23]
- Trawsfynydd – with a focus on the energy, environment and IT sectors; and
- Haven Waterway – further details awaited.[24]

The Welsh Government has stated that its plans are still in their early stages and no final decision has been made on whether to relax planning rules in these areas. The Welsh Government is initially making £10 million available over the next five years and companies investing in the sites will receive rate relief and may benefit from tax breaks to aid expansion.

'The new generation Enterprise Zones reflect the Government's core belief that economic growth and job creation should be led by the private sector. At the heart of these new Enterprise Zones is a desire to remove barriers to private sector growth through reduced burdens for businesses, particularly in terms of lower tax levels, planning and other regulatory and administrative burdens.'[25]

The *Enterprise Zone Prospectus*[26] outlines the following proposed benefits to businesses within an enterprise zone.

## Business rates discount

Local authorities with an enterprise zone in their area will have the power to provide discounts on rates of up to 100 per cent for every business within that zone, with the Government reimbursing the local authority the cost of the discount. The level of discount is limited by EU state aid law to €200,000 over a rolling three-year period, which is the equivalent of around £55,000 per year, and each business will receive a discount over a five-year period of up to £275,000, provided that it enters the zone by April 2015.

## Retention of business rates growth by local authorities

DCLG is carrying out its Local Government Resource Review. Consultation closed on 24 October 2011[27] on proposals to allow local authorities to keep

---

23 Welsh Government (20 September 2011) *Edwina Hart Announces Welsh Enterprise Zones* (available at http://wales.gov.uk/newsroom/businessandeconomy/2011/110920enterprisezones/?lang=en [accessed November 2011]).
24 Planning Portal (1 February 2012) *Two More Welsh Enterprise Zones* (available at http://www.planningportal.gov.uk/general/news/stories/2012/feb12/020212/020212_ [accessed February 2012]).
25 DCLG (2011) *Enterprise Zone Prospectus* (available at http://www.communities.gov.uk/documents/localgovernment/pdf/1872724.pdf [accessed March 2012]).
26 DCLG (2011) *Enterprise Zone Prospectus* (available at http://www.communities.gov.uk/documents/localgovernment/pdf/1872724.pdf [accessed March 2012]).
27 DCLG (2011) *Local Government Resource Review* (available at http://www.communities.gov.uk/documents/localgovernment/pdf/1947200.pdf [accessed November 2011]).

their business rates so as to provide better incentives for authorities to promote growth. All business rates growth within the enterprise zone for a period of 25 years is to be retained by the local authority, to support the LEP's economic objectives and ensure that enterprise zone growth is reinvested locally.

## Simplified planning approach

The *Enterprise Zone Prospectus* indicates that 'Enterprise Zone status is conditional upon putting in place a genuinely simplified approach to planning which should as a minimum cover the area zoned for business rate discounts'.[28] Local Development Orders ('LDOs') are stated to be the most likely planning mechanism by which local authorities can reduce the level of planning control in the enterprise zones. LDOs allow development to be undertaken without the need for planning permission to be obtained from the local planning authority. They can apply to a specific type of development or permit any development in a designated area and may grant planning permission outright or with conditions.

Local authorities already have the power to make LDOs under the Planning and Compulsory Purchase Act 2004 (as amended by the Planning Act 2008). To date, LDOs have been used relatively infrequently. The Planning Advisory Service ('PAS') has been providing guidance and support to a number of local authorities who are piloting LDOs in anticipation of an increase of their use. An example of such a scheme is in Cornwall where Cornwall Council is using LDOs at Newquay Cornwall Airport in partnership with Cornwall Development Company to provide the airport with private airport development rights and to develop an aviation business park.

On 5 March 2012, Eric Pickles approved the first set of LDOs for the Tees Valley Enterprise Zone. Six LDOs have been approved following a public consultation in December 2011. The introduction of these LDOs will provide simplified planning rules and business rate relief across eight sites and enhanced capital allowances across four. The director of policy and strategy at Tees Valley Unlimited stated that 'The LDOs grant pre-approved planning permission in line with key enterprise zone objectives, which critically saves time and money in the development process and will help make the sites attractive for investment'.[29] The simplified planning rules permitted by these LDOs will come into force on 1 April 2012 and it is anticipated that the Tees Valley Enterprise Zone will create 1,200 jobs and support 61 businesses by 2015.

## Broadband roll-out

The Government aims to accelerate the roll-out of superfast broadband to those business located in enterprise zones that require it by investing over half a billion pounds over the next four years into a new UK wide broadband network designed to be the best superfast broadband network in Europe by 2015.

---

28  DCLG (2011) *Enterprise Zone Prospectus,* page 10 (available at http://www.communities.gov.uk/documents/localgovernment/pdf/1872724.pdf [accessed March 2012]).
29  Tees Valley Unlimited (March 2012) *Enterprise Zone Secures First,* (available at http://www.teesvalleyunlimited.gov.uk/news-repository/ez-secures-first.aspx [accessed March 2012]).

*Local Enterprise Partnerships, enterprise zones*

## Enhanced capital allowances

The Autumn Statement 2011 announced that enterprise zones in six designated areas will qualify for enhanced capital allowances. Companies in these areas will be provided with 100 per cent first year allowances for plant and machinery, giving them an upfront cash flow benefit. These designated areas are assisted areas where there is a strong focus on manufacturing. Legislation to this effect will be included in the 2012 Finance Bill and will specify that:

> 'the qualifying expenditure must be incurred between 1 April 2012 and 31 March 2017 and the area in which the plant or machinery is to be used must be an assisted area at the time when the expenditure is incurred. In addition, the plant or machinery must not be held for use in an area outside of the designated assisted area for a period of five years.'[30]

Assisted areas are areas, which under the EC Treaty, Art 87, are eligible for EU grants under EU national regional aid 'where the standard of living is abnormally low or where there is serious underemployment'.[31]

The Chancellor's 2012 Budget announced that enhanced capital allowances would be made available from 1 April 2012 'for a designated site in the London Royal Docks Enterprise Zone, which has the potential to deliver 7,500 jobs', as well as 'at designated sites in enterprise zones in Scotland, including Irvine, Nigg and Dundee, and at Deeside in North Wales, with the potential to deliver more than 9,000 jobs in total'.[32]

## Additional options

The Government will also work with LEPs in considering additional options for enterprise zones[33] including:

- Tax Increment Finance, which enables borrowing against future increases in business rate receipts to help fund the development of infrastructure; and
- UKTI support for inward investment or trade opportunities in the enterprise zone.

So what really will be the main differences between this latest wave of enterprise zones and those seen in the 1980s? Dr Paul Greenhalgh, Reader in Property Economics at the School of the Built and Natural Environment, Northumbria University has carried out a good analysis.[34]

---

30 HM Revenues & Customs (2011) *Enterprise Zones: First-Year Allowances for Designated Areas* (available at http://www.hm-treasury.gov.uk/d/capital_allowance_enterprise_zones.pdf [accessed November 2011]).
31 European Union consolidated versions of the Treaty on European Union and of the Treaty Establishing the European Community, Art 87(3)(a), (available at http://eur-lex.europa.eu/LexUriServ/LexUriServ.do?uri=OJ:C:2006:321E:0001:0331:EN:pdf [accessed January 2012]).
32 HM Treasury, *Budget 2012*, pages 42 and 43.
33 DCLG (2011) *Enterprise Zone Prospectus*, page 6 (available at http://www.communities.gov.uk/documents/localgovernment/pdf/1872724.pdf [accessed March 2012]).
34 RTPI (2011) *Opportunity Knocks – What Prospects for the 'New Breed' of Enterprise Zones?* (available at http://www.rtpi.org.uk/download/11917/Opportunity-Knocks-Full-Article-on-EZs-070411.pdf [accessed December 2011]).

# Chapter 14

# National Planning Policy Framework

## BACKGROUND

The National Planning Policy Framework ('NPPF') is at the heart of the Government's planning reforms. The Conservative Party's Green Paper *Open Source Planning*, published before the 2010 General Election stated that:

'we will publish and present to Parliament for debate a simple and consolidated national planning framework, which will set out national economic and environmental priorities, and how the planning system will deliver them;

as part of this we will issue a reduced number of simplified guidance notes, setting out minimum environmental, architectural, design, economic and social standards for sustainable development;'[1]

This commitment to a consolidated framework was repeated in the Coalition Agreement[2] and on 20 December 2010 Greg Clark MP, Minister for Decentralisation and Cities, announced a review of national planning policy. To help with that review the Government established the Practitioners Advisory Group ('PAG').[3] PAG comprised four experts chosen by the Government to give a practitioner's perspective on what the NPPF should contain. PAG developed their own draft NPPF and this was submitted to the Government on 20 May 2011. A leaked draft NPPF dated 13 June was subsequently seen by Planning Magazine on 1 July and became widely available, but the DCLG refused to comment on the authenticity of the document.

## THE DRAFT NPPF

On 25 July 2011, after much speculation, the Government published for consultation a first official draft of the NPPF, which ran to just 58 pages and attempted to encapsulate national policy under the themes of planning for prosperity, planning for people and planning for places. It also provided guidance on plan-making and development management and introduced the concept of a presumption in the planning system in favour of sustainable development, which, as we will see, proved to be one of the more controversial aspects of the consultation.

---

1   The Conservative Party (February 2010) *Open Source Planning*, para 3 (available at http://www.conservatives.com/News/News_stories/2010/02/~/media/Files/Green%20Papers/planning-green-paper.ashx [accessed December 2011]).
2   'We will publish and present to Parliament a simple and consolidated national planning framework covering all forms of development and setting out national economic, environmental and social priorities.' HM Government (11 May 2010) *The Coalition: Our Programme for Government* (available at http://www.direct.gov.uk/prod_consum_dg/groups/dg_digitalassets/@dg/@en/documents/digitalasset/dg_187876.pdf [accessed January 2012]).
3   http://www.nppfpractitionersadvisorygroup.org.

*National Planning Policy Framework*

In the Introduction to the consultation document[4] the Government explained what the NPPF was intended to be:

'The [NPPF] is a radical streamlining of existing Planning Policy Statements, Planning Policy Guidance notes and some circulars to form a single consolidated document. The Framework condenses the near 900,000 words of national planning policies (over 1,000 pages) into a user-friendly and accessible document which can be understood and used by everybody who has an interest in shaping the development of their area.

This Framework sets out the Government's key economic, social and environmental objectives and the planning policies to deliver them. These policies will provide local communities with the tools they need to energise their local economies, meet housing needs, plan for a low-carbon future and protect the environmental and cultural landscapes that they value. We have sought to free communities from unnecessarily prescriptive central government policies, empowering local councils to deliver innovative solutions that work for that local area.

The Framework will have the same legal status as current Government policy documents …

Local and neighbourhood plans and policy should be prepared to have regard to the content of national planning policy. But there will be local circumstances where it is right for that community to depart from national policy. Those circumstances would need to be justified by robust evidence.'

The public consultation closed on 17 October 2011.

## WHAT MADE THE DRAFT NPPF SO DIFFERENT?

The most radical change to national policy, which appeared in the draft NPPF, was the presumption in favour of sustainable development, set in the context of a commitment by Government to ensure that 'the planning system does everything it can to support sustainable economic growth' (draft NPPF, para 13). The draft NPPF explained that the presumption was a 'golden thread' running through plan-making and decision-taking. The Government, it said, expected the default answer to development to be 'yes', unless this would compromise key sustainable development principles set out in the remainder of the document. This meant that:

'Local Planning authorities should:
- Prepare Local Plans on the basis that objectively assessed development needs should be met, and, with sufficient flexibility to respond to rapid shifts in demand or other economic changes;
- Approve development proposals that accord with statutory plans without delay; and
- Grant permission where a plan is absent, silent, indeterminate or where relevant policies are out of date.'[5]

---

4   DCLG (July 2011) *Draft NPPF* (available at http://www.communities.gov.uk/documents/planningandbuilding/pdf/1951811.pdf [accessed November 2011]).
5   DCLG (July 2011) *Draft NPPF*, para 14 (available at http://www.communities.gov.uk/documents/planningandbuilding/pdf/1951811.pdf [accessed November 2011]).

## What made the draft NPPF so different?

The draft NPPF provided that these policies should apply unless the adverse impacts of allowing development to proceed would significantly and demonstrably outweigh the benefits, when assessed against the policies in the NPPF taken as a whole.

One struggles to think of any stronger way of laying to rest the fears that localism would become a NIMBY's charter. In effect the draft NPPF was saying that localism can enable you to take control locally but only on the understanding that you embrace the need for development. If there were any doubt about that message, the draft NPPF went on to say[6] that the presumption had implications for the way communities engaged in neighbourhood planning:

- Neighbourhood plans should support the strategic development needs set out in local plans.
- Neighbourhoods should plan positively to support local development and have the power to promote more development than envisaged in the local plan.
- Neighbourhoods should identify opportunities to use neighbourhood development orders to grant planning permission for development consistent with an adopted neighbourhood plan.

It was the presumption in favour of sustainable development – more than anything else – that caused something of a media frenzy and staunch opposition from the likes of the National Trust and CPRE during the consultation on the draft NPPF. It left the National Trust asserting that:

> 'Government's planning reforms could lead to unchecked and damaging development in the undesignated countryside on a scale not seen since the 1930s.'[7]

Their response was to orchestrate an effective campaign ('Planning4People') to try to restore a higher degree of environmental protection to national policy, playing perhaps on the expectations of so many (which had arguably been raised by the parties in Government since their time in opposition) that with the introduction of localism they would have control over what development happened in their community and where. This left an exasperated Government in the unenviable position of having to fight a media pitch battle, culminating in the publication of the 'myth-buster' document.[8] That three-page document is itself useful for showing just how the Government saw the NPPF and its planning reforms. These are some of the Government's responses:

- planning reform is 'imperative for our economic recovery' – planning is acting as 'a serious brake on growth' and is 'slow, complex, bureaucratic and unresponsive' – but this is not 'a green light for any development anywhere' and the NPPF 'retains strong protections for the environment and heritage that we cherish';
- the democratically produced local plan 'will drive decision making' without 'top down housing targets';

---

6  DCLG (July 2011) *Draft NPPF*, para 17 (available at http://www.communities.gov.uk/documents/planningandbuilding/pdf/1951811.pdf [accessed November 2011]).
7  The National Trust (19 August 2011) *Planning reforms could damage the countryside* (available at http://www.nationaltrust.org.uk/what-we-do/news/view-page/item545109/ [accessed March 2012]).
8  DCLG (8 September 2011) *National Planning Policy Framework: Myth-Buster* (available at http://www.communities.gov.uk/documents/planningandbuilding/pdf/1984490.pdf [accessed April 2012]).

- the presumption in favour of sustainable development still means that 'all proposals need to demonstrate their sustainability' in line with the NPPF;
- Green Belt, Areas of Outstanding Natural Beauty ('AONBs') and other protections remain and 'local people and their councils decide where to locate development and how they want their area to grow';
- communities are to share the benefits of growth. 'Councils that choose growth will receive extra New Homes Bonus funding' and people will have a say about how a proportion of CIL is spent in their area.

Where the draft NPPF had perhaps been lacking in conveying the myth-buster's more balanced approach was in the definition of 'sustainable development' and the lack of emphasis on environmental protections. The draft NPPF was also not clear enough in recognising its own status as national policy and therefore no more than a material consideration in plan-making as well as planning decisions, albeit one with significant weight. The myth-buster document addressed this, making it clear that the Government had not unravelled the principle of a statutory plan-led system and that therefore, in planning decisions the local development plan would remain the starting point.[9] Whilst it remained open to LPAs to incorporate the presumption into their plan and make it part of the starting point for their decisions (the draft NPPF directed that local plans had to be consistent with the presumption), they did not need to do so. Therefore, in most cases the effect of the presumption was going to be dependent on how comprehensive and up to date the local development plan policies were: when policies were up to date and comprehensive the presumption would not dictate the outcome; when out of date or incomplete, the presumption would carry significant weight and might be determinative.

Regardless of these qualifications to its proposed introduction, there was no doubt in our mind that the presumption was going to have a significant indirect effect on the planning system. For example, it was almost certain to become an important determinant of issues at the plan-making stage and part of the assessment of a plan's 'soundness'. In planning decisions, it would become a fall-back position beyond the development plan which developers and objectors alike would draw upon for pro-growth or pro-environmental reasons. Perhaps more importantly, it was likely to act as a 'cultural sign-post' – an indication of the function that the planning system should be performing.

The presumption in favour of sustainable development and the inclusion in the draft NPPF of a direction to LPAs that the default to development should be 'yes' were bound to grab all the headlines. There were, however, more subtle but also significant proposed changes to national policy and they included the following:

- A modified 'Town Centre First' policy which retained its focus on town centres as the preferred location for retail and leisure development but removed office development from its scope. This meant that proposals for offices would be judged on their individual merit (including taking account of local and national policies on the location of development that generates significant movement of people and the supply of and demand for office space in different locations) and would no longer have to meet the sequential test where located in edge of or out of centre locations.

---

9   Under the Planning and Compulsory Purchase Act 2004, s 38.

## What made the draft NPPF so different?

- Extending the time horizon for assessing impacts of unplanned, retail and leisure schemes in edge of or out of centre locations from five years up to ten years.
- Removing the national maximum parking standards for non-residential uses and requiring local authorities to develop individual non-residential car parking standards which were appropriate to their local circumstances and communities.
- Relaxation of requirements for minerals land banks.
- Removing the target for 60 per cent of housing development to take place on previously developed land, so that LPAs were able to choose the most suitable locations for development based on local circumstances.
- The introduction of a new requirement for LPAs to allocate at least an additional 20 per cent of sites for housing against their five-year housing requirement (so that in the first five years, LPAs would have to identify sites to meet at least 120 per cent of their annual housing requirement).
- Removing the national minimum site threshold of 15 units for requiring affordable housing to be delivered so that LPAs could set their own threshold at which affordable housing contributions would be sought, which could be either higher or lower depending on local circumstances and viability.
- Removing the rural exception sites policy for affordable housing to give councils more flexibility (but without allowing rural housing that is distant from local services).
- Requiring considerations of the availability and viability of all community facilities as part of the plan-making process and policies to safeguard against their unnecessary loss.
- Various changes to the Green Belt policy (subject to the retention of the test to preserve the openness and purpose of land in the Green Belt) including:
  - allowing development on previously developed land on major developed sites whether or not identified in the local plan;
  - allowing local transport infrastructure as well as park and ride schemes;
  - allowing community right to build schemes in the Green Belt if supported by the local community;
  - extending the exception which allows the alteration or replacement of dwellings to other buildings;
  - providing that Green Belt boundaries should be altered only in exceptional circumstances and their appropriateness considered when a local plan is being prepared or reviewed.
- Planning positively for the creation, protection, enhancement and management of green infrastructure networks.
- The introduction of a new designation – Local Green Spaces – which would allow communities to designate locally significant green areas in their local and neighbourhood plans and thereby protect such areas from development other than in very special circumstances.
- Confirmation that the protections for European habitat sites[10] should apply to Special Areas of Conservation (SACs), Special Protection Areas (SPAs), Ramsar Sites, potential SPAs, possible SACs, proposed

---

10 Established by Council Directive 92/43/EEC on the conservation of natural habitats and of wild fauna and flora.

Ramsar Sites and sites identified as compensatory measures for adverse effects on other sites.
- Removal of required targets for decentralised energy but continued emphasis on policy support.
- Requiring LPAs to identify suitable areas for renewable and low carbon energy sources and supporting infrastructure.
- Condensed policies on heritage protection.

Of these additional policy changes, the removal of offices from the 'Town Centre First' approach and the requirement for LPAs to allocate 120 per cent of their annual housing requirement (the equivalent of a six-year supply for a five-year period) were particularly controversial.

Amidst all the campaigning, the media coverage and government myth-busters, a much needed voice of reason on the draft NPPF appeared in the form of the Communities and Local Government Select Committee who considered the draft NPPF and called for evidence to assist it in its deliberations. The Committee held a number of hearings in August 2011 and published its report towards the end of the year.

## COMMUNITIES AND LOCAL GOVERNMENT SELECT COMMITTEE REPORT

The Communities and Local Government Select Committee (the 'Select Committee') released their report on the draft NPPF shortly after midnight on 21 December 2011.[11] The report was very comprehensive and was generally well-received. DCLG also praised the report with the Minister, Greg Clark MP, saying:

'I warmly welcome the DCLG select committee's constructive recommendations to the draft Framework consultation. I invited the Committee to make specific suggestions to the draft Framework and am grateful for the practical and measured way they have approached the exercise.

The Government will consider carefully each of the suggestions that have been made, along with all responses to the consultation.

We are determined that the National Planning Policy Framework will put power into the hands of local people, through a simpler, clearer system, which safeguards our natural and historic environment while allowing the jobs and homes to be created that our country needs.'[12]

The recommendations included the following:

- The final version of the NPPF should begin with a clear narrative providing an overview of the planning policies that have been retained, modified or superseded by the NPPF. It should also explain what the

---

11 DCLG (15 December 2011) *Communities and Local Government Select Committee Report on Draft NPPF* (available at http://www.publications.parliament.uk/pa/cm201012/cmselect/cmcomloc/1526/152602.htm [accessed in December 2011]).
12 DCLG (21 December 2011) *Government Response to Select Committee Report on Draft National Planning Policy Framework* (available at http://www.communities.gov.uk/issuesandresponses/newsroom/2056346 [accessed in December 2011]).

## Communities and Local Government Select Committee Report

relationship is between the NPPF and other national policy documents, eg National Policy Statements (para 23).

- Existing technical guidance which is not included in the NPPF and which LPAs find most useful should be saved in some form to prevent 'reinventing numerous wheels'. Any new guidance produced by third parties should have government ownership to ensure consistency of approach (para 33).
- The brevity of the document does not achieve clarity. The loss of critical wording from existing policy means the draft NPPF is often vague. Consequently, the NPPF's 'drafting must be more precise and consistent, and sufficiently detailed to enable local authorities to write their own Local Plans. The Government should carefully consider the alternative drafts, submitted by many organisations as part of DCLG's consultation, in order to produce a tighter, clearer document, and should not make a fetish of how many pages it is. Examples of such words and phrases needing tighter definitions in the NPPF include: "significant weight"; "great weight"; "substantial weight"; "considerable weight"; "significant flexibility"; "a high degree of certainty"; "sustainable economic growth"; "absent"; "silent"; "indeterminate"; "out-of-date"; "certificate of conformity", "where practical"; and "where reasonable".' (para 29).
- The NPPF should acknowledge the possibility of local variations from the NPPF but with a sound evidence base, as well as the possibility of local plan issues not explicitly referred to in the NPPF being relevant to a local planning authority's plan-making and decision-making functions (paras 40 and 47).
- The Select Committee recommend that the definition of 'affordable housing' set out in PPS 3[13] should be retained (para 41), ie the definition of affordable housing should be:

    'Affordable housing includes social rented, affordable rented and intermediate housing, provided to eligible households whose needs are not met by the market. Affordable housing should:

    Meet the needs of eligible households including availability at a cost low enough for them to afford, determined with regard to local incomes and local house prices.

    Include provision for the home to remain at an affordable price for future eligible households or, if these restrictions are lifted, for the subsidy to be recycled for alternative affordable housing provision',[14]

    rather than the following more complicated definition set out in the draft NPPF:

    'Social rented, affordable rented and intermediate housing, provided to eligible households whose needs are not met by the market. Eligibility is determined with regard to local incomes and local house

---

13   DCLG (June 2011) *National Planning Policy Statement 3: Housing* (available at http://communities.gov.uk/publications/planningandbuilding/pps3housing [accessed December 2011]).
14   DCLG (June 2011) *National Planning Policy Statement 3: Housing*, Annex B (available at http://communities.gov.uk/publications/planningandbuilding/pps3housing [accessed December 2011]).

prices. Affordable housing should include provisions to remain at an affordable price for future eligible households or for the subsidy to be recycled for alternative affordable housing provision.

Social rented housing is owned by local authorities and private registered providers, for which guideline target rents are determined through the national rent regime. It may also be owned by other persons and provided under equivalent rental arrangements to the above, as agreed with the local authority or with the Homes and Communities Agency.

Affordable rented housing is let by local authorities or private registered providers of social housing to households who are eligible for social rented housing. Affordable Rent is subject to rent controls that require a rent of no more than 80% of the local market rent (including service charges, where applicable).

Intermediate housing is homes for sale and rent provided at a cost above social rent, but below market levels subject to the criteria in the Affordable Housing definition above. These can include shared equity (shared ownership and equity loans), other low cost homes for sale and intermediate rent, but not affordable rented housing.

Homes that do not meet the above definition of affordable housing, such as "low cost market" housing, may not be considered, for planning purposes, as affordable housing.'[15]

- There should be a new, clear definition of sustainable development. This should include an 'explicit statement of the need to address and to seek to achieve all of the aspects of sustainable development'[16] rather than starting with the assumption that one aspect can be traded off against the other (eg economic vs environmental well-being). The Select Committee suggest that the definition of sustainable development should also contain 'a) the clear and identifiable use of wording from the Brundtland report as this is well known and understood; b) the restating of the five guiding principles from the 2005 sustainable development strategy'.[17]

The definition of sustainable development in the Brundtland report is perhaps the most widely used definition of what is notoriously a hard concept to define and states that:

'Sustainable development is development that meets the needs of the present without compromising the ability of future generations to meet their own needs. It contains within it two key concepts:

the concept of "needs", in particular the essential needs of the world's poor, to which overriding priority should be given; and

---

15 DCLG (July 2011) *Draft NPPF*, page 53 (available at http://www.communities.gov.uk/documents/planningandbuilding/pdf/1951811.pdf [accessed November 2011]).
16 *CLG Select Committee Report on the Draft NPPF*, para 66 (available at http://www.publications.parliament.uk/pa/cm201012/cmselect.cmcomloc/1526/152602.htm [accessed December 2011]).
17 *CLG Select Committee Report on the Draft NPPF*, para 66 (available at http://www.publications.parliament.uk/pa/cm201012/cmselect.cmcomloc/1526/152602.htm [accessed December 2011]).

## Communities and Local Government Select Committee Report

the idea of limitations imposed by the state of technology and social organization on the environment's ability to meet present and future needs.'[18]

The following are the five guiding principles from the 2005 sustainable development strategy:

- 'Living within environmental limits'.
- 'Ensuring a strong, healthy and just society'.
- 'Achieving a sustainable economy'.
- 'Promoting good governance'.
- 'Using sound science responsibly'.[19]

- A presumption in favour of sustainable development is reasonable but it needs to avoid any ambiguity which might suggest that it is in fact a presumption in favour of sustainable economic growth and it should be amended to make it clear that this is a reference to sustainable development 'consistent with the local plan'. Confusion is added by the fact that the draft NPPF uses the terms 'sustainable development' and 'sustainable economic growth' interchangeably. The Select Committee suggests that these two terms are separate and should be clearly differentiated through the document. In addition, the sentence 'decision-takers at every level should assume that the default answer to development proposals is "yes", except where this would compromise the key sustainable development principles set out in this Framework'[20] should be removed from the NPPF because it is weighted too far towards a single interest and is inconsistent with a plan-led system and the presumption in favour of sustainable development. Otherwise the phrase 'significantly and demonstrably' cause harm should be removed from the NPPF so that the presumption in favour of sustainable development applies unless 'significant' harm is caused to the objectives, principles and policies in the NPPF (see paras 75 to 86).

- Any analysis of project viability must 'presuppose requirements to provide infrastructure and other measures necessary to the development, not simply returns deemed acceptable by the developer'.[21] This wording is necessary in order to clarify the confusion that has arisen from the wording of the draft NPPF which implies that LPAs may allow unsustainable development if insisting on sustainability measures would result in the development becoming unviable for the developer. The transport section of the draft NPPF is cited as an example of language which lends itself to this interpretation and which should be tightened.

- The relationship between the NPPF, local plans and neighbourhood plans must be clearly set out and the statutory supremacy of the local

---

18 UN (1897) *Report of the World Commission on Environment and Development: Our Common Future,* Ch 2, para 1 (available at http://www.un-documents.net/wced-ocf.htm [accessed December 2011]).
19 HM Government (March 2005) *The UK Government Sustainable Development Strategy,* page 16, para 4 (available at http://www.sd-commission.org.uk/data/files/publications/SecFut_complete.pdf [accessed December 2011]).
20 DCLG (July 2011) *Draft NPPF,* para 75 (available at http://www.communities.gov.uk/documents/planningandbuilding/pdf/1951811.pdf [accessed November 2011]).
21 *CLG Select Committee Report on the Draft NPPF,* para 91 (available at http://www.publications.parliament.uk/pa/cm201012/cmselect.cmcomloc/1526/152602.htm [accessed December 2011]).

## National Planning Policy Framework

plan better reflected. Further 'the NPPF should confirm that, in all planning decisions, it is a well evidenced Local Plan that provides the operational expression of the general presumption in favour of sustainable development'.[22]

- There should be guidance on the evidence base that will be necessary to show compliance by local authorities with the new 'duty to co-operate'; the effectiveness of this duty should also be monitored. In particular there should be consistency between LPAs when collecting evidence bases for the local plan as 'without consistency, it will not be clear what benchmark the Planning Inspectorate will use for judging the "soundness" of plans, especially when neighbouring local authorities have been unable to reach agreement about the need for or location of new housing. Therefore we recommend that the guidance being produced by practitioners on assembling an evidence base for housing be officially adopted by the Government. We also recommend that the Government commission groups of practitioners to produce similar, authoritative guidance on assessing needs for other types of infrastructure.'[23]

- There should also be another way for LPAs to demonstrate that they have fulfilled their duty to cooperate rather than waiting for the Planning Inspectorate to make a determination of 'soundness'. Whatever this alternative is, it should be informed by a report from the Planning Inspectorate on the degree of cooperation in development plans and then by an annual report on the effectiveness of the Localism Act 2011, s 110 (duty to co-operate in relation to planning of sustainable development).[24]

- Transitional arrangements for the introduction of the new system should be brought forward urgently. A timetable for the transition should also be agreed with local government. The Select Committee recommends that 'in the interests of ensuring that authorities put in place Local Plans compliant with the NPPF expeditiously, a strictly limited period is allowed during which the presumption in favour of sustainable development is not applied in cases of absent, silent or out-of-date plans until councils have had a realistic chance of putting such plans in place'.[25] Further, in order for local plans to be the main source of planning policy, there must be a mechanism by which these can be kept up-to-date. This could take the form of a 'light touch' approach that will allow LPAs to make discretionary changes to their local plans.

- The Select Committee also recommends that 'the Government consider as a matter of urgency whether the resources of the Planning Inspectorate are sufficient to prevent a bottleneck of unapproved plans building up,

---

22 *CLG Select Committee Report on the Draft NPPF*, para 112 (available at http://www.publications.parliament.uk/pa/cm201012/cmselect.cmcomloc/1526/152602.htm [accessed December 2011]).

23 *CLG Select Committee Report on the Draft NPPF*, para 117 (available at http://www.publications.parliament.uk/pa/cm201012/cmselect.cmcomloc/1526/152602.htm [accessed December 2011]).

24 *CLG Select Committee Report on the Draft NPPF*, para 118 (available at http://www.publications.parliament.uk/pa/cm201012/cmselect.cmcomloc/1526/152602.htm [accessed December 2011]).

25 *CLG Select Committee Report on the Draft NPPF*, para 132 (available at http://www.publications.parliament.uk/pa/cm201012/cmselect.cmcomloc/1526/152602.htm [accessed December 2011]).

particularly given the scope for a short term increase in challenge to Development Control decisions'.[26]
- The new six-year land supply requirement for housing risks a greater proportion of greenfield sites coming forward. It should be made clear that LPAs which adopt a target for use of brownfield land can prioritise it within the six year supply and this requirement should not result in the approval of unsustainable development where authorities have not allocated a full six-year supply. The Select Committee also recommend that windfall sites should be included alongside brownfield land as earmarked for redevelopment if the LPA can provide evidence of a history of such sites coming forward for development. This would help minimise the need to allocate greenfield sites for development. In order to encourage the use of brownfield sites for development, the NPPF should also explicitly set out the principle that brownfield land should be prioritised for development where possible and require LPAs to set their own targets for the use of brownfield land.[27]
- The NPPF should adhere to existing 'Town Centre First' policy and bring offices back within its ambit but allow exceptions that make a specific contribution to rural sustainability. In addition, in exceptional circumstances communities should be allowed to adopt an absolute protection for the town centre from out-of-town retail development. The sequential test for development should also be mandatory and any development proposal that fails this test should be deemed unsustainable.
- Finally, the Select Committee considered that there would be a strong case for further consultation once changes to the draft NPPF had been made by the Government.

## THE ENVIRONMENTAL AUDIT COMMITTEE REPORT

The Environmental Audit Committee ('EAC') undertook a linked but independent inquiry into the draft NPPF alongside that of the Select Committee. On 9 November 2011, the EAC sent a letter to the chair of the Select Committee setting out the main findings of the EAC inquiry, which focussed specifically on the extent that the draft NPPF reflected sustainable development principles.

Evidence was collected from a number of different independent third parties including Friends of the Earth, the Home Builders Federation and the British Property Foundation. The findings from the EAC inquiry have been fed into the Select Committee's report and in particular the EAC recommended the following:

- The Select Committee should ensure that they recommend that a final version of the NPPF does not allow for confusion in respect of the equal importance of the three elements of sustainable development, ie economic, social and environmental. The NPPF should not push local

---

26 *CLG Select Committee Report on the Draft NPPF*, para 135 (available at http://www.publications.parliament.uk/pa/cm201012/cmselect.cmcomloc/1526/152602.htm [accessed December 2011]).

27 *CLG Select Committee Report on the Draft NPPF*, paras 143–151 (available at http://www.publications.parliament.uk/pa/cm201012/cmselect.cmcomloc/1526/152602.htm [accessed December 2011]).

## National Planning Policy Framework

planning authorities 'to regard economic dimension as predominant'.[28] This recommendation stems from comments from a number of respondents to the inquiry who believe that the draft NPPF placed significant emphasis on the economic aspect of sustainable development. The Campaign to Protect Rural England, for example, responded that the NPPF 'is unacceptably weighted towards economic growth: it seems at almost any cost'.[29] The EAC noted that in response to such criticisms Decentralisation and Cities Minister, Greg Clark MP, stated that 'the economy has always been part of the definition of sustainability and we do need homes and jobs but any appearance in the NPPF of giving greater weight to the economic pillar was "not intentional"'.[30]

- Concern was raised by many respondents about the lack of any specific reference to brownfield land in the draft NPPF. Low-value brownfield land should therefore be specifically included in the definition of land of 'lowest environmental value' and preferably brownfield land should be referred to explicitly in the document and LPAs made aware that they may refer to brownfield land in their local plans.
- Many respondents expressed concerns about the lack of regional planning once regional strategies are abolished. Therefore, 'The finalised NPPF should be more specific about how local authorities should address "regional" and "larger than local" sustainable development factors – including for example food resilience, energy, climate change and some waste management functions ... The finalised NPPF should also specify how a duty to co-operate on such issues, as well as on developments on the boundaries between local authorities, would operate and be enforced. It should also address how the cumulative impacts of local development decisions will be monitored and controlled.'[31]
- A definition of sustainable development that goes beyond that in the Brundtland report should be introduced into the NPPF. Such a definition should include the five guiding principles of the 2005 Sustainable Development Strategy and wording for Planning Policy Statement 1 which refers to social progress that recognises the needs of everyone, effective protection of the environment, the prudent use of natural resources and the maintenance of high and stable levels of economic growth and employment. A more progressive definition of sustainable development is needed to take into account the changes in thinking that have taken place since the Brundtland report was published in 1987 and in order actually to encourage environmental improvement. As such the EAC recommend that the final NPPF should 'encourage local

---

28 DCLG (9 November 2011) *Letter from Chair to Chair of Communities and Local Government Committee*, Annex, para 10 (available at http://www.publications.parliament.uk/pa/cm201012/cmselect/cmenvaud/1480/1480i04.htm [accessed December 2011]).
29 DCLG (9 November 2011) *Letter from Chair to Chair of Communities and Local Government Committee*, Annex, para 7 (available at http://www.publications.parliament.uk/pa/cm201012/cmselect/cmenvaud/1480/1480i04.htm [accessed December 2011]).
30 DCLG (9 November 2011) *Letter from Chair to Chair of Communities and Local Government Committee*, Annex, para 9 (available at http://www.publications.parliament.uk/pa/cm201012/cmselect/cmenvaud/1480/1480i04.htm [accessed December 2011]).
31 DCLG (9 November 2011) *Letter from Chair to Chair of Communities and Local Government Committee*, Annex, para 19 (available at http://www.publications.parliament.uk/pa/cm201012/cmselect/cmenvaud/1480/1480i04.htm [accessed December 2011]).

## The National Planning Policy Framework (final form)

authorities to include in their Local Plans a requirement for some types of development to include environmental gain'.[32]

## THE NATIONAL PLANNING POLICY FRAMEWORK (FINAL FORM)

The final version of the NPPF was published on 27 March 2012.[33] It was a lesson in the art of politics, pleasing both the development industry and some of the fiercest critics of the draft NPPF. However, our view is that the NPPF remains unashamedly a pro-growth policy document and the changes between the draft and final versions largely provide clarification or a softening of language. Before considering more fully the context of the final NPPF, we summarise below the principal changes:

- As the Select Committee had recommended (when it considered the draft NPPF), the final NPPF describes the concept of Sustainable Development by reference to the Brundtland report[34] definition and to the five guiding principles from the 2005 UK Sustainable Development Strategy.[35] This appears in its own green box on page 2 and sits above the statement in para 6, which refers to achieving sustainable development as the purpose of the planning system. Paragraph 6 does not, however, cross-refer to the Brundtland report or the UK Sustainable Development Strategy (or the box). Instead it says 'The policies in paragraphs 18 to 219 [of the NPPF] constitute the Government's view of what sustainable development in England means in practice for the planning system'. In our view this is significant for at least two reasons. First, the prominent inclusion of the recognised definitions of 'sustainable development' coupled with the absence of any reference to those definitions in the text when it most counts, creates ambiguity; this will be exploited by both developers and objectors alike and the true meaning will only emerge through planning appeals, further ministerial statements and (probably) case law. Second, subject to this ambiguity, our best guess at what the Government seems to be saying is that insofar as there is a presumption in favour of sustainable development, this equates to a presumption in favour of development which accords with the NPPF; if that is right, we are back to where we were in the draft NPPF, albeit that the statement that the default answer to development should be 'yes' (another concern of the Select Committee) has been removed.

---

32  DCLG (9 November 2011) *Letter from Chair to Chair of Communities and Local Government Committee*, Annex, para 35 (available at http://www.publications.parliament.uk/pa/cm201012/cmselect/cmenvaud/1480/1480i04.htm [accessed December 2011]).
33  DCLG (March 2012) *NPPF* (available at http://www.communities.gov.uk/documents/planningandbuilding/pdf/2116950.pdf [accessed April 2012]).
34  'Sustainable development is development that meets the needs of the present without compromising the ability of future generations to meet their own needs.' UN (1987) *Report of the World Commission on Environment and Development: Our Common Future,* Ch 2 Towards Sustainable Development (available at http://www.un-documents.net/wced-ocf.htm [accessed April 2012]).
35  (1) Living within environmental limits, (2) Ensuring a strong healthy and just society, (3) Achieving a sustainable economy, (4) Promoting good governance, (5) Using sound science responsibly – HM Government (2005) *Securing the Future – The UK Government Sustainable Development Strategy* (available at http://www.defra.gov.uk/publications/files/pb10589-securing-the-future-050307.pdf [accessed April 2012]).

- A stronger emphasis on local variations in the way sustainable development is achieved, again reflecting a concern with the draft NPFF voiced by the Select Committee: para 10 of the NPFF reads 'Plans and decisions need to take local circumstances into account, so that they respond to the different opportunities for achieving sustainable development in different areas'.
- As recommended by the Select Committee, there is more of an explanation about how the NPPF sits within the planning system: under the Planning and Compulsory Purchase Act 2004, s 38(6) and the Town and Country Planning Act 1990, s 70(2), 'Planning law requires that applications for planning permission must be determined in accordance with the development plan unless material considerations indicate otherwise'[36] and 'The NPPF does not change the statutory status of the development plan as the starting point for decision making'.[37]
- Reference is now made to recognising the intrinsic character and beauty of the countryside[38] as part of the 12 core land-use planning principles. In addition, the list of core land-use planning principles includes the need for planning to 'encourage the effective use of land by reusing land that has been previously developed (brownfield land), provided that it is not of high environmental value'.[39] Campaigners against the draft NPPF had argued that there was insufficient protection for undesignated areas of countryside and this is a concession to those concerns.
- There is also reference in the core land-use planning principles to supporting cultural well-being for all and delivering sufficient community and cultural facilities and services to meet local needs.[40] The Theatres Trust among others had asked for reference to cultural facilities to be included.
- These core land-use planning principles also include 'actively manage growth to make the fullest possible use of public transport, walking and cycling'.[41]
- There are a number of changes in relation to town centres. In drawing up local plans LPAs should[42] 'promote competitive town centres that provide customer choice and a diverse retail offer and which reflect the individuality of town centres' and 'retain and enhance existing markets and, where appropriate, re-introduce or create new ones, ensuring that markets remain attractive and competitive'. Following another of the Select Committee's recommendations, the sequential approach/'Town Centre First' policy now again applies to all 'main town centre uses' (including offices and hotels). The only exceptions to this are small

---

36 DCLG (March 2012) *NPPF*, para 10 (available at http://www.communities.gov.uk/documents/planningandbuilding/pdf/2116950.pdf [accessed April 2012]).
37 DCLG (March 2012) *NPPF*, para 11 (available at http://www.communities.gov.uk/documents/planningandbuilding/pdf/2116950.pdf [accessed April 2012]). This is emphasised again at para 196.
38 DCLG (March 2012) *NPPF*, para 17 (available at http://www.communities.gov.uk/documents/planningandbuilding/pdf/2116950.pdf [accessed April 2012]).
39 DCLG (March 2012) *NPPF*, again at para 17 (available at http://www.communities.gov.uk/documents/planningandbuilding/pdf/2116950.pdf [accessed April 2012]).
40 DCLG (March 2012) *NPPF*, again at para 17 (available at http://www.communities.gov.uk/documents/planningandbuilding/pdf/2116950.pdf [accessed April 2012]).
41 DCLG (March 2012) *NPPF*, again at para 17 (available at http://www.communities.gov.uk/documents/planningandbuilding/pdf/2116950.pdf [accessed April 2012]).
42 DCLG (March 2012) *NPPF*, para 23 (available at http://www.communities.gov.uk/documents/planningandbuilding/pdf/2116950.pdf [accessed April 2012]).

scale rural offices and other small scale rural development.[43] Finally, the timescale for assessing the impact of a development proposal outside of town centres and not in accordance with an up-to-date local plan is now five years; a ten-year horizon should only be used for major schemes where the full impact won't be realised in five years.[44]

- The requirement in the draft NPPF for LPAs to identify five years' supply of housing sites plus an extra 20 per cent is modified:[45] the extra 20 per cent is only required where the LPA has had a 'record of persistent under delivery of housing', otherwise it is 5 per cent. In addition, as recommended by the CLG Select Committee, a 'realistic' allowance can be made for windfall within the five-year supply, where based on 'compelling evidence'.[46]
- In relation to design, the NPPF now says that it is proper for LPAs to 'seek to promote or reinforce local distinctiveness'.[47] The 'visual appearance and the architecture of individual buildings' are now not just important but 'very' important factors.[48] So important that individual building design would seem to trump the wider townscape:

  'Local planning authorities should not refuse planning permission for buildings or infrastructure which promote high levels of sustainability because of concerns about incompatibility with an existing townscape, if those concerns have been mitigated by good design (unless the concern relates to a designated heritage asset and the impact would cause material harm to the asset or its setting which is not outweighed by the proposal's economic, social and environmental benefits).'[49]

- There is more emphasis on co-location of housing and community facilities and services, sufficient choice of school places, replacement of lost open space, sports and recreational facilities and protection and enhancement of public rights of ways and access.[50]
- Apart from the emphasis on effective use of land by re-using previously development (brownfield) land and consideration by LPAs of the case for setting a locally appropriate target for the use of such land,[51] changes to policy on conserving and enhancing the natural environment also include a recognition of the economic and other benefits of the best and most versatile agricultural land.[52] There is also a little more detail on

---

43 DCLG (March 2012) *NPPF*, paras 24 and 25 (available at http://www.communities.gov.uk/documents/planningandbuilding/pdf/2116950.pdf [accessed April 2012]).
44 DCLG (March 2012) *NPPF*, para 26 (available at http://www.communities.gov.uk/documents/planningandbuilding/pdf/2116950.pdf [accessed April 2012]).
45 DCLG (March 2012) *NPPF*, para 47 (available at http://www.communities.gov.uk/documents/planningandbuilding/pdf/2116950.pdf [accessed April 2012]).
46 DCLG (March 2012) *NPPF*, para 48 (available at http://www.communities.gov.uk/documents/planningandbuilding/pdf/2116950.pdf [accessed April 2012]).
47 DCLG (March 2012) *NPPF*, para 60 (available at http://www.communities.gov.uk/documents/planningandbuilding/pdf/2116950.pdf [accessed April 2012]).
48 DCLG (March 2012) *NPPF*, para 61 (available at http://www.communities.gov.uk/documents/planningandbuilding/pdf/2116950.pdf [accessed April 2012]).
49 DCLG (March 2012) *NPPF*, para 65 (available at http://www.communities.gov.uk/documents/planningandbuilding/pdf/2116950.pdf [accessed April 2012]).
50 DCLG (March 2012) *NPPF*, paras 70–75 (available at http://www.communities.gov.uk/documents/planningandbuilding/pdf/2116950.pdf [accessed April 2012]).
51 DCLG (March 2012) *NPPF*, para 111 (available at http://www.communities.gov.uk/documents/planningandbuilding/pdf/2116950.pdf [accessed April 2012]).
52 DCLG (March 2012) *NPPF*, para 112 (available at http://www.communities.gov.uk/documents/planningandbuilding/pdf/2116950.pdf [accessed April 2012]).

## National Planning Policy Framework

protection for Sites of Special Scientific Interest[53] and on remediation of land,[54] as well as potentially a significant new passage on noise which recognises that some development will create noise and that existing businesses wanting to develop in continuance of their business should not have unreasonable restrictions put on them because of changes in nearby land uses since they were established.[55]

- There is a little more detail in the policies on conserving and enhancing the historic environment, particularly in relation to assessing the significance and impact on significance of designated and non-designated heritage assets.[56]
- The policies on the sustainable use of minerals have been expanded. Of particular note are the new provisions on strategic planning for the supply of aggregates which advise LPAs to prepare Local Aggregate Assessments based on a rolling average of ten years' data and taking into account the advice of the Aggregate Working Parties and the national and sub-national guidelines on future aggregates provision, among other things.[57]
- There is more guidance on plan-making. Local plans should be 'based on co-operation with neighbouring authorities, public, voluntary and private sector organisations';[58] an interesting point to note is that this policy advice is wider than the statutory duty to co-operate in relation to the planning of sustainable development.[59] In addition, LPAs are advised that 'Pursuing sustainable development requires careful attention to viability and costs in plan-making and decision making',[60] safeguards (mitigation and compensation measures) must be clearly justified 'and the options for keeping such costs to a minimum fully explored, so that development is not inhibited unnecessarily'.[61]
- Policy advice on neighbourhood plans has been altered slightly, emphasising that they should not promote less development than is set out in the local plan, or 'undermine its strategic policies'.[62] The provision for neighbourhood plans, once adopted, to take priority over local plans has been kept but with two important qualifications: first, the neighbourhood plan must have been demonstrated to be in general conformity with the strategic policies of the local plan and the policies it contains only take precedence over existing non-strategic policies in the

---

53 DCLG (March 2012) *NPPF*, para 118 (available at http://www.communities.gov.uk/documents/planningandbuilding/pdf/2116950.pdf [accessed April 2012]).
54 DCLG (March 2012) *NPPF*, paras 120–121 (available at http://www.communities.gov.uk/documents/planningandbuilding/pdf/2116950.pdf [accessed April 2012]).
55 DCLG (March 2012) *NPPF*, para 123 (available at http://www.communities.gov.uk/documents/planningandbuilding/pdf/2116950.pdf [accessed April 2012]).
56 DCLG (March 2012) *NPPF*, paras 126–141 (available at http://www.communities.gov.uk/documents/planningandbuilding/pdf/2116950.pdf [accessed April 2012]).
57 DCLG (March 2012) *NPPF*, para 145 (available at http://www.communities.gov.uk/documents/planningandbuilding/pdf/2116950.pdf [accessed April 2012]).
58 DCLG (March 2012) *NPPF*, para 157 (available at http://www.communities.gov.uk/documents/planningandbuilding/pdf/2116950.pdf [accessed April 2012]).
59 Localism Act 2011, s 110 inserting Planning and Compulsory Purchase Act 2004, new s 33A.
60 DCLG (March 2012) *NPPF*, para 173 (available at http://www.communities.gov.uk/documents/planningandbuilding/pdf/2116950.pdf [accessed April 2012]).
61 DCLG (March 2012) *NPPF*, para 176 (available at http://www.communities.gov.uk/documents/planningandbuilding/pdf/2116950.pdf [accessed April 2012]).
62 DCLG (March 2012) *NPPF*, para 184 (available at http://www.communities.gov.uk/documents/planningandbuilding/pdf/2116950.pdf [accessed April 2012]).

## The National Planning Policy Framework (final form)

local plan. This still seems to allow for a neighbourhood plan to differ from a local plan in the same area at least as far as non-strategic policies are concerned.

- The policy section on decision-making is now peppered with new passages which set the tone for the approach that should be taken by LPAs. For example, LPAs should 'approach decision-taking in a positive way to foster the delivery of sustainable development',[63] 'look for solutions rather than problems',[64] 'seek to approve applications for sustainable development where possible'[65] and 'work proactively with applicants to secure developments that improve the economic, social and environmental conditions of the area'.[66] The parallel processing of other, non-planning development consents is encouraged.[67] Interestingly, after reinforcing the plan-led nature of the planning system at para 196 of the NPPF, LPAs are nonetheless directed to apply the presumption in favour of sustainable development in assessing and determining development proposals;[68] this could be read still as a gloss on the duty to determine applications in accordance with the development plan unless material considerations indicate otherwise.

Having highlighted these changes we now turn to a more detailed consideration of the content of the final NPPF.

## Foreword and Introduction

In the Ministerial Foreword to the NPPF, Greg Clark opens with the statement that the purpose of the planning system is to help achieve sustainable development. He goes on to say that 'sustainable' means 'ensuring that better lives for ourselves doesn't mean worse lives for future generations' and that 'development means growth'; two paragraphs that follow further on in the Foreword sum up the main thrust of the NPPF:

'So sustainable development is about positive growth – making economic, environmental and social progress for this and future generations'; and

'Development that is sustainable should go ahead, without delay – a presumption in favour of sustainable development that is the basis for every plan and every decision. This framework sets out clearly what could make a proposed plan or development unsustainable'.

The Introduction to the NPPF makes clear that it:

- only applies in England;
- sets out government policies and requirements for the planning system to the extent it is relevant proportionate and necessary to do so;

---

63 DCLG (March 2012) *NPPF*, para 186 (available at http://www.communities.gov.uk/documents/planningandbuilding/pdf/2116950.pdf [accessed April 2012]).
64 DCLG (March 2012) *NPPF*, para 187 (available at http://www.communities.gov.uk/documents/planningandbuilding/pdf/2116950.pdf [accessed April 2012]).
65 DCLG (March 2012) *NPPF*, again at para 187 (available at http://www.communities.gov.uk/documents/planningandbuilding/pdf/2116950.pdf [accessed April 2012]).
66 DCLG (March 2012) *NPPF*, again at para 187 (available at http://www.communities.gov.uk/documents/planningandbuilding/pdf/2116950.pdf [accessed April 2012]).
67 DCLG (March 2012) *NPPF*, para 191 (available at http://www.communities.gov.uk/documents/planningandbuilding/pdf/2116950.pdf [accessed April 2012]).
68 DCLG (March 2012) *NPPF*, para 197 (available at http://www.communities.gov.uk/documents/planningandbuilding/pdf/2116950.pdf [accessed April 2012]).

## National Planning Policy Framework

- provides a framework within which distinctive local and neighbourhood plans can be produced;
- must be taken into account in the preparation of local and neighbourhood plans;
- is a material consideration in planning decisions.

The Introduction also qualifies the NPPF:

- It does not contain specific policies for Nationally Significant Infrastructure Projects – whilst the NPPF may have relevance to the decision-making process for such projects, that process will be governed by the Planning Act 2008 and National Policy Statements produced under that Act.
- Policies for traveller sites are contained in a separate policy document (see below).
- The NPPF does not contain specific waste policies – these will be part of the National Waste Management Plan for England and until then, Planning Policy Statement 10 continues to apply.

The NPPF recognises two official definitions of 'sustainable development' referring to 'development that meets the needs of the present without compromising the ability of future generations to meet their own needs'[69] (borrowing from the 1987 report of the Brundtland Commission, *Our Common Future*[70]) and the five 'guiding principles' of the UK Sustainable Development Strategy:[71] living within the planet's environmental limits, ensuring a strong, healthy and just society, achieving a sustainable economy, promoting good governance and using sound science responsibly.

Although these references to accepted principles of sustainable development appear in the NPPF and are clearly intended to convey generally the Government's acceptance of the concept of sustainable development, they are inherently vague and, as we have indicated above, are not referred to again in the remainder of the NPPF. Instead we have the following statement:

> 'The purpose of the planning system is to contribute to the achievement of sustainable development. The policies in paragraphs 18 to 219, taken as a whole, constitute the Government's view of what sustainable development in England means in practice for the planning system.'[72]

In other words, so far as the Government is concerned sustainable development in England is development that accords with the NPPF.

The NPPF goes on to recognise the roles which the planning system needs to play:

- an economic role – the planning system contributes to building a strong responsive and competitive economy;

---

69 DCLG (March 2012) *NPPF*, box above para 6 (available at http://www.communities.gov.uk/documents/planningandbuilding/pdf/2116950.pdf [accessed April 2012]).
70 UN (1987) *Report of the World Commission on Environment and Development: Our Common Future*, Ch 2 Towards Sustainable Development (available at http://www.un-documents.net/wced-ocf.htm [accessed January 2012]).
71 *UK Sustainable Development Strategy* (2005) (available at http://www.defra.gov.uk/publications/2011/03/25/securing-the-future-pb10589/ [accessed April 2012]).
72 DCLG (March 2012) *NPPF*, para 6 (available at http://www.communities.gov.uk/documents/planningandbuilding/pdf/2116950.pdf) [accessed April 2012]).

## The National Planning Policy Framework (final form)

- a social role – the planning system supports strong vibrant and healthy communities; and
- an environmental role – the planning system contributes to protecting and enhancing our natural, built and historic environment.[73]

Paragraph 8 of the NPPF makes it clear that these roles should not be undertaken in isolation because they are mutually dependent. It goes on to say that the planning system should play an active role in guiding development to sustainable solutions and provides at para 9 that pursuing sustainable development involves seeking positive improvement in the quality of the built, natural and historic environment, as well as improvement in people's qualify of life, giving examples of how to achieve this. Paragraph 10 recognises there will be local variations in how sustainable development might be achieved.

Paragraphs 11 to 16 deal with the presumption in favour of sustainable development. As indicated above, this has been one of the most controversial aspects of the NPPF and its final form is more balanced than it was, but, make no mistake, this is still a powerful statement of pro-growth policy.

Still seen as 'a golden thread running through plan-making and decision taking', para 14 details what it means for plan-making:

- LPAs should positively seek opportunities to meet the development needs of their area,
- local plans should meet objectively assessed needs with sufficient flexibility to adapt to rapid change unless adverse impacts 'significantly and demonstrably outweigh the benefits' (when assessed against the NPPF) or specific policies in the NPPF indicate development should be restricted,

and for decision-taking (unless material considerations indicate otherwise):

- development proposals that accord with the development plan should be approved without delay,
- where the development plan is silent or relevant policies are out of date, planning permission should be granted unless adverse impacts 'significantly and demonstrably outweigh the benefits' (when assessed against the NPPF) or specific policies in the NPPF indicate development should be restricted.

The NPPF expects local plans to follow the approach of the presumption in favour of sustainable development[74] and neighbourhood plans should support strategic development needs set out in local plans, plan positively to support local development and identify opportunities for neighbourhood development orders.[75]

The NPPF contains a set of 12 core land-use planning principles[76] to underpin plan-making and decision-making. These are that planning should:

---

73 DCLG (March 2012) *NPPF*, para 7 (available at http://www.communities.gov.uk/documents/planningandbuilding/pdf/2116950.pdf) [accessed April 2012]).
74 DCLG (March 2012) *NPPF*, para 15 (available at http://www.communities.gov.uk/documents/planningandbuilding/pdf/2116950.pdf) [accessed April 2012]).
75 DCLG (March 2012) *NPPF*, box above para 16 (available at http://www.communities.gov.uk/documents/planningandbuilding/pdf/2116950.pdf [accessed April 2012]).
76 DCLG (March 2012) *Draft NPPF*, para 17 (available at http://www.communities.gov.uk/documents/planningandbuilding/pdf/2116950.pdf) [accessed April 2012]).

(a) be genuinely plan-led, with succinct local and neighbourhood plans setting out a positive vision for the future of an area, based on joint working and co-operation and creating a practical framework within which planning applications can be made with a high degree of predictability and efficiency;
(b) be not just about scrutiny but instead a creative exercise finding ways to enhance places;
(c) proactively drive and support the developments that the country needs making every effort objectively to identify and meet the housing, business, and other development needs of an area and taking into account market signals;
(d) always seek to secure high quality design and a good standard of amenity for existing and future occupants of land and buildings;
(e) take account of different roles and characters of different areas, promoting the vitality of our main urban areas, protecting the Green Belts around them, recognising the intrinsic character and beauty of the countryside and supporting thriving local communities within it;
(f) support the transition to a low carbon future in a changing climate, taking full account of flood risk and coastal change, and encourage the reuse of existing resources and the use of renewable resources;
(g) contribute to conserving and enhancing the natural environment and reducing pollution (allocations of land for development should prefer land of lesser environmental value);
(h) encourage the effective use of land by reusing land that has been previously developed (brownfield land) provided it is not of high environmental value;
(i) promote mixed use developments and encourage multiple benefits from the use of land;
(j) conserve heritage assets in a manner appropriate to their significance;
(k) actively manage patterns of growth to make the fullest possible use of public transport, walking and cycling and focus significant development in locations which are or can be made sustainable;
(l) take account of and support local strategies to improve health, social and cultural well-being for all and deliver sufficient facilities and services to meet local needs.

Having set this context, the NPPF then adopts a topic-based approach to planning policies and these are dealt with in turn below.

# 1 Building a strong, competitive economy[77]

The Government sets out its commitment to secure economic growth and to meeting the twin challenges of global competition and a low carbon future. The NPPF states[78] that planning should operate to encourage and not act as an impediment to sustainable growth and significant weight should be placed on the need to support economic growth through the planning system.

To help achieve economic growth, LPAs should plan proactively to meet the development needs of business and support an economy fit for the 21st century.

---

77 DCLG (March 2012) *NPPF*, Section 1, paras 18–22 (available at http://www.communities.gov.uk/documents/planningandbuilding/pdf/2116950.pdf [accessed April 2012]).
78 DCLG (March 2012) *NPPF,* para 19 (available at http://www.communities.gov.uk/documents/planningandbuilding/pdf/2116950.pdf [accessed April 2012]).

## The National Planning Policy Framework (final form)

In addition, 'investment in business should not be over-burdened by the combined requirements of planning policy expectations'.[79] Planning policies should recognise and seek to address potential barriers to investment and when preparing their local plans. LPAs should:

- set out a clear economic vision and strategy for the area which positively and proactively encourages sustainable economic growth;
- set criteria or identify strategic sites for investment over the period of the plan;
- support existing business sectors and identify and plan for new or emerging sectors in their areas and ensure policies are flexible;
- plan positively for clusters or networks of knowledge-driven, creative or high technology industries;
- identify priority areas for economic regeneration, infrastructure provision or environmental enhancement; and
- facilitate flexible working practices such as integration of residential and commercial uses in the same units.

Paragraph 22 of the NPPF advises that planning policies should avoid long term protection of allocated employment land where there is no real prospect of it being used for that purpose.

## 2  Ensuring the vitality of town centres[80]

Planning policies should promote competitive town centres and set out policies for management and growth of town centres. The local plan should recognise town centres as the heart of their communities and support their vitality and viability. The local plan should define a hierarchy and network of centres resilient to future economic changes and define the extent of town centres and primary shopping areas and primary and secondary frontages. LPAs are also directed to 'promote competitive town centres that provide consumer choice and a diverse retail offer and which reflect the individuality of town centres' and to 'retain and enhance existing markets and, where appropriate, reintroduce or create new ones, ensuring that markets remain attractive and competitive'.[81]

In drawing up local plans, LPAs should also allocate a range of suitable sites to meet the scale and type of retail, leisure, commercial, office, tourism, cultural, community and residential development needed in town centres. Needs for retail, leisure, office and other main town centre uses should be met in full and not compromised by limited site availability. LPAs need therefore to ensure a sufficient supply of suitable sites. They should allocate town centre, edge of centre and other accessible sites using a sequential approach to site selection.

The NPPF directs LPAs to apply the sequential test to planning application proposals for main town centre uses that are not in an existing centre and not in accordance with an up-to-date local plan,[82] with the preference for town centre

---

79  DCLG (March 2012) *NPPF*, para 21 (available at http://www.communities.gov.uk/documents/planningandbuilding/pdf/2116950.pdf [accessed April 2012]).
80  DCLG (March 2012) *NPPF*, Section 2, paras 23–27 (available at http://www.communities.gov.uk/documents/planningandbuilding/pdf/2116950.pdf [accessed April 2012]).
81  DCLG (March 2012) *NPPF*, para 23 (available at http://www.communities.gov.uk/documents/planningandbuilding/pdf/2116950.pdf [accessed April 2012]).
82  The sequential approach should not apply to applications for small scale rural offices or other small scale rural development.

locations. LPAs and applicants are expected to demonstrate flexibility on format and scale. LPAs are free to set local floorspace thresholds for requiring impact assessments (the default figure is 2,500 sq m) and impact assessments should adopt a time horizon of five years or for major schemes where the impact would not be realised in five years, of up to ten years.[83]

## 3 Supporting a prosperous rural economy[84]

Planning policies should support economic growth in rural areas and seek to maintain a prosperous rural economy. Local and neighbourhood plans should: support the sustainable growth and expansion of rural businesses; promote development and diversification of agricultural and other land-based rural businesses; support the sustainable development of tourist and leisure facilities where appropriate; and promote the retention and development of local services and community facilities in villages.

## 4 Promoting sustainable transport[85]

The NPPF recognises that transport policies have an important role to play in facilitating development and contributing towards sustainability and health objectives. The transport system should be balanced in favour of sustainable transport modes in order that people have a real choice about how they travel, but the NPPF acknowledges different transport policies will be required in different communities and opportunities to maximise sustainable transport solutions will vary from urban to rural areas. If it is practical, 'encouragement' should be given to transport solutions which will support reductions in greenhouse gases and congestion. The pattern of development supported by local plans should facilitate the use of sustainable transport modes,[86] where it is reasonable to do so. In conjunction with neighbouring authorities and transport providers, LPAs are to develop strategies for provision of viable infrastructure to support sustainable development[87] and the NPPF sets out a brief list of examples.

In relation to individual planning applications, the NPPF provides that any development that generates significant amounts of movement will require a transport statement or transport assessment. Both local plans and decisions on planning applications should take into account whether opportunities for sustainable transport modes have been taken up, whether safe and suitable access can be achieved for all people and whether improvements can be undertaken to the transport network cost effectively, to limit any significant impacts of development. Importantly, the NPPF provides that development should only be prevented or refused on transport grounds 'when the residual cumulative impacts of development are severe'.[88]

---

83 DCLG (March 2012) *NPPF*, para 26 (available at http://www.communities.gov.uk/documents/planningandbuilding/pdf/2116950.pdf [accessed April 2012]).
84 DCLG (March 2012) *NPPF*, Section 3, para 28 (available at http://www.communities.gov.uk/documents/planningandbuilding/pdf/2116950.pdf [accessed April 2012]).
85 DCLG (March 2012) *NPPF*, Section 4, paras 29–41 (available at http://www.communities.gov.uk/documents/planningandbuilding/pdf/2116950.pdf [accessed April 2012]).
86 DCLG (March 2012) *NPPF*, para 30 (available at http://www.communities.gov.uk/documents/planningandbuilding/pdf/2116950.pdf [accessed April 2012]).
87 DCLG (March 2012) *NPPF*, para 31 (available at http://www.communities.gov.uk/documents/planningandbuilding/pdf/2116950.pdf [accessed April 2012]).
88 DCLG (March 2012) *NPPF*, para 32 (available at http://www.communities.gov.uk/documents/planningandbuilding/pdf/2116950.pdf [accessed April 2012]).

*The National Planning Policy Framework (final form)*

The NPPF places great emphasis on ensuring that development is designed and located in such a way as to minimise the need to travel and maximise the use of sustainable transport modes and suggests adapting policies, standards (including parking) and measures to the local circumstances. Travel plans are required for all developments that generate significant amounts of movement.[89]

## 5 Supporting high quality communications infrastructure[90]

Local plans should support the expansion of electronic communications networks. However, LPAs should aim to keep the numbers of telecommunications and radio masts and the sites of such installations to a minimum, consistent with the efficient operation of the networks. Existing masts, buildings and structures should be used unless the need for a new site is justified.

LPAs are advised not to impose blanket bans on telecommunications development in certain areas or insist on minimum distances between new telecommunications development and other existing development. Nevertheless, they should ensure that they have evidence to show that telecommunications infrastructure will not cause significant and irremediable interference with other electrical equipment, air traffic services or instrumentation operated in the national interest. LPAs should also consider the possibility that construction of new buildings could cause interference with broadcast and telecommunications services.

The NPPF stipulates the range of supporting evidence that will be needed for applications for telecommunications development (including applications for prior approval by operators using permitted development rights). Paragraph 46 of the NPPF also states in terms:

> 'Local planning authorities must determine applications on planning grounds. They should not seek to prevent competition between different operators, question the need for the telecommunications system or determine health safeguards if the proposal meets International Commission guidelines for public exposure.'

## 6 Delivering a wide choice of high quality homes[91]

Generally, the draft NPPF reflects the Government's key housing objective to increase significantly the delivery of new homes with wider choice of quality, wider opportunities for home ownership and the creation of sustainable and mixed communities.

In order to boost significantly the supply of housing, LPAs should:

- use their evidence-base to ensure that their Local Plan meets the full objectively assessed needs for market and affordable housing in the housing market area, as far as is consistent with the policies set out in this Framework, including identifying key sites which are critical to the delivery of the housing strategy over the plan period;

---

89 DCLG (March 2012) *NPPF*, para 36 (available at http://www.communities.gov.uk/documents/planningandbuilding/pdf/2116950.pdf [accessed April 2012]).
90 DCLG (March 2012) *NPPF*, Section 5, paras 42–46 (available at http://www.communities.gov.uk/documents/planningandbuilding/pdf/2116950.pdf [accessed April 2012]).
91 DCLG (March 2012) *NPPF*, Section 6, paras 47–55 (available at http://www.communities.gov.uk/documents/planningandbuilding/pdf/2116950.pdf [accessed April 2012]).

- identify and update annually a supply of specific deliverable sites sufficient to provide five years' worth of housing against their housing requirements, with an additional buffer of 5% (moved forward from later on in the plan period) to ensure choice and competition in the market for land. Where there has been a record of persistent under delivery of housing, local planning authorities should increase the buffer to 20% (moved forward from later in the plan period) to provide a realistic prospect of achieving the planned supply and to ensure choice and competition in the market for land;
- identify a supply of specific, developable sites or broad locations for growth, for years 6–10 and, where possible, for years 11–15;
- for market and affordable housing, illustrate the expected rate of housing delivery through a housing trajectory for the plan period and set out a housing implementation strategy for the full range of housing describing how they will maintain delivery of a five-year supply of housing land to meet their housing target;
- set out their own approach to housing density to reflect local circumstances.'[92]

LPAs may make allowance for windfall sites in the five-year supply provided there is compelling evidence that such sites have consistently become available in the local area and will provide a reliable source of supply. Any allowance should be realistic having regard to the Strategic Housing Land Availability Assessment, historic windfall delivery rates and expected future trends and should not include residential gardens.

As if to underscore the importance of housing delivery, the NPPF reminds LPAs that planning applications are to be considered in the context of the presumption in favour of sustainable development. In applying that presumption, housing policies will not be up to date if the LPA cannot demonstrate a five-year supply of *deliverable* housing sites (our emphasis).[93]

In order to deliver a wide choice of high quality housing, wider opportunities for home ownership and sustainable inclusive and mixed communities, LPAs should plan for a mix of housing based on current and future demographics, market trends and needs of different groups in the community; they should also identify the required size, type, tenure and range of housing reflecting local demand. If affordable housing is needed, local plan policies should require this to be provided for on-site unless provision off-site or an appropriate financial contribution can be robustly justified and the approach would still contribute to the objective of creating mixed and balanced communities; such policies should be flexible enough to deal with changing market conditions.

LPAs should identify and bring back into residential use empty housing and buildings in line with local housing and empty homes strategies and, where appropriate, acquire properties under compulsory purchase powers. In addition, planning applications for change of use from commercial to residential should normally be approved where there is an identified need for additional housing in that area, provided there are not strong economic reasons why this would be inappropriate. The NPPF recognises at para 52 that the supply of new homes

---

92 DCLG (March 2012) *NPPF*, para 47 (available at http://www.communities.gov.uk/documents/planningandbuilding/pdf/2116950.pdf [accessed April 2012]).
93 DCLG (March 2012) *NPPF*, para 49 (available at http://www.communities.gov.uk/documents/planningandbuilding/pdf/2116950.pdf [accessed April 2012]).

can sometimes be best achieved through planning for larger scale development, eg new settlements or extensions to settlements that 'follow the principle of Garden Cities'. LPAs should consider if such opportunities provide the best way of achieving sustainable development.

In rural areas, LPAs should respond to local circumstances working with their neighbouring authorities and plan housing development that reflects local needs. Housing should be located where it would enhance or maintain the vitality of rural communities: isolated homes in the countryside should be avoided unless there are special circumstances.

## 7 Requiring good design[94]

The NPPF emphasises the importance of good design – it is 'indivisible from good planning'.[95] Local and neighbourhood plans should develop robust and comprehensive policies setting out the expected quality of development in the local area. Design codes should be used where these would help ensure high standards but design policies should not contain unnecessary prescription or detail and instead should focus the overall scale, density, massing, height, landscape, layout, materials and access of new development in relation to neighbouring buildings and the local area.

The NPPF also states that planning policies should not 'stifle innovation, originality or initiative through unsubstantiated requirements to conform to certain development forms or styles ...' but that it is 'proper to seek to promote or reinforce local distinctiveness'.[96] There is recognition that inclusive design goes beyond aesthetic considerations: planning policies and decisions should address the connections between people and places and the integration of new development. In determining applications, the NPPF advises that great weight should also be given to truly outstanding or innovative designs and permission refused for development of poor design. There is also the following, potentially significant passage in support of sustainable innovative design:

> 'Local planning authorities should not refuse planning permission for buildings or infrastructure which promote high levels of sustainability because of concerns about incompatibility with an existing townscape, if those concerns have been mitigated by good design (unless the concern relates to a designated heritage asset and the impact would cause material harm to the asset or its setting, which is not outweighed by the proposal's economic, social and environmental benefits).'[97]

## 8 Promoting healthy communities[98]

The NPPF recognises the important role that the planning system can play in facilitating social interaction and creating healthy, inclusive communities.

---

94 DCLG (March 2012) *NPPF*, Section 7, paras 56–68 (available at http://www.communities.gov.uk/documents/planningandbuilding/pdf/2116950.pdf [accessed April 2012]).
95 DCLG (March 2012) *NPPF*, para 56 (available at http://www.communities.gov.uk/documents/planningandbuilding/pdf/2116950.pdf [accessed April 2012]).
96 DCLG (March 2012) *NPPF*, para 60 (available at http://www.communities.gov.uk/documents/planningandbuilding/pdf/2116950.pdf [accessed April 2012]).
97 DCLG (March 2012) *NPPF*, para 65 (available at http://www.communities.gov.uk/documents/planningandbuilding/pdf/2116950.pdf [accessed April 2012]).
98 DCLG (March 2012) *NPPF*, Section 8, paras 69–78 (available at http://www.communities.gov.uk/documents/planningandbuilding/pdf/2116950.pdf [accessed April 2012]).

## National Planning Policy Framework

It directs LPAs to create a shared vision with communities of the residential environment and facilities they wish to see. LPAs should involve all parts of the community in the development of local plans and in planning decisions and should facilitate neighbourhood planning. Planning policies and decisions should aim to achieve places which promote opportunities to meet, a safe and accessible environment and safe and accessible development.

In order to deliver the social, recreational and cultural facilities and services that the community needs, para 70 of the NPPF advises that planning policies and decisions should:

- plan positively for the provision of shared space, community facilities and other local services;
- guard against the unnecessary loss of valued facilities and services;
- ensure that existing facilities and services can develop sustainably and are retained for the benefit of the local community; and
- ensure an integrated approach to considering the location of housing, economic uses and community facilities and services.

LPAs are also directed to take a positive and collaborative approach towards Community Right to Build Orders. Specific mention is also made of the importance of a sufficient choice of school places to meet the needs of existing and new communities; LPAs are directed to take a proactive, positive and collaborative approach to meeting this requirement and to development that will widen choice in education.

The NPPF emphasises the importance to the health and well-being of communities of access to high quality open spaces and opportunities for sport and recreation. Planning policies should be based on robust and up-to-date assessments of the needs for these facilities in the local area and the opportunities for new provision. Existing areas of open space, sports and recreational facilities should not be built on unless an assessment has been made which shows that the open space, buildings or land are surplus to requirements, or the loss resulting from the proposed development would be replaced by equivalent or better provision or the development is for alternative sports and recreational provision, the needs for which clearly outweigh the loss.[99]

The NPPF also advises that planning policies should protect and enhance public rights of way and access; LPAs should seek opportunities to provide better facilities – for example by adding links to existing rights of way networks.[100]

Local communities should also be able to identify, for special protection, green areas of particular importance to them (through their local and neighbourhood plans); these are to be known as Local Green Spaces. These areas will be protected from new development other than in very special circumstances; the criteria for this designation are set out in the NPPF.[101]

---

99 DCLG (March 2012) *NPPF*, para 74 (available at http://www.communities.gov.uk/documents/planningandbuilding/pdf/2116950.pdf [accessed April 2012]).
100 DCLG (March 2012) *NPPF*, para 75 (available at http://www.communities.gov.uk/documents/planningandbuilding/pdf/2116950.pdf [accessed April 2012]).
101 DCLG (March 2012) *NPPF*, paras 76–77 (available at http://www.communities.gov.uk/documents/planningandbuilding/pdf/2116950.pdf [accessed April 2012]).

## The National Planning Policy Framework (final form)

## 9 Protecting Green Belt land[102]

Although the NPPF confirms that Green Belts are of great importance, it also states that new Green Belts should only be established in exceptional circumstances.[103]

The NPPF confirms that Green Belts serve five purposes:

- 'to check the unrestricted sprawl of large built-up areas;
- to prevent neighbouring towns merging into one another;
- to assist in safeguarding the countryside from encroachment;
- to preserve the setting and special character of historic towns; and
- to assist in urban regeneration, by encouraging the recycling of derelict and other urban land.'[104]

LPAs with Green Belts in their area should include in their local plans Green Belt boundaries and a framework of Green Belt and settlement policy. LPAs should plan positively to enhance the beneficial use of the Green Belt, eg by looking for opportunities to provide access or outdoor sport and recreation, to retain and enhance a landscape's visual amenity and biodiversity or to improve damaged or derelict land. Once established, Green Belt boundaries should only be altered in exceptional circumstances through preparation or review of the local plan.

As with previous Green Belt policy, inappropriate development is considered by definition to be harmful to the Green Belt and should only be approved in 'very special circumstances'[105] and in order for such circumstances to exist, the potential harm to the Green Belt must be clearly outweighed by the other considerations. Construction of buildings will normally be inappropriate in the Green Belt but, as with previous national policy, the NPPF sets out a list of exceptions.[106] The NPPF also identifies other forms of development that will not be inappropriate if it preserves openness and does not conflict with the purposes of including land in the Green Belt. These are mineral extraction, engineering operations, local transport infrastructure that is required in a Green Belt, reuse of buildings (of permanent and substantial construction) and development under a Community Right to Build Order. Very special circumstances such as wider environmental benefits from increased energy production from renewable sources might also justify elements of renewable energy projects in the Green Belt.[107]

---

102 DCLG (March 2012) *NPPF*, Section 9, paras 79–92 (available at http://www.communities.gov.uk/documents/planningandbuilding/pdf/2116950.pdf [accessed April 2012]).
103 DCLG (March 2012) *NPPF*, para 82 (available at http://www.communities.gov.uk/documents/planningandbuilding/pdf/2116950.pdf [accessed April 2012]).
104 DCLG (March 2012) *NPPF*, para 80 (available at http://www.communities.gov.uk/documents/planningandbuilding/pdf/2116950.pdf [accessed April 2012]).
105 DCLG (March 2012) *NPPF*, para 87 (available at http://www.communities.gov.uk/documents/planningandbuilding/pdf/2116950.pdf [accessed April 2012]).
106 DCLG (March 2012) *NPPF*, para 89 (available at http://www.communities.gov.uk/documents/planningandbuilding/pdf/2116950.pdf [accessed April 2012]).
107 DCLG (March 2012) *NPPF*, para 91 (available at http://www.communities.gov.uk/documents/planningandbuilding/pdf/2116950.pdf [accessed April 2012]).

## 10 Meeting the challenge of climate change, flooding and coastal change[108]

The NPPF recognises that the planning system plays a key role in shaping places to secure a radical reduction in greenhouse gas emissions, minimising vulnerability and providing resilience to the impacts of climate change and supporting the delivery of renewable and low-carbon energy infrastructure. LPAs are directed to adopt proactive strategies to mitigate and adapt to climate change, taking full account of flood risk, coastal change and water supply and demand considerations.

To support the move to a low carbon future, LPAs must plan for new development in locations and ways that reduce greenhouse gas emissions, actively support energy efficiency improvements to existing buildings and set any local requirements for sustainability of buildings in line with government policy and nationally described standards. In determining planning applications, the NPPF states that LPAs should expect new development to comply with adopted local plan policies on local requirements for decentralised energy supply unless it can be shown this is not feasible or viable and take account of land form, layout, building orientation, massing and landscaping to minimise energy consumption.[109]

In order to increase the use and supply of renewable and low carbon energy, the NPPF directs LPAs to recognise the responsibility of all communities to contribute to energy generation from renewable and low carbon sources. LPAs should have a positive strategy to support this type of energy generation, design policies to maximise renewable and low carbon energy development (ensuring adverse impacts are addressed satisfactorily), consider identifying suitable areas for renewable and low carbon energy sources and infrastructure, support community-led initiatives for renewable and low carbon energy and identify opportunities for development to draw its energy supply from decentralised low carbon or renewable energy supply systems. Planning applications for renewable or low carbon energy should not have to demonstrate the overall need for this type of energy and should be approved where these impacts are or can be made acceptable.[110]

The NPPF provides that local plans should take account of climate change over the longer term, including flood risk, coastal change, water supply and changes to biodiversity and landscape. New development should avoid increased vulnerability to the impacts of climate change and if development is to take place in vulnerable areas, risks should be managed by suitable adaptation measures.

The NPPF provides that inappropriate development in areas at risk of flooding should be avoided by directing development away from areas at highest risk, but where development is necessary, making it safe without increasing flood risk elsewhere. Local plans should be supported by Strategic Flood Risk Assessment and should adopt a sequential risk-based approach to the location

---

108 DCLG (March 2012) *NPPF*, Section 10, paras 93–108 (available at http://www.communities.gov.uk/documents/planningandbuilding/pdf/2116950.pdf [accessed April 2012]).
109 DCLG (March 2012) *NPPF*, para 96 (available at http://www.communities.gov.uk/documents/planningandbuilding/pdf/2116950.pdf [accessed April 2012]).
110 DCLG (March 2012) *NPPF*, para 98 (available at http://www.communities.gov.uk/documents/planningandbuilding/pdf/2116950.pdf [accessed April 2012]).

## The National Planning Policy Framework (final form)

of development in order to avoid flood risk to people and property where possible and manage any residual risks, taking account of the impacts of climate change. The same sequential risk-based approach is to be followed in both site allocations and site-specific planning decisions supported by a site-specific flood risk assessment. Paragraphs 100 to 104 of the NPPF deal with this in more detail and technical guidance on flood risk was published in parallel with the NPPF (see below).

In coastal regions, LPAs must take into account the UK Marine Policy Statement and Marine Plans and apply integrated Coastal Zone Management. LPAs are directed to reduce risk from coastal change by avoiding inappropriate development in vulnerable areas or adding to the impacts of physical changes to the coast. Those areas that are at risk from physical coastline changes should be designated as Coastal Change Management Areas. Development should only be permitted in these areas in appropriate circumstances, defined locally and by reference to advice in para 107 of the NPPF.

## 11 Conserving and enhancing the natural environment[111]

The NPPF states that the planning system should contribute to and enhance the natural and local environment in a number of ways (para 109). In preparing plans, the aim should be to minimise pollution and other adverse effects on the local and natural environment. Land with the least environmental or amenity value should be allocated; policies and decisions alike should encourage the effective use of land by reusing brownfield land provided it does not have high environmental value itself and LPAs may set locally appropriate targets. LPAs should also take into account the economic and other benefits of the best and most versatile agricultural land, directing any necessary development to areas of poorer quality land.

LPAs should set policies against which development affecting protected wildlife or geodiversity sites or landscapes will be judged; the level of protection for these features should be commensurate with their international, national or local status. They should also plan positively for networks of biodiversity and green infrastructure and maintain the character of the undeveloped coast and improve public access and enjoyment. Great weight is to be given to conserving landscape and scenic beauty in National Parks, the Broads and Areas of Outstanding Natural Beauty; conservation of wildlife and cultural heritage is also important and should be given great weight in National Parks and the Broads. Planning permission for major developments in these designated areas should be refused other than in exceptional circumstances.

When determining planning applications LPAs should aim to conserve and enhance biodiversity by applying a number of principles set out in the NPPF at para 118. They include the following:

- If significant harm cannot be avoided, adequately mitigated or as a last resort compensated for, planning permission should be refused.
- Planning permission should be refused for development resulting in loss or deterioration of irreplaceable habitats, eg ancient woodland,

---

[111] DCLG (March 2012) *NPPF*, Section 11, paras 109–125 (available at http://www.communities.gov.uk/documents/planningandbuilding/pdf/2116950.pdf [accessed April 2012]).

## National Planning Policy Framework

unless the loss is clearly outweighed by the need for/benefits of the development in that location.
- The following should have the same protection as is given to European sites under the Habitats Directive –[112]
  - potential Special Protection Areas,
  - possible Special Areas of Conservation,
  - listed or proposed Ramsar sites, and
  - sites identified for compensatory measures for adverse effects on these and other European sites.
- The presumption in favour of sustainable development does not apply where development requiring appropriate assessment under the Birds or Habitats Directives[113] is being considered, planned or determined.[114]

LPAs are also directed by the NPPF to prevent unacceptable risks from pollution and land instability in their policies and decisions and to ensure development is appropriate for its location, taking into account cumulative effects of pollution on health, the natural environment, general amenity, the potential sensitivity of the area or the proposed development to adverse effects from pollution. They should ensure suitability of the site for its new use and focus on whether the development itself is an acceptable use of the land and the impact of the use; in doing so, LPAs should ensure that other regimes which control processes and emissions will operate effectively. The NPPF makes specific reference to:

- noise from a new development – this should not give rise to significant adverse impacts on health and quality of life; other adverse impacts should be mitigated and reduced to a minimum. However, it should be recognised that development will often create some noise and existing businesses wanting to develop in continuance of their business should not have unreasonable restrictions placed on them due to changes in nearby land uses since they were established. Areas of tranquillity should be identified and protected;
- air quality – policies should ensure compliance with and contribution to EU limit values and national objectives for pollutants and new development in Air Quality Management Areas should be consistent with the local air quality action plan;
- the impact of light pollution from artificial light on amenity, intrinsically dark landscapes and nature conservation should be limited.

## 12 Conserving and enhancing the historic environment[115]

The NPPF sets out the Government's objectives for planning and the historic environment as the conservation of heritage assets in a manner appropriate to their significance and the contribution to our knowledge and understanding of our past by capturing evidence and making it publicly available. LPAs should

---

112 Directive 92/43/EEC on the conservation of natural habitats and of wild fauna and flora.
113 Directive 92/43/EEC on the conservation of natural habitats and of wild fauna and flora and Directive 2009/147/EC on the conservation of wild birds, which is the consolidated version of Directive 79/409/EEC.
114 This is significant because it appears to disapply the presumption in favour of sustainable development even before the outcome/findings of the appropriate assessment.
115 DCLG (March 2012) *NPPF,* Section 12, paras 126–141 (available at http://www.communities.gov.uk/documents/planningandbuilding/pdf/2116950.pdf [accessed April 2012]).

## The National Planning Policy Framework (final form)

set out in their local plans a positive strategy for conservation and enjoyment of the historic environment in their areas taking into account:

- the desirability of sustaining and enhancing the significance of heritage assets and putting them to viable uses consistent with their conservation;
- the wider social, cultural, economic and environmental benefits that conservation can bring;
- the desirability of new development making a positive contribution to local character and distinctiveness; and
- the opportunities to draw on the contribution made by the historic environment to the character of a place.

In the determination of planning applications, the NPPF advises that LPAs should require the significance of any heritage assets affected by the development to be described and assessed; the level of detail must remain proportionate to the importance of the asset and no more than is sufficient to understand the potential impact. LPAs should identify and assess the particular significance of any heritage assets that may be affected by a proposal (including the setting of a heritage asset) taking account of available evidence and any necessary expertise. LPAs should also take into account:

- the desirability of sustaining and enhancing the significance of heritage assets and putting them in viable use consistent with their conservation;
- the positive contribution heritage assets can make to sustainable communities including their economic vitality; and
- the desirability of new development making a positive contribution to local character and distinctiveness.[116]

When considering the impact of development on the significance of a designated heritage asset, great weight should be given to its conservation. Any harm or loss will require clear and convincing justification. Substantial harm or loss of a grade II listed building, park or garden should be exceptional and substantial harm or loss of designated assets with a higher level of protection (eg scheduled monuments, grade I and II* listed buildings, World Heritage Sites etc) should be wholly exceptional.

The NPPF further advises that if proposals lead to substantial harm or loss of a designated heritage asset, consent should be refused unless the loss or harm is necessary to deliver substantial public benefits that outweigh the harm or loss or certain criteria are met.[117] Where proposals affect non-designated heritage assets, this will be taken into account in determining the planning application and a balanced judgement will be required having regard to the scale of any harm or loss and the significance of the asset. Where loss of all or part of a heritage asset is permitted, LPAs should try to ensure that the new development will, in practice, proceed after the loss has occurred.

Enabling development which would otherwise conflict with planning policies but would secure the future conservation of a heritage asset should be assessed in terms of whether the benefits outweigh the disbenefits of departing from the planning policies.

---

116 DCLG (March 2012) *NPPF*, para 131 (available at http://www.communities.gov.uk/documents/planningandbuilding/pdf/2116950.pdf [accessed April 2012]).
117 DCLG (March 2012) *NPPF*, para 133 (available at http://www.communities.gov.uk/documents/planningandbuilding/pdf/2116950.pdf [accessed April 2012]).

## 13 Facilitating the sustainable use of minerals[118]

The NPPF expresses the Government's overall objective for the minerals planning system, namely ensuring a sufficient supply to support sustainable economic growth whilst making the best use of resources to secure their long term conservation.

LPAs are directed to comply with a number of requirements when preparing local plans[119] including:

- identify and include policies for extraction of locally and nationally important minerals in their area but not identify sites or extensions to existing sites for peat extraction;
- so far as practicable, take account of supply from substitute, secondary and recycled materials and minerals waste before considering extraction of primary materials, with the aim of sourcing minerals supplies indigenously;
- define minerals safeguarding areas and related minerals consultation areas to ensure that known locations of specific minerals resources of local and national importance are not needlessly sterilised by non-mineral development;
- safeguard rail heads, rail links and other storage, handling and processing facilities for bulk transport by rail, sea or inland waterways;
- include policies to encourage prior extraction of minerals, where practicable and environmentally feasible, if it is necessary for non-mineral development to take place;
- set out environmental criteria in line with the NPPF for determination of minerals planning applications; and
- put in place policies to ensure early reclamation and high quality restoration and aftercare.

Minerals planning authorities are advised to plan for a steady and sufficient supply of land-won aggregates, by adopting a number of measures,[120] including preparing annual local aggregate assessments based on a rolling ten years' sales data and other local information and assessing all supply options, as well as taking account of apportionment in the national and sub-national guidelines and the advice of aggregate working parties.

Paragraph 146 sets out measures by which MPAs should plan for a steady and adequate supply of industrial minerals to support their use in manufacturing processes. Paragraphs 147 to 149 give advice to MPAs on energy minerals supply, including on-shore oil and gas development, underground gas and carbon storage, coal extraction (planning permission should not be given unless the proposal is environmentally acceptable or it provides national, local or community benefits that clearly outweigh the likely impact), the capture and use of methane from coalfields and fireclay.

When determining planning applications in respect of mineral development, LPAs should give great weight to the benefits of mineral extraction, including

---

118 DCLG (March 2012) *NPPF*, Section 13, paras 142–149 (available at http://www.communities.gov.uk/documents/planningandbuilding/pdf/2116950.pdf [accessed April 2012]).
119 DCLG (March 2012) *NPPF*, para 143 (available at http://www.communities.gov.uk/documents/planningandbuilding/pdf/2116950.pdf [accessed April 2012]).
120 DCLG (March 2012) *NPPF*, para 145 (available at http://www.communities.gov.uk/documents/planningandbuilding/pdf/2116950.pdf [accessed April 2012]).

## The National Planning Policy Framework (final form)

benefits to the economy, but also ensure that there are no unacceptable adverse impacts on the natural and historic landscape, human health or aviation safety, and take into account cumulative effects. They must also ensure the control and mitigation of environmental impacts of development including any noise, dust, particle emission and vibrations. So far as practicable, LPAs must provide for maintenance of landbanks of non-energy minerals from reserves outside National Parks, the Broads, AONBs, World Heritage Sites, Schedule Monuments and Conservation Areas. This and other advice on the determination of minerals planning applications appear at para 144 of the NPPF.

## Plan-making[121]

The NPPF recognises that in a plan-led system local plans are key to delivering sustainable development that reflects the visions and aspirations of local communities. However, it emphasises the need for consistency between a plan and the contents of the NPPF (including the presumption in favour of sustainable development).[122] Plans should be prepared with the objective of contributing to the achievement of sustainable development and LPAs should seek opportunities to achieve each of the economic, social and environmental dimensions of sustainable development and indeed net gains across all three. LPAs should produce one local plan for its area which can be renewed in whole or in part to respond flexibly to changing circumstances. Additional development plan documents should only be used where clearly justified. Any supplementary planning documents should only be introduced where they can facilitate successful applications or aid infrastructure delivery; these documents should not add unnecessarily to the financial burdens on development.

The NPPF advises that local plans should be 'aspirational but realistic'[123] and address the spatial implications of economic, social and environmental change. Local plans should set out the opportunities for development and clear policies on what will or will not be permitted and where. The NPPF also regards early and meaningful engagement and collaboration with neighbourhoods, local organisations and businesses as essential. A wide section of the community should be 'proactively engaged' so that 'Local Plans, as far as possible, reflect a collective vision and a set of agreed priorities for the sustainable development of the area …'.[124]

Paragraph 156 of the NPPF advises that each local plan should set out the strategic priorities for the area which should include the following strategic policies:

- '• the homes and jobs needed in the area;
- • the provision of retail, leisure and other commercial developments;
- • the provision of infrastructure for transport, telecommunications, minerals, waste management, water supply, waste water, flood risk

---

121 DCLG (March 2012) *NPPF*, Plan-Making at paras 150–185 (available at http://www.communities.gov.uk/documents/planningandbuilding/pdf/2116950.pdf [accessed April 2012]).
122 DCLG (March 2012) *NPPF*, para 151 (available at http://www.communities.gov.uk/documents/planningandbuilding/pdf/2116950.pdf [accessed April 2012]).
123 DCLG (March 2012) *NPPF*, para 154 (available at http://www.communities.gov.uk/documents/planningandbuilding/pdf/2116950.pdf [accessed April 2012]).
124 DCLB (March 2012) *NPPF*, para 155 (available at http://www.communities.gov.uk/documents/planningandbuilding/pdf/2116950.pdf [accessed April 2012]).

## National Planning Policy Framework

and coastal change management and the provision of minerals and energy (including heat);
- the provision of health, security, community and cultural infrastructure and other local facilities; and
- climate change mitigation and adaptation, conservation and enhancement of the natural and historic environment, including landscape.'

The NPPF also considers it to be crucial that local plans should:

'• plan positively for the development and infrastructure required in the area to meet the objectives, principles and policies of this Framework;
- be drawn up over an appropriate time scale, preferably a 15-year time horizon, take account of longer term requirements, and be kept up to date;
- be based on co-operation with neighbouring authorities, public, voluntary and private sector organisations;
- indicate broad locations for strategic development on a key diagram and land-use designations on a proposals map;
- allocate sites to promote development and flexible use of land, bringing forward new land where necessary and provide detail on form, scale, access and quantum of development where appropriate;
- identify areas where it may be necessary to limit freedom to change the uses of buildings, and support such restrictions with a clear explanation;
- identify land where development would be inappropriate, for instance because of its environmental or historic significance; and
- contain a clear strategy for enhancing the natural, built and historic environment and supporting Nature Improvement Areas[125] where they have been identified.'[126]

The NPPF also requires that the LPA should base their local plan on an adequate up-to-date and relevant evidence base concerning the economic, social and environmental characteristics and prospects of the area, taking full account of market and economic signals. Paragraphs 159 to 177 of the NPPF highlight a number of areas where a clear understanding of the characteristics and needs of the area will be needed. They include:

- On housing need, LPAs should prepare a Strategic Housing Market Assessment to assess their full housing needs, working with neighbouring authorities where housing market areas cross boundaries. This assessment should identify the scale and mix of housing and the types of tenures which will be required over the plan period. LPAs should also prepare a Strategic Housing Land Availability Assessment to establish availability suitability and likely economic viability of land to meet the identified need.
- In relation to business needs, within the economic markets operating in and across their area, LPAs should work together with LEPs and county and neighbourhood authorities to prepare a robust evidence

---

125 Nature Improvement Areas are inter-connected networks of wildlife habitats intended to re-establish thriving wildlife populations and help species respond to the challenges of climate change.
126 DCLG (March 2012) *NPPF*, para 157 (available at http://www.communities.gov.uk/documents/planningandbuilding/pdf/2116950.pdf [accessed April 2012]).

## The National Planning Policy Framework (final form)

base to understand the existing needs of business and market changes. They should work closely with the business community to understand their changing needs and address barriers to investment, such as lack of housing infrastructure or viability. This evidence should be used to determine the existing and future need for land for economic development, sufficiency of land supply, the role and function and capacity of existing town centres, locations of deprivation that would benefit from development and the needs of the food production industry.[127]

- LPAs should work with other authorities and providers to assess the quality and capacity of infrastructure in their area and its ability to meet forecast demand; they should also take account of the need for strategic infrastructure (including nationally significant infrastructure) within their areas.[128]

- LPAs should work with other relevant organisations to use the best available information to understand the extent and locations of mineral resource in their areas and assess projected demand, taking full account of opportunities to provide suitable alternatives to extraction of primary materials.[129]

- LPAs should work with the Ministry of Defence Strategic Planning Team to determine the most up-to-date information about defence and security needs in their area; they should also work with local advisers and others to take into account information about higher risk sites and threats and national hazards, including steps that could reduce vulnerability and increase resilience.[130]

- Policies and decisions should be based on up-to-date information about the natural environment and other characteristics of the area. LPAs should ensure that a sustainability appraisal is an integral part of the plan preparation process. Local plans may also require other assessments, eg under the Habitats Regulations[131] and the Strategic Flood Risk Assessments. Any assessment processes should, however, be proportionate to the plan and should not repeat any previous assessment of policy.[132]

- LPAs should have up-to-date information about the historic environment in their area to assess the significance of heritage assets, any contribution these make to the environment and the likelihood of any currently unidentified historical assets; where appropriate, landscape character assessments should also be prepared.[133]

---

127 DCLG (March 2012) *NPPF*, paras 160–161 (available at http://www.communities.gov.uk/documents/planningandbuilding/pdf/2116950.pdf [accessed April 2012]).
128 DCLG (March 2012) *NPPF*, para 162 (available at http://www.communities.gov.uk/documents/planningandbuilding/pdf/2116950.pdf [accessed April 2012]).
129 DCLG (March 2012) *NPPF*, para 163 (available at http://www.communities.gov.uk/documents/planningandbuilding/pdf/2116950.pdf [accessed April 2012]).
130 DCLG (March 2012) *NPPF*, para 164 (available at http://www.communities.gov.uk/documents/planningandbuilding/pdf/2116950.pdf [accessed April 2012]).
131 Conservation of Habitats and Species Regulations 2010 (SI 490/2010), as amended.
132 DCLG (March 2012) *NPPF*, paras 165–168 (available at http://www.communities.gov.uk/documents/planningandbuilding/pdf/2116950.pdf [accessed April 2012]).
133 DCLG (March 2012) *NPPF*, paras 169–170 (available at http://www.communities.gov.uk/documents/planningandbuilding/pdf/2116950.pdf [accessed April 2012]).

## National Planning Policy Framework

- LPAs should work with the local health organisations to determine the health needs of their local populations, expected changes and barriers to improving health and well-being.[134]
- LPAs should also have up-to-date information on location of major hazards and mitigation of the consequences of major accidents.[135]

The NPPF states that pursuing sustainable development requires careful attention to viability and cost in both plan-making and decisions. Plans should be deliverable and therefore the sites and scale of developments identified by a local plan must not 'be subject to such a scale of obligation and policy burdens that their ability to be developed viably is threatened'.[136] Development must still be capable of providing competitive returns to a willing landowner and willing developer, taking into account normal development costs and mitigation. This means that CIL charges should be worked up and tested in parallel with the local plan. It also means that local planning authorities, parishes and neighbourhood forums must assess the likely *cumulative* impacts on development in their area of all existing and proposed national and local standards and policy requirements. Viability and deliverability are dealt with in detail in paras 173 to 177 of the NPPF. This includes the following key passage at para 176:

> 'Where safeguards are necessary to make a particular development acceptable in planning terms (such as environmental mitigation or compensation), the development should not be approved if the measures required cannot be secured through appropriate conditions or agreements. The need for such safeguards should be clearly justified through discussions with the applicant and the options for keeping such costs to a minimum fully explored, so that development is not inhibited unnecessarily.'

Under s 110 of the Localism Act, LPAs (alongside other public bodies) have a duty to co-operate on planning issues that relate to strategic matters (the sustainable development or use of land, where there are impacts on at least two planning areas). The NPPF reiterates this requirement at paras 178 to 181 emphasising the importance of collaborative working and the need to ensure that strategic priorities are properly co-ordinated and clearly reflected in individual local plans. Evidence will be expected from LPAs when local plans are submitted for examination to demonstrate that they are co-operating with other public bodies to plan for these cross-boundary issues.

The section on neighbourhood plans in the NPPF (paras 183 to 185) is surprisingly short. It states that these plans give communities power to develop a shared vision for neighbourhood and deliver the sustainable development they need. These plans can be used to set policies for determination of planning applications and to give planning permission through Neighbourhood Development Orders and Community Right to Build Orders. This part of the NPPF also emphasises the need for the ambition of the neighbourhood to be aligned with the strategic needs and priorities of the wider local area – in other words neighbourhood plans should complement local plans and generally conform to the strategic policies of local plans. This draws upon the statutory

---

134 DCLG (March 2012) *NPPF*, para 171 (available at http://www.communities.gov.uk/documents/planningandbuilding/pdf/2116950.pdf [accessed April 2012]).
135 DCLG (March 2012) *NPPF*, para 172 (available at http://www.communities.gov.uk/documents/planningandbuilding/pdf/2116950.pdf [accessed April 2012]).
136 DCLG (March 2012) *NPPF*, para 173 (available at http://www.communities.gov.uk/documents/planningandbuilding/pdf/2116950.pdf [accessed April 2012]).

## The National Planning Policy Framework (final form)

requirement for Neighbourhood Development Plans and Neighbourhood Development Orders to be in general conformity with the strategic policies contained in the development plan for the area of the local authority.[137] Neighbourhood plans should not promote less development than is set out in the local plan or undermine its strategic policies.

It is particularly important to note that the NPPF states that once general conformity with the local plan's strategic policies is demonstrated and they have been brought into force, policies within an adopted neighbourhood plan will take precedence over non-strategic policies in the local plan in that area if there is a conflict. This priority given to Neighbourhood Development Plans is consistent with the philosophy of localism but of course it assumes that consistency with the NPPF and strategic policies of the local plan is rigorously adhered to by neighbourhoods, the LPA and the independent examiner and that there is always a clear distinction between strategic and non-strategic policies. As most users of the planning system know, that assumption will not always be a reliable one – especially where there are no active opponents to a neighbourhood plan or where decisions are taken by the local planning authority, for example, for political expediency. More importantly perhaps, this provision of the NPPF fails to appreciate that local plans may be revised subsequently to the neighbourhood plan being put into place. Should not the later local plan take priority where there is a conflict, as a more up-to-date response to local circumstances?

## Decision-taking[138]

The NPPF advises LPAs to approach decision-taking in a positive way to foster the delivery of sustainable development. The NPPF envisages a seamless relationship between plan-making and development management.

There is clear endorsement in the NPPF of pre-application engagement and 'front-loading' with good quality pre-application discussions and engagement with other LPAs, statutory consultees, consenting bodies (with a view to encouraging parallel processing of other development consents) and local communities. This is consistent with the new duty of pre-application consultation which is placed on developers by s 122 of the Localism Act.[139] The NPPF emphasises the importance of the right information to enable good decision-making, especially in cases where formal assessments are required such as environmental impact assessments[140] or an assessment under the Habitats Regulations.[141]

There is a small crumb of comfort to those who may be concerned that planning applications could become even more voluminous as a result of the new pre-application duty of consultation and the NPPF's requirements for adequate information. The NPPF reminds LPAs that the information required should be:

---

137 See Town and Country Planning Act 1990, new Sch 4B, para 8(2), inserted by Localism Act 2011, Sch 10, as also applied to Neighbourhood Development Plans by Localism Act 2011, Sch 9, para 7.
138 DCLG (March 2012) *NPPF*, paras 186–206 (available at http://www.communities.gov.uk/documents/planningandbuilding/pdf/2116950.pdf [accessed April 2012]).
139 Inserting new ss 61W, 61X and 61Y into Town and Country Planning Act 1990.
140 Under Town and Country Planning (Environmental Impact Assessment) Regulations 2011 (SI 2011/1824).
141 Conservation of Habitats and Species Regulations 2010 (SI 2010/490), as amended.

## National Planning Policy Framework

'proportionate to the nature and scale of the development proposal and reviewed on a frequent basis. Local planning authorities should only request supporting information that is relevant, necessary and material to the application in question.'[142]

When determining planning applications, the NPPF emphasises the nature of the plan-led system so that applications are determined in accordance with the development plan (which will now include any neighbourhood development plan for the area in which the development is situated and still includes the London Plan in Greater London) unless material considerations indicate otherwise.[143] The NPPF also directs LPAs (at para 197) to apply the presumption in favour of sustainable development. The NPPF itself is also noted as a material consideration in planning decisions. Importantly, the NPPF also states (para 198):

> 'Where a planning application conflicts with a neighbourhood plan that has been brought into force, planning permission should not normally be granted.'

Attention is also drawn to other vehicles through which planning permission can be granted and the degree of control exercised by LPAs can be relaxed, including Local Development Orders,[144] Neighbourhood Development Orders and Community Right to Build Orders.[145]

In dealing with planning conditions and obligations, the NPPF repeats previous policy and existing law. Planning conditions should only 'be imposed where they are necessary, relevant to planning and to the development to be permitted, enforceable, precise and reasonable in all other respects'.[146] Planning obligations should only be used where it is not possible to address unacceptable impacts through a planning condition and only where they are necessary to make the development acceptable in planning terms, directly related to the development and fair and reasonably related in scale and kind to the development. The NPPF adds that where obligations are being sought or revised, LPAs should take account of changes in market conditions over time and, wherever appropriate, be sufficiently flexible to prevent planned development being stalled.[147]

Finally, in a very short passage (para 207), the NPPF comments that effective enforcement of planning control is important as a means of maintaining public confidence in the planning system. The NPPF advises LPAs to act proportionately to suspected breaches of planning control and consider publishing a local enforcement plan to manage enforcement appropriately and proactively in their area.

---

142 DCLG (March 2012) *NPPF*, para 193 (available at http://www.communities.gov.uk/documents/planningandbuilding/pdf/2116950.pdf [accessed April 2012]).
143 Planning and Compulsory Purchase Act 2004, s 38 and Town and Country Planning Act 1990, s 70(2).
144 Under Town and Country Planning Act 1990, ss 61A–61D and Sch 4A, inserted by Planning and Compulsory Purchase Act 2004, ss 40 and 41.
145 DCLG (March 2012) *NPPF*, paras 199–202 (available at http://www.communities.gov.uk/documents/planningandbuilding/pdf/2116950.pdf [accessed April 2012]).
146 DCLG (March 2012) *NPPF*, para 206 (available at http://www.communities.gov.uk/documents/planningandbuilding/pdf/2116950.pdf [accessed April 2012]).
147 DCLG (March 2012) *NPPF*, para 205 (available at http://www.communities.gov.uk/documents/planningandbuilding/pdf/2116950.pdf [accessed April 2012]).

## TRANSITIONAL ARRANGEMENTS FOR THE NPPF

Annex 1 of the NPPF sets out a number of provisions relating to implementation – including transitional arrangements.

It is made clear that the NPPF takes effect immediately so that the policies within it are material considerations in the determination of planning applications and must be taken into account in preparing local plans.[148] In recognition of this, the Planning Inspectorate issued advice to inspectors in relation to the handling of appeals and local plan examinations, for which the procedures had already begun at the time of publication.[149]

In relation to local plan preparation and review, although Annex 1, para 211 of the NPPF states that policies in local plans should not be considered out of date simply because they were adopted prior to the NPPF, Annex 1, para 213 of the NPPF makes it clear that plans may need to be revised to take the NPPF into account and this should be progressed as quickly as possible. Paragraph 214 advises that 'For 12 months from the date of publication, decision-takers may continue to give full weight to relevant policies adopted since 2004[150] even if there is a limited degree of conflict with this Framework'. In other cases, and after the 12-month period, 'due weight should be given to relevant policies in existing plans according to their degree of consistency'[151] with the NPPF, the principle being that the greater the consistency between development plan policy and the NPPF, the greater the weight that may be given to that policy.

On the face of it, this measurement of consistency with the NPPF is a significant gloss on the principle of a plan-led system that other parts of the NPPF are so keen to say remains unaffected. We could face a significant period of uncertainty as plans are brought up to date and the exact meaning of this part of the NPPF becomes clearer through appeal decisions and ministerial pronouncements. The 12-month transition period during which full weight can be given to policies adopted since 2004 seems only to apply where there is a 'limited degree of conflict' with the NPPF; when is the degree of conflict more than 'limited'? In addition, does the principle of giving weight to development plan policy according to its consistency with the NPPF after 12 months (or before with a pre-2004 plan) apply to 'existing plans' in the sense of plans existing at the date of the NPPF but not revised or plans existing from time to time going forward? In other words, is this part of the NPPF an ongoing check on the consistency of local (and neighbourhood) plans with the NPPF, in case inconsistencies creep through the plan-preparation process?

Also significant is the reference in Annex 1 of the NPPF to the soon-to-be-abolished regional strategies and their evidence base – both may be reflected

---

148 NPPF, Annex 1, para 219 does however make it clear that the NPPF has been drafted on the assumption that the Localism Act 2011 represents the current law so that any policies dependent on certain provisions being in force should be taken to apply only when the relevant part of the legislation is brought into effect.
149 The Planning Inspectorate (27 March 2012) *Advice Produced by The Planning Inspectorate for Use by Inspectors: National Planning Policy Framework* (available at http://www.planningportal.gov.uk/uploads/pins/advice_for_inspectors/nppf.pdf [accessed April 2012]).
150 The footnotes to the NPPF make it clear that this means development plan documents adopted pursuant to the Planning and Compulsory Purchase Act 2004 and policies in the London Plan.
151 DCLG (March 2012) *NPPF*, Annex 1, para 215 (available at http://www.communities.gov.uk/documents/planningandbuilding/pdf/2116950.pdf [accessed April 2012]).

*National Planning Policy Framework*

in local plan policies where appropriate[152] and there is recognition (albeit in a footnote accompanying this reference) that until abolished, a regional strategy remains part of the development plan.

## DOCUMENTS REPLACED BY THE NPPF

Annex 3 of the NPPF sets out the documents that are replaced by the policies in the NPPF; this is replicated in Appendix 4 to this book. It lists virtually all of the Planning Policy Statements ('PPSs'), Planning Policy Guidance Notes ('PPGs') and Minerals Policy Guidance ('MPGs'), Circular 05/2005 on planning obligations, the (former) Government Office for London's Circular 1/2008 on strategic planning in London and a series of letters to Chief Planning Officers. The notable exceptions from this list are:

- PPS 10 (Sustainable Waste Management), updated 30 March 2011[153] – this is acknowledged by the NPPF[154] as remaining in place until the National Waste Management Plan is published;
- MPG 4 (Revocation, Modification, Discontinuance, Prohibition and Suspension Orders);[155]
- MPG 8 (Interim Development Order Permissions: Statutory Provisions and Procedures);[156]
- MPG 9 (Interim Development Order Permissions: Conditions);[157] and
- MPG 14 (Review of Mineral Planning Permissions).[158]

Whilst it was always the intention of the Government to achieve this outcome, the wholesale replacement of policy documents wipes away a significant amount of helpful technical guidance that appears nowhere else. Equally, the list of replaced documents omits not only PPS 10 and the MPGs listed above but also an awful lot of circulars, practice notes and other guidance that may still potentially be of relevance and which are unlikely to sit comfortably in every respect with the NPPF.

This will need to be addressed far more urgently than perhaps the Government recognises; failure to do so quickly will give rise to the risk of developers, objectors and LPAs alike reinventing the wheel to cover replaced technical guidance or disagreeing on whether or not remaining guidance is consistent with the NPPF and therefore capable of being relied upon or, worse still, introducing local variations to what have previously been understood to be robust and sound methods and benchmarks for the assessment of development proposals. So far,

---

152 DCLG (March 2012) *NPPF*, Annex 1, para 218 (available at http://www.communities.gov.uk/documents/planningandbuilding/pdf/2116950.pdf [accessed April 2012]).
153 Available at http://www.communities.gov.uk/publications/planningandbuilding/planningpolicystatement10 [accessed April 2012].
154 DCLG (March 2012) *NPPF*, page 1, footnote 5 (available at http://www.communities.gov.uk/documents/planningandbuilding/pdf/2116950.pdf [accessed April 2012]).
155 Available at http://www.communities.gov.uk/documents/planningandbuilding/pdf/157896.pdf [accessed April 2012].
156 Available at http://www.communities.gov.uk/documents/planningandbuilding/pdf/157464.pdf [accessed April 2012].
157 Available at http://www.communities.gov.uk/documents/planningandbuilding/pdf/156048.pdf [accessed April 2012].
158 Available at http://www.communities.gov.uk/documents/planningandbuilding/pdf/155844.pdf [accessed April 2012].

## Documents published alongside the NPPF

the Government has simply indicated, in response to the Select Committee,[159] that it will:

'... now embark on a new exercise to consider what underpinning guidance continues to be needed, involving practitioners and other interested parties. The outcome of this process will be an appropriate and easy to use set of guidance, focussing on issues that require national expression, to support implementation of the Framework. It will not always be the case that the guidance should come from Government – in some cases professional bodies may be the most appropriate bodies to publish guidance. The Government has been clear that until such time as the guidance review is complete, the existing guidance where relevant can still be used.'[160]

Technical guidance was published alongside the NPPF but this is limited to detailed advice on flooding and minerals issues[161] and was described as an interim measure pending a wider review of guidance to support planning policy.

## DOCUMENTS PUBLISHED ALONGSIDE THE NPPF

As indicated above, Technical Guidance to the NPPF, restricted to flooding and minerals issues, was published alongside the NPPF and a few days earlier than publication of the NPPF the Government also published *Planning Policy for Traveller Sites*.[162] In addition, the Government presented to Parliament its response to the *Communities and Local Government Select Committee Report: National Planning Policy Framework*.[163] We summarise each of these in turn.

### Technical Guidance to the NPPF

The Technical Guidance aims to provide additional advice to LPAs in applying the policies set out in the NPPF where they deal with development in areas at risk of flooding and in relation to mineral extraction. The guidance retains key elements of (now superseded) Planning Policy Statement 25 *Development and Flood Risk* and certain of the superseded Minerals Policy Statements and Minerals Planning Guidance notes, and is said to be an interim measure pending a wider review of technical guidance to support the NPPF.

In relation to flood risk, the guidance starts from the principle in the NPPF that development is to be directed away from areas at highest risk to areas with the lowest possibility of flooding. Where Strategic Flood Risk Assessment exists, the flood zones identified in the assessment are to provide the basis for applying

---

159 DCLG (March 2012) *Government Response to the Communities and Local Government Select Committee Report: National Planning Policy Framework* (available at http://www.official-documents.gov.uk/document/cm83/8322/8322.pdf [accessed April 2012]).
160 DCLG (March 2012) *Government Response to the Communities and Local Government Select Committee Report: National Planning Policy Framework*, para 10 (available at http://www.official-documents.gov.uk/document/cm83/8322/8322.pdf [accessed April 2012]).
161 DCLG (March 2012) *Technical Guidance to the National Planning Policy Framework* (available at http://www.communities.gov.uk/documents/planningandbuilding/pdf/2115548.pdf [accessed April 2012]).
162 DCLG (March 2012) (available at http://www.communities.gov.uk/publications/planningandbuilding/planningpolicytravellers [accessed April 2012]).
163 DCLG (March 2012) *Government Response to the Communities and Local Government Select Committee Report: National Planning Policy Framework* (available at http://www.official-documents.gov.uk/document/cm83/8322/8322.pdf [accessed April 2012]).

the sequential test; otherwise, the Environment Agency's flood zones apply. Development is to be steered to Flood Zone 1, and only where there are no reasonably available sites in Flood Zone 1 should LPAs (when allocating land in local plans or determining planning applications) consider reasonably available sites in Flood Zone 2 (applying the exception test[164] if required by reference to Table 3 of the document). Only where there are no reasonably available sites in either Flood Zones 1 or 2 should LPAs consider the suitability of sites on Flood Zone 3, having regard to the flood risk vulnerability of land uses (as set out in the guidance) and applying the exception test if required (by reference to Table 3 of the document).

The guidance also sets out appropriate land uses, flood risk assessment requirements, and policy aims for LPAs and developers in relation to each of the Flood Zones, it guides LPAs and developers as to what development may be appropriate in each of the Flood Zones. Climate change is to be taken into account with contingency allowances for net sea level rises and peak rainfall intensities. The guidance also provides advice on managing residual flood risk.

The guidance stresses and elaborates on the NPPF policies that local plans should be supported by Strategic Flood Risk Assessments; and that LPAs should only consider development in flood risk areas where informed by site-specific flood risk assessments.

In relation to minerals, the guidance stresses that minerals planning authorities are expected to ensure that plan proposals do not have an unacceptable adverse effect on the natural or historic environment or human health. Care must be taken in relation to conditions to be attached to planning permissions for working close to communities. A programme of work should also be agreed, although it is recognised that working in proximity to residential property may be necessary where there are specific objectives (such as preparing land for future development). Such workings should be for a limited and specified period, without scope for extension.

In relation to the NPPF policies, which require minerals planning authorities to ensure that unavoidable dust and noise emissions are controlled, mitigated or removed at source, the guidance adds that dust assessments and noise emissions assessments should be carried out. Appropriate noise limits should also be established by minerals planning authorities for extraction in proximity to noise sensitive properties.

The guidance also sets out how stability issues in surface mine workings and tips are to be dealt with; and how planning authorities and applicants for minerals operations should provide for the restoration and aftercare of minerals sites (including financial guarantees).

---

164 The exception test is passed if development provides wider sustainability benefits to the community that outweigh flood risk, informed by Strategic Flood Risk Assessment where one has been prepared *and* a site-specific flood risk assessment demonstrates that the development will be safe for its lifetime, taking account of the vulnerability of its users, without increasing flood risk elsewhere and where possible will reduce flood risk overall. See *NPPF*, para 102 (available at http://www.communities.gov.uk/documents/planningandbuilding/pdf/2116950.pdf [accessed April 2012]).

*Documents published alongside the NPPF*

## Planning Policy for Traveller Sites

This document sets out the Government's planning policy for traveller sites and came into force on the same day as the NPPF. Where LPAs are making decisions in respect to traveller sites in their area, they must have regard to this policy document alongside the relevant NPPF policies.

The policy document begins by setting out the Government's aims in respect of traveller sites which include that:

- LPAs, working collaboratively, must develop fair and effective strategies to meet need through the identification of land for traveller sites;
- plan-making and decision-taking should aim to reduce the number of unauthorised developments and encampments and make enforcement more effective;
- LPAs ensure that their local plans include fair, realistic and inclusive policies; and
- the number of traveller sites in appropriate locations with planning permission is increased, to address under-provision and maintain an appropriate level of supply.

The remainder of the document goes on to set out a number of policies that LPAs must comply with when making plans and taking decisions in respect of traveller sites. In particular, LPAs must base all planning decisions on relevant evidence. When preparing such evidence, the LPA must pay particular attention to effective community engagement with both local settled and traveller communities and ensure that they prepare and maintain an up-to-date understanding of the likely permanent and transit site accommodation needs in their areas.

Local plans should identify, and be annually updated to include, a supply of specific deliverable sites sufficient to provide five years' worth of sites against locally set targets. LPAs should also identify a supply of specific deliverable sites, or broad locations for growth, for years six to ten and where possible for years 11 to 15. Where there is an identified need for traveller sites, critcria should be set to guide land supply allocations. Where there is no such identifiable need, fair criteria-based policies that facilitate the traditional and nomadic life of travellers whilst respecting the life of settled residents should be included to help guide decision-making in case applications. LPAs should also ensure that traveller sites are economically, socially and environmentally sustainable and consider, wherever possible, mixed use sites.

In rural locations, the policy document states that, when assessing the suitability of sites in rural or semi-rural settings, LPAs should ensure that the scale of such sites does not dominate the nearest settled community. Further, where viable and practical, LPAs should consider using a rural exception site policy for traveller sites which will enable small sites to be used in small rural communities, specifically for affordable traveller sites, that would not normally be used in such a manner. The rural exception cannot however be used for mixed use sites.

In support of the NPPF's policies on the green-belt, the policy document specifies that traveller sites, whether temporary or permanent, are inappropriate development in the Green Belt and Green Belt boundaries should only be altered in exceptional circumstances. LPAs should also strictly limit traveller site development in the open countryside away from existing settlements or outside areas allocated in the development plan.

Where a traveller site is to be relocated as a result of a major redevelopment project, LPAs must work with the planning applicant and the affected traveller community to identify sites suitable for relocation. The applicant will be expected to identify and provide an alternative site provided that the traveller site requiring relocation is authorised.

The policy document also sets out a number of considerations that LPAs must take into account when considering applications for new traveller sites. They include the effective use of brownfield, untidy or derelict land. In addition, where an LPA has not identified an up-to-date five-year supply of deliverable sites, this must be a material consideration in any subsequent planning decision when considering applications for the grant of temporary planning permissions. LPAs are also encouraged to use planning conditions and planning obligations in order to make a traveller site acceptable in planning terms.

## Government's response to the CLG Select Committee's Report

We have summarised earlier in this chapter the recommendations concerning the draft NPPF which were made by the Communities and Local Government Select Committee and the principal changes made to the NPPF by the Government between draft stage and its final publication. The Government's formal response to the Select Committee's recommendations provides another useful summary of those changes and some commentary which gives an indication of the Government's thinking. We highlight here the most helpful parts of the commentary:

- In accepting the recommendation that current technical guidance should remain in place after publication of the NPPF, the Government confirms that it will start to consider what technical guidance is needed to underpin the NPPF and until then existing guidance, where relevant, can still be used (para 10). However, clearly this can not include any technical guidance previously contained in planning policy statements which are listed in Annex 3 of the NPPF as having been replaced entirely. Nor, logically, can it include any advice or guidance which might still exist but which is not consistent with the NPPF. Paragraphs 40 to 42 of the Government's response make it clear that it will not always be the case that new underpinning guidance should come from government; in some cases it will be more appropriate for this to come from professional bodies.
- In accepting the Committee's recommendation to recognise the differential impacts of the NPPF policies in different parts of the country, the Government makes it clear that local areas should be able to set local policies that reflect their local circumstances and enable them to respond to different opportunities for achieving sustainable development in their areas (para 18). This is a very localist statement but, of course, it is tempered by the actual content of the NPPF and in particular the presumption in favour of sustainable development.
- On the meaning of sustainable development, the Government indicates that it amended the NPPF to refer to both the Brundtland report and the UK Sustainable Development Strategy 2005, but there follows a very

*Documents published alongside the NPPF*

telling statement reflecting our view that in practice the presumption in favour of sustainable development is still effectively a presumption in favour of development that complies with the NPPF:

> 'The policies in this Framework reflect the Government's views of how the principles of sustainability should be applied in preparing local and neighbourhood plans and in making planning decisions' (para 22)

although the Government also goes on to acknowledge that the economic social and environmental roles of the planning system should not be pursued in isolation because they are mutually dependent.

- In agreeing to remove the direction that the default answer to development proposals should be 'yes', the Government explains that this gave rise to unwarranted concerns that development should be allowed at all costs, which was not their intention. However, this is followed by the comment that 'the Government remains committed to ensuring that the planning system does everything it can to support economic growth' (para 27).
- The Government fully accepts that the NPPF and the presumption in favour of sustainable development operate within the plan-led legislative framework (paras 31 and 36).
- At paras 32 and 33, in defending reference in the presumption in favour of sustainable development to adverse impacts which 'significantly and demonstrably outweigh the benefits'[165] as part of the caveat to the requirement for local plans to meet objectively assessed needs and the requirement to grant planning permission where the development plan is absent, silent or out of date, the Government rejected the view that the burden of proof for this should shift to the applicant. Instead, the Government says that the word 'demonstrably' simply means based on more than assertion and it is up to LPAs to require the right information to take its planning decision.
- In relation to viability and the affordability for the developer of mitigation measures, the Government accepted that this needed clarification and so altered the NPPF to state that where such measures were necessary to make a development acceptable in planning terms, the development should not be approved if the measures cannot be secured; however, the Government adds that the need for these measures should be clearly justified and the options for keeping the cost of such measures to a minimum need to be fully explored: it does not want development to be inhibited unnecessarily (para 34).
- The Committee had expressed the view that local plans would inevitably have to be longer to fill significant gaps left by the reduction in detail of national policy and the loss of regional strategies; the Government rejected the idea that there would be significant gaps and considered that where it was necessary to do so locally, LPAs could reflect policies from regional strategies in their plans and that LPAs could also continue to draw on evidence that informed the regional strategies to support their policies, supplemented by up-to-date robust local evidence, as needed (para 37).

---

165 DCLG (March 2012) *NPPF*, para 14 (available at http://www.communities.gov.uk/documents/planningandbuilding/pdf/2116950.pdf [accessed April 2012]).

- Paragraph 44 of the Government's response provides some indication of the rationale behind the presumption in favour of sustainable development – in particular the state of local plans across the country:

  'The Government ... agrees the lack of up-to-date Local Plans has contributed to the shortage of homes that communities need and is determined to ensure up-to-date plans are put in place more quickly than in the past and maintained. This is one reason why the Government has embarked on its ambitious programme of reforms to the planning system. A key aim of the new Framework is to support and encourage local planning authorities and their communities to put in place up-to-date Local Plans as soon as possible to enable them to deliver the homes, jobs and quality environment they need.'

- Paragraph 45 of the response refers to the Government's decision that the local plan should be given weight 'according to whether or not it is clearly contrary to the Framework' – as we have said this could in time become a significant gloss on the plan-led system. Paragraph 46 goes on to explain the transitional arrangements for the relationship between the NPPF and local plans – there will be an additional 12-month period during which LPAs who have adopted plans since 2004 can rely on them even if there is a conflict with the NPPF 'to give them a realistic chance to bring up-to-date their Local Plan'; this 12-month period is quite a challenging timescale but clearly the Government has attempted to strike a balance between the time taken for local plan reviews and the need to stimulate action and growth through the delivery of much needed development. The Government goes on to refer to a support network which it has set up with the Local Government Association, the Planning Inspectorate and the DCLG (para 48) and the availability of additional resources for the Planning Inspectorate (para 51) which it considers will facilitate speedy reviews.
- On housing, the Government says that LPAs can reflect a priority for re-use of brownfield land within their five-year supply of sites for new housing (para 53). They can also make allowance for windfall sites within the five-year supply but only where there is 'compelling' evidence (para 54) that such sites have consistently become available and will continue to be a reliable source of supply.
- On town centres, whilst the Government confirms its commitment to strong policy protections for town centres (para 56), it rejected out of hand the recommendation of the Committee to allow communities in certain exceptional circumstances to adopt an absolute protection of a town centre from out-of-town retail development. It did not consider this to be justifiable or lawful (para 59).
- Finally, at paras 61 and 62 of its response, the Government firmly rejected the suggestion of further consultation on the NPPF before its final publication but added:

  'The Government strongly believes that Parliament and its Select Committees, having contributed to the development of this Framework, should supervise its implementation with debates in both Houses during the new session' (para 62).

  It will be worth keeping an eye out for these debates and whether they give further clarification or explanation for the NPPF.

## CONCLUDING THOUGHTS ON THE NPPF

The Localism Act has radically changed the structure of the planning system, providing for the removal of the regional tier of planning policy and introducing a new set of neighbourhood planning tools, together with new powers and rights for the community. The NPPF provides a vital guiding force for these reforms, directing local authorities and neighbourhoods in the use of their new powers.

Without the key message of the NPPF that the planning system must be used positively to meet objectively assessed needs through the delivery of sustainable development, the reforms bringing local empowerment might have favoured NIMBY-ism,[166] as some had feared. As it is, the NPPF (even with the Government's concessions following consultation) is a statement of support for growth and for new development but developers will not be popping champagne corks just yet. There remain questions about how effective the NPPF will be.

The Government started with a determination to reduce the amount of national policy guidance significantly and it has certainly succeeded in that. It also wanted to make the planning system more accessible and inclusive and again, the signs so far are good: the controversy that the NPPF caused between its publication in draft and in its final version, was driven by front page headlines in our daily newspapers and engaged a wide range of organisations and individuals, all of whom were able to express a view on what the NPPF meant for them.

The question is whether the NPPF will meet the objective of fostering a positive, pro-growth climate for the delivery of development that meets the needs of the country. It will be some time before we know but whilst, judging by the controversy of the consultation, the brevity of the NPPF appears to have increased the influence of national policy, the same brevity may not lend itself to a quicker, more efficient planning system.

We see three principal problem areas:

- The scope still for confusion around what the presumption in favour of sustainable development means in practice. The Government has acknowledged international and national definitions of sustainable development but, as we have mentioned, it has also made clear that the NPPF itself is the Government's view of what sustainable development means in practice in England. So whilst those acknowledged definitions incorporate environmental protections and the NPPF guides LPAs to seek opportunities to achieve each of the economic, social and environmental dimensions of sustainable development and indeed net gains across all three, the analysis as to whether the presumption applies might not need to extend beyond the question of whether, overall, a proposal complies with the NPPF – if it does the presumption could well be relied upon.
- The relationship between the NPPF and local plans has scope for different interpretations. First, the policies in the NPPF are very directive in parts but the NPPF also recognises that there should and

---

166 Not In My Back Yard-ism. NIMBYs are also sometimes referred to as BANANAS (Build Absolutely Nothing Anywhere Near Anything) or NOPES (Not On Planet Earth).

*National Planning Policy Framework*

      will be local variations in how sustainable development is achieved – what degree of variation is acceptable? Secondly, the NPPF recognises that it sits within a plan-led system and that therefore the starting point for decision-making is the local plan, with the NPPF as a material consideration; however, elsewhere the NPPF provides that the weight to be given to local plan policies depends on their consistency with policies in the NPPF, appearing to place a qualification on the principle of a plan-led system.

- Thirdly, the loss of technical guidance in some of the previous planning policy statements and circulars that are listed in Annex 3 to the NPPF as having been replaced has been allowed to happen before the Government has undertaken a review of what underpinning guidance may be necessary or desirable for the NPPF. As an example, Planning Policy Guidance 24 *Planning and Noise* is one of those that has been replaced and with it the advice on the use of Noise Exposure Categories in the planning system and the measurement and assessment of noise. There is of course a large amount of technical guidance which has not yet been replaced but that which has been lost will leave a gap in accepted practice and could open the door for different approaches to technical issues and locally endorsed variations of methodology and standards.

Each of these issues has the potential to cause delays in both plan-making and decision-taking while differences in opinion are resolved. Far from the NPPF being a charter for lawyers (as some have claimed), applicants, objectors and LPAs are more likely to turn to town planners and other experts to exploit the ambiguities and gaps to their own advantage. The predictability of the system which is so vital for investment could be adversely affected and with this potential debate on policy, one has to wonder whether the planning system will remain as accessible as the Government had hoped when it published its 59 pages of national policy.

# Chapter 15

# Funding LPAs

Reform of the local government finance system is a necessary part of the Government's localism programme. *Control Shift*[1] talked of a 'five-pillar strategy':

- 'Giving local communities a share in local growth';
- 'Freeing local government from central control';
- 'Giving local people more power over local government';
- 'Giving local people more ability to determine spending priorities'; and
- 'Removing regional government'.

In this Chapter we address the following:

1. the Government's proposals for local government business rate retention;
2. the potential introduction of Tax Increment Financing;
3. the replacement of the Housing and Planning Delivery Grant mechanism with the New Homes Bonus;
4. the Government's proposal that LPAs should be allowed to set their own planning application fees;
5. the idea of Community Land Auctions;
6. the relevance of 'local finance considerations' for decision makers.

The Community Infrastructure Levy is addressed in Chapter 9 and the Regional Growth Fund is addressed in Chapter 13.

We set out the Government's own overview of the current local government finance system as follows:

'Under the current system, local government has three main sources of income: grants from central government; council tax; and other locally generated income (such as fees and charges for services).

On average, councils receive 53 per cent of their income from central government grants, of which there are two types. First, 'specific grants', which may be ringfenced for specific purposes, or unringfenced. Second, 'formula grant', which is an unringfenced revenue grant distributed to local authorities through the Local Government Finance Settlement.

Formula grant funds a wide range of local services, including children's services, adult social services, police, fire, highways maintenance, environmental, protective and cultural services. It includes funding from central government, known as "Revenue Support Grant"; Police Grant from the Home Office; and National Non-Domestic Rates, commonly known as business rates. Business rates are collected by local authorities, paid into a

---

1   The Conservative Party (February 2009) *Control Shift: Returning Power to Communities* (available at http://www.conservatives.com/~/media/Files/Green%20Papers/Localism-Policy-Paper.ashx?dl=true [accessed March 2012]).

central government pool and redistributed through the Local Government Finance Settlement. Billing authorities (district councils and unitary authorities) collect business rates from the occupiers of non-domestic properties – mainly businesses such as shops, offices, warehouses and factories. There are approximately 1.7 million properties liable for business rates in England. Each property has a rateable value which is assessed by the Valuation Office Agency on the basis of the annual rent that a tenant would be willing to pay for it on the open market.

Every five years there is a revaluation to ensure a property's rateable value reflects changes to the property market. The business rates owed are calculated as a function of the rateable value and a multiplier. The national multiplier currently stands at 43.3p in England. So a property with a rateable value of £100,000 would have an annual bill of £43,300. The multiplier is increased each year by the Retail Prices Index (RPI). The multiplier is also adjusted at each revaluation so that the overall tax yield remains the same in real terms before and after revaluation. There are a number of reliefs (with mandatory and discretionary elements) available to occupants to reduce their liability – for example reliefs for charities, community amateur sports clubs, certain businesses in rural areas and Small Business Rate Relief.'

## LOCAL RETENTION OF BUSINESS RATES

Since the Local Government Finance Act 1988, business rates have been set centrally and collected locally, to be pooled centrally for redistribution back to authorities in accordance with a formula which does not incentivise each authority to increase, through development and increases in rental values, its local taxation base.

On 18 July 2011 as part of Phase 1 of the Local Government Resource Review, DCLG published a consultation on proposals to allow local government to retain the business rates collected in its local area.[2] Eight technical papers were added to the consultation on 19 August 2011.[3] The Government's response to the consultation process was published on 19 December 2011.[4] The Government has now deposited the Local Government Finance Bill in Parliament, with a view to Royal Assent by Summer 2012, which will enable business rates retention to be introduced from April 2013. Its proposals can be summarised as follows:

- No changes are proposed to the system of business rate taxation as far as businesses are concerned. The proposals relate solely to the way that revenues are distributed.
- Billing authorities (ie district/borough councils and unitary authorities) will still bill and collect business rates as they do now. However, an element of the business rates that they collect will be retained locally.

---

2   DCLG (July 2011) *Local Government Resource Review: Proposals for Business Rates Retention* (available at http://www.communities.gov.uk/documents/localgovernment/pdf/1947200.pdf [accessed in December 2011]).
3   Various titles, available at http://www.communities.gov.uk/localgovernment/localgovernment finance/lgresourcereview/ [accessed December 2011].
4   DCLG (19 December 2011) *Local Government Resource Review: Proposals for Business Rates Retention: Government Response* (available at http://www.communities.gov.uk/documents/localgovernment/pdf/2053502.pdf [accessed March 2012]).

The level to be retained will depend upon the extent to which the business rates base in its area grows over time. A baseline level of funding will be set so that, at the start of the system, the authority's budget will be equivalent to what it would have been under the current system. From then on, the authority's funding will grow if the business rates base in its area is to grow, but conversely could fall if its business rates base were to decline.

- County councils (which currently receive a share of business rates revenues from districts/boroughs in their area) will similarly find that their funding will depend upon whether the business rates base in their area rises or falls. They are encouraged to consider with their district/borough councils and/or any relevant LEP in the area, whether decisions should be made jointly about the distribution of funding.
- Revenue elements of the GLA general grant will be rolled in, 'ensuring that the GLA is funded through the business rates retention scheme and is under the same incentive to go for growth as other authorities'.[5]
- The 'baseline level of funding' would be set for 2013/14 for each authority following the 2011 Autumn Statement.
- The Government will calculate a tariff or top up amount for each local authority. Those authorities with business rates in excess of their baseline level of funding will pay a tariff to government; those authorities with business rates yield below their baseline will receive a top-up from government.
- To manage the possibility that some local authorities with high business rate tax bases could see disproportionate financial gains, the Government will recoup a share of disproportionate benefit through a levy.
- There will be revaluations every five years.
- The Government will have the option of resetting the system every ten years, although, in exceptional circumstances, a reset could be required outside of this period.
- 'Local authorities, for example those in local enterprise partnerships, or districts and counties, could choose to form voluntary pools within the system, allowing them to share the benefits of growth and smooth the impact of volatility over a wider economic area.'[6]

Although there has been concern that the introduction of the top-up and tariff safeguards may not result in fair outcomes, a number of local authorities appear to be supportive of the concept of locally retained business rates. For example, Colin Barrow, leader of Westminster City Council, which collects £1.4 billion of business rate revenue a year, has stated that:

'A business rate retention scheme will encourage us to go even further, to attract even more business. Competition between councils to become more business-friendly will force us all to pay more attention to our local business communities. That is healthy for local government, for businesses, for residents and for the national economy.'[7]

---

5  DCLG (19 December 2011) *Local Government Resource Review: Proposals for Business Rates Retention: Government Response* (available at http://www.communities.gov.uk/documents/localgovernment/pdf/2053502.pdf [accessed March 2012]).
6  DCLG (19 December 2011) *Local Government Resource Review: Proposals for Business Rates Retention: Government Response* (available at http://www.communities.gov.uk/documents/localgovernment/pdf/2053502.pdf [accessed March 2012]).
7  The Guardian (2 August 2011) *Westminster Deserves its Share of Local Business Rates.*

*Funding LPAs*

London Councils, the group representing the 32 London boroughs and the Corporation of London, has produced a model for a scheme whereby authorities would combine their retained business rates and would allocate this money to different boroughs depending on the needs of their residents.[8] Although this model is currently simply a working draft, setting out one possible way in which business rate retention may be approached in London, London Councils' executive committee has agreed the following set of guiding principles in the approach to dealing with business rate retention:

> '(a) London would continue to pay a share of its business rates yield to the rest of England, to ensure fairness across England by reflecting London's historic position as a major generator of business rates.
> (b) Recognising London's position as a driver of growth in the national economy, and the fact that London is an economic whole, any scheme for business rate retention in London should drive and incentivise growth by directly rewarding councils for local growth through a retention mechanism, as well as sharing the benefits of growth across the capital.
> (c) Any London scheme would fund the withdrawal of the London boroughs, the Corporation of London, LFEPA and the MPA from the government's formula grant system.
> (d) Any London scheme would pool business rates across the city and allocate them, at least at the outset, according to the 2012/13 damped formula grant distribution – i.e. the year before the government's proposed introduction year.
> (e) The distribution formula for any London scheme would be reviewed in the future to develop a new version, designed by those involved in London's governance, which better reflected the evolving needs of each authority area. Any such formula would:
>  (i) be consistent with policy goals in this area and ensure that every borough has an incentive to drive growth;
>  (ii) recognise and improve the definition of need and take account of this in the distribution methodology;
>  (iii) hedge risks through pooling;
>  (iv) be subject to review and reform at regular intervals, but, recognising that there is a premium in stability, this period should be sufficiently long (say five years) to allow the proceeds of any growth to flow through. In the first phase, a review of operation after three years may be appropriate.
> (f) Governance and operation:
>  (i) any London scheme should be administered by a small independent body, funded by the pool;
>  (ii) there should be a small, independent board with "expert" participation, to oversee and guide day-to-day operations;
>  (iii) the body and board will be ultimately accountable to the democratically elected leaders of London;
>  (iv) an arbitration procedure would be adopted as the route of last resort to resolve disagreements.'[9]

---

8 London Councils (22 June 2011) *Resourcing London – A Model for Retained Business Rates.*
9 London Councils (22 June 2011) *Resourcing London – A Model for Retained Business Rates*, page 18.

## TAX INCREMENT FINANCING

Allowing local authorities to retain the business rates generated in their area may also assist in the introduction of Tax Increment Financing ('TIF'). TIF is a funding mechanism, pioneered in the United States, to provide financing for major infrastructure and redevelopment schemes. TIF operates by anticipating increases in future tax revenue and using these to finance the development that is designed to lead to these increases. The concept behind TIF is that investment in infrastructure, or development, will attract business and lead to improvement, and an increase in value, of surrounding land and buildings. Such increases in value should then, in turn, lead to increased taxation. By pledging this anticipated increase in taxation, it therefore becomes possible to finance the initial development.

At the Liberal Democrat party conference in September 2010, Nick Clegg announced that councils would be allowed to use TIF as a new borrowing mechanism. This was confirmed in the October 2010 publication, *Local Growth: Realising Every Place's Potential*, which stated that 'we will introduce new borrowing powers to enable authorities to carry out Tax Incremental Financing' in order to 'fund key infrastructure and other capital projects'.[10] The July 2011 consultation document proposes two options for the implementation of TIF in the UK.[11] The first of these would allow local authorities to decide independently whether or not to use TIF against their retained business rate revenues. However any growth in business rate revenue would be subject to the levy and be used to calculate any appropriate top-ups or tariffs. Under the second option there would be central government controls on the ability to use TIF but the additional business growth rates arising from any TIF funded project would be retained for a certain period of time and would not be used in the calculation of the levy or the top-ups or tariffs. The second option would provide greater certainty for prospective lenders as they would be assured that any revenue generated would be protected. However it would reduce the amount of money available nationwide to provide the levy rebalancing system. As such, if the second option is implemented there would have to be strict centralised controls on the number of TIF schemes implemented.

The Chancellor's 2011 Autumn Statement referred to TIF:[12]

> 'As part of its commitment to enable TIF, the government will ... consider allowing city mayors, to borrow against future CIL receipts where this can make a significant contribution to national infrastructure.'

The document went on to state that the Government would consider allowing local borrowing (presumably by the London Borough of Wandsworth) against future receipts of the CIL to support the proposed Northern Line extension to Battersea via Nine Elms.

---

10 HM Government (October 2010) *Local Growth: Realising Every Place's Potential* (available at http://www.bis.gov.uk/assets/biscore/economic-development/docs/l/cm7961-local-growth-white-paper.pdf [accessed November 2011]).
11 DCLG (July 2011) *Local Government Resource Review: Proposals for Business Rates Retention* (available at http://www.communities.gov.uk/documents/localgovernment/pdf/1947200.pdf [accessed in December 2011]).
12 HM Treasury (November 2011) *National Infrastructure Plan 2011*, page 7 (available at http://cdn.hm-treasury.gov.uk/national_infrastructure_plan291111.pdf [accessed February 2011]).

*Funding LPAs*

The proposals still, however, have some way to go. For example, the potential for the Government to 'reset' business rates every ten years, as set out in the Local Government Finance Bill and the Government's December 2011 response document in relation to its business rate retention proposals has raised concerns as to whether this will prejudice authorities' ability to achieve long-term borrowing against business rates in a TIF system.

Further announcements were made in the Chancellor's 2012 Budget,[13] including that up to £150 million would be made available from 2012 to 2014, including through additional funding, for larger scale projects in core cities to be financed through TIF2, which would enable local authorities to borrow against future growth in business rates. Further details of a competition for allocating funding are awaited.

## THE NEW HOMES BONUS

The Conservative Green Paper *Open Source Planning* stated as follows:

'We have already set out in a previous green paper[14] our commitment that when your community builds more homes, central government will match pound-for-pound the extra money that your area gets through council tax for six years […]. Now, in this green paper, we also commit to allowing neighbourhoods to keep some of the money contributed by developers to councils at the time when planning approval is given. This will generate real cash for local communities, be a real incentive for local people to welcome new homes and new businesses, and be a powerful symbol of the new collaborative approach we want to take to development.'[15]

The framework for the scheme was set out in a consultation document in Autumn 2010.[16] On 17 February 2011, Minister for Housing and Local Government Grant Shapps announced its final structure,[17] which will operate by matching the council tax generated from every new home for each of the following six years. This funding, designed to replace the Housing and Planning Delivery Grant, has been described by the Government as 'the cornerstone of the new framework for incentivising housing growth'.[18]

The New Homes Bonus is designed to incentivise and encourage local authorities and communities to build houses in their area by providing local authorities and communities with financial assistance in proportion to the amount of new homes built. As stated in a letter from Grant Shapps to council

---

13  HM Treasury, *Budget 2012*, page 42.
14  The Conservative Party (February 2009) *Control Shift: Returning Power to Communities* (available at http://www.conservatives.com/~/media/Files/Green%20Papers/Localism-Policy-Paper.ashx?dl=true [accessed March 2012]).
15  The Conservative Party (February 2010) *Open Source Planning*.
16  DCLG (November 2010) *New Homes Bonus: Consultation* (available at http://www.communities.gov.uk/documents/housing/pdf/1767788.pdf [accessed in December 2011]).
17  DCLG (February 2011) *New Homes Bonus: Final Scheme Design* (available at http://www.communities.gov.uk/documents/housing/pdf/1846530.pdf [accessed in December 2011]).
18  DCLG (February 2011) *New Homes Bonus: Final Scheme Design*, para 3.28 (available at http://www.communities.gov.uk/documents/housing/pdf/1846530.pdf [accessed in December 2011]).

leaders, 'local authorities ... who take action now to give planning consent and support the construction of new homes will receive direct and substantial benefit from their actions'.[19]

The funds raised by the New Homes Bonus will not be ringfenced, and can therefore be used as the local authority sees fit. The New Homes Bonus will also apply to empty homes that are brought back onto the market. It will apply as well to affordable homes, for which a flat rate of £350 will be paid each year. Local authorities will also receive funding for the provision of travellers sites.[20]

£200 million has been assigned to fund the scheme in 2011/2012, with £250 million per year allocated for the following three years. Any additional funding required will be provided by the Formula Grant. The money will be paid to local authorities through the Local Government Act 2003, s 31 alongside normal government financing. Where, in areas outside of London, there are two tiers of local authority, the lower tier (ie district or borough councils) will receive 80 per cent of the bonus whilst the upper tier (ie county councils) will receive 20 per cent. In London, 100 per cent of the New Homes Bonus will be paid to the borough in which the homes are built.

## THE PROPOSAL THAT LPAS SHOULD BE ALLOWED TO SET THEIR OWN PLANNING APPLICATION FEES

In November 2010, DCLG consulted as to whether local authorities should be able to set their own fees for handling planning applications rather than these being set at a national level, so as to allow local authorities to cover the actual costs of handling planning applications (whilst not making a profit). The original consultation document stated that these changes to the fee-setting structure should be implemented from April 2011, with a transition period until October 2011. As yet however there is no indication of when these changes will be implemented.

The lack of progress is leading to concern on the part of many authorities. In the interim, Westminster City Council (with the support of the Westminster Property Association) is encouraging the use of Planning Performance Agreements for large or complex developments. Entering into such an agreement is completely voluntary, as is the payment of the suggested fee of £26,000 plus VAT. Any large scheme that is submitted without a Planning Performance Agreement will be determined without the benefit of any lengthy pre-application discussions. However pre-application advice may still be obtained on payment of a standard fee.

---

19 DCLG (9 August 2010) Press Notice *Grant Shapps: Extra Funding for Councils who Go for Growth Now* (available at http://www.communities.gov.uk/news/corporate/1681467 [accessed December 2011]).
20 DCLG (29 August 2010) *Eric Pickles: Fair Deal for Travellers and the Settled Community* (available at http://www.communities.gov.uk/newsstories/newsroom/1701109 [accessed December 2011]).

## COMMUNITY LAND AUCTIONS

The 2011 Budget[21] presented by Chancellor George Osborne, included an announcement of new plans for 'land auctions'[22] to encourage local development. DCLG hopes that auctioning parcels of land with planning permission will have the potential to 'bring forward more land for development, increase competition in development and provide greater certainty for developers'.[23]

The idea behind community land auctions stems from a paper written in 2007 by Dr Tim Leunig,[24] reader in economic history at the London School of Economics. In 2007 Leunig also jointly wrote an article on the same subject with Liberal Democrat MP Ed Davey (now Minister for Employment Relations, Consumer and Postal Affairs).[25]

A community land auction would work by encouraging local land owners to submit sealed bids to the LPA stating the price at which they would be willing to sell their land. The offer would be binding, giving the LPA an option to buy the land for a specified length of time, such as a year. The LPA would consult with the local community to decide which land they would like to see developed and would then grant that land planning permission and then auction it to developers. The successful bidder would pay the land owner the price that the land owner had set and the rest of the money would go to the LPA, capturing a large proportion of the increase in land value created by allowing development. In urban areas the scheme would also encourage the reallocation of land from industrial to residential use. The LPA would then be able to use these profits for the benefit of the community, for example, by offering subsidies for affordable housing or by supporting local services.

The Government's *Plan for Growth*[26] published alongside the March 2011 Budget states that:

> 'The land auctions model seeks to capture a greater share of the land value uplift created by the granting of planning permission than is currently the case. This may bring a number of benefits compared to the current system of allocating land for development, potentially making significantly more land available for development, increasing competition and bringing greater certainty and reduced risks for developers. It would work alongside existing mechanisms such as the Community Infrastructure Levy. The model would generally involve local authorities auctioning planning permission on parcels of land, owned either by the public sector or private landowners who want to participate.

---

21 HM Government (June 2011) *Budget 2011* (available at http://cdn.hm-treasury.gov.uk/2011budget_complete.pdf [accessed December 2011]).
22 HM Government (June 2011) *Budget 2011*, para 1.82 (available at http://cdn.hm-treasury.gov.uk/2011budget_complete.pdf [accessed December 2011]).
23 DCLG (23 March 2011) Press notice *Eric Pickles: Radical Changes in Housing and Planning will Drive Local Growth* (available at http://www.communities.gov.uk/news/newsroom/1871038 [accessed December 2011]).
24 Centre Forum (2007) *In My Back Yard: Unlocking the Planning System* (available at http://www.centreforum.org/assets/pubs/in-my-back-yard.pdf [accessed December 2011]).
25 Financial Times (24 July 2007) *Auction Land to Ease the Housing Crisis* (available at http://www.ft.com/cms/s/0/516ecf08-3a0f-11dc-9d73-0000779fd2ac.html#axzz1gQjcnSgj [accessed December 2011]).
26 HM Treasury (March 2011) *Plan for Growth* (available at http://cdn.hm-treasury.gov.uk/2011budget_growth.pdf [accessed December 2011]).

*Local finance considerations*

The Government will pilot elements of this approach on publicly owned land within 12 months, in order to test the land disposal elements of the model. The Government will give further consideration to the wider land auctions model over the coming months, with a view to wider use.'[27]

A small number of LPAs have been approached to volunteer for what is described as a pilot scheme. However, it is still uncertain exactly how this will work. It appears strange to be piloting the scheme with land that is already owned by the public sector, a point which Tim Leunig has himself made.

A number of matters appear to be unresolved in relation to the proposals, for example:

- The LPA would need to do full due diligence before entering into each option. The idea only works if there are options over more land than is ultimately required (otherwise the land owner will see he is in pole position for the allocation and price accordingly) and so one has the notion of an LPA negotiating a number of different option agreements to a stage where it is satisfied that it has secured an option that will be marketable to bidders in an auction.
- What restrictions would the land owner be under in dealing in his land in the meantime?
- A developer would not wish to draw down land under an option arrangement simply on the basis of an allocation, as opposed to having the benefit of detailed planning permission for specific parcels.
- Do many LPAs have the resources and commercial experience to bring forward a viable, marketable opportunity which maximises planning uplift – requiring investment in up-front master-planning, infrastructure planning and site assembly?

## LOCAL FINANCE CONSIDERATIONS

Section 143 of the Act introduces an amendment to the Town and Country Planning Act, s 70 to add 'local finance considerations' to the list of considerations to be taken into account by a decision maker when determining applications for planning permission.

Prior to its amendment, s 70 provides that in determining planning applications local authorities 'shall have regard to the provisions of the development plan, so far as material to the application, and to any other material considerations'. The courts have interpreted the meaning of 'other material considerations' in many cases over the years. On this formulation, the courts have held that an applicant cannot 'buy' a permission. Further, as already mentioned, from 6 April 2010, the Community Infrastructure Levy Regulations 2010 (SI 2010/948) made it unlawful for an authority in determining a planning application to have regard to a planning obligation which was not necessary to make the development acceptable in planning terms, directly related to the development, and fairly and reasonably related in scale and kind to the development.

---

27 HM Treasury (March 2011) *Plan for Growth*, para 2.18 (available at http://cdn.hm-treasury.gov.uk/2011budget_growth.pdf [accessed December 2011]).

*Funding LPAs*

When the amendment, inserting reference to 'local finance considerations' into s 70, was introduced at the Report Stage in the House of Commons, Greg Clark commented that the provision:

> 'makes it clear that local finance matters that are relevant to planning considerations can be taken into account. It does not change the law in any way, and it is not some stealthy way in which to introduce a new basis for planning policy. Everyone knows that section 106 payments that are material in planning matters can be taken into consideration. The new clause reflects the fact that the introduction of the community infrastructure levy, and, potentially, other rebates to the local community, as I like to call them, can be used for planning purposes. It is important to be clear, lest there is any doubt on the part of local authorities, that such rebates, just like under section 106, can be made when they are relevant to planning considerations.'[28]

Because of concerns raised that the amendment would pave the way for planning permissions being 'bought', the following additional provisions were tabled at the House of Lords stage, which have made their way into s 143(5):

> '(5) The amendments made by this section do not alter –
> (a) whether under subsection (2) of section 70 of the Town and Country Planning Act 1990 regard is to be had to any particular consideration, or
> (b) the weight to be given to any consideration to which regard is had under that subsection.'

Lord Atlee in the House of Lords (for the Government) commented in relation to the new local finance consideration that:

> 'I can categorically confirm that the Government are in no doubt that the clause as drafted does not represent any change in the current law whatever. It is declaratory of the current law, which is that where local financial considerations are material to a planning application they should be taken into account in the determination of that planning application.
>
> Furthermore – this is of direct relevance to the concerns raised previously by noble Lords – the Government are absolutely certain that the clause does not require greater consideration to be given to local finance considerations than to any other material consideration …
>
> As noble Lords will see, Amendment 223CA makes it absolutely explicit that the new reference to local finance considerations does not affect the weight to be given to any particular consideration. We have provided even greater reassurance by additionally confirming that the clause does not alter whether regard is to be had to any consideration. Apportioning weight remains a matter for the decision-maker.'[29]

Baroness Parminter (also for the Government) in her response gave an example of the mixed views on the amendment:

> 'As we know, this clause, which outlines that financial considerations can be material to a planning application, was added in the Commons as an incidental measure for clarification. As the noble Earl, Lord Attlee, indicated, the Government have argued that it is the new homes bonus that

---

28   Hansard, 17 May 2011, col 270.
29   Hansard, 17 October 2011, cols 124–125.

has necessitated such clarification. However, by using statute rather than the traditional route of guidance, the Government are undoubtedly creating further uncertainty.

The clause elevates financial considerations above all other legitimate planning considerations, which are not mentioned here or anywhere else in statute. As such, the courts will be used to decide just what Parliament means by putting financial considerations up front as a material condition. While the government amendment goes some way to try to tackle that ambiguity, there still remains a lack of clarity about when such financial considerations could be considered material.'[30]

---

30  Hansard, 17 October 2011, cols 126–127.

# Chapter 16

# Navigating the system

So what will this new localist planning system look like and how will it feel? What in practice will you need to do now which you might not have had to do before? How might this differ if you are a landowner, a developer, an LPA or one of the people for whom the system is being reformed – local residents and local businesses?

In this Chapter we have tried to put ourselves in the shoes of those who need to navigate the planning system and who want to get the most (or the least) out of it. We highlight the five most important things we think you need to have in mind and we conclude with one key message.

## THE LANDOWNER

### Audit developer interest

If you are a landowner with a development opportunity, hoping to profit from developer interest, choose your developer wisely. Make sure they appreciate the change in culture that the reforms are bringing: test their track record and check that they understand and have researched the local context. Before you agree to an option and lock yourself out of dealing with your land for one or two years, do your homework. What is the policy justification for the development's proposal and, given the abolition of regional strategies, the revision of local plans and the possibility of Neighbourhood Development Plans, for how long can that policy justification be relied upon? If there is not a local plan in your area that is compliant with the National Planning Policy Framework, then in theory that could provide an opportunity where the presumption in favour of sustainable development may apply. Similarly the opportunity presented by a favourable regional strategy policy or evidence base may yet have some life left in it: transitional arrangements for the abolition of regional strategies may result in certain regional level policies being saved for a period of time and in certain circumstances those policies may be reflected in local plans when they are reviewed. However, as a general rule, reliance on these 'non-localist' sources of policy support is likely to prove short-lived. Even at the early stage of preparation, a replacement local plan or a local plan review is likely now to be given significant weight, in order not to deprive local communities of their role in identifying the level and location of development in their areas. We draw attention to one of a number of recent planning appeal decisions which emphasised this point:

> '… Government has made it clear that its intention is to return decision making powers in housing and planning to local authorities. This is a key planning priority for the Government and the Secretary of State considers

that in this particular case it is important to give Winchester the opportunity to complete its blueprint process.'[1]

## Everybody needs good neighbours

Regardless of developer interest in your land and particularly if you are in a non-parished area, be alert to the coalescence of interests, organisations for individuals which gain momentum. At the very least they could become a powerful influence on local public opinion and the LPA's decision-making; they may also form themselves into a Neighbourhood Forum and gain the ability to bring forward a Neighbourhood Development Plan, a Neighbourhood Development Order or a Community Right to Build Order.

Think about joining or influencing any Neighbourhood Forum or parish council, but do in any event track their activity. Time invested in community relationships will also be well-spent – those relationships will help you to influence outcomes; remember that your community is not just local residents but also your tenants, other landowners, businesses and other public bodies.

Through their Neighbourhood Development Plans, Neighbourhood Development Orders and Community Right to Build Orders, Neighbourhood Forums and parish councils will have the ability to allocate sites for development or introduce designations or protections, which can have significant implications for the development prospects for your land. However, they too must engage with and consult the wider community, so if you are not involved in the early stages of production of a plan or order, then you should actively protect your interests by responding to consultation and seeking modifications where appropriate. Where this fails, there are various pitfalls for parishes and Neighbourhood Forums (and local planning authorities) which may lead to the unravelling of any neighbourhood planning document or at least its delay, either at the examination stage or later on in the courts. For example:

- compliance with mandatory requirements for content and scope[2] such as 'excluded development';[3]
- adequacy of consultation undertaken for the Neighbourhood Development Plan, Neighbourhood Development Order or Community Right to Build Order;

---

1 Secretary of State's decision letter (28 September 2011) para 20 in the appeal by Cala Homes (South) Limited relating to land at Barton Farm (APP/L1765/A/10/212622) (available at http://www.communities.gov.uk/documents/planning-callins/pdf/1997209.pdf [accessed January 2012]). Although the Secretary of State has since consented to judgment on this appeal decision so that it has been formally quashed and must be re-taken, it is symptomatic of the Government's approach and we refer later in this chapter to other appeal decisions where the same philosophy is underlined.
2 Localism Act 2011, Schs 9–11.
3 In the context of Neighbourhood Development Orders see Town and Country Planning Act 1990, new ss 61J and 61K, inserted by Localism Act 2011, Sch 9, para 2 and Planning and Compulsory Purchase Act 2004, s 38B inserted by Localism Act 2011, Sch 9, para 7 in relation to Neighbourhood Development Plans.

*The landowner*

- environmental impact assessment (for Neighbourhood Development Orders[4]) and strategic environmental assessment[5] (for Plans);
- the requirement for general conformity with strategic priorities in the Local Development Plan; and
- the need to contribute to the achievement of sustainable development.

## The promotion of sites

The pitfalls of the neighbourhood planning processes are a good place to start for considering the approach that is needed towards the promotion of sites.

These pitfalls are faced not only by the parish council or the Neighbourhood Forum in terms of aspiration, time and expense, but also by the LPA in terms of administration time and expense; it is the LPA which in the majority of cases will take the administrative decisions that are vulnerable to judicial review, ie the adoption of any Neighbourhood Development Plan or the making of any Neighbourhood Development Order. For the LPA, these functions are not replaced by others which it no longer has to perform; this is additional work and therefore a further drain on resources.

All of this points towards the need to promote sites in a way which relieves the parish council/Neighbourhood Forum and the LPA of as much of the burden as possible. As far as practicable, we consider the landowner should be handing Neighbourhood Forums/parish councils and LPAs a 'ready-made' allocation. By this we mean a proposal that evidences:

- consultation with the community and partnership working with other stakeholders (including the Neighbourhood Forum, parish council and local planning authority concerned);
- compliance with strategic priorities in the Local Development Plan;
- impact assessment;
- viability and availability; and
- an audit check against the requirements of the Localism Act 2011.

This will provide LPAs in particular and also Neighbourhood Forums/parish councils with a solid base from which to conduct their own processes.

## Unlocking potential

This co-operative approach towards realising the development potential of a site deserves some emphasis.

Its consequence goes beyond making it easier for the Neighbourhood Forum/parish council or the LPA. Achieving an allocation, particularly at neighbourhood level (with the implication of community support and acceptance) will render your site a very attractive proposition.

---

4   A Neighbourhood Development Order must not include any project which falls within Annex 1 to the 'Environmental Impact Assessment Directive' (Council Directive 85/337/EEC) but it can include projects which fall within Annex 2 to that Directive. However, the local planning authority must decline to consider a proposal for the Community Right to Build Order if they consider that it is likely to require environmental impact assessment.
5   As required by Council Directive 2001/42/EC on the assessment of plans and programmes which we consider may well extend to Neighbourhood Development Plans.

In addition, the LPA, bolstered by its general power of competence in s 1 of the Localism Act, and as the ringmaster for Community Infrastructure Levy receipts, income from business rates growth,[6] New Homes Bonus[7] and potentially other sources,[8] could play an important part in unlocking your site, by committing to infrastructure funding, pooling land resources or leading a process of collaboration with other landowners and interests.

To some extent this may also be true of parish councils and Neighbourhood Forums where they are in receipt of funds (eg their 'meaningful proportion'[9] of Community Infrastructure Levy) or other sources or where they have ownership of land.

## New designations

By contrast you also need to be alert to the desire of the parish council/Neighbourhood Forum or other parts of the community to acquire or designate your site as an asset, either through the allocation of land in local and neighbourhood plans as Local Green Space or other restrictive policy allocations, or through the List of Assets of Community Value (or indeed other statutory designations that exist already such as public rights of way and town/village greens).

Local Green Space is a concept that is referred to in the National Planning Policy Framework and it is intended for use by communities in local and neighbourhood development plans as a means by which they can protect green spaces of particular importance to them. The effect of such a designation in policy terms will be 'to rule out new development other than in very special circumstances'[10] on a comparable basis to Green Belt policy.[11] However, the NPPF is clear that Local Green Spaces should be used sparingly and only when a plan is prepared or reviewed. Identifying land as Local Green Space is to be 'consistent with the local planning of sustainable development and complement investment in sufficient homes, jobs and other essential services'.[12] Furthermore its use will not be appropriate for most green spaces and only:

---

6 The Local Government Finance Bill introduced to Parliament on 19 December 2011 includes a business rates retention scheme whereby a percentage share of business rates will be localised and, subject to future adjustment by the Government, will be applied to any growth in business rates revenue generated in the local area.
7 New Homes Bonus commenced in April 2011. The effect of the initiative is that the Government will match-fund the additional Council Tax raised for new homes and empty properties brought back into use for a period of six years. A premium amount is payable for affordable homes.
8 For example Tax Increment Financing.
9 Planning Act 2008, s 216A inserted by Localism Act 2011, s 115, which allows Community Infrastructure Levy Regulations to include a requirement that the amount of the CIL received in respect of the development of land is to be passed to other persons. In the consultation document *Community Infrastructure Levy – Detailed Proposals and Draft Regulations for Reform* (DCLG, 10 October 2011), the Government confirmed on page 11 that it intends to use this power to allocate a meaningful proportion of the revenue generated from the Levy to the locally elected council for the area where the development takes place.
10 DCLG (March 2012) *NPPF*, para 76 (available at http://www.communities.gov.uk/documents/planningandbuilding/pdf/2116950.pdf [accessed April 2012]).
11 DCLG (March 2012) *NPPF*, para 79 ff (available at http://www.communities.gov.uk/documents/planningandbuilding/pdf/2116950.pdf [accessed April 2012]).
12 DCLG (March 2012) *NPPF*, para 76 (available at http://www.communities.gov.uk/documents/planningandbuilding/pdf/2116950.pdf [accessed April 2012]).

*The landowner*

- '• where the green space is in reasonably close proximity to a centre of population or urban area
- • where the green space is demonstrably special to a local community and holds a particular local significant because of its beauty, historic importance, recreational value, tranquillity or richness of its wildlife
- • where the green area concerned is local in character and is not an extensive tract of land and
- • if the designation does not overlap with Green Belt.'

The List of Assets of Community Value is a register which LPAs will be obliged to maintain.[13] The consequence of land being included in the list is that (absent any successful review or later appeal of that decision[14]) there is a moratorium[15] on the disposal of the land without notice to the LPA; that notice triggers a six week window for expressions of interest to be made by community interest groups and where any interest is received, the extension of that window to six months to allow the relevant groups to bid on the open market to acquire the asset. Some disposals are exempt from the moratorium and the Government has indicated that certain classes of property will not be capable of being included in the list.[16] However, subject to that, land will be of community value[17] and eligible for inclusion in the list if:

- • the building or land is currently used to further the social well-being or social interests of the local community (not in a way that is ancillary to another use) and it is realistic to think that such a use can continue (albeit that it may further the social well-being or social interests of the local community in another way); or
- • the building or land has recently been used to further the social well-being or social interests[18] of the local community (not in a way that is ancillary to another use) and it is realistic to think that such a use could resume in the next five years (albeit that it may further the social well-being or social interests of the local community in another way).

Although it might be thought that the inclusion of land on the list of community assets has little teeth, if a community group secures this outcome it is likely to deter market interest, have an adverse (albeit temporary) effect on value and delay the realisation of development potential.

Clearly, if as a landowner you are unfortunate enough to have an allocation or listing imposed upon you, there is scope to use these criteria in a defensive way – ie to defeat a proposed allocation of Local Green Space or a nomination for inclusion as a community asset either through review, appeal, representations or judicial challenge – but this will be time-consuming and potentially costly. Prevention is better than cure: the earlier you bring forward development

---

13  Localism Act 2011, s 87. See Chapter 4.
14  Localism Act 2011, s 92.
15  Localism Act 2011, s 95.
16  Localism Act 2011, s 87(3) provides power to make regulations which deem land not to be of community value and the Government has indicated that this is likely to include residential land and operational land belonging to statutory undertakers: see DCLG (September 2011) *Assets of Community Value Policy Statement* (available at http://www.communities.gov.uk/documents/localgovernment/pdf/1987150.pdf [accessed January 2012]).
17  Localism Act 2011, s 88.
18  Including cultural interests, recreational interests and sporting interests: Localism Act 2011, s 88(6).

proposals the better and in the meantime, try to regulate any public access that may occur on your land, reaffirming your rights as owner to the extent that you can within the law (eg occasionally closing off public access where there is no existing public right, erecting notices to indicate the land is private and is not accessible without the landowner's consent, etc).

# THE DEVELOPER

## Community demographics

It is probably no exaggeration to say that major retailers are obsessive about acquiring knowledge of their customers – their social background, their income, their shopping habits, etc. In particular, when considering store openings, retailers will tend to establish the profile of the people in the catchment area in order to determine whether their store will perform well – ie whether there is a close correlation between the catchment and their usual type of customers. This may be a rather sophisticated example of what we have in mind but we would suggest that developers can learn from this, when it comes to promoting development in this new localist environment.

You should know your community before you start to promote your development. Taking time to research the residents, businesses and other stakeholders in the area where you have a development opportunity will arm you with invaluable information.

Perhaps most important of all you will ascertain the needs of that area. Aside from influencing the type of development you bring forward, this will help you to understand what will motivate your audience and where the key concerns of the community lie: is it the low number of school places, the loss of small local shops or the absence of facilities for young people or other parts of the community and what effect will your development have on them? This information may also help you to devise solutions to the current problems and deliver those solutions or contribute towards their delivery through your development.

This sort of exercise should also enable you to establish the track record of the LPA, other public bodies and different groups in the community in terms of their attitude to development. This will tend to illuminate 'no go areas' or approaches that are welcomed. It should also enable you to target your time and resources towards the relationships that are likely to be most important to the success of your proposals.

Finally, investing in this process should help you to understand how extensively you need to consult on your proposals, the methods you will need to use and how best to engage successfully with the majority of people in the community and not just the minority who keep an eye out for the weekly planning application list or those who make it their business to read the minutes of every parish council meeting. This may mean embracing new ways of reaching people such as social networking – a tool that could be particularly important, for example, in an area with a large commuting population.

*The developer*

## Consultation, consultation, consultation

This brings us to another key change in the reforms for developers: the new duty to undertake consultation before applying for planning permission.[19]

We have covered the detail of these changes elsewhere in this book[20] and drawn attention to the likelihood that the duty will only apply to a certain scale of proposals but it is likely nonetheless to have a significant effect on the expectations of the local community and the local planning authority about the level of their involvement in the development process. More than that, pre-application consultation is now enshrined as a legal duty and the degree to which that duty is discharged could prove to be a fruitful area for judicial review claims against the grant of planning permission, right at the end of the process – either because the LPA has failed to give consideration to the adequacy of the consultation or because, having done so, it has overlooked a key aspect of the consultation that did not meet the requirements of the Act. This combination of changes in expectation and the vulnerability to legal challenge will, we believe, bring about changes in practice, even among those developers who undertake exemplary pre-application consultation under the existing voluntary system. Certainly the inclusion of a similar duty in the context of the planning system for Nationally Significant Infrastructure Projects[21] is one of the reasons for the anecdotal evidence that front-loading for those types of schemes – ie the time and cost spent at the pre-application stage – has increased significantly and beyond all expectation.[22]

The new duty can be broken down into different components. There is the ability to introduce further, more detailed requirements through regulations but in their present form the key components are:

- publicise the application in such manner as you reasonably consider is likely to bring it to the attention of a majority of persons who live at or otherwise occupy premises in the vicinity of the land;
- in doing so, set out how you may be contacted by anyone wishing to comment on or collaborate with you on the design of the proposed development and give sufficient information about the proposed timetable for consultation to ensure those wishing to comment may do so in good time;
- consult each specified person (identified for example in the Development Management Order[23]);
- in doing this, have regard to the advice (if any) given by the LPA; and
- following this, have regard to any responses to the consultation that you receive in deciding whether to bring forward the proposals in the same form.

---

19 Localism Act 2011, s 122, which inserts Town and Country Planning Act 1990, ss 61W, 61X and 61Y.
20 See Chapter 7.
21 Planning Act 2008, ss 47–49.
22 The other being the near perfect condition that the application for a development consent order has had to be in for acceptance, which to some extent should be relieved by the new flexibility given to the Secretary of State to accept applications if they are of a standard that he considers acceptable, which has been introduced by Localism Act 2011, s 137 (amending Planning Act 2008, s 55).
23 The Town and Country Planning (Development Management Procedure) (England) Order 2010 (SI 2010/2184), which may be amended in order to accommodate these changes.

*Navigating the system*

This is one of the reasons why we say it is so important to know your community before you initiate a development proposal – you will need to invest sufficient time and resources to identify who you should consult, when you should consult them and how and to what extent. However, to provide you with a degree of certainty early on and to minimise the risk of the pre-application consultation becoming a ground of challenge for judicial review of a planning permission later on, rather than waiting for any advice from the local planning authority on this we suggest that the better approach is to engage them actively in a 'screening' and 'scoping' exercise.[24] In other words, you should prepare a statement setting out clearly:

- the nature of the proposal and its likely effects;
- the people, businesses and other organisations who you are intending to consult and the geographical extent of the area that you are targeting for consultation;
- what you are intending to consult on;
- the methods you are intending to use; and
- the timescale that you are intending to adopt.

You will need to bear in mind the well-established case law on consultation requirements that we have drawn attention to earlier in this book;[25] whilst these cases primarily concern public authorities the principles they establish should inform how you approach pre-application consultation. For example:

- you should consult at a stage when there is scope to influence the outcome (especially in light of the fact that in the context of the obligation to give contact details in publicity[26] the new duty envisages people collaborating with you on matters such as design);
- people should have adequate time to be consulted – the guideline adopted by Government and other public authorities is at least 12 weeks[27] although this length of time may not be necessary in every case;
- you should be clear about the scope of the consultation and the ability to influence the development proposals;
- you should make the process as easy as possible for the people you are consulting; and
- you should build in time to analyse the responses and provide feedback and if necessary, a further period of consultation on significant changes that may be made in response to the first round of consultation.

We think a practice will develop of consulting the LPA on this sort of 'consultation scoping' statement and securing a written opinion from the authority on its adequacy. It is interesting to note in this regard that the planning system for Nationally Significant Infrastructure Projects expressly provides for such a procedure as part of the pre-application duty to consult.[28]

---

24 Not dissimilar to the concept of screening and scoping that is now common practice for environmental impact assessment: see the Town and Country Planning (Environmental Impact Assessment) (England) Regulations 2011 (SI 2011/1824), Pts 2 and 4.
25 See Chapter 7.
26 Town and Country Planning Act 1990, s 61W(4).
27 See, for example, HM Government Code of Practice on Consultation (July 2008) published by the then Department for Business Enterprise and Regulatory Reform (now BIS) (now archived).
28 See Planning Act 2008, s 47(1) and (2).

*The developer*

To continue the audit trail for compliance with this pre-application duty of consultation, you should also include with your planning application, as a matter of course, an evidence-based report on the consultation exercise which draws on the scoping statement, records how in fact the consultation exercise was undertaken, the level of response, the nature of the responses and how those responses were taken into account. Some developers already prepare a report of this nature under the existing system where it is either voluntary or a local policy requirement or a local requirement for validation of a planning application. In many cases, those statements may be adequate for the sort of audit trail we have in mind but they must be written with the new legal duty in mind, with evidence to support any assertions that may be made, eg concerning influence on design.

To sum up, consultation has to be taken seriously and it must be genuine: 'This is a hall for mutual consultation and discussion; not an arena for the exhibition of champions.'[29]

## Collaboration

As we have seen, the word 'collaborate' is used in the context of the duty of pre-application consultation, with regard to influencing design.[30] It is by no means the only context in which the concept of collaboration will be important for the successful delivery of a project. Given the political philosophy behind the Localism Act and the effect that this will have – indeed already has had – on the culture and the climate of the planning process, developers will be well-advised to explore opportunities for partnership in the local community. This could take place in some small way – for example, by including in your development proposals the delivery of some much needed community facilities or accepting that part of the site will become Local Green Space or a community asset, protected by policy or other provisions in the Localism Act. Alternatively, it may be appropriate to think on a larger, more ambitious scale by pooling land, finances or other resources with the parish council, the LPA or other landowners to make a bigger, more positive difference.

You should see this as a two-way street and not just another form of planning gain.[31] In some instances, there could be constraints which are outside your control but which are preventing you from realising the full development potential of your site; these might be relieved by the LPA, not only in the conventional sense that we have come to understand (use of compulsory purchase powers, undertaking improvements to the road network as local highway authority, etc) but also in more innovative deployment of the many funding pots that the authority will be co-ordinating – whether Community Infrastructure Levy, business rates retention, New Homes Bonus, regional grant funding and so on. More generally, those developers that explore and take up opportunities for partnership in the local community will, we believe, benefit from a greater level of support and acceptance – in effect an unwritten licence to operate.

---

29   Daniel Webster, American Statesman, Senator and Orator (1782–1852).
30   Town and Country Planning Act 1990, s 61W(4).
31   Ie a planning obligation which would be secured by an agreement or undertaking pursuant to Town and Country Planning Act 1990, s 106.

Critics of this approach will argue that this is to endorse the buying and selling of planning permission. That is not the case. It is undoubtedly a policy objective of Government that the local community should benefit more from the investment that development brings to its area; the collaborative approach is more about recognising and responding to the needs of communities and ensuring that development is 'sustainable' – again it is a matter of knowing your community.

We think this principle will be all the more important in the early stages of the new localist planning system when expectations will be higher, when government funding is being cut, because of national debt and the state of the economy, and when the principal reference points for decision making (the development plan and other planning policies) are likely to be in a state of flux for some time. Although they are not carried through to the final NPPF, the words near the beginning of the draft National Planning Policy Framework[32] best conveyed this sentiment:

> 'Those responsible for bringing forward development are expected to play their part by recognising and responding to the needs of communities. Development should be of good design and appropriately located. National incentives and relevant local charges will help ensure local communities benefit directly from the increase in development that this Framework seeks to achieve. The revenue generated from development will help sustain local services, fund infrastructure and deliver environmental enhancement.'

## The policy landscape

We have alluded to this already[33] but it is a significant feature of these reforms that planning policy will be in a state of flux for the short to medium term. Establishing policy support for a development proposal will be challenging at best and even once established may prove to be short-lived.

The problem stems from the removal of one tier of policy (regional strategies),[34] the insertion of another *optional* tier of policy (Neighbourhood Development Plans[35]) and the consolidation of national policy into the National Planning Policy Framework with the presumption in favour of sustainable development and the need for local development plans to be reviewed for their compliance with the Framework. The interplay between all these factors will be complicated. We predict a good deal of inconsistency around the country in these early years.

Nor do we see planning appeals as an answer to this inconsistency. Called-in and recovered appeal decisions thus far in the shadow of these reforms (including the draft form of the NPPF) suggest that these decisions will also be led by the specific local circumstances. We have already referred to the *Cala Homes* decision by the Secretary of State.[36] This decision has since been quashed as a result of the Secretary of State consenting to judgment but it remains illustrative of the Government's willingness to allow localism to run its course so that important strategic decisions are taken locally. It might also

---

32  DCLG (July 2011) *Draft NPPF*, para 18 (available at http://www.communities.gov.uk/documents/planningandbuilding/pdf/1951811.pdf [accessed November 2011]).
33  See above under 'The Landowner' – 'Audit developer interest'.
34  Localism Act 2011, s 109.
35  Localism Act 2011, s 116 and Sch 9.
36  APP/LI765/A/10/2126522 (28 September 2011).

be argued that the decision was tainted by the backdrop of litigation between Cala Homes and the Secretary of State concerning the abolition of regional strategies[37] but the emphasis placed on the importance of allowing the local processes for the determination of the amount and location of development to take their natural course is consistent with other decisions. In particular, in the appeal by Wainhomes (South West) Holdings Limited for a mixed use extension of St Austell,[38] despite finding that there was a probable absence of a five year supply of housing land, the Secretary of State said this:

> '... the grant of planning permission now would deny the local community the opportunity of determining its preferred choice of housing sites for St Austell and that, without full public consultation on all potential options, a complete representation of local opinion would not emerge.
>
> The Government has made it clear that its intention is to return decision making powers in housing and planning to local authorities. This is a key planning priority for the Government and the Secretary of State considers that in this particular case it is important to give Cornwall the opportunity to complete its Core Strategy process ...'[39]

The same approach was evident in an appeal concerning at least 1,000 dwellings at Belton Lane Grantham[40] where prematurity was a reason for refusal, albeit in circumstances where the Grantham Area Action Plan was at an advanced stage of preparation. In another appeal, the Secretary of State refused a 280 dwelling scheme on a greenfield site at Middlewich Road, Sandbach[41] partly because, although the Local Development Framework was at an early state of preparation, allowing the appeal 'would send the wrong message to other developers' and discourage development of previously developed land. This appeal decision has since been quashed[42] but in principle the Secretary of State was considered entitled to rely on prematurity as a reason for refusal; the problem arose in the inconsistency between this and an earlier appeal decision in the same geographic area.

In a further example of the importance placed on local determination and formation of policy, a mixed use scheme including up to 1,200 dwellings at Hatchfield Farm, Fordham Road, Newmarket[43] was refused notwithstanding an established need for more general and affordable housing in the district and an inadequate five-year housing land supply. One of the reasons for this was that a local plan review would properly compare the long term sustainable alternative locations for housing developments in a way that could not be carried out when determining a planning appeal. Even though the review still had a long way to go until adoption, the appeal proposals would pre-empt the proper operation of

---

37 Culminating in *R (Cala Homes (South) Limited) v Secretary of State for Communities and Local Government* (No.2) [2011] EWCA Civ 639.
38 APP/D0840/A/10/2130022 (31 October 2011) (available at http://www.communities.gov.uk/documents/planning-callins/pdf/2020508.pdf [accessed January 2012]).
39 APP/D0840/A/10/2130022 (31 October 2011), paras 18 and 19 (available at http://www.communities.gov.uk/documents/planning-callins/pdf/2020508.pdf [accessed January 2012]).
40 Decision letter (1 March 2012), APP/E2530/A/11/2150609 (available at http://www.communities.gov.uk/documents/planning-callins/pdf/2098380.pdf [accessed March 2012]).
41 Decision letter (29 September 2011), APP/R0660/A/10/2141564 (available at http://www.communities.gov.uk/documents/planning-callins/pdf/1998448.pdf [accessed March 2012]).
42 *Fox Strategic Land and Property Ltd v Secretary of State for Communities and Local Government* [2012] EWHC 444 (Admin).
43 Decision letter (22 March 2011) APP/H3510/A/10/2142030 (available at http://www.communities.gov.uk/documents/planning-callins/pdf/2112445.pdf [accessed April 2012]).

the development plan process which could give local residents an opportunity to influence the planning of their own communities.

By contrast, however, the Secretary of State was prepared to allow a 500-plus dwellings scheme at Binhamy Farm, Stratton Road, Bude[44] notwithstanding the concerns raised by others about prematurity and the fact that allowing the appeal could frustrate localism in the area; a factor seems to have been the need for housing in the local area and the suitability of the site for development in advance of adoption of local development plan documents which were still at an early stage.

So in this changing landscape what do you need to be aware of?

In some areas, regional strategies[45] may remain part of the development plan for the purposes of the Planning and Compulsory Purchase Act 2004, s 38(6) for a short time to come. Notwithstanding the provision in the Localism Act for revocation of regional strategies,[46] the Secretary of State has power to revoke all or parts only of a regional strategy[47] and the Government decided voluntarily to undertake and consult on an assessment of the likely significant environmental effects of revocation of the strategy in each region (outside of London where the London Plan will remain in force).[48] This may mean that adverse effects are identified and some parts of a strategy will need to be saved pending the evolution of local development plans. It may also lead to legal challenges (some of them successful) to the decision of the Secretary of State to revoke a strategy in any given case. However, any reliance placed on a regional strategy policy or even its evidence base must come with a health warning. Not only is there a significant risk that the policy will cease to have any effect in the short term but also that it will have an ever-reducing weight in decision-making, especially where the local plan is undergoing a review in compliance with the National Planning Policy Framework and the new duty to co-operate between LPAs and other bodies.[49]

Following publication of the National Planning Policy Framework, all local plans will to varying degrees need to be reviewed to ensure that among other things they:

- aim to achieve the objective of sustainable development;
- are consistent with the objectives principles and policies set out in the National Planning Policy Framework (including the presumption in favour of sustainable development); and
- set out the strategic priorities for the area in co-operation with other local planning authorities and other public bodies.

This process will need to be followed closely not only for the obvious reason that site allocations favourable to your development proposal will need to

---

44 Decision letter (28 July 2011), APP/D0840/A/09/2115945 (available at http://www.communities.gov.uk/documents/planning-callins/pdf/1955047.pdf [accessed March 2012]).
45 As provided for by Local Democracy, Economic Development and Construction Act 2009, Pt 5.
46 Localism Act 2011, s 109.
47 Localism Act 2011, s 109(3).
48 See the various environmental reports on the revocation of regional strategies published for consultation ending on 20 January 2012 and available at http://www.communities.gov.uk/planningandbuilding/planningenvironment/strategicenvironmentassess/ [accessed March 2012].
49 Localism Act 2011, s 110, which inserts Planning and Compulsory Purchase Act 2004, s 33A.

## The developer

be protected or secured, but also in order to ensure that the evidence base established in the local plan (replacing the evidence base which existed at regional level) along with the rest of the policy framework remain supportive and robust. It may also be the case that these local plan reviews provide an early expression of localism in the sense that community groups may jettison the possibility of using neighbourhood planning tools in favour of pursuing their objectives in the local plan.

In relation to those neighbourhood planning tools, the take up of Neighbourhood Development Plans will vary across the country but they will have significant force when they are in place: the National Planning Policy Framework provides that once made, policies in a Neighbourhood Development Plan will take precedence over existing non-strategic policies in the local plan for that neighbourhood where they are in conflict.[50] This is tempered by the fact that the neighbourhood level plan must also contribute to the achievement of sustainable development, be in general conformity with the strategic policies of the development plan for the area and be appropriate having regard to national planning policy.[51] Nevertheless, given the priority which they will have, it will be important to monitor whether these requirements are met and whether the Neighbourhood Development Plan supports or hinders your development proposals.

What of the National Planning Policy Framework? Well, the Framework, with its presumption in favour of sustainable development[52] and its emphasis on the importance of economic growth,[53] promises much for developers and undoubtedly it will become a starting point for policy justification. However, it will be important not to lose sight of the philosophy of the localism reforms and to keep in mind just how important this Government regards the shift of power to local authorities and communities; as the call-in decisions in Winchester,[54] Grantham,[55] Sandbach,[56] St Austell[57] and Newmarket[58] show, where the initiative is being grasped locally and the process of a locally-driven decision about the amount and location of development has begun, allowances will be

---

50  DCLG (March 2012) *NPPF*, para 185 (available at http://www.communities.gov.uk/documents/planningandbuilding/pdf/2116950.pdf [accessed April 2012]).
51  See Town and Country Planning Act 1990, Sch 4B, para 8(2), inserted by Localism Act 2011, Sch 10, applied to neighbourhood development plans by Planning and Compulsory Purchase Act 2004, s 38A(3) (inserted by Localism Act 2011, Sch 9, para 7).
52  DCLG (March 2012) *NPPF*, para 14 (available at http://www.communities.gov.uk/documents/planningandbuilding/pdf/2116950.pdf [accessed April 2012]) which directs local planning authorities to grant permission where the development plan is absent, silent or where relevant policies are out of date (unless the adverse impacts of allowing development would significantly and demonstrably outweigh the benefits, when assessed against the policies in the Framework as a whole or specific policies indicate that development should be restricted). Paragraph 15 also confirms that all plans should be based upon and reflect the presumption in favour of sustainable development.
53  Eg 'The Government is committed to ensuring that the planning system does everything it can to support sustainable economic growth' DCLG (March 2012) *NPPF*, para 19 (available at http://www.communities.gov.uk/documents/planningandbuilding/pdf/2116950.pdf [accessed April 2012]).
54  APP/L1765/A/10/2126522 (28 September 2011) (since quashed but still relevant in this context).
55  APP/E2530/A/11/2150609 (1 March 2012).
56  APP/R0660/A/10/2141564 (29 September 2011) (since quashed but still of relevance in this context).
57  APP/D0840/A/10/2130022 (31 October 2011).
58  APP/H3510/A/10/2142030 (22 March 2012).

made and this local process will carry significant weight and should not be ignored.

In summary, it will remain important for you to identify support for your proposals in the development plan (the regional strategy for so long as it continues to exist and local development plan documents) and in national planning policy (in particular the National Planning Policy Framework) but it is vital to appreciate that the policy landscape will be subject to major changes for at least the first two or three years of the new system and that local circumstances will continue to be the key determinant of success. You will need to follow developments in policy very closely and look towards the collaborative approach that we have referred to for assurance and a way of establishing a more stable basis for your objectives. Our fear, which we hope will not be realised, is that rather than 'plan-led' many decisions will become led more by the moment, ie the community's reaction and the political priorities of the LPA at the relevant time.

## Turn socio-economic benefits into headline issues

Over the past ten years or more, it has become common practice to incorporate socio-economic assessments in planning applications often as part of environmental impact assessment. However, in our view, the socio-economic benefits of development merit greater focus and perhaps a more sophisticated approach than we sometimes see.

Given the prognosis for the economy and the associated cuts in public expenditure, in the next few years these benefits – the private investment in jobs, services and facilities – will offer convincing reasons to grant planning permission. The full scope of benefits should be examined such as:

- employment, education and training;
- housing supply;
- health/physical well-being;
- relieving poverty/deprivation and social exclusion;
- improved facilities and services; and
- increased values for existing properties and businesses.

The value of this approach is reinforced by the National Planning Policy Framework which places the economic and social roles of planning on an equal footing with the environmental role of planning as the three components of delivering sustainable development, which the Government sees as the central purpose of the planning system.[59] As described earlier in this book,[60] the Government goes on to emphasise the importance of ensuring that the planning system does everything it can to support sustainable economic growth.[61]

Elsewhere in this book we have also drawn attention to new and changing forms of local finance.[62] Developers should project the value of any increases in local

---

59 DCLG (March 2012) *NPPF*, paras 7 and 8 (available at http://www.communities.gov.uk/documents/planning and building/pdf/2116950.pdf [accessed April 2012]).
60 See Chapter 14.
61 DCLG (March 2012) *NPPF*, para 19 (available at http://www.communities.gov.uk/documents/planningandbuilding/pdf/2116950.pdf [accessed April 2012]).
62 'New Homes Bonus' (Chapter 15), 'Community Infrastructure Levy' (Chapter 9), 'Regional Growth Fund' (Chapter 13), 'Business rates retention' (Chapter 15), 'Tax Increment Financing' (Chapter 15).

finance brought about by new development and what might be achieved with such increases and include this in the assessment of socio-economic benefits. It should be borne in mind that the Localism Act now expressly requires local planning authorities to have regard to 'local finance considerations' (so far as they are material) in the determination of planning applications.[63] These include Government grants and financial assistance (such as the New Homes Bonus) and sums receivable in payment of the Community Infrastructure Levy. It is therefore entirely legitimate for developers to emphasise these benefits of their developments and to expect the local planning authority to take them into account. We also see no reason why in appropriate cases local planning authorities could not also consider the projected generation of receipts by the LPA from business rates growth and other funds, even though these fall outside the ambit of 'local finance considerations' as defined above.

It does of course remain open to developers to persuade the LPA to 'ringfence' the equivalent of receipts from local finance considerations and other funding generated by their development for the purposes of delivering infrastructure to support that development or unlocking other constraints. Whilst this may provide an innovative way of maintaining the viability of development, where this happens care will need to be taken not to 'double count' – in other words, not to claim the value of increases in local finance as socio-economic benefits when in fact they may be neutral if the equivalent amount of funding is being diverted to support or mitigate the development.

## THE LOCAL PLANNING AUTHORITY

## L is for local plan

There is one key area of the existing planning system which remains unchanged by the Localism Act and ironically, in our view, it is likely to become the easiest and most common expression of localism in action: the local plan (or local development plan documents).

This was acknowledged by the Government. In its *Myth-Buster* document[64] there are various references to the control which communities have through the local plan:

'**Myth: This isn't localism – the Framework takes control away from local communities**

**Fact:** Not true. The Framework puts local people in the driving seat of decision making in the planning system. Communities will have the power to decide the areas they wish to see developed and those to be protected, through their Local Plan. Once a local plan is in place which has the support of the local community that is what will drive decision making …'

---

63 Localism Act 2011, s 143, which amends Town and Country Planning Act 1990, s 70 (determination of applications for planning permission: general considerations).
64 DCLG (8 September 2011) *National Planning Policy Framework: Myth-Buster* – see Chapter 14.

*Navigating the system*

And later on:

> 'The Presumption [in favour of sustainable development] is principally about plan-making. Once a local plan is put in place local decisions should be made in line with it.'

The continuing importance of the local plan was also endorsed by CLG Select Committee in their report on the draft National Planning Policy Framework.[65] They concluded that the Framework should unambiguously reflect the statutory supremacy of local plans and that the presumption in favour of sustainable development should be qualified by the need for consistency with the local plan. The Select Committee also recommended that the Framework should acknowledge the possibility of the local plan containing locally justified variations from the Framework.[66] Ultimately this was reflected in the final NPPF: the fact that the local plan-led system was left intact was made clear in paras 11 to 13, for example, and the possibility of local variations is recognised in paras 10 and 15.

Aside from this, there are good practical reasons why the local plan may well become the route of choice for the expression of localism and giving effect to community aspirations:

- it is compulsory, not voluntary – LPAs are under a duty to bring these forward[67] and remain in control of the process;
- even though there remain a number of LPAs which have not yet adopted a core strategy or other local development documents[68] it is a tried and tested process and therefore carries fewer risks;
- there ought to be existing budget allocations for bringing forward new or revised local plans or alternatively a more predictable budgetary outcome.

For LPAs there is the additional advantage of remaining in control of the process and the content. However, contrast this with the Neighbourhood Development Plan which is voluntary not compulsory, new and untested and without any certainty of cost or budget; we suspect that even with neighbourhood planning grants[69] and the Neighbourhood Planning Front Runners initiative, the untested nature of neighbourhood plans and cost exposure will be a significant deterrent to communities and take up will be sporadic in the early years. Neighbourhood development plans are also led principally by the parish council or the Neighbourhood Forum and yet the administrative burden falls to the LPA, so from that authority's perspective too, these plans will be a less attractive option.

Our view is that these planning reforms will give local plans a new lease of life. LPAs should accelerate their preparation in order to avoid the potential

---

65  DCLG (21 December 2011) *Communities and Local Government Select Committee Report on the Draft National Planning Policy Framework* – see Chapter 14.
66  DCLG (21 December 2011) *Communities and Local Government Select Committee Report on the Draft National Planning Policy Framework,* paras 40 and 47.
67  Planning and Compulsory Purchase Act 2004, Pt 2.
68  Planning and Compulsory Purchase Act 2004, s 17.
69  On 13 April 2011, Planning Minister Greg Clark announced that four organisations (The Prince Foundation, Locality, The Royal Town Planning Institute and the National Association of Local Councils in partnership with the Council for the Protection of Rural England) would share a £3.2 milion fund to provide assistance to local groups developing neighbourhood plans. Communities wishing to take up free advice and guidance are to contact these organisations – http://www.communities.gov.uk/news/corporate/1886583.

## The local planning authority

for the National Planning Policy Framework to have a controlling influence on development management decisions but also widen their appeal so that they can encapsulate the needs and aspirations of local communities in their area.

## Resources

LPAs will find that the changes brought about by the Localism Act will place additional demands on their time and resources.

In the context of Neighbourhood Development Plans, Neighbourhood Development Orders and Community Right to Build Orders, as we highlighted in Chapter 6, LPAs will be required:

- in areas without a parish council, first to select Neighbourhood Forums and in doing so identify the appropriate boundaries for neighbourhood areas, choose between the applications made to them by groups in their area and monitor the performance of those groups and their constitution following their designation as Neighbourhood Forums;[70]
- to give appropriate advice or assistance to the parish council or the Neighbourhood Forum for the purposes of facilitating the making of any plans or orders in their area;[71]
- in practice to assist with the preparation of orders and plans before they are submitted including assisting technically and procedurally, eg with pre-submission consultation and potentially matters such as strategic environmental assessment and environmental impact assessment;
- once submitted to process any plans or orders, including organising publicity and post-submission consultation and considering any representations;
- consider the adequacy of plans and orders and submit them to and arrange independent examination;
- potentially to make representations to the independent examination and following receipt of the report of the examiner to publish the report, consider its recommendations and decide what action to take in response to each recommendation including limited modifications to the plan or order;
- where conditions are met, to arrange a referendum on the making of the order or plan giving specific consideration to the area that should be covered by the referendum;
- to make the order or the plan if the referendum vote results in a majority in favour and the basic conditions for the order or plan are met, and subsequently arrange for its publicity;
- to defend the decision to make the order or the plan if a legal challenge is made to its validity.

There is provision in the Localism Act[72] for charges to be introduced for the LPA's neighbourhood planning functions but it remains to be seen first whether

---

70 Town and Country Planning Act 1990, ss 61F and 61G, inserted by Localism Act 2011, Sch 9, para 2.
71 This is a duty imposed by Town and Country Planning Act 1990, Sch 4B, para 3, inserted by Localism Act 2011, Sch 10 (Neighbourhood Development Orders) and applied to Neighbourhood Development Plans by Planning and Compulsory Purchase Act 2004, s 38A(3) (inserted by Localism Act 2011, Sch 9, para 7) and to Community Right to Build Orders by Town and Country Planning Act 1990, Sch 4C, para 7 (inserted by Localism Act 2011, Sch 11).
72 Localism Act 2011, s 117.

*Navigating the system*

such charges will be introduced and secondly, if they are, whether local communities (other than perhaps business Neighbourhood Forums) will be able to afford them. We consider it essential that the Government continues with and expands its neighbourhood planning funding initiatives. Without this, given their own budgetary constraints (even without these additional functions), as well as cuts in public expenditure, many authorities will find themselves in a very difficult position and many communities will become frustrated.

Aside from the impact of these new neighbourhood planning functions, there are other reforms that could have significant resource implications for LPAs:

- We have drawn attention to the National Planning Policy Framework (Chapter 14) and the emphasis in that document on supporting (sustainable) economic growth; in light of this and the presumption in favour of sustainable development, there could in the short term, be an increase in planning applications from developers seeking to take advantage of this policy emphasis particularly where local development plan documents are non-existent or out of date.
- The National Planning Policy Framework, the abolition of regional strategies[73] and the new duty to co-operate in relation to the planning of sustainable development will require LPAs to bring forward or review development plan documents to ensure strategic priorities for the area are encapsulated in the development plan and that the development plan is consistent with the Framework.[74] This will be the case even for the most efficient and conscientious of LPAs who may have already adopted core strategies and other development plan documents.
- The Localism Act extends the purposes for which the Community Infrastructure Levy may be used and makes provision for a meaningful proportion of CIL receipts to be passed down to parish councils or Neighbourhood Forums. This will require authorities to reassess projected CIL receipts and their deployment – those authorities that have already progressed their CIL charging schedules will need to revisit them.
- We have already postulated the likely response of developers to the new duty to undertake pre-application consultation[75] which includes involving LPAs in establishing the extent of consultation and could become as sophisticated although perhaps not quite so burdensome as screening and scoping exercises for environmental impact assessment.
- In some cases, LPAs will no doubt welcome the new power to obtain a planning enforcement order where breaches of planning control have been concealed from them and the usual time limit for enforcement has expired.[76] However, the availability of this power may lead to increased pressure from the community to take enforcement action and further demand on officers. Authorities may also find themselves being asked to

---

73  Localism Act 2011, s 109.
74  It will be recalled that Annex 1 of the National Planning Policy Framework (Implementation) states that local plans may need to be revised to take into account the policies in the Framework and that this should be prepared as quickly as possible. Although for 12 months full weight can continue to be given to policies adopted since 2004, in other cases and after that 12-month period the weight given to policies in local plans will depend on their degree of consistency with the Framework (paras 212–215).
75  Localism Act 2011, s 122.
76  Localism Act 2011, s 124 which inserts Town and Country Planning Act 1990, ss 171BA, 171BB and 171BC.

## The local planning authority

opine on their state of awareness of particular circumstances and/or the likelihood of their exercising this power by prospective purchasers and funders of properties in their area.
- Two further changes which will also require a review of procedure and training in LPAs are the duty to have regard to local finance considerations[77] and the express provision for members (decision-takers) to be allowed to express a view on a matter without being taken to have a closed mind.[78]

These are not exhaustive but they are an indication of the additional demands that will be placed on LPAs particularly in the early years of the new localist system when practices and procedures are being established and public finances and the economy are at their worst. Continued and extended funding for neighbourhood planning, increased use of planning performance agreements (with provisions for developer funding of officer time) and incentives such as the New Homes Bonus may help, but it is unrealistic to think they represent the answer to this. We think the Government will have to give serious consideration to further injection of funds and other forms of support if it wishes to see its planning reforms take hold: local planning authorities are pivotal to the success of localism in planning and even the most enthusiastic authorities will need centralist intervention on resources.

## Be open and inclusive

We think LPAs will have to take decisions in an ever more open and inclusive manner. Arguably existing legislation has already compelled LPAs to conduct themselves in this way – thinking in particular of the freedom of information and equalities legislation[79] – but in our view the localism reforms imply a new benchmark.

This is based partly on our belief that the local plan will be the most important and most common expression of localism and will be favoured by communities in preference to neighbourhood development plans. This can only be the case if the local plan-making process engages with all communities and it will only be effective if communities can see how and why decisions are taken about their future. In this regard it is significant that the National Planning Policy Framework says this:

- 'Local plans are the key to delivering sustainable development that reflects the vision and aspirations of local communities.'[80]
- 'Early and meaningful engagement and collaboration with neighbourhoods, local organisations and businesses is essential. A wide section of the community should be proactively engaged, so that Local Plans, as far as possible, reflect a collective vision and a set of agreed priorities for the sustainable development of the area,

---

77 Localism Act 2011, s 143 which amends Town and Country Planning Act 1990, s 70.
78 Localism Act 2011, s 25.
79 Freedom of Information Act 2000, Environmental Information Regulations 2004 (SI 2004/3391), Equality Act 2010.
80 DCLG (March 2012) *NPPF*, para 150 (available at http://www.communities.gov.uk/documents/planningandbuilding/pdf/2116950.pdf [accessed April 2012]) – see Chapter 14.

*Navigating the system*

including those contained in any neighbourhood plans that have been made.'[81]

We also note – as this chapter bears out – the fact that the localism reforms draw LPAs into closer relationships with their communities and other stakeholders, including developers. Without the discipline of openness and inclusiveness, such relationships may not engender decisions that stand up to legal scrutiny or provide the best outcome in planning terms.

Furthermore, this need to be ever more open and inclusive will be more marked in the early years of the new system when, as we have suggested, policies will be in a state of flux and the certainty and predictability that the development plan usually brings will not always be there. In addition, expectations among communities will be at their highest and they will demand action from their LPAs. Decisions will come under more scrutiny than usual and will need to be based upon the best available evidence from all sections of the community and particularly those affected by the decisions.

## Ringmaster

Not just in planning but in a range of public services, the Localism Act shifts powers and competence to act away from central Government to the local level – to LPAs and, beyond that, to local communities. This is an opportunity that the Government expects local authorities and local people to seize in order to meet locally determined needs.

This is underlined by the very first provision of the Act – the general power of competence, which although later limited in scope by cross-reference to other existing constraints in the legislation, is intended to switch emphasis away from the requirement for a specific power to act to a requirement for a specific restraint to stop action. In one of a number of speeches made by Ministers of the Department for Communities and Local Government, the Secretary of State, Eric Pickles MP, said this:[82]

> 'There's nothing milk and honey about localism. There's nothing easy about it – there's no guidance manual. That isn't really the point. Localism won't deliver homogenous, bland, uniform public services. This is about pushing power outwards, downwards as far as possible. And all the possibilities that arise from local communities seizing power themselves …
>
> …
>
> Now the Government is putting councils back into the driving seat. So they can go their own way …
>
> …
>
> My role, the role of central government is to remove any obstacles and create the right conditions for local decision making. Our Localism Bill … will give councils the legal confidence to act in their residents' best interests

---

81  DCLG (March 2012) *NPPF*, para 155 (available at http://www.communities.gov.uk/documents/planningandbuilding/pdf/2116950.pdf [accessed April 2012]).
82  Speech by the Rt Hon Eric Pickles MP, Secretary of State for Communities and Local Government, at a Reform Conference on 15 June 2011, London.

*The local planning authority*

rather than relying on specific powers. Councils will get a "general power of competence" – legal shorthand for cutting central government's leash.

…

… And we're handing over control of the purse strings and ending ringfencing. Community Budgets are the start of councils and local areas getting a single pot of funding from Government, to spend as they see fit. But I have to say one thing that struck me on Community Budgets. At first I thought it was about putting money together. But it's about power. It's actually about one agency accepting and agreeing with another.

Retention of business rates will give councils a direct stake in the local economy. Councils will get the powers and incentives to do what local people want them to do.

…

… This is a time of big challenges and big opportunities. It's not a time for sleepwalkers. Localism is happening and if you want to grasp it – the sky is the limit. This is a real opportunity to be responsible to local needs …'

The sentiment is clear – LPAs are expected to make things happen and they will be both an originator and a co-ordinator of funding and ideas.

In a planning context, that potentially means a number of things for LPAs:

- as suggested above, as planning authority, facilitating the expression of local communities' preferences and aspirations through the local plan and other tools at their disposal or within the influence of the authority;
- again as already touched upon, working with developers and landowners to bring forward development opportunities and unlock constraints;
- acting as ringmaster for obtaining and prioritising the expenditure of the various pots of funding that are available: Community Infrastructure Levy, New Homes Bonus, planning obligation payments, business rates retention, Regional Growth Fund, etc.

Expectations of LPAs will be high and often misplaced but the fact is that this co-ordinating role will be vital in meeting the needs of local communities and delivering growth in the planning system. The decentralisation of power and the removal of regional government, which are heralded by the localism reforms, mean that the local authority – working in partnership with other authorities and public bodies – is uniquely placed to maintain an overview of their entire area. That overview is vital for ensuring that needs are recognised, understood and prioritised. It is also critical to devising and delivering solutions – to securing investment and resources and deploying them in the most effective way – and thereby maintaining public confidence in the planning system.

## Pitfalls

A number of factors suggest that LPAs will be facing increased risks in carrying out their functions as well as a greater level of scrutiny:

- We have alluded to a number of new functions and responsibilities which local authorities will have as well as a change in approach. It will take time for local authorities to get to grips with this.

- Regardless of how they play out on the ground, the philosophy of community empowerment that lies behind the reforms will have raised expectations in many communities across the country for more influence, more accountability and better outcomes (in their eyes).
- The development plan and other areas of planning policy are likely to be in a state of flux for the short term at least.
- The state of the economy and gaps in funding for public services mean that there is an increasing pressure to attract private sector investment and deliver growth through development.
- To attract private sector investment against a background of (a) low economic growth, (b) reduced levels of return on developer investment, and (c) reduced availability of development finance means that we are likely to see more collaboration between local authorities and the private sector and with it a closer relationship.
- At the same time, closer relationships will be developing between the local authority and their communities through neighbourhood planning initiatives (whether formalised or not). In such situations there will be occasions when the roles and responsibilities of different parties may become blurred.

Our view is that for the foreseeable future there will be an increase in the incidence of judicial review as various interested parties interrogate the decisions and actions taken by local authorities in these challenging circumstances. If we look closer at some of the new functions which will be assumed by LPAs under the Localism Act then the scope for greater use of judicial review becomes clear. Indeed, each of the additional demands on local authority resources which we described above provides fertile ground for litigation.

- Think about the selection of Neighbourhood Forums. Both the choice of neighbourhood area and the choice of Forum may prove to be very controversial in some cases, particularly where there is competition between community groups. A careful reading of the Act will be required to ensure mandatory requirements are met and local authorities will need to ensure adequate publicity and consultation in their decision-making process.
- The LPA has a duty to provide assistance in relation to neighbourhood planning matters. It will need to take care that in this process it does not compromise its later administrative functions of accepting and making orders or plans.
- Once submitted plans or orders need to be subject to adequate publicity and post-submission consultation – a judgment will need to be made about the scope of that exercise. In addition any representations will need to be given adequate consideration.
- Following independent examination of neighbourhood plans and orders, the LPA will need to consider and act upon the report of the examiner. The manner in which it does so will be an area for scrutiny, particularly where the authority makes (or refuses to make) modifications to the plan or order.
- LPAs responsible for arranging a referendum will need to take well-informed decisions around the area that should be covered, the adequacy of information given to voters and the framing of the referendum questions. Care will also need to be taken around the staging of the poll

and the processing of the vote. Given that neighbourhood plans and orders are likely to have a more immediate impact on everyday life, it is likely that the process of these referendums will attract more interest than say polling for general or local elections.

- The making of the order or the plan following a referendum sounds straightforward enough but it will be necessary to conduct a final audit of the process before this last administrative decision is taken. As well as the matters already mentioned, authorities will need to make sure that common pitfalls under the present system (such as habitats regulations assessment, environmental impact assessment and strategic environmental assessment) have been thought about and adequately addressed.
- The state of flux in policy (the National Planning Policy Framework, the abolition of regional strategies, the new duty to co-operate, the consequential review of local plans etc) is likely to present difficulties both in terms of plan-making and decision-making. Taking all relevant policy considerations and evidence bases into account and attributing appropriate weight to such matters will be particularly challenging.
- The new duty on developers to undertake pre-application consultation is a particular problem since, like environmental impact assessment, it is a procedural requirement upon which an LPA's decision will be based but which ultimately is a matter outside of the authority's control. Decisions based on inadequate pre-application consultation will be vulnerable to legal challenge.
- The use and particularly the refusal to use new planning enforcement orders to open up investigations into concealed breaches of planning control are likely to be contentious and the subject of legal challenges; LPAs will need a robust audit trail when it considers matters such as these which are likely to prove very sensitive.
- How LPAs handle the new duty to have regard to local finance considerations and express themselves when considering such matters will be important; these are areas where the community in particular will want some assurance that planning permissions are not being bought and sold and any suspicions are likely to lead to judicial review.
- We have referred to the new provision which states that decision-takers may express a view on a matter without being taken to have a closed mind. Inasmuch as this is a welcome reinforcement of the ability for members to engage early on in the planning process, fundamentally it does not change the law and LPAs will need to ensure that members remain aware of the circumstances in which they risk having a 'closed mind' before determining a planning application or face further legal challenges on the point.

Local authorities faced with this increase in risk will have little option other than to identify these and other areas of vulnerability and seek to manage risk through training, sharing of best practice and audit procedures – a mode of operation which most will be well-used to but which is no easy task at a time of significant change and budgetary restraint.

## LOCAL RESIDENT/LOCAL BUSINESS

## Initiate or join a Neighbourhood Forum

If you are a business or a resident in an area without a parish council, the Neighbourhood Forum[83] is the vehicle through which the principal neighbourhood planning powers[84] are exercisable. Although the lifetime of a specific Forum is intended to be temporary,[85] its legacy in terms of the orders and plans it makes may continue for some time since their validity is unaffected by the Forum ceasing to exist. As we have explained elsewhere, whilst Neighbourhood Development Plans and Neighbourhood Development Orders do need to be[86] in general conformity with the strategic priorities of the development plan and appropriate having regard to national policy and also need to contribute to the achievement of sustainable development, once made they may take priority over the local plan and they can make provision for land use restrictions or allocations for development on a significant scale.[87]

This makes the Neighbourhood Forum a potentially powerful vehicle through which your local area can be shaped and influenced and clearly there is every possibility that a Forum could bring forward a proposal that is against your interests. There is of course some protection built into the legislation through various requirements to be satisfied before an organisation or body is designated to act as a Forum:[88]

- it must be established for the express purpose of promoting or improving the social economic and environmental well-being of an area;
- its membership must be open to individuals who live in the neighbourhood area, who work there and who are elected member of a council in whose administrative area the neighbourhood is located;
- its membership must have a minimum of 21 individuals who live in the area, work there or are elected members as mentioned above;
- it must have a written constitution.

---

83 Town and Country Planning Act 1990, ss 61F to 61I, inserted by Localism Act 2011, Sch 9, para 2.
84 Ie Neighbourhood Development Plans (Planning and Compulsory Purchase Act 2004, ss 38A–38C inserted by Localism Act 2011, Sch 9, para 7) and Neighbourhood Development Orders (Town and Country Planning Act 1990, ss 61E and 61J–61P, inserted by Localism Act 2011, Sch 9, para 2). Community Right to Build Orders (Town and Country Planning Act 1990, s 61Q and Sch 4C, inserted by Localism Act 2011, Sch 9, para 2 and Sch 11) can be initiated by any 'community organisation' – see Town and Country Planning Act 1990, Sch 4C, para 4.
85 Town and Country Planning Act 1990, s 61F, inserted by Localism Act 2011, Sch 9, para 2 provides at sub-s (8) that a designation ceases to have effect at the end of a period of five years beginning with the day on which it is made.
86 See the basic conditions described at Town and Country Planning Act 1990, Sch 4B, para 8(2) (Process for making of Neighbourhood Development Orders), inserted by Localism Act 2011, Sch 10 and which is also applied to Neighbourhood Development Plans by Planning and Compulsory Purchase Act 2004, s 38C, inserted by Localism Act 2011, Sch 9, para 7.
87 Although not 'excluded development' – see Town and Country Planning Act 1990, s 61K, inserted by Localism Act 2011, Sch 9, para 2.
88 Town and Country Planning Act 1990, s 61F(5), inserted by Localism Act 2011, Sch 9, para 2.

*Local resident/local business*

In addition, it is clear that any plan or order produced by the Forum will need to be the subject of proper consultation,[89] an independent examination[90] and a referendum[91] in which the majority of votes support the making of the plan or order before being accepted and made by the local planning authority. However, reliance on these safeguards alone is high risk; the various requirements are capable of being met quite easily and, by the time proposals are advertised, it may be too late to bring your influence to bear on them because of the amount of political momentum they have gained. We advise you to get involved early on, help form a Neighbourhood Forum for your area to gain some control or at least join a Forum where you might be able to exert some influence in the genesis of ideas and the early stages of the process.

## Beware the cost of formal localism structures

Having said this, no one should be under the illusion that the decision to establish a Forum or bring forward a Neighbourhood Development Plan or Neighbourhood Development Order can be taken lightly. The Forum itself will involve set up and running costs and significant volunteer time. With regard to the orders or plans themselves, the Government has estimated that these could cost anything between £17,000 and £200,000[92] to put into place – with possibly additional costs to operate where the parish council or the Neighbourhood Forum have a continuing role in later stages of the planning process that follow the plan or order.

The funding for these structures must be found by local communities, but there are options for assistance with this:

- LPAs can apply to the Government for funding as part of the Neighbourhood Planning Front Runners initiative. You will need to initiate this – do not wait for the local authority to approach you.
- As indicated earlier, the Government has awarded £3.2 million of grant funding to four organisations who may be approached by communities for free advice and guidance.[93]
- LPAs themselves may wish to use neighbourhood planning tools to achieve objectives in their own development plan and may be willing to fund (at least partly) the set up costs of a Neighbourhood Forum and the neighbourhood plan- or order-making process.

---

89 There is provision for Regulations to be made which will cover such matters both before and after submission to the local planning authority: see the Town and Country Planning Act 1990, Sch 4B, para 4 (Process for making of Neighbourhood Development Orders), inserted by Localism Act 2011, Sch 10 and which is also applied to Neighbourhood Development Plans by Planning and Compulsory Purchase Act 2004, s 38C, inserted by Localism Act 2011, Sch 9, para 7.
90 Town and Country Planning Act 1990, Sch 4B, para 7.
91 Town and Country Planning Act 1990, Sch 4B, para 14.
92 DCLG (January 2011) *Localism Bill: Neighbourhood Plans and Community Right to Build – Impact Assessment* (available at http://www.communities.gov.uk/documents/localgovernment/pdf/1829678.pdf [accessed January 2012]).
93 On 13 April 2011, Planning Minister Greg Clark announced that four organisations (The Prince Foundation, Locality, The Royal Town Planning Institute and the National Association of Local Councils in partnership with the Council for the Protection of Rural England) would share a £3.2 million fund to provide assistance to local groups developing neighbourhood plans. Communities wishing to take up free advice and guidance are to contact these organisations – http://www.communities.gov.uk/news/corporate/1886583.

- Inclusion of local businesses in the membership of a Forum could provide your organisation with logistical and financial support for set up and operational phases. They may also be willing to fund the plan- and order- making processes, but will of course expect to influence the content/output.
- Developers or landowners themselves may view these neighbourhood planning tools as a means by which they can promote development proposals; if you are willing to partner with them you are likely to gain access to funding and logistical support and, whilst accepting their proposals, you may also be able to achieve further objectives across a wider geographic area.

Finally, as an alternative to bringing forward Neighbourhood Development Plans and Neighbourhood Development Orders, you may wish to consider relying on existing structures to express your community's objectives and aspirations. As we have said, local plans will need to be revised and refreshed to take account of these reforms and in particular the final National Planning Policy Framework, and these could provide the best vehicle through which to achieve your objectives, at the LPA's cost; start speaking to your authority early on.

## Power of opinion

As a local resident or business it is important to realise that these reforms are borne out of a political philosophy that is looking to empower you. The structures that the Localism Act puts into place – the community right to challenge,[94] the list of community assets,[95] Neighbourhood Development Plans,[96] Neighbourhood Development Orders[97] and Community Right to Build Orders[98] – all signal this power shift and, as a result, even at an early stage these processes will carry significant weight in decisions by the LPA and the Secretary of State. As we have seen, in the shadow of these reforms, this is even true of the existing local plan process where there is evidence of LPAs engaging with their communities in seeking to identify the amount and location of development.[99]

Added to this, there is the new pre-application duty on developers to undertake consultation (including a duty to take any responses into account).[100] Politically, the Government is also committed to the philosophy that local communities should share the benefits of economic growth and development in their area; the draft National Planning Policy Framework made this clear (although this passage did not make it into the final NPPF):

> '… National incentives and relevant local charges will help ensure local communities benefit directly from the increase in development that this Framework seeks to achieve. The revenue generated from development will

---

94  Localism Act 2011, ss 81–86.
95  Localism Act 2011, ss 87–108.
96  Localism Act 2011, Sch 9, Pt 2.
97  Localism Act 2011, Sch 9, Pt 1.
98  Localism Act 2011, Sch 11.
99  See our earlier discussion in this chapter (under 'The Developer', 'The policy landscape') concerning the Secretary of State's called-in and recovered appeal decisions in Winchester, Grantham, Sandbach, St Austell and Newmarket.
100 Localism Act 2011, s 122.

*Local resident/local business*

help sustain local services, fund infrastructure and deliver environmental enhancement.'[101]

In addition, the rationale for the New Homes Bonus is to ensure that local communities see the benefit of embracing new development:

> '... Now, communities will see the economic and social benefits of having the housing they want. Communities could benefit from reductions in council tax, or a redeveloped town centre or a new community centre or play park as a consequence of accepting new homes. It will be up to them.
>
> The New Home Bonus will have localism at its heart. It will re-energise communities. It will encourage local politicians to lead a debate with communities about the benefits of new homes. Local authorities will be expected to work with local people to develop their housing plans in ways that meet their needs and concerns ...'[102]

The Localism Act also provides for a proportion of receipts from the CIL to be passed to specified persons[103] and the Government has confirmed that they will use this to direct a meaningful proportion of CIL receipts to local neighbourhoods.[104]

All of these changes give local communities a greater stake and a greater say in development proposals than ever before and in our view, harnessing representative opinions from the local communities where development is being promoted will have increased weight in decision-making. Social networking and the internet in general provide powerful and yet accessible platforms from which to build this opinion. With or without formal localism structures, you should not lose sight of this if you are a local resident or local business. As we have indicated, in years to come, we envisage the power of local opinion becoming an unwritten licence to operate or develop in a local area.

## If you don't ask, you don't get

This power of opinion and the determination that local communities should share in the benefit of new development leaves concerned local residents and businesses, as a collective, in a very strong position to secure investment in your community. Added to this, the Government's policy of decentralisation and community empowerment, the availability of new neighbourhood planning tools, the pre-application duty on the part of developers to consult and the political expectation that developers should recognise and respond to the needs of local communities, means there has never been a better time to embrace development, shape your community and secure genuine and lasting benefits: the opportunities are there for the taking.

So if you wish to steer or influence planning policy in your area, find like-minded people in your community and consider asking the local authority to

---

101  DCLG (July 2011) *Draft NPPF*, para 18 (available at http://www.communities.gov.uk/documents/planningandbuilding/pdf/1951811.pdf [accessed November 2011]) – see Chapter 14.
102  DCLG (Feburary 2011) Ministerial Foreword, *New Homes Bonus: Final Scheme Design*.
103  Localism Act 2011, s 115.
104  For example, see DCLG (October 2011) *Community Infrastructure Levy – Detailed Proposals and Draft Regulatory Reform Consultation*, Chapter 1 – Neighbourhood Funds (available at http://www.communities.gov.uk/documents/planningandbuilding/pdf/1997385.pdf [accessed January 2012]).

*Navigating the system*

accept you as a Neighbourhood Forum; ask the LPA, voluntary organisations, businesses or even developers for help with the funding and the logistical support to bring forward neighbourhood plans and orders. In conjunction with this, ask questions about the next revision of the LPA's development plan and whether your community's plans and aspirations could be conveyed more efficiently through that vehicle.

If you wish your community to benefit more from development in your area, press the LPA for a proportion of the funding that they receive (from planning obligations, the CIL, the New Homes Bonus and the like) to be spent locally. This is sanctioned by both legislation and policy but if you have an established 'need case', a budget and a clear statement about how funds would be spent and the benefit that is expected to accrue locally, so much the better.

Likewise, if you are consulted about a significant development proposal, make clear in your response to the consultation any deficiencies in facilities or services in the community, which you wish to see addressed. You may find that the developer, mindful of the influence of local opinion, addresses them or makes a significant contribution towards doing so.

## Opposition tactics

The Government's aspiration is for localism to revolutionise the way in which the planning system operates so that the adversarial approach which pitches communities against developers and communities against LPAs (applying top-down targets) becomes a thing of the past. The National Planning Policy Framework, for example, advises that engagement by communities should take place firmly in the context of the local plan (which itself is shaped by the presumption in favour of sustainable development); it urges that 'The ambition of the neighbourhood should be aligned with the strategic needs and priorities of the wider local area' and that neighbourhood plans should reflect the strategic policies of the local plan and 'plan positively to support them'.[105]

Notwithstanding this, the tensions in the planning process that we see all too frequently today, between those who want change and those who would prefer the status quo, still seem to us to be inevitable. The difference with localism is that this tension may become more common within the community itself – for example, where a parish council or Forum exercising its neighbourhood planning functions fails to carry local opinion with it – rather than being just an issue between the community and the developer or LPA.

Where this tension occurs in the new localist planning system and you find yourself in the objectors' camp, how might you oppose development differently? The first thing to say is that the same tactics as those that are used today will continue to be deployed: issues such as environmental impact assessment[106] will continue to be fertile ground for objecting to schemes and challenging decisions; likewise, judicial review[107] will continue to be the principal means by which objectors seek closure regarding a difference of view and will continue to be deployed tactically to defeat or delay projects. Nevertheless, the Localism Act

---

105  DCLG (March 2012) *NPPF*, para 184 (available at http://www.communities.gov.uk/documents/planningandbuilding/pdf/2116950.pdf [accessed March 2012]) – see Chapter 14.
106  In England see the Town and Country Planning (Environmental Impact Assessment) Regulations 2011 (SI 2011/1824).
107  Civil Procedure Rules, Pt 54.

*Local resident/local business*

and its associated reforms will give rise to new pressure points that are capable of being exploited by determined objectors, many of which we have highlighted in the section above under the 'The local planning authority', 'Pitfalls'. As an objector we would draw your attention to the following in particular:

- If you wish to oppose the formation of a Neighbourhood Forum, the Act contains various legal requirements with which groups or organisations must comply[108] and requires LPAs to direct their minds specifically to the question of whether the boundaries of the neighbourhood area proposed by the Forum are appropriate.[109] Furthermore there is a continuing requirement for the Forum to meet certain conditions by reference to which it was designated[110] and the local planning authority should be monitoring compliance.
- If you are opposing a Neighbourhood Development Plan or Neighbourhood Development Order, the Act specifies basic conditions[111] which need to be met and the Neighbourhood Planning Regulations specify further requirements.[112] In addition, the process for making plans and orders incorporates various administrative acts by the LPA and these will be vulnerable to scrutiny: for example, the consideration of the report of the independent examination and the geographic extent of the referendum.
- We have alluded earlier in this chapter to the likelihood of an increase in the incidence of collaboration and partnership and thus a closer relationship between the LPA and other players such as developers, landowners and even the parish council/neighbourhood Forum. Any objector should explore the nature of these relationships through freedom of information requests[113] and other means with a view to establishing whether the authority has compromised its judgement in any given situation – ie whether the relationships have tainted or otherwise adversely affected the decision-making process.
- As they are revised to take account of these reforms and in particular the National Planning Policy Framework, areas of potential challenge to local development plans include the extent to which the LPA has complied with its new duty to co-operate with other public bodies in relation to the planning of sustainable development.[114] In addition, given the policy objective of empowering communities and the new presumption in favour of sustainable development in the National Planning Policy Framework, there may be other grounds of challenge in relation to the adequacy of consultation exercises with local communities and the approach taken towards strategic environmental

---

108 Town and Country Planning Act 1990, s 61F, inserted by Localism Act 2011, Sch 9, para 2.
109 Having regard to the provisions of Town and Country Planning Act 1990, s 61G, inserted by Localism Act 2011, Sch 9, para 2.
110 The local planning authority has power to withdraw a designation under Town and Country Planning Act 1990, s 61F(9), inserted by Localism Act 2011, Sch 9, para 2.
111 See Town and Country Planning Act 1990, Sch 4B, para 8(2), inserted by Localism Act 2011, Sch 10 (Process for Making of Neighbourhood Development Orders) and applied to Neighbourhood Development Plans by Planning and Compulsory Purchase Act 2004, s 38A(3), inserted by Localism Act 2011, Sch 9, para 7.
112 Neighbourhood Planning (General) Regulations 2012 (SI 2012/637).
113 Requests made to public bodies under the Freedom of Information Act 2000 and/or the Environmental Information Regulations 2004.
114 Localism Act 2011, s 110, which inserts Planning and Compulsory Purchase Act 2004, s 33A.

- assessment (focusing in particular on the extent to which social economic and environmental issues are balanced).
- In relation to development management decisions and planning appeals, the extent to which the developer has properly discharged the duty to undertake pre-application consultation may provide a basis for challenging a planning permission. Regulations will be made which set out the scale of applications to which this duty applies but where it does apply, we suggest that you look in particular at the extent to which the developer has publicised the application in a manner '*likely* to bring the proposed application to *the attention of a majority* of the persons who live at or otherwise occupy, premises *in the vicinity of the land*'[115] [emphasis added] and consulted other specified persons.[116] We also suggest you examine the information that accompanied the publicity for the application and whether it clearly identifies how the developer could be contacted to comment on or collaborate on the design of the development and the timetable for consultation;[117] you should also consider whether there is sufficient evidence that the developer has complied with the duty to have regard to consultation responses.[118]
- Again in relation to development management decisions on applications and appeals, the duty to have regard to 'local finance considerations'[119] is new and decision-makers will not be accustomed to the practicalities of discharging this duty. Objectors should take note that this term has a specific meaning[120] and decisions should be examined to make sure that the LPA or the inspector on appeal have not included financial considerations that fall outside the statutory definition or if they have, that such financial considerations are proper material considerations.

## CONCLUDING THOUGHTS

In our view, there is one essential message that you need to take on board whoever you are and whatever outcome you are hoping for: the Localism Act and its associated package of reforms represent a fundamental cultural change in the planning system.

The introduction of localism structures for planning, such as Neighbourhood Forums, Neighbourhood Development Plans and the Neighbourhood Development Orders, are voluntary; in other words, in any given area of the country you will only find these structures if local people have decided to initiate them. However, do not be fooled into thinking that the absence of these structures means that you can ignore the reforms. The structures may be

---

115 Town and Country Planning Act 1990, s 61W(2), inserted by Localism Act 2011, s 122.
116 Town and Country Planning Act 1990, s 61W(3), inserted by Localism Act 2011, s 122.
117 Town and Country Planning Act 1990, s 61W(4), inserted by Localism Act 2011, s 122. Note this also suggests, and common law principles of consultation would also require, that the consultation takes place at a sufficiently early or formative stage of the development when matters such as design can be influenced.
118 Town and Country Planning Act 1990, s 61X(2), inserted by Localism Act 2011, s 122.
119 Localism Act 2011, s 143, which amends Town and Country Planning Act 1990, s 70.
120 Town and Country Planning Act 1990, s 70(4) inserted by Localism Act 2011, s 143(4) which states that '"local finance considerations" means – (a) a grant or other financial assistance that has been, or will or could be, provided to a relevant authority by a Minister of the Crown, or (b) sums that a relevant authority has received, or will or could receive, in payment of Community Infrastructure Levy'.

*Concluding thoughts*

voluntary, but a localist approach is compulsory: the philosophy and rhetoric of the Government that lies behind the reforms and the symbolic value of the Localism Act mean that in most areas you will come across a different set of expectations and new ways of approaching things. Failure to appreciate this will reduce significantly the chances of achieving your desired outcome: if you don't 'get it', you won't get it.

# Appendix 1

# Territorial extent of the Act

The majority of the Localism Act applies to England only, however significant portions also apply to Wales. The competence of the National Assembly for Wales increased substantially as the Act passed through Parliament as Welsh legislation providing the Assembly with more powers came into force during this period. As such, certain provisions in the Act required legislative consent motions to be passed by the Assembly. The Welsh Ministers were also required to approve the inclusion of provisions which relate to matters over which they already had authority. The Act also includes provisions which relate to non-devolved matters in Wales, eg the Community Infrastructure Levy and Nationally Significant Infrastructure Projects.

A small number of provisions, for example Pt 2 on EU financial sanctions, apply to the whole of the UK and the sections relating to Nationally Significant Infrastructure Projects also apply to Scotland in respect of cross border pipelines. A number of other general sections, for example in relation to commencement and repeals and revocations, apply to Scotland and Northern Ireland.

The table below sets out the territorial extent of each chapter of the Act.

| **Part 1: Local government** | |
|---|---|
| Chapter 1: General power of authorities | England only, apart from: Section 5: Powers to make supplemental provisions – limited application to Wales |
| Chapter 2: Fire and rescue authorities | England and Wales |
| Chapter 3: Other authorities | England only |
| Chapter 4: Transfer and delegation of functions to certain authorities | England only |
| Chapter 5: Governance | England only |
| Chapter 6: Predetermination | England and Wales |
| Chapter 7: Standards | England and Police Authorities in Wales, apart from: Section 35: Delegation of Functions by the Greater London Authority – England only |
| Chapter 8: Pay accountability | England and Wales |
| Chapter 9: Commission for Local Administration in England | England only |
| Chapter 10: Miscellaneous appeals | England and Wales, apart from: Section 47: Schemes to encourage domestic waste reduction by payment and charges – England only |

*Territorial extent of the Act*

| Part 2: EU financial sanctions | UK-wide |
|---|---|
| Part 3: EU financial sanctions: Wales | Wales only |
| Part 4: Non domestic rates | England and Wales, apart from: Section 70: Small business relief; and Section 71: Cancellation of liability to backdated non-domestic rates – England only |
| **Part 5: Community empowerment** | |
| Chapter 1: Council tax | England only, apart from: Section 72: Referendums relating to council tax increases – mainly England only but part Wales only; and Section 80: Council tax revaluations in Wales – Wales only |
| Chapter 2: Community right to challenge | England only |
| Chapter 3: Assets of community value | England and Wales, apart from: Section 103: Advice and assistance in relation to land of community value in England – England only; and Section 104: Advice and assistance in relation to land of community value in Wales – Wales only |
| **Part 6: Planning** | |
| Chapter 1: Plans and strategies | England only |
| Chapter 2: Community Infrastructure Levy | England and Wales |
| Chapter 3: Neighbourhood planning | England only |
| Chapter 4: Consultation | England only |
| Chapter 5: Enforcement | England only, apart from: Section 125: Assurance as regards prosecution for person served with enforcement notice – England and Wales |
| Chapter 6: Nationally Significant Infrastructure Projects | England, Scotland and Wales, apart from: Section 132: Secretary of State's direction in relation to projects of national significance – England only |
| Chapter 7: Other planning matters | England only, apart from: Section 144: Application of this Part to the Crown – England, Scotland and Wales |

## Territorial extent of the Act

| **Part 7: Housing** | |
|---|---|
| Chapter 1: Allocation and homelessness | England only, apart from:<br>Section 148: Duties to homeless persons – England and Wales; and<br>Section 149 – Duties to homeless persons: further amendments – England and Wales |
| Chapter 2: Social housing: tenure reform | England only, apart from:<br>Section 162: Secure and assured tenancies recovery of possession after tenant's death – mainly England only but in part Wales only |
| Chapter 3: Housing finance | England only |
| Chapter 4: Housing mobility | England only |
| Chapter 5: Regulation of social housing | England only |
| Chapter 6: Other housing matters | England only, apart from:<br>Section 183: Abolition of home information packs – England and Wales;<br>Section 184: Tenancy Deposit Schemes – England and Wales; and<br>Section 185: Exemption from HMO licencing for buildings run by co-operatives – England and Wales |
| **Part 8: London** | |
| Chapter 1: Housing and regeneration functions | England only |
| Chapter 2: Mayoral Development Corporations | England only |
| Chapter 3: Greater London Authority governance | England only |
| **Part 9: Compensation for compulsory acquisition** | England and Wales |
| **Part 10: General** | UK wide, apart from:<br>Section 234: Pre-commencement consultation – England and Wales |

# Appendix 2

# From a Bill to an Act: The stages undergone by the Localism Bill

| Stage | Date |
|---|---|
| 1st reading: House of Commons | 13.12.2010[1] |
| 2nd reading: House of Commons | 17.01.2011 |
| Programme motion: House of Commons | 17.01.2011 |
| Money resolution: House of Commons | 17.01.2011 |
| Committee debate 1st sitting: House of Commons | 25.01.2011 |
| Committee debate 2nd sitting: House of Commons | 25.01.2011 |
| Committee debate 3rd sitting: House of Commons | 27.01.2011 |
| Committee debate 4th sitting: House of Commons | 27.01.2011 |
| Committee debate 5th sitting: House of Commons | 01.02.2011 |
| Committee debate 6th sitting: House of Commons | 01.02.2011 |
| Committee debate 7th sitting: House of Commons | 03.02.2011 |
| Committee debate 8th sitting: House of Commons | 03.02.2011 |
| Committee debate 9th sitting: House of Commons | 08.02.2011 |
| Committee debate 10th sitting: House of Commons | 08.02.2011 |
| Committee debate 11th sitting: House of Commons | 10.02.2011 |
| Committee debate 12th sitting: House of Commons | 10.02.2011 |
| Committee debate 13th sitting: House of Commons | 15.02.2011 |
| Committee debate 14th sitting: House of Commons | 15.02.2011 |
| Committee debate 15th sitting: House of Commons | 17.02.2011 |
| Committee debate 16th sitting: House of Commons | 17.02.2011 |
| Committee debate 17th sitting: House of Commons | 01.03.2011 |
| Committee debate 18th sitting: House of Commons | 01.03.2011 |
| Committee debate 19th sitting: House of Commons | 03.03.2011 |
| Committee debate 20th sitting: House of Commons | 03.03.2011 |
| Committee debate 21st sitting: House of Commons | 08.03.2011 |
| Committee debate 22nd sitting: House of Commons | 08.03.2011 |
| Committee debate 23rd sitting: House of Commons | 10.03.2011 |
| Committee Debate 24th sitting: House of Commons | 10.03.2011 |
| Bill 161 2010-11 as amended in Public Bill Committee[2] | 13.03.2011 |

1  Bill 126 2010–2011 as introduced (available at http://www.publications.parliament.uk/pa/cm201011/cmbills/126/11126part1.pdf (volume 1) and http://www.publications.parliament.uk/pa/cm201011/cmbills/126/11126part2.pdf (volume 2)).
2  Available at http://www.publications.parliament.uk/pa/cm201011/cmbills/161/11161.i-vii.html.

*From a Bill to an Act: The stages undergone by the Localism Bill*

| Stage | Date |
|---|---|
| Report: 1st sitting: House of Commons | 17.05.2011 |
| Programme (No 2) motion: House of Commons | 17.05.2011 |
| Ways and Means resolution: House of Commons | 17.05.2011 |
| Report: 2nd sitting: House of Commons | 18.05.2011 |
| 3rd reading: House of Commons | 18.05.2011 |
| HL Bill 71 2010-12 (as brought from the Commons)[3] | 23.05.2011 |
| 1st reading: House of Lords | 07.06.2011 |
| 2nd reading: House of Lords | 20.06.2011 |
| Committee: 1st sitting: House of Lords | 20.06.2011 |
| Committee: 2nd sitting: House of Lords | 23.06.2011 |
| Committee: 3rd sitting: House of Lords | 28.06.2011 |
| Committee: 4th sitting: House of Lords | 30.06.2011 |
| Committee: 5th sitting: House of Lords | 05.07.2011 |
| Committee: 6th sitting: House of Lords | 07.07.2011 |
| Committee: 7th sitting: House of Lords | 12.07.2011 |
| Committee: 8th sitting: House of Lords | 14.07.2011 |
| Committee: 9th sitting: House of Lords | 19.07.2011 |
| Committee: 10th sitting: House of Lords | 20.07.2011 |
| HL Bill 90 2010-12 [as amended in Committee][4] | 22.07.2011 |
| Report: 1st sitting: House of Lords | 05.09.2011 |
| Report: 2nd sitting: House of Lords | 07.09.2011 |
| Report: 3rd sitting: House of Lords | 12.09.2011 |
| Report: 4th sitting: House of Lords | 14.09.2011 |
| Report: 5th sitting: House of Lords | 10.10.2011 |
| Report: 6th sitting: House of Lords | 12.10.2011 |
| Report: 7th sitting: House of Lords | 17.10.2011 |
| 3rd reading: House of Lords | 31.10.2011 |
| Bill 244 2010-12 (Lords Amendments to the Bill)[5] | 02.11.2011 |
| Ping Pong: House of Commons | 07.11.2011 |
| Programme (No 3) motion: House of Commons | 07.11.2011 |
| Money (No 2) resolution: House of Commons | 07.11.2011 |
| Royal Assent | 15.11.2011 |

3 Available at http://www.publications.parliament.uk/pa/bills/lbill/2010-2012/0071/lbill_2010-20120071_en_1.htm (volume 1); http://www.publications.parliament.uk/pa/bills/lbill/2010-2012/0071/2012071pt2.pdf (volume 2).
4 Available at http://www.publications.parliament.uk/pa/bills/lbill/2010-2012/0090/2012090v1.pdf (volume 1); http://www.publications.parliament.uk/pa/bills/lbill/2010-2012/0100/lbill_2010-20120100_en_1.htm (volume 2).
5 Available at http://www.publications.parliament.uk/pa/bills/cbill/2010-2012/0244/12244.1-6.html.

# Appendix 3

# Is it in force?

## PROVISIONS THAT CAME INTO FORCE ON 15 NOVEMBER 2011

*The following sections of the Act came into force on 15 November 2011:*

Section 23 – Transitional provisions: changes to local authority governance in England

Schedule 4, paras 57 and 58 and s 26 (to the extent it relates to these paragraphs) – Secretary of State powers to provide for abolition of Standards Board for England.

Section 37 – Transitional provision: standards

Part 5, Ch 2 (to the extent it confers powers on the Secretary of State to make regulations) – Community right to challenge

Section 86 – Community right to challenge: provision of advice and assistance

Part 5, Ch 3 (to the extent it confers power on the Secretary of State, or the Welsh Ministers, to make regulations or orders) – Assets of community value

Sections 103 and 104 – Assets of community value: advice and assistance

Section 109(1)(b) and (2) to (6), Sch 8, paras 1, 13(1), 18 and 19 and s 109(7) (so far as relating to those provisions of that Schedule) – Abolition of regional strategies

Section 110 – Duty to co-operate in relation to planning of sustainable development

Sections 116 and 121 and Schs 9 to 12 (so far as those sections or Schedules confer power on the Secretary of State to make regulations or publish documents setting standards) – Neighbourhood planning

Sections 117 to 120 – Neighbourhood planning

The provisions inserted by s 122 (so far as they require or authorise the making of provision in a development order) – Consultation before applying for planning permission

Section 144 – Other planning matters: application to the Crown

Sections 168 to 175 – Housing finance

Section 233 and Sch 24 (so far as they confer power on the Treasury to make regulations or orders) – General: tax

Sections 234, 235, 236, 238, 239, 240 and 241 – General: various

Sch 25, Pt 15 and s 237 (so far as relating to that Part) – Repeals and revocations (regional strategies)

*Is it in force?*

## PROVISIONS THAT CAME INTO FORCE ON 16 NOVEMBER 2011

Section 114 – CIL: approval of charging schedules

## PROVISIONS THAT CAME INTO FORCE ON 3 DECEMBER 2011

*The Localism Act 2011 (Commencement No 1 and Transitional Provisions) Order 2011 (SI 2011/2896) brought the following provisions into force on 3 December 2011:*

Section 8(2) – What is an eligible parish council for the purposes of the general power of competence

Sections 15, 19 and 20 – The power to transfer local public functions to permitted authorities

Sections 21, 22, Schs 2 and 3 (para 70) (partly) – The new arrangements for the governance of English local authorities

Section 69(8) – Discretionary relief for non-domestic rates in England

Sections 72 to 79 and Schs 5 to 7 – Referendums relating to council tax increases

Sch 3, para 70 and s 22 (so far as relating to that Part) – Section 105 orders

## PROVISIONS THAT CAME INTO FORCE ON 15 JANUARY 2012 (UNDER THE TERMS OF THE ACT)

*The following provisions came into force on 15 January 2012:*

Section 25 – Predetermination

Part 1, Ch 8 (so far as relating to England) – Pay accountability

Section 44 – Commission for Local Administration in England: arrangement for provision of services and discharge of functions

Section 45 – Repeals: duties relating to promotion of local democracy

Section 47 – Repeals: schemes to encourage domestic waste reduction by payments and charges

Section 71 – Cancellation of liability to backdated non-domestic rates

Section 80 – Council tax: revaluations in Wales

Sections 111 to 113 – Local development schemes

Section 143 – Applications for planning permission: local finance considerations

Section 177 – Assisting tenants to become home owners

Section 183 and Sch 18 – Abolition of HIPs

Part 8, Ch 2 (excluding ss 197(3)(e) and (f) and 197(5)) – Mayoral development corporations

Schedule 25, Pts 6, 8, 14, 17 and 29 and s 237 (to the extent it relates to these parts) – Repeals and revocations (various)

## PROVISIONS THAT CAME INTO FORCE ON 15 JANUARY 2012 (UNDER A COMMENCEMENT ORDER)

*The Localism Act 2011 (Commencement No 2 and Transitional and Saving Provision) Order 2012 (SI 2012/57) brought the following provisions into force in England and Wales on 15 January 2012 (except for those marked E (England only) and those marked EWS (England, Wales and Scotland)):*

Part 1, Ch 4 – Make provision for the further transfer and delegation of functions to certain authorities

Section 21 and Sch 2 (to the extent that insert certain provisions in the Local Government Act 2000) – Concern the new arrangements relating to the governance of English local authorities

Section 22 and Sch 3 (in part) – Make minor and consequential amendments to take account of the new local governance arrangements

Section 24 – Sets out the timetables for changing English district councils' electoral schemes

Section 36 (in part) – Deletes section 27(6)(f) from the Act

Section 68(E) –Amends the Business Rates Supplements Act 2009 concerning ballots for the imposition and variation of a business rate supplement

Section 69(1) to (7)(E) – Amends the Local Government Finance Act 1988, s 47 concerning discretionary relief from non-domestic rates

Section 70 – Amends the Local Government Finance Act 1988, s 43 concerning small business rate relief

Section 115 – Allows regulations to be made governing use of the community infrastructure levy

Sections 116, 121 and 124(2) and Schs 10, 11 and 12 (to the extent that the amendments made to the Town and Country Planning Act 1990 give the Secretary of State the power to prescribe matters in a development order) – Relate to the introduction of neighbourhood development plans and planning enforcement

Section 128(2) and Sch 13 (in part) (EWS) – Make consequential amendments to allow for the Infrastructure Planning Commission to be abolished

Section 129 (to extent necessary to give the Secretary of State the power to give directions) (EWS) – Allows for transitional provisions relating to the Infrastructure Planning Commission being abolished

Sections 138(5) and 142(3) (to the extent necessary to give the Secretary of State the power to make regulations) (EWS) – Make amendments to the Planning Act 2008 concerning development consents

Section 145 (to the extent that it allows local housing authorities to draft and consult on allocation schemes) – Amends the Housing Act 1996 (HA 1996) changing the way social housing can be allocated

*Is it in force?*

Section 146 (to the extent necessary to allow the Secretary of State the power to make regulations) – Amends the HA 1996 changing the way social housing can be allocated

Section 147(1) and (6) – Amends the HA 1996 changing the way social housing can be allocated

Section 150 (except sub-s (3)) – Requires local housing authorities to prepare and publish tenancy strategies

Sections 151 and 152 – Provide further detail on tenancy strategies

Section 153 (in part) – Provides further detail on tenancy strategies

Section 154 (to the extent necessary to amend the Housing Act 1985 and give the Secretary of State the power to make regulations) – Will amend the Housing Act 1985 to introduce flexible tenancies

Section 158 (to the extent necessary to allow the Secretary of State the power to make regulations) – Will allow for the transfer of secure and assured tenancies between tenants

Section 165 (to the extent necessary to amend the Housing and Regeneration Act 2008 and give the Secretary of State the power to make regulations) – Amends the social housing 'right to acquire'

Section 176 – Amends the Housing and Regeneration Act 2008 to facilitate the exchange of tenancies by social housing tenants

Section 178 (in part) – Will transfer functions of the Office for Tenants and Social Landlords to the Homes and Communities Agency

Section 186 (in part) – Will amend the Greater London Authority Act 1999 to remove limitations on the authority's general power

Section 187 (in part) – Will provide the Greater London Authority (GLA) with new housing and regeneration powers

Section 190 – Allows the Secretary of State to make provisions transferring the property of the Homes and Communities Agency

Section 191(2) to (5) – Allows for transitional provisions relating to the abolition of the London Development Agency (LDA)

Sections 193 and 194 – Make further provisions about the transfer schemes that may be necessary under ss 190 and 191

Section 195 (in part) – Makes further consequential amendments concerning changes to the powers of the GLA and abolition of the LDA

Section 197(3)(e), (f) and (5) – Relates to a new power for the Mayor of London to designate an area as a mayoral development area under s 197(1)

Sections 223 and 224 – Make amendments to the Greater London Authority Act 1999 concerning the delegation of further powers to the Mayor of London and the carrying on of commercial activities by the GLA

Section 230 – Relates to the sharing of administrative services by London authorities

Section 237 and Sch 25 (in part) (E to a lesser extent only) – Makes various repeals

## PROVISIONS THAT CAME INTO FORCE ON 31 JANUARY 2012 IN ENGLAND AND WALES

*The Localism Act 2011 (Commencement No 2 and Transitional and Saving Provision) Order 2012 (SI 2012/57) brought the following provisions into force on 31 January 2012 in England and Wales:*

Section 26 and Sch 4 (in part) – Make changes to the requirements for the conduct of local government members and employees in England, and ends the involvement of the Standards Board for England in investigating complaints

Section 30 (to the extent necessary to allow the Secretary of State the power to make regulations) – Relates to the requirement for local government members to disclose pecuniary interests

Section 237 and Sch 25, Pt 5 (in part) – Repeal provisions regarding miscellaneous provisions about powers to make regulations under the Localism Act 2011

*The Localism Act 2011 (Commencement No 1) (Wales) Order 2012 (SI 2012/193) brought the following provisions into force on 31 January 2012 in Wales only:*

Sections 38 to 43 – Pay accountability and the requirement on local authorities to produce an annual statement setting out the remuneration of certain employees

Section 69 – Amends the Local Government Finance Act 1988, s 47 concerning the circumstances in which local authorities can give discretionary relief from non-domestic rates

## PROVISIONS THAT CAME INTO FORCE ON 18 FEBRUARY 2012

*The Localism Act 2011 (Commencement No 3) Order 2012 (SI 2011/411) brought the following provisions into force on 18 February 2012:*

Section 1 (except subsection (7)) – Local authority's general power of competence

Sections 2 to 8 – Boundaries, limits and interpretation of the general power of competence

Sections 9 and 10 (in part) – General powers of fire and rescue authorities

Sections 11 to 14 – General powers of other authorities

Section 237 and Sch 25, Pts 2 and 3 (in part) – Repeal provisions regarding fire, rescue and other authorities

## PROVISIONS THAT CAME INTO FORCE ON 9 MARCH 2012

*The Localism Act 2011 (Commencement No. 4 and Transitional, Transitory and Saving Provisions) Order 2012 (SI 2012/628) brought the following provisions into force on 9 March 2012:*

*Is it in force?*

Section 21 and Sch 2 (in part) – Election as elected mayor and councillor

Section 22 and Sch 3 (in part) – Elected mayors etc

Section 237 and Sch 25, Pt 4 (in part) – Repeal the Local Government Act 2000, s 39(2), (3) and (6)

## PROVISIONS THAT CAME INTO FORCE ON 30 MARCH 2012 IN ENGLAND AND WALES

*The Localism Act 2011 (Commencement No 4 and Transitional, Transitory and Saving Provisions) Order 2012 (SI 2012/628) brought the following provisions into force on 30 March 2012:*

Section 233 – Tax

Schedule 24 – Transfers and transfer schemes: tax provisions

## PROVISIONS THAT CAME INTO FORCE ON 31 MARCH 2012 IN ENGLAND AND WALES

*The Localism Act 2011 (Commencement No 4 and Transitional, Transitory and Saving Provisions) Order 2012 (SI 2012/628) brought the following provisions into force on 31 March 2012:*

Sections 191(1) and 195(2) and Sch 20 – Abolition of the London Development Agency

Schedule 25, Pt 32 and s 237 (so far as relating to that part) – Repeal provisions regarding abolition of the London Development Agency

## PROVISIONS THAT CAME INTO FORCE ON 1 APRIL 2012

*The Localism Act 2011 (Commencement No 4 and Transitional, Transitory and Saving Provisions) Order 2012 (SI 2012/628) brought the following provisions into force in England and Wales on 15 January 2012 (except for those marked E (England only) and those marked EWS (England, Wales and Scotland)):*

Section 46 (E) – Repeal of provisions about petitions to local authorities

Section 64 (E) – EU Financial sanctions – warning notices

Sections 128 to 142 and Sch 13 (EWS) – Nationally significant infrastructure projects

Sections 154 to 161 – Flexible tenancies and social housing

Section 162(1), (2), (3)(a), (4) and (5) – Secure and assured tenancies: recovery of possession after tenant's death

Sections 163 to 166 – Assured shorthold tenancies (in part)

Sections 178 and 179 – Regulation of social housing

Sections 185 to 187, 189 and 195(1) – Exemption from HMO licensing for buildings run by co-operatives and London specific sections

Schedule 4 and s 26 (in part) – Conduct of local government members

Schedules 16, 17 and 19 – Transfer of functions from the Office for Tenants and Social Landlords to the Homes and Communities Agency, regulation of social housing and housing and regeneration: consequential amendments

Schedule 25, Pts 7 and 10 and s 237 (so far as relating to that part) (E) – Repeal provisions regarding petitions and non-domestic rates: discretionary relief

Schedule 25, Pts 20 and 21 and s 237 (so far as relating to that part) (EWS) – Repeal provisions regarding abolition of Infrastructure Planning Commission and nationally significant infrastructure projects

Schedule 25, Pts 26, 27 and 31 (in part) and s 237 (so far as relating to that part) – Repeal provisions regarding Office for Tenants and Social Landlords, regulation of social housing and London (housing and regeneration)

## TRANSITIONAL PROVISIONS THAT CAME INTO FORCE ON 3 APRIL 2012 IN ENGLAND AND WALES

*The Localism Act 2011 (Commencement No 5 and Transitional, Savings and Transitory Provisions) Order 2012 brought the following transitional provisions into force in England and Wales on 3 April 2012:*

Amendments to Local Government Act 2000 – Amendments to the Local Government Act 2000 brought about by the Localism Act, Sch 1, paras 2 and 3 are to come into force subject to an additional amendment to the Local Government Act 2000, s 2 (power to promote well-being) for eligible parish councils. Further, the power under the Local Government Act 2000, s 2 shall remain a function of the Greater Manchester Combined Authority, and the constituent councils of the Greater Manchester Combined Authority shall continue to have the power under that section to the extent necessary for it to be a function of the Greater Manchester Combined Authority.

Economic Development Strategy for London – On the day on which the Greater London Authority Act 1999, s 333F (Economic Development Strategy for London) comes into force, the Economic Development Strategy for London is to consist of the London Development Agency Strategy. This transitional provision also confirms that the duties of the Mayor of London imposed by s 333F(1) to (3) are deemed to be satisfied in respect of the strategy.

London Environment Strategy – On the day on which the Greater London Authority Act 1999, s 351(A) (the London Environment Strategy) comes into force, the London Environment Strategy is to consist of strategies set out in Greater London Authority Act 1999, s 41(1)(d) to (g) (general duties of the Mayor in relation to his strategies). Further, any guidance or direction under the Greater London Authority Act 1999 repealed by the Localism Act, Sch 23 applicable to these strategies remain effective as guidance or as directions to the relevant part of the London Environmental Strategy. This transitional provision also confirms that the duties of the Mayor of London imposed by s 351(A)(1) to (4) have been complied with.

London Housing Strategy – The Greater London Authority Act 1999, s 42B does not apply to the draft revision of the London housing strategy which was published for consultation in December 2011.

Tenancy Strategies – Where, on or before 14 January 2013, a local housing authority has published its tenancy strategy under the Localism Act, s 150(1),

*Is it in force?*

it must have regard to that strategy in exercising its housing management functions.

## PROVISIONS THAT CAME INTO FORCE ON 4 APRIL 2012 IN ENGLAND AND WALES

*The Localism Act 2011 (Commencement No 5 and Transitional, Savings and Transitory Provisions) Order 2012 brought the following provisions into force in England and Wales on 4 April 2012:*

Section 1(7) – Schedule 1 (General Power of Competence: Consequential Amendments)

Schedule 1 – General Power of Competence: Consequential Amendments

Schedule 14 – Grounds on which landlord may refuse to surrender and grant tenancies under s 158

Schedule 25, Pt 1 and s 237 (so far as relating to that part) – Repeals and revocations (general power of competence)

## PROVISIONS THAT CAME INTO FORCE ON 6 APRIL 2012 IN ENGLAND AND WALES

*The Localism Act 2011 (Commencement No. 4 and Transitional, Transitory and Saving Provisions) Order 2012 (SI 2012/628) brought the following provisions into force on 6 April 2012:*

Sections 116 and 121 and Sch 9 to 12 (but not for the purpose of holding a referendum) – Neighbourhood planning and consequential amendments

Sections 123 to 127 – Enforcement

Section 184 – Tenancy deposit schemes

Section 232 – Taking account of planning permission when assessing compensation

Schedule 25, Pts 18, 19, 30 and 34 and s 237 (so far as relating to those parts) – Neighbourhood planning, unauthorised advertisements and defacement of premises, tenants' deposits and compensation for compulsory acquisition

## PROVISIONS THAT WILL COME INTO FORCE ON 3 MAY 2012 IN ENGLAND AND WALES

*The Localism Act 2011 (Commencement No 5 and Transitional, Savings and Transitory Provisions) Order 2012 will bring the following provisions into force in England and Wales on 3 May 2012:*

Section 188 – The London housing strategy

Section 192 – Mayor's economic development strategy for London

Section 225 – The London Environment Strategy

Section 226 – Abolition of Mayor's duty to prepare state of the environment reports

*Provisions that will come into force on 15 January 2013*

Section 227 – Mayoral strategies: general duties

Section 228 – Simplification of the consultation process for the Mayor's strategies

Section 229 – London Assembly's power to reject draft strategies

Section 231 – Transport for London access to meetings and documents etc

Schedule 23 – The London Environment Strategy: Minor and consequential amendments of the Greater London Authority Act 1999

Schedule 25, Pt 33 and s 237 (so far as relating to that part) – Repeals and revocations (Greater London authority governance)

## PROVISIONS THAT WILL COME INTO FORCE ON 4 MAY 2012 IN ENGLAND AND WALES

*The Localism Act 2011 (Commencement No 5 and Transitional, Savings and Transitory Provisions) Order 2012 will bring the following provisions into force in England and Wales on 4 May 2012:*

Section 21 – New arrangements with respect to governance of English local authorities

Section 22 – New local authority governance arrangements: amendments

Schedule 2 – New arrangements with respect to governance of English local authorities

Schedule 3 – Minor and consequential amendments relating to local authority governance in England

Schedule 25, Pt 4 and s 237 (so far as relating to that part) – Repeals and revocations (local authority governance)

## PROVISIONS THAT WILL COME INTO FORCE ON 31 MAY 2012 IN ENGLAND, WALES, SCOTLAND AND NORTHERN IRELAND

*The Localism Act 2011 (Commencement No 5 and Transitional, Savings and Transitory Provisions) Order 2012 will bring the following provisions into force in England, Wales, Scotland and Northern Ireland on 31 May 2012:*

Sections 48 to 57 – EU financial sanctions

## PROVISIONS THAT WILL COME INTO FORCE ON 15 JANUARY 2013 IN ENGLAND AND WALES

*The Localism Act 2011 (Commencement No 5 and Transitional, Savings and Transitory Provisions) Order 2012 will bring the following provisions into force in England and Wales on 15 January 2013:*

Section 150(3) – Tenancy strategies and local housing authorities

# Appendix 4

# List of documents replaced by the NPPF[1]

1. Planning Policy Statement: *Delivering Sustainable Development* (31 January 2005)
2. Planning Policy Statement: *Planning and Climate Change – Supplement to Planning Policy Statement 1* (17 December 2007)
3. Planning Policy Guidance 2: *Green Belts* (24 January 1995)
4. Planning Policy Statement 3: *Housing* (9 June 2011)
5. Planning Policy Statement 4: *Planning for Sustainable Economic Growth* (29 December 2009)
6. Planning Policy Statement 5: *Planning for the Historic Environment* (23 March 2010)
7. Planning Policy Statement 7: *Sustainable Development in Rural Areas* (3 August 2004)
8. Planning Policy Guidance 8: *Telecommunications* (23 August 2001)
9. Planning Policy Statement 9: *Biodiversity and Geological Conservation* (16 August 2005)
10. Planning Policy Statement 12: *Local Spatial Planning* (4 June 2008)
11. Planning Policy Guidance 13: *Transport* (3 January 2011)
12. Planning Policy Guidance 14: *Development on Unstable Land* (30 April 1990)
13. Planning Policy Guidance 17: *Planning for Open Space, Sport and Recreation* (24 July 2002)
14. Planning Policy Guidance 18: *Enforcing Planning Control* (20 December 1991)
15. Planning Policy Guidance 19: *Outdoor Advertisement Control* (23 March 1992)
16. Planning Policy Guidance 20: *Coastal Planning* (1 October 1992)
17. Planning Policy Statement 22: *Renewable Energy* (10 August 2004)
18. Planning Policy Statement 23: *Planning and Pollution Control* (3 November 2004)
19. Planning Policy Guidance 24: *Planning and Noise* (3 October 1994)
20. Planning Policy Statement 25: *Development and Flood Risk* (29 March 2010)
21. Planning Policy Statement 25 Supplement: *Development and Coastal Change* (9 March 2010)
22. Minerals Policy Statement 1: *Planning and Minerals* (13 November 2006)
23. Minerals Policy Statement 2: *Controlling and Mitigating the Environmental Effects of Minerals Extraction in England*. This includes its Annex 1: *Dust* and Annex 2: *Noise* (23 March 2005 – Annex 1: 23 March 2005 and Annex 2: 23 May 2005)
24. Minerals Planning Guidance 2: *Applications, permissions and conditions* (10 July 1998)

---

1 DCLG (March 2012) NPPF, Annex 3 (available at http://www.communities.gov.uk/documents/planningandbuilding/pdf/2116950.pdf [accessed April 2012]).

*List of documents replaced by the NPPF*

25  Minerals Planning Guidance 3: *Coal Mining and Colliery Spoil Disposal* (30 March 1999)
26  Minerals Planning Guidance 5: *Stability in Surface Mineral Workings and Tips* (28 January 2000)
27  Minerals Planning Guidance 7: *Reclamation of Minerals Workings* (29 November 1996)
28  Minerals Planning Guidance 10: *Provision of Raw Material for the Cement Industry* (20 November 1991)
29  Minerals Planning Guidance 13: *Guidance for Peat Provision in England* (13 July 1995)
30  Minerals Planning Guidance 15: *Provision of Silica Sand in England* (23 September 1996)
31  Circular 05/2005: *Planning Obligations* (18 July 2005)
32  Government Office London Circular 1/2008: *Strategic Planning in London* (4 April 2008)
33  Letter to Chief Planning Officers: *Town and Country Planning (Electronic Communications) (England) Order 2003* (2 April 2003)
34  Letter to Chief Planning Officers: *Planning Obligations and Planning Registers* (3 April 2002)
35  Letter to Chief Planning Officers: *Model Planning Conditions for Development on Land Affected by Contamination* (30 May 2008)
36  Letter to Chief Planning Officers: *Planning for Housing and Economic Recovery* (12 May 2009)
37  Letter to Chief Planning Officers: *Development and Flood Risk – Update to the Practice Guide to Planning Policy Statement 25* (14 December 2009)
38  Letter to Chief Planning Officers: *Implementation of Planning Policy Statement 25 (PPS25) – Development and Flood Risk* (7 May 2009)
39  Letter to Chief Planning Officers: *The Planning Bill – Delivering Well Designed Homes and High Quality Places* (23 February 2009)
40  Letter to Chief Planning Officers: *Planning and Climate Change – Update* (20 January 2009)
41  Letter to Chief Planning Officers: *New Powers for Local Authorities to Stop 'Garden-Grabbing'* (15 June 2010)
42  Letter to Chief Planning Officer: *Area Based Grant: Climate Change New Burdens* (14 January 2010)
43  Letter to Chief Planning Officers: *The Localism Bill* (15 December 2010)
44  Letter to Chief Planning Officers: *Planning Policy on Residential Parking Standards, Parking Charges, and Electric Vehicle Charging Infrastructure* (14 January 2011)

# Index

## A

**Accident prevention**
  local plans 184
**Advertising**
  unauthorised
    action notices 89
    defacement of premises 89
    display structures 89
    removal notices 89
    time limit for proceedings 90
**Aggregates**
  National Planning Policy
      Framework 164
  planning permission, generally 75, 81
**Agricultural building**
  change of use 132
**Agricultural land**
  National Planning Policy
      Framework 163
**Air Quality Management Area**
  National Planning Policy
      Framework 178
**Appeal system**
  developers' rights 9
  third party appeals 9, 12
**Area of Outstanding Natural Beauty**
  National Planning Policy
      Framework 152, 177, 181
**Asset of community value**
  *Assets of community value* Policy
      Statement 54
  buildings 51
  community empowerment 47
  Community Right to Buy 29, 50–56
    concept generally 50
    Scottish scheme 54–55
  definition 31, 50–51
  empty land and buildings, information
      on 56
  excluded assets 52
  land 51
  local authority list
    effect of inclusion in 52, 212–214
    nominations for inclusion 51, 52–53
    notification of owners 53
    removal from 52–53
    requirement to maintain 50
  Localism Bill 29

**Asset of community value** – *contd*
  nomination of assets as 51
  public request to order disposal
      distinguished 55–56
  sale of listed asset 50
    full moratorium period 53–54
    interim moratorium period 53–54
    notification of intention by
        owner 53, 54
    relevant disposal 53–54
  straddling local authority areas 29
**Atlee, Lord** 206
**Autumn Statement 2011**
  planning reform proposals 131–132

## B

**Bailiffs**
  protection against 15
**Barker Report**
  generally 109
**Behavioural thinking**
  influence on Conservative policy 4
***Better Homes, Greener Cities***
  Policy Exchange report 3–4
***Big Bang Localism***
  Policy Exchange report 3
**'the Big Society'**
  government policy formulation 2–3,
      10, 21–22
**Biodiversity**
  national Planning Policy
      Framework 177–178
**Blight**
  compensation for 10
**Broadband roll-out**
  enterprise zones 147
**Brownfield land**
  National Planning Policy
      Framework 160, 163, 168, 194
**Brundtland Report**
  definition of sustainable
      development 156–157, 160, 161,
      166, 192
**Bullock, Hugh**
  *Localism and Growth* 10–11
**Business**
  financial benefit to local authority 5
  local plans 183

259

*Index*

**Business** – *contd*
  neighbourhood development orders 25
  neighbourhood plans 25
**Business area**
  Localism Bill 29
**Business rates**
  backdated 45
  billing authorities 198
  collection 197–198
  discretionary relief 45
    London 124
  enterprise zones 146–147
  generally 197–198
  local authority powers 5, 45
  local retention, proposed 198–200
  London 124, 199–200
  redistribution from central pool 198
  reliefs 198
  revaluations 198

C

**Cameron, David** 3, 14, 21–22
**Change of use regulations**
  proposed changes 26, 127–130
**Charity**
  Community Infrastructure Levy 103–104
  non-domestic rates 45
**Churchill, Winston** 11
**Civil Aviation Authority**
  duty to co-operate on planning issues 135
**Clark, Greg** 11, 16, 49, 111, 149, 160, 165
  *Total Politics: Labour's Command State* 2–3
**Clegg, Nick** 14, 201
**Climate change**
  measures to tackle
    duty to co-operate 66
    pre-existing planning system 2
    National Planning Policy Framework 176–177, 190
**Co-operation**
  abolition of regional strategies 65–67
  bodies with duty to co-operate on planning issues 135, 184
  local authority duty as to 23, 26, 65–67
**Coalition Agreement**
  abolition of regional strategies 59–63
  communities and local government 14–16
  Community Right to Challenge 49
  deficit reduction 13, 16
  environmental measures 13, 15
  housing 15
  localism 13, 14–16, 47
  national planning framework 14, 149

**Coalition Agreement** – *contd*
  neighbourhood planning 69
  publication 14
  Standards Board, abolition 41
**Coastal change and erosion**
  Coastal Change Management Areas 177
  National Planning Policy Framework 168, 176–177
  planning, duty to co-operate 66
**Coastal Zone Management**
  National Planning Policy Framework 177
**Collaborative democracy**
  concept of 9
**Combe, Malcolm** 55
**Commercial development**
  minor 26
**Commercial premises**
  conversion to residential use 26, 127–130
**Committee system**
  local authorities 15, 37–38
**Communications infrastructure**
  National Planning Policy Framework 171
**Community**
  National Planning Policy Framework 173–174
**Community consultation**
  pre-planning application 85–86, 185, 215–217
**Community empowerment**
  community right to challenge 15, 17, 47, 49–50
  local referendums 47–49
  Localism Act, generally 228–229, 234–235
  *See also* ASSET OF COMMUNITY VALUE
**Community facilities**
  Community Right to Build Orders 80, 174
  National Planning Policy Framework 153, 174
**Community Infrastructure Levy (CIL)**
  appeals 106–107
  authorities which have adopted 107–108
  basis of charge 93–94
  calculation 96–97
    apportioned CIL 97–98
  chargeable amount 96–97
    review and appeal 106–107
  chargeable developments 98–99
  charging authorities 92–93
  charging schedule 93–94
    adoption procedures 94–96
    errors in 96

# Index

**Community Infrastructure Levy (CIL)**
– *contd*
  charging schedule – *contd*
    examination 94–95
    formulation 94–95
    publication 96
  charities exemption 103–104
    appeals 107
    claw back provisions 103
  collecting authorities 93
  commencement date
    deemed 101
    incorrectly determined 107
  commencement notice 100–101
  exceptional circumstances relief 105
  excluded developments 96
  full planning permission 99
  generally 91–92
  indexation 97
  legislative basis 91
  liability for 97–99
    apportionment 97–98
    generally 98–99
    joint owners 98
    owners 98
    reviews and appeals 107
    transfer of 97
  liability notice 97, 99, 100
    service of 100
  London 92, 93, 95, 107–108
  meaning of development 96
  minor developments 103
  notices chargeable development 100
  outline planning permission 99
  payment 100–101
    in instalments 101
    outstanding payments 101
    payments in kind (land payments) 101–102
  planning obligations and 102–103
  procedural issues 99–100
  proposed replacement 9
  purpose 91–92
  reliefs and exemptions 103–105
    reviews and appeals 107
  reviews 106–107
  social housing relief 104
  stop notices, appeals 107
  surcharges, appeals against 107
  temporary planning permissions 99
  uses 31, 91–92, 235
**Community land auctions**
  proposals for 25, 204–205
**Community Right to Build Order (CRBO)**
  community organisations 79
  generally 210, 225
  National Planning Policy Framework 174, 184, 186

**Community Right to Build Order (CRBO)** – *contd*
  neighbourhood planning 70, 79–82
  proposals for
    generally 79
    publicising 76
    referendums 48, 80
    refusal 79–80
  role 70, 79, 80
  rural areas 80
  site-specific developments 79
**Community right to build scheme**
  Green Belt 153, 175
**Community Right to Buy**
  assets of community value 29, 50–56
    excluded assets 52
    nomination as 51
  buildings 51
  full moratorium period 53–54
  interim moratorium period 53–54
  land 51
  notification of intention to sell 53
  Scottish scheme 54–55
**Community Right to Challenge**
  Coalition Agreement 49
  creation of right 49
  procurement exercises 49, 50
  saving local facilities and services 15, 17, 47, 49–50
  scope 30, 49–50
**Community Right to Reclaim Land**
  generally 56
**Competition**
  local authority newspapers 15
**Comprehensive Area Assessment**
  proposed abolition 5, 15
**Compulsory purchase**
  compensation 30
**Conservation Area**
  demolition of unlisted buildings 134
  National Planning Policy Framework 181
**Conservation Credit**
  proposed 10
**Consultation**
  Code of Practice 86
  pre-application 85–86, 185, 215–217
**Contamination**
  land affected by 129
*Control Shift: Returning Power to Local Communities*
  Policy Green Paper 4–6, 47, 197
**Council officials**
  salary packages 15
  publication 18
**Council tax**
  capping 5

*Index*

**Council tax** – *contd*
excessive increases
referendums 5, 47–48
veto 5, 18
freeze 15
**Councillor**
devolved funding to 5
discussions with planning applicants 9
**County council**
Community Infrastructure Levy 93
**Crime maps**
publication 5
**Cultural facilities**
National Planning Policy
Framework 162, 174
**Cycling**
National Planning Policy
Framework 162, 168

**D**

**Davey, Ed** 204
**Decentralisation**
generally 2–3, 228–229
**Decentralisation and Localism Bill** *See* LOCALISM BILL
**Defence and security requirements**
local plans 183
*Delivering Sustainable Development*
Planning Policy Statement 11
**Department for Communities and Local Government (DCLG)**
budget reduction 22
**Developer**
appeal, right of 9
choosing a developer 209–210
collaborative approach 217–218
community demographics 214, 216
emphasising socio-economic benefits 222–223
LPA charges, liability for 83
matters to be considered by 214–223
pre-application consultation 85–86, 185, 215–217
**Development**
CIL *See* COMMUNITY INFRASTRUCTURE LEVY
development plan documents 135
General Development Procedure Order, changes to 137–138
local development documents 135
permitted development rights, changes to 127–130
stalled developments 132, 134
sustainable *See* SUSTAINABLE DEVELOPMENT
**Development control (management) system**
pre-existing planning system 1–2

*Development and Flood Risk*
Planning Policy Statement 189
**Development Management Procedure Order**
generally 137–138
**Development plans**
duty to co-operate 65–67

**E**

**Eco-town**
government policy 7
**Economic growth**
Coalition Agreement, deficit reduction 13, 16
localist and growth agendas, potential clash 29
planning policy, and 22, 127, 150–151, 165, 166–167
National Planning Policy Framework 168–169
**Eddington Report**
generally 109
**Employer**
emissions reduction targets 8
**Energy Performance Certificate**
generally 7
**Energy supply**
micro-renewable energy development rights 32
National Planning Policy Framework 154, 168, 176
National Policy Statements 110
*See also* INFRASTRUCTURE PROVISION
**Enforcement notice**
land owners 29–30
**English Heritage**
proposed changes to remit 134
**Enterprise zone**
benefits to businesses 146–148
broadband roll-out 147
business rates 146–147
capital allowances 148
Community Infrastructure Levy 93
designation 144
enhanced capital allowances 32
introduction 2
legislative framework 144
new generation 26, 144–145
listed 145
simplified planning approach 147
Tax Increment Finance 148
Wales 145
**Environment Agency**
duty to co-operate on planning issues 135
proposed changes to remit 134

## Index

**Environmental protection**
abolition of regional strategies 63–64
Coalition Agreement 13, 15
compensatory sites 154
impact assessment
   development where required 129
   procedures 26, 75
National Planning Policy
   Framework 152, 153–154, 162,
   163, 168, 176–178, 183
   Environmental Audit Committee
     Report 159–161
Nature Improvement Areas 138
planning, duty to co-operate 66
role of planning system 167
Strategic Environmental Assessment
   Directive 63
**Equality legislation**
local authorities subject to 36
**European Convention on Human Rights**
local authorities subject to 36
**European legislation**
local authorities subject to 36
   EU fines passed on by
     government 44–45
   failure to comply 44–45

### F

**Fire and rescue authority**
code of conduct, requirement to
   adopt 42
pay accountability 42–44
**Fire Service**
regionalisation 6, 15
**Flooding**
control measures
   duty to co-operate 66
   National Planning Policy
     Framework 168, 176–177, 183,
     189–190
*Development and Flood Risk* 189
Flood Zones 190
Strategic Flood Risk Assessment 176–177, 183, 189–190

### G

**Garden grabbing**
measures to prevent 7, 12, 14, 59
**General Development Procedure Order**
changes to 137–138
**Get Britain Building Investment Fund**
purpose 134
**Government Office for London**
abolition 6, 15
**Government Offices for the Regions**
proposed abolition 22

**Green Belt**
abolition of regional strategies 64
Coalition Agreement 15
community right to build schemes 153, 175
National Planning Policy
   Framework 152, 153, 168, 175
new, creation of 175
purposes 175
*Strong Foundations: Building Homes and Communities* 7
**Green Space, locally significant** *See* LOCAL GREEN SPACE
**Greenhalgh, Paul**
*Opportunity Knocks* 148

### H

**Habitats Directive**
compliance with 132, 178
**Habitats Regulations**
compliance with 183
**Hanham, Baroness** 17, 65, 72–73, 74, 78, 81, 82
**Hazard**
location of major, local plan 184
**Health and Safety Executive**
proposed changes to remit 134
**Heritage protection**
National Planning Policy Framework 154, 164, 168, 178–179, 183
**Heseltine, Lord**
independent spending review 32
**Highway authority**
duty to co-operate on planning
   issues 135
**Highway consent**
proposed changes 134
**Highways Agency**
proposed changes to remit 134
**Historic Buildings and Monuments Commission for England**
duty to co-operate on planning
   issues 135
**Home on the Farm scheme**
Coalition Agreement 15
**Home Information Pack (HIP)**
abolition 7, 18, 20
**Homes and Communities Agency**
duty to co-operate on planning
   issues 135
**Homes and Communities Agency (HCA)**
Community Infrastructure Levy 93
London 119
**Housing**
affordable
   government commitment to
     deliver 22

263

*Index*

**Housing** – *contd*
  affordable – *contd*
    government incentives  6, 9, 134–135
    local targets  9
    minimum site threshold  153
    National Planning Policy Framework  155–156, 172
    pre-existing planning system  2
    rural exception sites policy  153
  *Better Homes, Greener Cities*  3–4
  'build now, pay later' schemes  135
  co-location of community facilities and services  163
  Coalition Agreement  15
  Community Right to Build Orders  80
  community-led  6–7, 18
  empty properties  7, 15, 172
  energy efficiency  8
  Energy Performance Certificates  7
  financial benefit to local authority  5
  Get Britain Building Investment Fund  134
  Home Information Packs  7
  housebuilder indemnity fund  134
  Housing Strategy for England  134–135
  large scale developments  172–173
  local decision-making powers  17, 22
  Local Enterprise Partnerships  141
  Local Housing Trusts  7
  Local Planning Authorities (LPAs)  9, 59
  London  118–120
  Merton Rule  8
  national building targets  59
  National Planning Policy Framework  153, 155–156, 159, 171–173, 194
    co-location of community facilities and services  163
    identification of housing sites  163, 171–172, 194
  New Homes Bonus  22, 24–25, 202–203, 235
  previously developed land, percentage on  153
  public sector land
    accelerated release  32, 134–135
    pre-auction planning permission  135
    surplus  7, 26
  regional building targets  6, 59
  rural areas, National Planning Policy Framework  173
  shops, accommodation above  130
  social housing *See* SOCIAL HOUSING
  stalled developments  132, 134

**Housing** – *contd*
  Strategic Housing Land Availability Assessment  172
  Strategic Housing Market Assessment  182
  *Strong Foundations: Building Homes and Communities*  6–8
**Housing Revenue Account**
  proposed review  15, 18
**Howell, John**  10
**Hutton Review of Fair Pay in the Public Sector**  43

**I**
**Infrastructure Planning Commission (IPC)**
  abolition  14, 17, 111–112
    transitional provisions  111–113
  establishment  110
  generally  6, 9, 12
**Infrastructure provision**
  CIL *See* COMMUNITY INFRASTRUCTURE LEVY
  consenting regime, simplification  32
  fast track planning process  26, 131
  forecast demands  183
  funding  91
  local plans  183
  London  122–123
  LPA duty as to  183
  Major Infrastructure Unit  9
  National Infrastructure Directorate  111
  National Policy Statements  110, 111, 114
  Nationally Significant Infrastructure Projects
    applications, validation  115
    approval  110
    background to  9, 30, 75, 81, 109–111
    compensation payments  115
    development consent  109
    development consent orders  110
    environmental impact assessment  115
    flexibility  132
    habitats regulations assessment  115
    notification of accepted application  115–116
    NPPF and  166
    *Planning for a Sustainable Future*  109
    pre-application consultation  114–115
    publicity requirements  114–115
    rights of entry for surveying etc  115
    section 35 directions  114
    timetable for decision-making  110
  pre-existing planning system  2
  private sector funding  21
  section 35 directions  114

**Infrastructure UK**
establishment 21

**J**

**Jenkins, Simon**
*Big Bang Localism* 3

**L**

**Land**
assets of community value *See* ASSET OF COMMUNITY VALUE
public sector *See* PUBLIC SECTOR LAND

**Landowner**
choosing a developer 209–210
community relationships 210–211
enforcement notices, service on 29–30
LPA charges, liability for 83
matters to be considered by 209–214
Neighbourhood Forum, participation in 210
parish council, joining or influencing 210
promoting sites 211
unlocking site potential 211–212

**Leisure development scheme**
out of centre location 153

**Letwin, Oliver** 3

**Leunig, Tim** 204, 205

**Libertarian paternalism**
influence on Conservative policy 4

**Listed building**
certificates of immunity 133
extent of special interest to be legally defined 133
generally 129
National Planning Policy Framework 179
statutory management agreements 133

**Liverpool**
directly elected mayor 38–39
Mayoral Development Council 39

**Local authority**
business rates, discretionary relief 5, 45
code of conduct, requirement to adopt 41–42
committee system, operating through 15, 37–38
delegation of government functions to 36–37
European legislation
EU fines passed on by government 44–45
failure to comply 44–45
Human Rights Convention 36
local authorities subject to 36
public procurement rules 36

**Local authority** – *contd*
general power of competence 5, 15, 18, 19, 33–36, 39
limits 33–34, 36
supervision 34
governance arrangements, change of 37–38
legal capacity 33
member's register of interests 42
pay accountability 42–43
bonuses 44
*Hutton Review* 43
policy statements 42
redundancy packages 44
prayers, holding 36
pre-determination of decisions by 39–41
Standards Board, abolition 5, 15, 17, 39, 41–42
transfer of government functions to 36–37
well-being power, replacement 35

**Local development documents**
generally 135

**Local Development Framework**
generally 24

**Local Development Order (LDO)**
enterprise zones 147
generally 186
simplified planning consents 21, 147

**Local Enterprise Partnership (LEP)**
Capacity Fund 143–144
constitution 142
economic areas, representing 142
enterprise zones 26, 145
funding 142–144
governance structure 140, 142
housing 141
listed 140–141
localism and 12
powers 24
proposed 18, 21, 22, 24
Regional Growth Fund 141, 142–143
role 139–140, 141–142
in planning system 26
size 140
Start-up Fund 144

**Local government**
financial autonomy 18
financial benefits, right to retain 5
financing
bond market, through 6
business rates, local retention 198–200
generally 197–198
New Homes Bonus 202–203, 235
Tax Increment Financing 201–202
freeing from central control 5

265

## Index

**Local government** – *contd*
  organisational structure 5
  planning authorities *See* LOCAL PLANNING AUTHORITY
  ring fencing 6, 15
  spending priorities, determination 6
**Local Green Space**
  effect of designation 212–214
  generally 153, 212–214
  identification and protection 12, 15, 174
  National Trust concerns 27–29
*Local Growth: Realising Every Place's Potential*
  White Paper 22–23, 141, 201
**Local Housing Trust**
  generally 7
**Local plan-making process**
  amendments to 135–137
**Local plan** *See* LOCAL PLANNING AUTHORITY
**Local Planning Authority (LPA)**
  assistance, duty to provide 230
  charges for neighbourhood planning functions 83–84
  co-operation
    with neighbouring authorities 164
    on planning issues 184
  effect of Localism Act on time and resources 225–227
  funding
    business rates, retention 198–200
    community land auctions 204–205
    generally 197–198
    New Homes Bonus 202–203, 235
    planning application fees 203
    Tax Increment Financing 201–202
  housing policies 9, 59
    business needs 182–183
    identification of housing sites 163, 171–172
    infrastructure 183
    Strategic Housing Market Assessment 182
  list of assets of community value *See* ASSET OF COMMUNITY VALUE
  local distinctiveness, promoting or reinforcing 163
  local plan
    co-operation with neighbouring authorities 164
    defence and security needs 183
    departure from national policy 150
    draft 67, 136–137
    duty to draw up 224
    generally 136, 223–224
    hazards and accidents, information on 184

**Local Planning Authority (LPA)** – *contd*
  local plan – *contd*
    health needs of population 184
    housing 182
    independent examination 137, 230
    National Planning Policy Framework 150, 157–158, 166, 181–185
    notification of 136
    submission to Secretary of State 136–137
  monitoring reports
    availability 137
    preparation 137
  National Planning Policy Framework
    effect on LPA's time and resources 226–227
    requirements and technical guidance 165, 185–186, 189–190
  national policy considerations 60
  neighbourhood areas 70
  openness and inclusivity 227–228
  potential problems facing 229–231
  pre-existing planning system 1
  renewable and low carbon energy, requirements as to 154
  windfall land 172
**Localism**
  *Better Homes, Greener Cities* report 3–4
  CLG Select Committee 11
  Coalition Agreement 13, 14–16, 47
  concept generally 11–12, 20, 22
  *Control Shift: Returning Power to Local Communities* 4–6, 47, 197
  Liberal Democrat policy 12
  localist and growth agendas, potential clash 29
**Localism Act**
  Royal Assent 30
**Localism Bill**
  amendments 29–30
  Essential Guide 23
  Media Background Note 23
  Parliamentary reports 23–25
  proposals 17–18
**London**
  business rates, pooling and redistribution 200
  Community Infrastructure Levy 92, 93, 95, 107–108
    exceptional circumstances relief 105
  delegation of functions to Mayor 124–125
  *Devolution Package for London* 118
  economic development strategy 119–120

## Index

**London** – *contd*
  Environment Strategy 125
  governance structure 117
  Government Office for London,
    abolition 6, 15, 118
  Greater London Authority 6, 117, 118
    funding 199–200
    governance changes 124–125
    housing and regeneration
      functions 118–120
  housing and regeneration 118–120, 123
  infrastructure provision 122–123
  London Development Agency 117, 139
  London Fire and Emergency Planning
    Authority 117
  London Legacy Development
    Corporation 39, 118, 120–121
  London Plan 117
  Mayor *See* Mayor of London
  Mayoral Development Areas 120
  Mayoral Development
    Corporations 30, 120–124
    acquisition of land 123
    business rates, discretionary
      relief 124
    compulsory acquisition of land 123
    disposal of land 123–124
    dissolution 124
    financial assistance, power to
      give 124
    object 122
    powers and duties 122–124
    review of designation 124
    revocation of designation 124
    rights of way 123
  Mayoral Development Council 39
  Metropolitan Police Authority 117
  *A New Settlement for London's
    Government* 117–118
  Olympic legacy 18, 39, 118, 120–121
  Port of London Authority 118
  potentially strategic important planning
    applications 117
  Royal Docks Enterprise Zone 32
  Transport for London 117
    duty to co-operate on planning
      issues 135

### M

**Major Infrastructure Unit**
  proposed 9
**Marine Management Organisation**
  duty to co-operate on planning
    issues 135
**Marine Plans**
  duty to co-operate 65–67
  LPA's duty as to 177

**Marine Policy Statement**
  LPA's duty as to 177
**Mayor**
  directly elected city mayors 5, 15, 18, 38–39
  elections 38
  referendums on decision 38
  transfer of functions to 38
  London *See* Mayor of London
  mayoral cities 38
**Mayor of London**
  Community Infrastructure Levy 92, 93, 95, 107–108
    exceptional circumstances relief 105
  delegation of functions to 124–125
  duty to co-operate on planning
    issues 135
  economic development strategy 119–120
  Localism Bill 30
  London Environment Strategy 125
  role 117
  strategies 12
**Mayoral Development Corporation**
  Liverpool 39
  localism and 12, 30
  London 39
**Merton Rule**
  generally 8
**Military land**
  surplus 26
**Minerals**
  land banks 153
  minerals consultation areas 180
  minerals safeguarding areas 180
  National Planning Policy
    Framework 164, 180–181, 183, 188, 190
  planning permission, generally 75, 81
  sustainable use 180–181
  transport facilities 180
**Minerals Policy Guidance (MPG)**
  replacement by NPPF 188

### N

**National Parks**
  National Planning Policy
    Framework 177, 181
**National Planning Policy Framework
  (NPPF)**
  agricultural land 163
  air quality 178
  Areas of Outstanding Natural
    Beauty 152, 177, 181
  biodiversity 177–178
  the Broads 177, 181
  brownfield land 160, 163, 168, 194

*Index*

**National Planning Policy Framework (NPPF)** – *contd*
building a strong, competitive economy 168–169
climate change 176–177, 190
Coalition Agreement 14, 149
coastal change 168, 176–177
communications infrastructure 171
community facilities 153, 174
community role 173–174
Conservation Areas 181
cultural facilities 162, 174
    sports and recreational facilities 174
decision-taking 185–186, 223
design, policy as to 168, 173
documents published alongside 189–194
documents replaced by 188–189
draft 27, 149–154
    Environmental Audit Committee Report 159–161
    objections raised 27–29, 151
    Select Committee Report 154–159, 192–194, 224
energy supply 154, 168, 176
England only, application to 165
environmental issues 152, 153–154, 162, 163, 168, 177–178, 183
    Environmental Audit Committee Report 159–161
final form 161–165
flood control 168, 176–177, 183, 189–190
forward and introduction 165–168
generally 25, 132, 218, 220, 221–222
Green Belt 152, 153, 168, 175
heritage protection 154, 164, 168, 178–179, 183
housing 153, 159, 171–173, 194
    affordable 155–156, 172
    co-location of community facilities and services 163
    identification of housing sites 163, 194
land-use, core planning principles 167–168
legal status 150
light pollution 178
listed buildings 179
local distinctiveness, promoting or reinforcing 163
Local Green Spaces, identification and protection 153, 174, 212
local plans 150, 157–158, 166
    co-operation with neighbouring authorities 164
    departure from national policy 150
    strategic policies 181–185

**National Planning Policy Framework (NPPF)** – *contd*
minerals 164, 180–181, 183, 190
*Myth-Buster* document 151–152, 223
National Parks 177, 181
neighbourhood plans 81, 151, 157–158, 164–165, 166, 184–185
noise 164, 178
NSIPs, and 166
open spaces
    existing 174
    Local Green Spaces, identification and protection 153, 174, 212
parking standards 153
pollution 168, 178
problem areas 195–196, 218
public rights of way and access 174
publication 31–32, 161
purpose 150
role and character of each area 168
rural economy 170
rural housing 173
Sites of Special Scientific Interest 164
sustainable development 164, 165
    definition 156–157, 160–161, 166
    presumption in favour of 32, 149, 150–152, 156–157, 160–162, 167, 184, 193, 224
technical guidance to LPAs 189–190
town centres 152, 154, 159, 162–163, 169–170, 194
transitional arrangements 187–188
transport 153, 168, 170–171
traveller sites 189, 191–192
unplanned retail or leisure schemes 153
World Heritage Sites 179, 181
**National Trust**
concerns over proposed planning reforms 27–29, 151
**Nationally Significant Infrastructure Project (NSIP)** *See* INFRASTRUCTURE PROVISION
*The Natural Choice: Securing the Value of Nature*
White Paper 138
**Natural England**
duty to co-operate on planning issues 135
proposed changes to remit 134
species licences 134
**Nature Improvement Area (NIA)**
areas listed 138
funding 138
purpose 138
**Neighbourhood area**
application for designation as 71
refusal 71–72

**Neighbourhood area** – *contd*
   business areas  72
   formation  71–72
   generally  70
   Neighbourhood Development Plans  81
   Neighbourhood Forums *See*
      NEIGHBOURHOOD FORUM
   planning permission  74–75
   residential areas  72
**Neighbourhood Development Order (NDO)**
   business areas  78–79
   cost and funding  233
   CRBOs *See* COMMUNITY RIGHT TO
      BUILD ORDERS
   generally  210, 225
   judicial review  79
   National Planning Policy
      Framework  184, 186
   national policy and  77
   objecting to  237
   planning permission granted by  74–75
      conditional  75
      excluded types and classes  75
   proposals for  75–79
      consultation requirements  76
      independent examination of  77–78
      publicising  76, 84
      referendums on  48, 78
      refusal  79–80
      repeat  76
      who may request  75
   role  70, 74–75
**Neighbourhood Development Plan (NDP)**
   conformity with strategic policies  82
   cost and funding  233
   excluded subjects  81
   generally  210, 218, 221, 225
   independent examination  82, 230
   judicial review  82
   meaning  81
   National Planning Policy
      Framework  81, 151, 157–158
   neighbourhood areas  81
   objecting to  237
   publicising  84
   referendums  48, 82
   role  70, 81–82
   voluntary nature  218, 224
**Neighbourhood Forum**
   consultation on NDOs  76
   cost and funding  233
   designation as  70
      application for  73
      publicity  73
      withdrawal  73–74
   duration  74

**Neighbourhood Forum** – *contd*
   generally  70, 210
   initiating or joining  210, 232–233
   judicial review  74
   local businesses
      consultation with  25
      inclusion in  232–233, 234
   minimum membership  72–73
   neighbourhood planning  69, 70, 72–74
   objecting to  237
   one per neighbourhood area  73
   potential problems for LPAs  230
   purpose and role  70, 74
**Neighbourhood planning**
   Coalition Agreement  69
   Community Right to Build  70
   CRBOs *See* COMMUNITY RIGHT TO
      BUILD ORDERS
   Front Runners initiative  224
   funding  83–84
   LPA charges  83–84
   measures, generally  69–70
   National Planning Policy
      Framework  81, 151, 157–158,
      164, 166, 184–185
   neighbourhood areas  70–72
   qualifying bodies  70, 72–74
**Neill, Bob**  17, 21, 63–64, 87
**New Homes Bonus**
   introduction  22
   Parliamentary committee
      recommendations  24–25
   purpose  22, 24, 202–203, 235
**Newspaper**
   local authority  15
**Noise**
   National Planning Policy
      Framework  164, 178
**Non-planning consents**
   Penfold Review  133
   proposed maximum timescale  132
**Nuclear power**
   Coalition Agreement  13–14

**O**

**Olympic legacy**
   government proposals  18
***Open Source Planning***
   Policy Green Paper  4, 8–10, 14, 39,
      47, 59, 69, 149, 202
**Opposing planning policy**
   tactics, generally  236–238
**Osborne, George**  21, 25, 31, 204

**P**

**Parish council**
   code of conduct, requirement to
      adopt  42

*Index*

**Parish council** – *contd*
consultation with local businesses  25
consultation on NDOs  76
general power of competence  33–36, 39
  limits  33–34
  supervision  34
generally  210
legal capacity  33
neighbourhood planning  69, 70, 72–74
pre-existing planning system  1
**Parking standards**
National Planning Policy Framework  153
**Parminter, Baroness**  206–207
**Pay accountability**
local authorities  42–43
**Penfold Review**
aim  133
implementation  26, 133
Implementation Report  131, 133–134
recommendations  133
**Pickles, Eric**  16, 19–21, 147, 228
**Pidgley, Tony**  135
*The Plan for Growth*  25, 127–128, 130–131, 204
**Planning appeal**
award of costs  132
review of appeals procedure  132
**Planning application**
12-month planning guarantee  26, 127, 130–131
decision-taking
  local finance considerations  205–207, 231
  National Planning Policy Framework  185–186
information requirements, proposed review  130, 131
local finance considerations  26, 31, 205–207, 231
Penfold Review  26
pre-application consultation  85–86, 185, 215–217
retrospective, where enforcement notice already served  87
streamlining measures  127, 132–133
**Planning control**
breach
  deliberate concealment  29, 87–89
  Planning Enforcement Orders  88, 231
  retrospective planning applications  87
  time limit for action  87
  unauthorised display structures  89
**Planning Enforcement Order (PEO)**
potential problems  231
where deliberate concealment of breach  29, 88

**Planning guarantee**
concept of  26, 127, 130–131
**Planning Inspectorate**
power to alter draft local plans  9
**Planning Policy Guidance Notes (PPGs)**
replacement by NPPF  188
**Planning Policy Statements (PPSs)**
*Delivering Sustainable Development*  11
*Development and Flood Risk*  189
replacement by NPPF  188
*Planning for a Sustainable Future*
White Paper  109
*Planning for Sustainable Growth*
Policy Statement  10
**Planning system**
localisation  3–4
pre-existing  1–2
**Planning4People campaign**
generally  151, 154
**Police**
accountability  5
elected commissioners  5
**Policy Exchange**
*Better Homes, Greener Cities*  3–4
*Big Bang Localism*  3
**Policy Green Papers**
*Control Shift: Returning Power to Local Communities*  4–6, 47, 197
*Open Source Planning*  4, 8–10, 14, 39, 47, 59, 69, 202
*Strong Foundations: Building Homes and Communities*  6–8
**Pollution**
National Planning Policy Framework  168, 178
light pollution  178
noise pollution  178
**Ports Review**
backdated rates  45
**Practitioners Advisory Group (PAG)**
generally  149
**Pre-determination**
decision-making process, in  39–41
application of legislation  41
meaning  39
test for  40
**Primary Care Trust**
duty to co-operate on planning issues  135
**Public request to order disposal (PROD)**
generally  55–56
**Public sector land**
access to databases  7
pre-auction planning permission  135
surplus  7, 26
  accelerated release  32, 134–135

270

## Q
**Quartermain, Steve** 61

## R
**Radio masts**
 National Planning Policy
  Framework 171
**Rail Regulation, Office of**
 duty to co-operate on planning
  issues 135
**Ramsar Site**
 National Planning Policy
  Framework 153–154, 178
**Rates**
 non-domestic *See* BUSINESS RATES
**Recreational facilities**
 National Planning Policy
  Framework 174
**Recycling**
 sustainable use of minerals 180
**Referendum**
 local
  community empowerment 47–49
  Community Right to Build
   Orders 48, 80
  excessive council tax rises 5, 47, 48
  Neighbourhood Development
   Orders 48, 78
  Neighbourhood Development
   Plans 48, 82
  potential problems 230–231
  power to instigate 5, 18, 47–48
  special-case petitions 29
 local authority governance
  arrangements 38, 48
**Regional Development Agencies
 (RDAs)**
 abolition 21, 139, 142, 160, 218, 220
 proposed changes 6, 18
 purpose 58, 59
**Regional Growth Fund**
 extension 22
 generally 21
 Local Enterprise Partnerships 141,
  142–143
**Regional planning bodies**
 pre-existing planning system 1
**Regional strategies**
 abolition 5, 14, 17, 20, 21, 22, 31,
  63–65
  concerns raised 23–24
  duty to co-operate 65–67
  environmental protection 63–64
  existing development schemes and
   plans 59–62
  Strategic Environmental Assessment
   Directive 63
 background to 57–59

**Regional strategies** – *contd*
 Coalition Government's stance 59–63
 economic 59
 London Plan 117
 part only revoked 31
 spatial 59
**Regulation of Investigatory Powers Act
 (RIPA)**
 powers in, use by council 15
**Repossession**
 Coalition Agreement proposals 15
**Retail development**
 out of centre location 153
 planning application competition
  test 12
**Retrospective planning permission**
 proposed changes 10
*Review of Sub-national Economic
  Development and Regeneration* 58
**Reynolds, Dame Fiona** 27–29
**Richards, Steve**
 *Can the Big Society work?* 3
**Right to Buy scheme**
 social housing 7
**Right to Move scheme**
 social housing 7
**Right of way**
 public, National Planning Policy
  Framework 174
**Ring fencing**
 proposed phasing-out 6, 15
**Rural economy**
 National Planning Policy
  Framework 170, 173

## S
**Safety hazard zone**
 generally 129
**Scheduled monument**
 generally 129
 National Planning Policy
  Framework 181
**Secretary of State**
 ministerial team 16–17
 pre-existing planning system 1
**Services**
 Community Right to Challenge
  provision 15, 17, 47, 49–50
 state-run, community bid to take
  over 49–50
**Shapps, Grant** 16, 80
**Shop**
 accommodation above 130
 Community Right to Build Orders 80
**Silkin, Lewis** 11
**Site of Special Scientific Interest (SSSI)**
 Coalition Agreement 15

271

*Index*

**Site of Special Scientific Interest (SSSI)** – *contd*
  National Planning Policy Framework 164
**Skeffington, Arthur** 11
**Social housing**
  Coalition Agreement 15
  Community Infrastructure Levy 104
  Localism Bill 30
  national mobility scheme 7
  proposed changes 7
  Right to Buy 7
  Right to Move scheme 7
  waiting lists policy 7
**Social role of planning system**
  importance 167
**Special Area of Conservation (SAC)**
  National Planning Policy Framework 153–154, 178
**Special Protection Area (SPA)**
  National Planning Policy Framework 153–154, 178
**Sports facilities**
  Community Right to Build Orders 80
  National Planning Policy Framework 174
**Stamp duty**
  Coalition Agreement 15
**Standards Board**
  abolition 5, 15, 17, 39, 41–42
**State-run services**
  community bid to take over 15, 17, 47, 49–50
**Strategic Environmental Assessment Directive**
  abolition of regional strategies 63
**Strategic Flood Risk Assessment**
  generally 176–177, 183, 189–190
**Strategic Housing Land Availability Assessment**
  generally 172
**Strategic Housing Market Assessment**
  preparation by LPA 182
*Strong Foundations: Building Homes and Communities*
  Policy Green Paper 6–8
**Stunell, Andrew** 16
**Sustainable Communities Act**
  Coalition Agreement 15
**Sustainable development**
  Brundtland Report 156–157, 160, 161, 166, 192
  Coalition Agreement 15
  definition 156–157, 160–161, 166, 192
  Delivering Sustainable Development (PPS1) 11
  local variations 162

**Sustainable development** – *contd*
  Penfold Review 131–132
  presumption in favour of 9, 25
    DCLG statement on 26–27
  National Planning Policy Framework 32, 149, 150–152, 156–157, 160–162, 164, 165, 167, 184, 193, 224

**T**

**Tax Incremental Financing (TIF)**
  enterprise zones 148
  generally 32, 201–202
**Telecommications masts**
  National Planning Policy Framework 171
**Thaler, Richard H and Sunstein, Cass R**
  *Nudge* 4
**Thatcher, Margaret** 3
**Town centres**
  National Planning Policy Framework 152, 154, 159, 162–163, 169–170, 194
**Town council**
  pre-existing planning system 1
**Transport**
  bodies with duty to co-operate on planning issues 135
  bulk transport of minerals 180
  Local Enterprise Partnerships 141
  National Planning Policy Framework 153, 170–171
  public transport 162, 168
  park and ride schemes 153
**Transport** *See* INFRASTRUCTURE PROVISION
**Traveller sites**
  funding for provision of 203
  planning policy 189, 191–192
**Tree preservation**
  time limit for prosecutions 90

**U**

**Urban development corporations**
  Community Infrastructure Levy 93
**Use Classes Order**
  review 32, 128, 130

**V**

**Village, Peter** 21
*Voluntary Action in the 21st Century*
  policy paper 4

## W

**Walking**
National Planning Policy
 Framework 162, 168
**Waste**
National Policy Statements 110
planning permission, generally 75, 81
**Water** *See* INFRASTRUCTURE PROVISION
**Wild Bird Directive**
compliance with 132, 178

**World Heritage Site**
National Planning Policy
 Framework 179, 181

## Y

**Young of Scone, Baroness** 66
*Your Region, Your Choice* White
 Paper 58